T0302361

Agricultural Growth, Productivity and Regional Change in India

Agriculture productivity, growth and regional change in post-colonial India from a spatial perspective are yet to be rigorously examined. In particular, the impacts of economic liberalisation, globalisation and deregulation are not being empirically investigated at a small-area level using advanced statistical and spatial techniques. Understanding the process of regional formation and the rapid transitioning of agricultural landscapes in the Post-Liberalisation phase is pivotal to developing and devising regional economic development strategies.

This book employs advanced methods to empirically examine the key characteristics and patterns of regional change in agricultural growth and productivity. It offers insights on changes in agricultural production and practices since the colonial period through to the Post-Liberalisation phase in India. It also incorporates the key public policy debates on the progress of India's agricultural development with the aim of formulating spatially integrated strategies to reduce rapid rise in the regional convergence and to promote equitable distribution of strategic government investment.

Surendra Singh is formerly Professor at North-Eastern Hill University, Shillong, India. He is Visiting Professor at several premier organisations, including the Polish Academy of Sciences, Warsaw, the Asian Institute of Technology, Bangkok, and the Disaster Prevention Research Institute, Kyoto. He has published both books and research papers in reputed international journals on various aspects of Indian agriculture. He was formerly coordinator of the Indo-Polish Inter-Governmental Program on the study of degraded landscape in extremely humid areas of Northeast India. He is also the recipient of the Career Award from the University Grants Commission New Delhi (1982–1985).

Prem Chhetri is Professor of Logistics and Geographic Systems at RMIT University, Australia. He was Deputy Head for Industry Engagement and Program Director for Open Australia Universities. He has received a number of Australian Research Council and federal and state government grants. His recent publications include articles in *Transportation Research Part E, European Journal of Transport and Infrastructure Research* and *International Journal of Physical Distribution and Logistics Management*. He is the recipient of several awards, including the RMIT University 2013 Research Excellence Award, and the RMIT 2009 Learning and Teaching Award. His research focuses include city logistics, urban modelling, tourism potential mapping, emergency response and the application of GIS in transport, infrastructure and logistics planning.

Routledge Studies in the Modern World Economy

For a full list of titles in this series, please visit www.routledge.com/series/SE0432

Agricultural Growth, Productivity and Regional Change in India

Challenges of globalisation, liberalisation and food insecurity

Surendra Singh and Prem Chhetri

LONDON AND NEW YORK

First published 2017
by Routledge
2 Park Square, Milton Park, Abingdon, Oxon OX14 4RN

and by Routledge
711 Third Avenue, New York, NY 10017

Routledge is an imprint of the Taylor & Francis Group, an informa business

© 2017 Surendra Singh and Prem Chhetri

British Library Cataloguing in Publication Data
A catalogue record for this book is available from the British Library

Library of Congress Cataloging in Publication Data
A catalog record for this book has been requested

ISBN: 978-1-138-92517-5 (hbk)
ISBN: 978-1-315-39342-1 (ebk)

Typeset in Galliard
by Apex CoVantage, LLC

Contents

Figures

Tables

Preface

Agriculture is a *way of life* in India. It is indeed more than a mode of business as it defines cultural identity, drives individual and collective behaviour, shapes socio-economic practices and creates a sense of community. Over 56 per cent of workers are engaged in agricultural and allied activities, producing food for over 1.21 billion people and exporting products with a return of $US39B. Despite the economic significance of this major industry it is widely conceded that agriculture received the least priority in implementing key liberalisation policies and regulatory reforms to facilitate access to competitive global markets to boost trade through more efficient global supply networks. The evidence shows agricultural practices in India remain rudimentary, primitive and ill-equipped to react to global change.

Media reports and informed commentary continually highlighted the duality in the Indian government policy, which provided substantial subsidies to farmers while simultaneously controlling the agriculture commodity prices until 1991. With the collapse of the *Nehruvian socialist model* with a higher priority for public sector investment, industrialisation and protectionism, India entered into a new era of economic reforms towards liberalisation, globalisation and privatisation. Agriculture transitioned through various waves of policy changes and regulatory adjustments to achieve the goals set by the neo-liberal agenda. Yet, agriculture continued to operate in a highly restrictive export-import regime, coupled with the impositions of the licensing Raj.

The outcomes of the first six decades of planned development in India's Post-Independence era aimed at achieving self-sufficiency, propelled by the Green Revolution, land reforms and the introduction of HYV seeds during the 1960s were not entirely unsatisfactory. Nevertheless, increased population pressure on finite land resources, continuous sub-division and fragmentation of landholdings, and reduced land and labour productivity presented many problems. But the challenges were also exacerbated by added complexities such as the use of primitive agricultural tools such as wooden ploughs and bullocks, the uncertainty of the vital monsoon rains, the predominance of subsistence farming, an absence of productive investment in rural infrastructure and the lack of institutional credit. All these factors combined to thwart the performance of the agriculture industry in India.

Rural India has been enormously affected by the neo-liberal reforms which have implemented measures to reduce per capita government expenditure on rural areas, cut subsidies on fertiliser, decrease public investment in rural infrastructure, agriculture and irrigation, and reduce access to rural credit. Not all of the reforms introduced in the Liberalisation phase were inimical or unfavourable to the agriculture sector. Internal trade, for example, has been liberalised by removing restrictions on agricultural commodities across states in India. International trade barriers on export and the import of agricultural commodities including import tariffs were reduced. Trade barriers to restrict the export of cultivated items such as Wheat and Rice were also reduced. Through these measures, the agriculture industry now has the opportunity to compete in the global marketplace and be able to harness the potential of free and unrestricted global trade.

Liberalisation policies and regulatory reforms in India aimed at helping the agriculture to alleviate rural poverty and unemployment, promote free and fair trade practices, improve the quality of life of farmers, secure food supplies, and create a buoyant market to compete in a global marketplace. Were small and marginal farmers being supported through regulatory reforms? Or were these regulations formulated to help larger farmers practicing commercial farming to produce commodities for export? It is vital to understand the mechanism through which economic growth and development percolated through to deprived regions and disadvantaged households. For example, was agriculture growth equitably dispersed or strategically concentrated in few high-performing growth areas to achieve high-efficiency standards? Did economic liberalisation and trade deregulation result in the convergence or divergence of agriculture growth?

The issue of farmer suicides is at the forefront of the policy agenda. One of the common reasons cited in the media for farmer suicides is soaring debt which farmers accrue due to the rising input costs, the plummeting price of produce and the interest that they pay to private moneylenders. A rigid and inadequate banking and credit system for agriculture loans in India has created situations for farmers to get caught in a debt trap. This is more prominent among small and marginal farmers who are enabled to get loans from institutional credit agencies. Only 20 per cent of available credit is funded from institutional credit providers, which offer low-interest loans to farmers for investment in agriculture projects. Predatory private moneylenders generally charge exorbitant interest rates, which make repayment difficult for small and marginal farmers. Thus, about 48 per cent of all farmers are in debt (NSSO2 Survey result), which shows farming reaching a toxic 'advanced stage of crisis', as concluded by the Commission of Farmer's Welfare. Given that agriculture wages in India are near a paltry $US3.5 – $US4.0 a day, and with the rising debt crisis, there is no mystery to explaining the disconcerting financial stress that has led the soaring numbers of farmers to commit suicide in rural India.

To place these key issues and other factors in context, this book examines the impacts of globalisation, liberalisation and farm commercialisation on regional restructuring of agricultural production networks in India. Time, space and the embedded events across various stages of social evolution are integrated to capture key changes in agriculture and land management in rural India. The transitional phases of Indian agriculture systems are analysed from the beginning of the Indus Valley Civilisation through to the era of post-industrialisation and the globalisation of the world economic system. The focus of this analysis is placed on spatio-temporal re-organisation of agriculture growth, productivity and regional change. The book is structured to probe key policy debates, government interventions, or the lack thereof, and planning directions to achieve inclusive growth and balanced regional economic development in a globalised competitive marketplace.

This book is specifically designed to fulfil three key purposes: the *first* is to investigate the above listed challenges thwarting the growth of Indian agriculture in a globalised competitive world; the *second* is to generate an evidence base to empirically evaluate the effects of economic liberalisation and regulatory reforms on agriculture growth and productivity; and the *third* is to provide a regional perspective to explain agriculture as a spatial phenomenon to aid policy formulation in terms of planning, strategic development and implementation.

This book incorporates creative ideas, new approaches and innovative methods to analyse, model and visualise key regional changes and spatial restructuring of agricultural landscape. Readers will appreciate the details captured at a small geographic area level while synthesising the results at a national and strategic level. Case studies are embedded that describe the hidden stories from local communities to highlight the cumulative impact of global change on local learning and to add depth and context to the readers' understanding. Crop-wise data coupled with land use data is also a key feature to enrich the analytic power to quantify and visualise spatial re-organisation of agriculture systems over several decades of change.

All chapters in this book are issue-based, outcome-oriented and policy-led interpretation of agriculture growth, productivity and regional change in India.

Chapter 2 describes the historical development of agriculture systems as an evolving and adaptive system of change since pre-historical periods through to the emergence of contemporary India. It discusses the underlying structures that created spatially fragmented, socially stratified and culturally fractured land management systems in response to value-based division of land and labour in India.

Chapter 3 examines the national and state level changes and emerging regional patterns in area, production and yield of food grains and other crops, while Chapter 4 analyses agricultural growth trends, identifies the key growth determinants and demarcates areas of growth concentration.

Chapters 5 and 6 explore various dimensions of land and labour productivity and evaluate the impact of economic liberalisation on convergence or divergence of regional growth processes in India respectively.

Chapter 7 investigates the ontological basis of delineating regional boundaries of agricultural sub-systems in India. A new spatial methodology develops the procedures and criteria required to delimit the agricultural regions to maximise differences in agriculture performance. It is vital to identify the way agricultural regions are hierarchically structured and functionally organised in India.

Chapter 8 presents the modelling and simulation of agriculture growth to predict the impact of any change in an agriculture system and its performance. Understanding the key drivers shaping the agriculture growth at a farm level where farm households are required to invest in farm assets and agriculture inputs is paramount to regional planning initiatives.

Chapter 9 analyses the production and consumption patterns and the resultant food availability in India at a disaggregate level. Consumption patterns in rural and urban areas in India are examined using National Sample Survey data, which highlight the key trends and changing consumption behaviour. This new regional approach to food insecurity helps identify areas of food deficiency or surplus. This in turn enables the generation of evidence to help devise and deploy area-specific strategies to mitigate challenges associated with food insecurity in India.

The authors' aims are for researchers, students and policy-makers interested in the spatiality of agriculture systems and regional development to find this book instructive. Some readers may be encouraged to explore new frontiers by applying the creative ideas, novel tools and innovative methods to analyse the transformative processes continually changing the Indian agriculture landscape. This research is purposely designed to be useful for policy-makers in initiating new public debates through heightened discourse and evidence-based policy responses to the challenges of globalisation, liberalisation and social change in India and the world around us. With all modesty we will not conceal that we, as the authors, feel we are motivated by a deep desire coupled with the ethical responsibility in our work to improving the well-being and quality of life of Indian farmers through the contribution of this book.

Professor Surendra Singh, North-Eastern Hill University, Shillong, India
Professor Prem Chhetri, RMIT University, Melbourne, Australia
May 2016

1   Introduction

1.01 Introduction

Agriculture is a *'way of life'* as it provides the livelihood for most rural people as well as drives the mainstream culture of Indian society. It is the employment engine of rural economies and the main source of basic food supply for rural households. Farming however in India has largely remained primitive despite the advancement in modern farming technology. Not until recent years, farmers started to adopt technological innovations to help increase food production and farm productivity. However, it is often difficult to overcome constraints such as small farm holding size, increasing population pressure and of course the uncertainty of monsoon. In agriculture-based countries like India, agriculture is considered as a means to sustain rural households as a self-functioning unit but its scope now has extended to offer new opportunities to adopt commercial farming through animal husbandry, cultivation of high-value crops (e.g. fruits, vegetables and other horticulture crops) and the linkages to non-farming activities in rural areas (World Bank Report 2008).

To tackle the challenges of rural living, it is imperative to shift the policy focus predominately from urban to rural economy. Agriculture could provide a strong economic base for employment generation if it embraces innovative farming techniques, commercialises food production, modernises its production line, helps achieve the economy of scale and diversifies its industrial structure. In recent decades, there were major regulatory reforms and structural changes in India, but it is yet to be examined whether they were successful in integrating rural economies with urban economies and being embedded seamlessly with the global marketplace. Further public debate is now needed to help devise a comprehensive global approach to food production and distribution through establishing inter-industry linkages that connect rural economy, ranging from food grains production to allied farm activities to the processing of agricultural products through to non-farm activities such as cottage industry, with global commodity markets. However, there are many unexplained benefits of globalised rural economies in terms of providing stimulus required to generate rural employment to help supply agricultural commodities to domestic and global markets.

The effect of liberalisation policies on agriculture growth, productivity and the convergence of regional structure are of a particular interest to policy-makers and regional planners. The deregulation and privatisation of the Indian economy driven by a neo-liberal agenda posits numerous challenges for the agriculture sector, which operates within a non-competitive market of more traditional subsistence farming. Are farmers in India ready to export their produce to spatially fragmented global production networks, which require more responsive and agile commodity chains? This book highlights some of the debates and provides empirical evidence to examining the key concerns and challenges for the agriculture sector in India. In this chapter, the policy context within which the agriculture development processes and growth mechanisms are conceptualised, measured, and visualised is established. This chapter discusses the key themes which will form the basis for defining the scope of the rest of the chapters.

1.02 Agriculture dynamics in India

Historically, agriculture was considered as a source of food supply to fulfil the demand of the local people. Only a small part of total farm produce was traded in the market. Farming was therefore subsistence in most parts of India. Since farming has been largely conducted to produce for domestic consumption, farmers continue to alter farming practices and land use as per their food requirements using traditional means of farm irrigation, crop harvesting and use of indigenous seeds and manures. Low productivity, insufficient use of technology, high labour intensity and disorganised spatial markets continue to underpin the performance and efficiency of the Indian agriculture system. However, India has tremendous potential to produce sufficient food to fulfil the national requirements and simultaneously generate food surpluses for the global market. However, the prerequisite for such a growth model would be a stronger industrial base, fairer farmer-market relationship, more matured and integrated market, and stronger associations and cooperatives. Few of these challenges were taken up after the Independence during the first five-year plan, which placed greater emphasis on agriculture. The Green Revolution further provided the impetus to increase agricultural productivity, which occurred during the first phase of agricultural development in India in the 1970s. Changing cropping patterns, variegated agro-ecological conditions and unpredictability of monsoon, regional variation in soil fertility levels (biophysical factors of land) and changing food consumption habits are major factors which drive the extent of food supply and consumption requirements in India.

The new economic policy favoured deregulation and undertook numerous open market reforms during the 1990s. India became a member of World Trade Organisation (WTO) and reported high economic growth especially in non-agricultural sectors. However, the agricultural growth remained constant at about 2.5 per cent per annum as it was recorded during the Green Revolution. Nonetheless, India expanded the Gross Cropped Area (GCA) by about 20 per cent during the periods of economic liberalisation. Cropping patterns were diversified with the cultivation of a variety of food grains, fruits and vegetables. The food-processing industry became a common link between the farmers and the final consumers in the domestic and international markets.

The demand for high-value food products in the global market had grown when the annual growth of GDP reached to 8 per cent to 9 per cent during the middle of first decade of this century. Indian food suppliers responded positively to increasing consumer demand. However, the global market is more competitive. In India, there has been structural transformation in food supply chains to strengthen its retail segment and to regulate food processing and wholesale/logistic segments. According to the study conducted by the International Food Policy Research Institute, rural–urban food supply chains and its transformation in terms of volume has tripled in the last three decades, consumption has diversified and the marketing has doubled (Reardon and Minten 2011). However, agro-supply chains are weaker in India because of the lack of sophisticated farm technology and advanced manufacturing techniques among food producers, processors, packagers and distributors. It is one way of looking at the increasing volume of food supply, which has shifted the focus from low-value locally consumed food commodities to high-value market-based products. However, the government reduced fertiliser subsidies from 3.2 per cent of GDP to 2.5 per cent during the Liberalisation period (1990–1 to 2000–1) resulted in an increase of fertiliser price index from 99 to 228 during the same period. As a result, incremental input output ratio (IIOR) rose sharply from 1.65 to 2.25 after the implementation of new economic policies. Furthermore, recent analysis by the Re-emerging World Advisory Services using the NSSO Household Expenditure Survey data (66th round July 2009 – June 2010) concluded that the income and consumption disparities after the implementation of new economic policies (1993–4 to 2004–5) have increased, which has in turn widened the urban–rural divide (Re-emerging World Advisory Services 2012).

1.03 Income inequalities and regional disparities

This rising regional disparity is of a particular concern for marginal and vulnerable communities in India that fall below the poverty line. For instance, the proportion of people living on a daily per capita consumption between Rs 12 and 20, increased from 51.2 to 55 per cent during the Liberalisation period (1990–1 to 2000–1). Whilst on the other side of the spectrum, the rich population went up to 56 per cent in the Post-Liberalisation phase, while for the high-income groups who spend Rs 93 or more per capita per day increased from 2.7 per cent to 4.0 per cent. This shows an increasing disparity at the extreme ends of the spectrum whereby the rich are consuming substantially more, while the poor, though not necessarily consuming less, tend to have marginal increase in their consumption levels. The upliftment of the marginalised communities requires government interventions as 88 per cent of scheduled castes and scheduled tribes, 85 per cent of Muslims, and 80 per cent of Other Backward Class population are deemed socially deprived. Moreover, 86 per cent of socially disadvantaged communities are illiterates, 79 per cent have not attained primary level of education and 79 per cent of them are working in informal sectors of the economy. This inequality in accessing economic opportunities, education and infrastructure amenities between rural and urban India necessitates spatially embedded economic development planning interventions to create functionally integrated economic systems that close the gap between rural production systems and urban systems.

This regional argument is further reinforced through the rising rural–rural and urban–rural disparities in Monthly Per Capita Expenditure (MPCE). The analysis of survey data shows the increasing rural differences in MPCE at the state level. Kerala (Rs 1835) had the highest rural MPCE, followed by Punjab (Rs 1649) and Haryana (Rs 1510). The gap in the consumption between rural and urban is also less. On the other hand, Jharkhand, Orisha, Chattisgarh and Bihar had very low rural and urban MPCEs. Maharashtra's urban MPCE interestingly is 110 per cent of that of its rural counterpart. On the other hand, the state of West Bengal also had substantial differences in urban–rural MPCE.

The annual growth of per capita State Domestic Products (SDP) was reported lowest (0.65 per cent) in the state of Assam, which experienced a moderate population growth (1.75 per cent annually) in the year 2010. It is highest (6.38 per cent) in Gujarat, which also recorded high population growth (1.59 per cent annually). The ratio between the average per capita SDP of the bottom three states (Bihar, Odisha and Assam) and the top three states (Punjab, Haryana and Maharashtra) was 1:2 in 1980s, which became 1:7 in the 1990s. This shows a significant level of regional disparity across the states. The widening gap in inter-regional income is seen as a major policy concern. The per capita income gap, for instance, between the top state (Punjab Rs 6487) and the state ranked at the bottom (Bihar Rs 2253) rose from 2.88 in 1988–9 to 4.75 times in 1996–7 and further to 5.50 times in 2003–4 (Suryakant 2010, Table 1.1). This concern led to the introduction of various new investment strategies and industrial and trade policies in 1991 such as liberalisation reforms and trade agreements. Such widening regional inequalities across the nation and deepening rural–urban divide necessitate deploying spatially integrated market reforms and policies to enhance efficiency of food production and distribution and curtailment of excessive and wasteful consumption.

The Post-Independence phase of economic development in India placed greater emphasis on heavy industries. They were established as growth poles to diffuse economic growth and propel economic prosperity in India. There were several benefits of this approach, but it failed to secure the overall prosperity of

Table 1.1 Widening regional gaps in per capita income

Period	Highest per capita income State	Lowest per capita income State	Ratio
1960–1	Maharashtra (Rs 409)	Bihar (Rs 215)	1.9
1970–1	Punjab (Rs 1,070)	Bihar (Rs 402)	2.66
1980–1	Punjab (Rs 2,674)	Bihar (Rs 917)	2.92
1988–9	Punjab (Rs 6,487)	Bihar (Rs 2,253)	2.88
1996–7	Punjab (Rs 18,213)	Bihar (Rs 3,835)	4.75
2003–4	Haryana (Rs 29,504)	Bihar (Rs 5,362)	5.5

Source: Economic Survey of different years, Ministry of Finance, New Delhi, compiled by Suryakant (2010)

Indian society. The richer regions became more prosperous whilst more deprived economies in rural India struggled to propel the economic growth. This linked to the earlier theoretical work in regional economics on growth poles and Hirshman and Myrdal's models on regional economic development. The national economy of India is now controlled and regulated by few powerful city economies, which regulate resource allocation and deploy regional economic development strategies.

Agriculture, in a globalised and competitive world, has overly marginalised to merely providing food supply with little investment and opportunity for innovation and creativity. Two key forces have played a key role in such a global change. First is the increasing policy focus on agglomeration economies as a strategic tool of economic growth, and second is the strengthening of economies of urbanisation. The first places greater emphasis on specialisation while the latter argues for industrial diversification. There are opportunities that could potentially be shifted to accelerate rural economies through agglomeration economies, which are based on decentralised spatial market clusters around agro-businesses, which provide services to the agriculture sector. The argument is to shift the location away from major metropolitan cities to highly productive farming areas, which are strategically located.

However, there is little evidence to support whether farm-based rural infrastructure can be developed through an integrated transport and logistics network that allows food to be seamlessly transported, stored, processed, packaged, consolidated and distributed (Minten 2011). The end-to-end supply chain solution however requires a better integration with urban economies. This is because cities are key nodes of mass consumption as well as transformation of raw materials from farm to finished or semi-finished products. This would then help achieve the economies of scale once a critical mass is achieved in the production scale. This will deter the increasing gap between rural and urban economies while decelerating the polarisation of agricultural growth in few key pockets (Nurul-Amin 1994).

Intra- and inter-regional disparities can be addressed through commercialisation of agriculture with a greater focus on the production of fruits and vegetables, dairy farming, and increased share of non-farming allied activities to support agro-farming businesses in rural areas. But the success of such propositions is yet to be tested. Agricultural-based rural economies are more likely to get commercialised with the expansion of exchange economy with greater industrial linkages in metropolitan cities. Agricultural policies such as the National Policy for farmers and Comprehensive District Agriculture Plan (C-ADP) 2007 were implemented to establish linkages between farming and urban-marketing, meaning the push towards a demand- driven production for greater economic returns. The aims of C-ADP include:

- Agricultural development at a grass-roots level,
- Greater collaboration among stakeholders involved in the development and planning activities,

- Active participation and engagement of local expertise,
- Proper coordination of Government departments and
- Improved linkages between rural sectors and urban economy to enhance functional interdependency between city economies and their rural hinterlands.

Despite the policy-push for better integration, the rural–urban linkages remained confined to the hinterlands of the key metropolitan economies in India whilst the peripheral economies were marginalised from the national benefits of policy change.

The interactions between rural and urban sectors are not uni-directional as commodities flow from rural to urban and urban to rural markets. However, farm-based rural economies have less income elasticity of demand for urban goods. Urban goods in large market centres need limited space for production. Linking farming with the market economy to support centre-oriented agglomeration would be a challenge because of space and biophysical constraints. However, post-production linkages can be established similar to the industrial production system to help optimise unit production. The World Bank also highlighted the need to bring agriculture to market to help promote the perspective on 'agriculture for development' (World Development Report 2008). They suggested the following instruments for using agriculture for overall development: '*bringing agriculture to market*', '*agri-business for development*' and '*environmentally sustainable agriculture*'.

1.04 Rural employment and labour force mobility

A relatively slow growth of the agricultural sector and its continually declining contribution to the country's GDP exert tremendous pressure on the rural labour force. As a result the elasticity of employment with respect to output diminishes faster as rural labour pressure grows (Table 1.2). There are some structural adjustments on account of reduced employment in the public sector in urban economies. Consequently, a shift of rural labour force from farming to non-farming activities in rural areas is evident. This form of rural labour tapped the employment opportunities in infrastructure projects such as road and rail network expansion and new township construction projects in rural–urban fringe areas. There is also a frequent mobility of traditionally farm labour force to work in non-farming occupations. Consequently, the employment in the rural non-farm sector grew at 9.5 per cent per year from 14.3 per cent in 1972–3 to 23.8 per cent in 1999–2000 of the total employment. The emergence of a 'new' labour force in rural India, but employed in non-farming occupations such as processing, procurement, distribution and retail of food commodities is also changing the configuration of supply-and-demand relationships.

Surprisingly, male non-farm rural employment increased faster than female particularly in manufacturing, wholesale and rural trades. However, as expected, female non-farming rural employment has a greater dominance in the services sector, though there are substantial differences between states. For example,

Table 1.2 Shift in sectoral shares and labour growth rates in India

Year	Annual compound growth rate + (%)	Total population (millions)	Working population (millions)	Annual compound growth rate + (%)	Size of labour force (millions)		Average annual growth rate # (%)		% Distribution of labour force	
					1	2	1	2	1	2
1951	1.25	361.1	140	–	97.2	42.8	–	–	69.4	30.6
1961	1.96	439.2	188.7	3.02	131.1	57.6	3.48	3.45	69.5	30.5
1971	2.2	548.9	180.5	-0.5	125.8	54.7	-0.4	-0.5	69.5	30.5
1981	2.25	658.2	222.5**	2.11	148	74.5	1.76	3.62	69.7	30.3
1991	2.43	836.6	285.4	2.5	185.2	100.2	2.51	3.62	66.5	33.5
2001	2.09	1028.7	313	0.93	167.1	145.9	-0.98	4.56	53.4	46.6
2011	1.64	1210.56	481.74	4.41	182	299.73	0.89	20.54	37.78	62.21

N.B.; 1=Agricultural Sector, 2=Non-Agricultural Sector

* Provisional figures compiled from Provisional Population Table, paper-3, Census of India, 1991 (series 1)

** Figures related to main worker only.

+ Compound growth rate, r, is computed by simplifying the following formula P1=P0(1+r)t; and

Average annual growth rate as r= (P1–P0)/P0t, where p1 and p0 are the population figures of current and base years respectively, r is annual rate, and t is the number of years.

Source: Census of India. Office of the Registrar General of India, Government of India, New Delhi

Kerala had 52 per cent share of total rural employment in the non-farming sec-tor whilst Madhya Pradesh had only 12 per cent in 1998–2000 (Panda 2006). Many progressive states have promoted agro-based industries and the supporting services as economic development strategy for creating employment for rural households. The magnitude is however largely driven by the levels of urbanisa-tion, wage differentials between rural and urban labour force and agricultural productivity (Srivastav and Dubey 2002). For instance, the states where the wage difference is less between urban and rural workforce, the incentives to shift to non-farming employment are not many. Despite the increasing significance of non-farm employment in rural areas, there is scant literature on the labour force dynamics and the embedded regional variability. Industrial diversification is a vital employment generation strategy, which not only transforms the economic base but also makes the rural economies more resilient to national and international economic shocks.

1.05 Globalised agriculture commodity markets

Market is an economic system for matching production and consumption of goods and services and for maintaining the equilibrium between demand and supply. While state is an 'institution' to support and regulate market by setting out a set of rules (Hayami 2001: 221–229) to ensure the market operate effi-ciently and effectively. Regulating the market means greater control on market failure. Linking farmers to an efficient market system would strengthen the inte-gration of food supply chains, especially for rural markets which act as collection centres of food surplus, while helping in making of agricultural inputs such as fertilisers, high-yield seeds or technology readily available to farmers at a lower cost. The traditional agricultural market was solely based on the collection of surpluses at a local (village) level using multi-layered distribution channels. These intermediaries acted as agents or were wholesalers and exporters. The State had little control and power to regulate the open market mechanisms through which prices of goods were determined. Commodities were also exchanged in a barter system in various parts of the country during the periods of early planning. As the production surplus increased during the Green Revolution, the role of the Public Distribution System (PDS) in India evolved through regulating the price control mechanism of food grain commodities to purchase and supply of essential food grain commodities to disadvantaged communities. The functions of PDS extended across food supply chains through a series of reforms including the food-procurement policy by the government. Food distribution is controlled by two systems in India: one is PDS, which procures and distributes basic food com-modities at subsidised rates to low-income households; second is support of a competitive market that connects various links of commodity supply chains from procurement, storage, distribution through to retailing to reach the end consum-ers. Recent economic reforms are targeted to promote the open and deregulated commodity market to help operate more efficiently and optimally within the ambit of supply and demand price mechanism.

An efficient market system in India however has to consider whether the open and competitive market provides a 'fair' and 'just' price for farm produce to farmers, who operate under high market uncertainty and within the stringent biophysical constraints of land, weather and technology. The market also needs to be wary of consumption variability with substantial vertical and horizontal differences. Farmers want higher prices for their produce, whilst intermediaries procuring the goods in an open market always negotiate a lower price. A lack of a fully functioning and competitive commodity market however favours intermediaries and provides few choices to farmers to sell their products in a poorly understood market. Furthermore, an international market where the opportunities for farmers to directly access international markets is limited but growing at an unprecedented rate. The ability of small farmers to negotiate better prices for their commodities in overseas markets is rather restricted as is their bargaining power. The importation of goods from overseas markets however could drive down the prices in the local market. In many cases, prices are set out by the Government, which could be deemed as an 'unnecessary interference' in an open market. Distribution of agriculture produce in India operates under two parallel consumer markets where high-quality products are supplied to consumers who are willing to pay higher prices whilst lower-quality food products are offered to low-income households.

1.06 Operational inefficiency and food waste

With increasing urban population and the concomitant re-configuration of food supply chains, an efficient food freight network is required to provide food where needed while minimising waste and storage costs. However, there are a number of constraints that are thwarting the development of efficient supply chains including inadequate and low capacity infrastructure, insufficient cold storage and transport vehicles, and poor accessibility to and remoteness of wholesale markets. It is now imperative to map various categories of food commodities (e.g. dairy products, meat, poultry and sea food, grains, fruits and vegetables), which are area-specific while processing of food is location-specific. Spatial organisation of locations within different agricultural regions should therefore be the basis for agricultural development and planning. Spatially integrated agriculture planning would integrate production, distribution and consumption as a set of nodes in a complex commodity supply chain. This will make the supply chains more efficient, effective and resilient to any perturbation in the distribution network.

Sustainable food supply chains are dependent on the reduction of food waste. Traditional methods of crop harvesting and crop collection at farms by farmers operating on smaller landholdings increase the chance of food wastage. Food is often stored at home with no food storage or refrigeration facility. This is particularly vital for fresh and perishable food. Farm produce is also exposed to infestation and other hazards. Lack of refrigeration and long-haul non-refrigerated transportation further escalates the chance of food waste. Two-thirds of food produced on a subsistence farm is often kept for household consumption. Chakravarty (1976) in an earlier study reported about 16 per cent waste of food from farm to the kitchen. Wheat crop harvesting in the western part of the Great Plains and Paddy-harvesting in the Bengal plains of India are two examples which show how traditional manual harvesting results in food-grain waste. The matured crops of Wheat when ready for harvesting are cut down by labour in March–April and kept in the field until completely dried. At the time of threshing, it is estimated that about 5 per cent of total volume of Wheat grains falls from dried branches onto the ground. Some of it is collected by the farm workers, but the rest remains unusable or left on the ground. The process of waste continues when dried crops are transported to a place where they are thrashed or winnowed. About 2 per cent of total grains is wasted in loading/unloading or handling. Furthermore, threshing is traditionally done by domestic animals; they eat forage with grains causing a further loss of about 4–5 per cent. Grains are then separated from forage but some cannot be separated due to the use of primitive techniques or adverse weather conditions such as high-speed wind or heavy rain. About 5 per cent of grains remain in forage. When food grains are sent to flour mills, 2 per cent wastage is often reported.

Likewise, the process of paddy crop cutting and manual grain-separation make up about 7 to 9 per cent waste, where in a Paddy-husking process contributes to about 2 to 4 per cent. Food wastage is also a significant issue in food-processing, procurement and retailing. Inadequate cold-storage facilities and insufficient protection of food grains from insects and pests cause more than 10 per cent of food grains to become wet and eventually infested from fungal and other bacteria. Overall, the disjointed food-supply chains (as production price delinked from market) increase the likelihood of food wastage up to 30 per cent, which ironically is significantly high by the world standard.

Technology plays a critical role in shaping our economy and societal pursuits. Technology however is a means not the end. Is it the solution for our problems in rural India, which has deep-rooted social and cultural values and structures that resist change? Nonetheless, there are two main ways of reducing the waste and efficiently managing the food supply chain in India. First is the adoption of 'cutting-edge' modern technology to help improve storage, transportation and distribution of food, in addition to reducing waste during agro-processing activities. Table 1.3 lists the techniques which are widely used in various stages of

Table 1.3 Technology and food supply chain

Agricultural production	Biological and bio–process technology
	Agricultural mechanisation
	Soil and water engineering
	Livestock technology
	Fruits and cultivation systems
	Harvest management
Storage and food procurement	Cold chain technology
	Storage and warehouse
	Fermentation technology

Food processing and packaging	Agro–industry and its location
	Agro–business management
	Transport and logistics
	Drying technology
	Packing technology
Retailers and food shops	Technologies related to providing clean and safe food

food production, storage, transportation and distribution. Second is to promote behavioural change particularly related to the perception of consumption habits, and recognition of waste during the religious events and social festivities. Nevertheless, the solution to food wastage is well beyond the scope of these changes as it requires significant operational changes and structural reforms.

1.07 Carrying capacity, land potential and monsoon-dependency

Land potential, environmental risk and climatic uncertainty, both short and long term, are the key drivers of agriculture production economics. Agricultural productivity heavily relies on land capability and weather conditions. India is a monsoon country, thus it is highly dependent on the arrival of monsoon, which sets the sowing season. Any early arrivals or delays of monsoon could either destroy the harvesting of crops or push out the sowing season of crops. Natural disasters, land degradation and overutilisation of land have strong effects on land potential and thus on farm productivity. This in turn also affects production prices and input costs. Known weather conditions particularly the arrival of monsoon and the anticipated rainfall would be useful pieces of information for farmers in making evidence-based farming decisions such as the type and combination of crops, farming techniques and amount of fertiliser. For example, Rice production and its growth period are determined by environmental conditions such as the suitable temperature and the amount of moisture in soil, which in turn determine the land potential. Increasing population pressure and delays in monsoon season affect the entire crop season, alter crop pattern, and reduce crop production and productivity.

Environmental conditions in India, given its physiographic diversity, vary over time and space. Understanding agro-ecological specificities provides a broader framework to provide farmers a better knowledge of the biophysical conditions of land and weather which would enable them to choose the correct measures to help achieve the optimal result. Such a framework has to be developed and implemented at a farm level as well as integrated at a regional scale, linked to national policy goals and objectives. Mapping and monitoring of regional growth and productivity patterns and linking them with the constantly changing local agroclimatic conditions are fundamental to promoting sustainable growth and environmental protection of land. The regional approach for managing agriculture growth and productivity thus provides a sound base of a long-term sustainability of farming.

Stagnation of agricultural production is a threat to producing surplus food for export in the global market place. This is seen as an opportunity to harness the potential of trade in countries which import food for domestic consumption. Some however argue for fulfilling the domestic demand prior to exporting food for foreign earnings. The production in India is barely satisfying the growing population size and changing consumption behaviour. Despite the adoption of innovative farming technology during the Pre-Liberalisation phase (1960s to 1990s), leading to the Green Revolution or the implementation of new economic policies and reforms in the 1990s, the agricultural growth has by and large remained constant. This indicates the effect of the 'diminishing law of return', as IIOR increases over time. It could mean the declining profitability of agriculture in comparison to other alternatives. As the Planning Commission (now National Institute for Transferring India, NITI Aayoug) adopted the agro-climatic region as a planning unit in its policy frame, the regional disparity in agricultural productivity and growth remained a challenging task for agriculture planners in building more resilient national food supply chains. In recent decades, agriculture growth and productivity are increasingly becoming more dependent on market rather than on biophysical conditions of farm land.

1.08 Agriculture supply chain complexity

Agriculture as a practice in India is complex, so is its planning. It is complex due to the long historical evolution and the resulting embeddedness of socio-cultural values that resist any major structural changes. Multitude of food commodities, processing, transport and logistics and the disconnected market raise another layer to this complexity. Ideally, if what is being produced and what is being consumed occur within the same region, most of the issues would disappear. However, the areas of production are often not the same as those of consumption, which requires transportation and distribution of food. This creates a complex maze of food supply chains, which are reflected in the physical flow of food commodities and are seamlessly connected through modal and intermodal facilities such as transportation networks and hubs.

Establishing a market-based agriculture system operating within a public sector infrastructure posits a range of challenges for producers, agents, distributors and retailers. Poor road condition and network connectivity, embryonic market information systems, premature commodity exchange market mechanism, and production-price risk management systems are the main drivers that link agriculture to market. Conversion of agricultural products to high-value goods for urban markets or international markets requires optimal spatial market networks which facilitate the selection of food processing locations to minimise transport and storage costs of food, development of new farm towns in close proximity to areas of agriculture surplus and strengthening of the market facilities in rural areas. Such optimal spatial agriculture market systems would provide employment to rural population and minimise out migration of rural labour force to urban areas.

1.09 The policy shift

Indian agriculture system has gone through the throes of significant policy changes since Independence. Land use and crop production patterns were changed under the regulatory reforms or market during the colonial period when feudalism was prevalent in the country and later in subsequent planning phases of economic development after Independence. Major policies were formulated to encourage land consolidation, provision of low-interest rate loans/credits to farmers, and strengthening agricultural research institutes/organisations.

Indian agriculture is now at the forefront of major policy change. It is at a crossroads of experiencing a 'transitional phase' of technological change and heading for market-based policy changes to help commercialise food production. The policy shift is aiming to increase competitiveness in the global commodity markets and to create innovative farming practices. Evidence of such policy shift is seen in a few highly productive areas which have started to produce food surplus for the market. However, there are still major hurdles that need to be tackled in order to ensure that farming remains productive, competitive, efficient and more importantly fair. Supply of food commodities from one part of the country to another is a main issue that is linked to unconnected and disorganised spatial markets inefficiently controlling and regulating the flows of commodities from areas of production to areas of consumption. Consequently, the Indian commodity market is unable to maintain a demand-and-supply equilibrium, which is causing market failures and food shortages in some areas while excess in others (Berry et al. 1993).

One of the key policy changes is a shift in modelling framework from agro-meteorological- to agro-economic-based agriculture planning. Agro-meteorological-based planning is guided by the physiographical characteristics of land such as land capability potential, climatic conditions and geomorphological properties to determine the potential for crop cultivation. While the agro-meteorological properties are important determinants of land productivity, the economic and socio-institutional structures such as the efficiency of commodity markets, consumption behaviour, market accessibility, consumer behaviour and the potential of international export of farm produce are equally vital. During the Liberalisation phase, the planning paradigm has shifted from agro-climatic-driven agricultural planning to agro-economic regions, which integrate more functional criteria in defining regional homogeneity over the earlier, more formal and static definition. The success of central Government-sponsored schemes particularly for the development of agro-based industries was dependent on three key factors: the centre-state relations (federal structure), the bureaucratic setup with heavy administrative burden at a grass-roots level and the ability of recipients to adopt new approaches and techniques to increase productivity levels.

Empirical evidence is now required to evaluate the effectiveness of this shift that substantiates the benefits of agro-economic-based planning on regional agricultural performance. Agriculture production and productivity and their relationships with biophysical factors of land such as soil properties, availability of water, and geomorphological processes have been analysed by a number of studies (Kumar et al. 2015, Singh et al. 2009–10) including a seminal study by the Indian Council of Agriculture Research (ICAR). When agriculture is considered as a production activity and capital to boost productivity, the econometric approaches for modelling input–output relationships are useful in gathering empirical evidence necessary to formulate effective agricultural policies. However, there is little empirical evidence to show whether such policies and planning interventions were effective in improving the current farming practices and in enhancing farm productivity in vulnerable and less resilient regions, requiring further investigation. There is no doubt that sustainable agriculture production requires a well-planned and coordinated strategic framework, which connects production, availability, distribution and consumption of food as an integrated commodity supply chain. A 'regional approach' to making food available where it is needed at an affordable price could be a way forward in the integration of these key dimensions of a sustainable food production system. The failure to manage commodity flows from the areas of production to areas of consumption could potentially lead to market failure, price rise (or fall) and food waste. This could also create food insecurity for a nation which has no single policy framework to strategically and spatially plan food distribution in emergency situations such as natural disasters.

1.10 Challenges of food insecurity

The food production index in India, which represents the food crops that are palatable and contain nutrients, has increased from 91.7 in 2000 to 138.8 in 2013. Moreover the crop production index in India has also increased from 92.3 in 2000 to 141.9 in 2013 (The World Bank 2016). Over the last five decades (between 1961–3 and 2007–9) the food production has increased enormously by around 170 per cent, which shows the increased performance of agriculture. But with the growing population of India, which is expected to reach around 1,800 million in 2050, India will need to produce more in 2050 than what we produced in 2006 to satisfy the burgeoning demand of food and to attain the amount of calories required (WRI 2013). The proportion of malnourished people in India has dropped by 1 per cent from year 1990 to 2000 but the absolute number has increased by 18 million people in that decade. The latest statistics show that around 194 million people were undernourished in India in 2015 where as 795 million people were undernourished worldwide, which represents a significant proportion that is around 25 per cent lies only in India (FAO 2015).

In recent decades, food insecurity is at the forefront of public debate in India. Figure 1.1 demonstrates the interlocking relationships between food supply chains, market demand and food security/insecurity. It shows that food security entails making food availability where it is needed, providing it at a reasonable rate so that it is affordable and distributing it so that it is economically and geographically accessible.

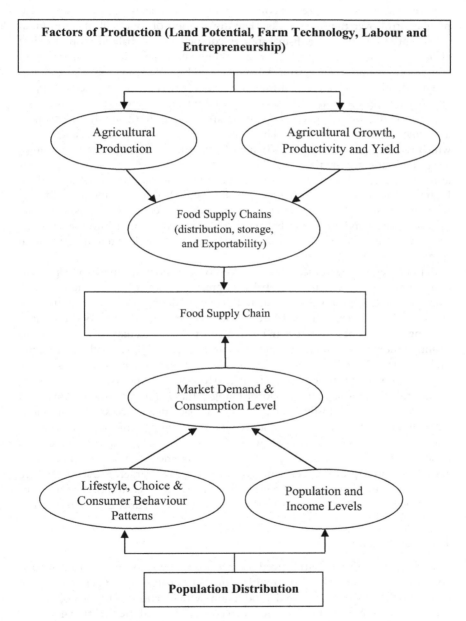

Figure 1.1 Food supply chains, market linkages and food security/insecurity

Despite the introduction of food security bill in the parliament to help strengthen the optimum balance between demand–supply of agriculture commodity, the distribution, availability and accessibility of food remains a major challenge for the Indian Government. PDS and the market-led open system operate mostly in different economic models. The prevalence of two contradictory yet parallel systems creates confusion about the benefits of government-led price control over the free market. The distribution of food still operates in an inefficient mode and is in a dismal state to compete in a globalised economy. The efforts to regulate food supplies to help eliminate market inefficiency through legislation are not yet successful (Chaudhary and Bhattacharyya 2012).

The identification of areas of food shortages (where demand exceeds supply) allows mapping the potential transportation and logistics requirements to optimised food distribution over a large geographic space. Both supply and demand are *inter alia* affected by space. There are often areas of food surplus and deficit, which requires geostrategic approach to distribution planning to minimise food waste and storage. Spatial variability is not just a feature of food supply, but also an inherent characteristic of food demand. Consumption is often high in high population density urban areas, which have higher disposal income and consumptive lifestyle. Food consumption is therefore affected by disposal income, lifestyle choices and consumer behaviour. A systematic approach to food insecurity in India is now called upon to help develop spatially integrated agricultural planning and policy framework.

Better access to market-led pricing system of demand and supply to help maintain the production-consumption balance, greater choices of marketing channels, strengthened transport linkages, demand-driven production of food, and changing consumer behaviour and lifestyle are prerequisites for tackling the food insecurity challenges. The problems associated with access to and availability of basic foods to maintain the bare minimum nutritional requirements of human body are creating 'hidden hunger' (i.e., poor diet and malnutrition) among the populace, despite the sufficient production of food within India. More than 20 per cent of Indians are malnourished according to the Global Hunger Index report by the International Food Policy Research Institute in 2011. The availability and accessibility of food is certainly a geographic problem as they require the optimum utilisation of economic space. It is a problem which is often overlooked but requires urgent attention of policy-makers. Would in-depth spatial analysis of empirical data on food production and consumption provide an evidence base to prepare geo-targeted strategies? There is certainly an urgency to minimise high levels of food-wastage in India and to establish efficient food distribution networks to manage food security more effectively.

1.11 Summary

This chapter has briefly introduced agriculture as a way of life for Indian society. Key issues were discussed to initiate further debates on the performance of agriculture. With the globalised production systems and the rising population pressure on finite land, there is urgency to cognate beyond the traditional ways of cultivating land. A policy shift from agro-climatic region-based planning to more economically embedded planning paradigm would certainly better link farmers with the market. Nonetheless, it requires careful integration of land potential based on the biophysical carrying capacity of land and adjustment to the techno-institutional evolutionary structures that construct agriculture as a socio-cultural phenomenon.

Agriculture in India is conceived as a holistic system which is deeply rooted in nature and is embedded in social values and beliefs. Economic liberalisation and market-centred deregulation have the potential to enhance the competitiveness of an open market system but they have to transform traditional agriculture into an economically driven, modern farming production operation. Regional issues and income inequality have produced new challenges for rural India. Food production and consumption require bridging the geographic distance through better and improved freight transportation networks to create more agile and lean commodity supply chains. Any spatial mismatch might potentially create a situation of food insecurity and could jeopardise the economic prosperity, progress, inclusive growth and the overall well-being of Indian society.

2 Evolution of agriculture development in India

2.01 Introduction

Agriculture is the 'culture' of Indian society. It has evolved through various phases of Indian history. Changes in production mode and land ownership have long been affected by social evolution and technological changes. Food is not just a commodity for consumption; it is also an object of worship. Some foods have remedial or healing power and, thus, are often used as herbal medicines for curing diseases. Hence, cultivation of crops has high cultural and social value in Indian society. Value systems however are complex, structured and rigid in Indian society. Historically, the value systems in India determined what types of food are grown on land, who grows them, what methods should be employed and who consumes what products. Agriculture therefore is spatially fragmented, socially stratified and culturally fractured in response to value-based division of labour and land. Changes in socio-ecological systems have thus shaped and regimented the agriculture landscape in India.

Food production is also regulated and institutionalised. There are institutional frameworks, social rules and cultural norms from ancient times on division of labour. The interwoven systems, entailing socio-cultural beliefs, individualised altitudes and collective societal values, have exerted significant influence on agricultural production practices in the past and present. In recent decades, agricultural systems and the underlying norms and farm practices in India are shaped by the ideology of modernity, connectedness through globalisation and progress via technological transitioning. This chapter therefore traces the historical developments of agriculture systems since pre-historical periods through to the emergence of Modern India.

2.02 Agriculture as a construct

Historically, the expansion of Aryan settlements in the middle Ganga valley and the concomitant spatial diffusion of Vedic knowledge (ancient literature) led to the adoption of sedentary farming. Cultivation of Rice and indigenous crops became part of the Ganga culture in Northern India. Numerous socio-religious movements and reforms through the classical Vedic age resulted in changes in land ownerships, tenancy and farming methods. Vedic knowledge, which accrued through experiences of practicing sedentary agriculture and value-systems, laid a stronger base for the transformation of Indian agriculture systems. Sedentary lifestyle and high-land dependency during the late ancient period created regional identities (*mahajanapadas*) and power to control land. This place-bound regionalism and place-based social coherence were shaped by the growing influence of 'brahamanism', which established and then regulated socio-religious practices and institutional structures. It surpassed the ritualistic culture and social norms in the middle Ganga plains (present days Bihar and Bengal areas) through assimilating Aryans with indigenous tribes (Schwartzberg 1978: 162–163). As a result, socio-cultural systems were coalesced, which in turn led to the creation of a new set of rules and norms. In areas of ancient settled agriculture in India, Rice and Cotton were the dominating crops, which are of high socio-cultural importance. For instance, Cotton for weaving and making cloths and Rice for food are still used as 'God gifts'. They are still used to symbolically represent the 'source of life' in social events and religious festivals. Use of rice during puja (worship) is a known socio-cultural activity in contemporary modern India. Given the predominance of food grains in ancient India, the socio-economic set up of the communes was shaped by the necessities of agrarian economy.

The emergence of the feudal system and changes in land use from an 'open' land system to a 'closed' land system for revenue collection in the Mughal period had diversified the agrarian economy and rural society. It developed class systems, reinforcing the rigid structure of caste systems, from *zamindar* (landlord) to peasants (small farmers). Other artisans whose economic occupations were entirely dependent on the functional organisation of village economy were also cemented with virtually no possibility of vertical mobility. Carpenters, iron smiths, washer-men, barbers, cleaners and *banjies* (scavengers) and other castes belonging to lower social strata were engaged as helpers. They were given a small share of food produced in each season so as to feed their families. This socially disintegrated and economically exploitative system was created and established in rural India prior to the emergence of urban settlements during the medieval period. During the time of colonial British rule, agriculture was considered as a backbone of Indian society with its social relevance in defining its identity, character and belief system.

Increasing population and growing size of non-agricultural sectors of the economy during the recent decades compelled landless or near landless labourers operating on marginal farms to migrate to nearby towns in search of jobs on account of wage differentials and better job opportunities. This was despite the increasing land and labour productivity in the agricultural sector. With intensive resource use and technological enhancement, agriculture in India has gradually evolved from hunting and gathering to pastoral agriculture and through to modernisation of agriculture. There are, however, regions where hunting and gathering are still prevalent particularly in tribal areas. With the challenges associated with increasing population and finite resources, the use of farm technology has become essential to increase farm productivity. Nonetheless, in most parts of India, agriculture is still subsistence-oriented, which is organised and practiced to largely fulfil the daily household food requirements. However, the recent trends toward commercialisation of farming on a larger scale started to emerge in more advanced regions of India, nevertheless the majority of farms remained small, fragmented and primitive. The initial mode of production was animal husbandry and cattle raising in ancient India, which later shifted to pasture-based agriculture with open farming. Thus, farming practices and its associated value-systems shifted from 'cow-culture' during the late ancient period (circa 500 BC) to 'plough-culture'. This led to sedentary farming, transitioned from animal grazing or slash-and-burn farming.

The right to land ownership has a significant impact on modern farming practices in India. The power of owning land was institutionalised in the feudal system, which empowered few landlords to own and collect revenues for the government while the majority works on farms as labourers or '*bandhwa majdoor*'. Farm production, thus, has three key purposes: first was to produce food to feed families, second to pay land tax and third to generate excess food to barter trade with other essential commodities. Often, it was difficult for farmers to achieve all, which resulted a continuous class structure in rural India.

McCarty and Lindburg's optima-limit theory of agricultural resource use (1967) could explain the spatial organisation of agriculture. The technological inputs in farm and capital accumulation were the key drivers that have increased the productive land capacity and established proper institutional structures, particularly rural banking and finance. Adoption of new production technology and bringing social change in agrarian society are dependent on the development of institutions in modern times where agriculture is considered as an industrial activity, rather than a means to fulfilment of domestic needs for food or mere survival in India. Transitioning of agriculture is evident in the changing social forms and modes from food-grains-based production primarily for household consumption to production of commercial crops for the accumulation of capital and to market-based production to increase surplus. Such transformation of Indian agriculture has brought a significant change in land use patterns, which was monotonous in the early 20th century but later diversified in the beginning of 21st century due to deregulation and liberalisation of the Indian economy.

2.03 Historical evolution of Indian agriculture

The history of Indian agriculture is complex, culturally intertwined and complicated. The narratives have several unresolved controversies, bias judgements, contradictory interpretations of events and incomplete historical records (Gopal and Srivastawa 2008). The evolution of the agricultural landscape in India is the result of poly-cultural traits and their changing socio-economic environments and continuous alterations in people's requirements over time. However, numerous scholars investigated the cultural and political history of Indian society to understand the roots of present-day agricultural landscapes. The social mosaics and cultural embeddedness are produced in response to the geographic vastness, diversity and disconnectedness of communities within the Indian sub-continent. Arguably, the history of India is the collective reflection of multiple 'histories' of parallel societies, coexisting within their own socio-ecological milieu. Among many available writings on the history of India, three key documents were consulted to present the historical accounts of Indian agriculture. These include: *A Historical Atlas of South Asia* edited by Schwartzberg (1978), the *Themes in Indian History* compiled by the National Council of Educational Research and Training (NCERT 2007) and the *History of Agriculture in India up to c 1200 AD* edited by Gopal and Srivastawa (2008).

Pre-historic texts (Neolithic period before the Harappan civilisation that flourished between c. 2600 and 1900 BC) contain little evidence of settled agriculture in India. They have evidence of hunting, cattle rearing and food gathering activities, but little to show the widespread prevalence of sedentary farming. However, the Harappan civilisation, which developed in the adjacent areas of the middle and lower Indus valley, had civilised rural societies who practiced settled agriculture.

The historical texts and narratives help divide the evolution of Indian agriculture from the Harappan civilisation to the modern system of agriculture. It is broadly divided into four phases: the Harappan civilisation, the medieval period of feudalism (Mughal empire and agrarian society of the 16th and 17th century), and the colonial British era (19th till mid 20th century) with the beginning of modern agriculture in independent India (1947 till present).

2.03.1 Agriculture in the Harappan civilisation (c. 600 to 2600 BCE) – the beginning of settled cultivation

The Harappan civilisation was a dispersed planned settlement along the middle Indus valley including its delta along with the coastal areas of the Arabian Sea (Figure 2.1). Due to the favourable sub-humid and sub-arid climate and fertile alluvial soils of the Indus and Ganga valleys, there is evidence to suggest that the people of the Harappan civilisation cultivated Wheat, Barley and Sesamum. Millets were also grown in Harappan sites, which were located in Gujrat and coastal areas of Sindh (now in Pakistan).

Agricultural technology during this phase was simple and primitive. Domestication of animals was commonplace. The use of oxen for ploughing of land was the major development in farm technology. Archaeologists found that plough (a tool for digging land) and ploughed fields at the sites located at the confluence of Indus and Jamuna River (now the plains of Punjab and Haryana). Iron blade was used in the plough. Indigenous seeds were typically broadcasted (scattered) in ploughed fields for crop production. Of course, a section of Harappan society ate meat of wild animals such as deer and *gharyal*. However, some evidence indicates that the majority of people had a vegetarian diet. Food grains were the staple food. The key technological developments in farming include:

- Application of harvesting tools made of stone with wooden handle;
- Development of terraces of channel for irrigation in the Harappan sites located in semi-arid lands; and
- The possible use of a device to draw water from a well.

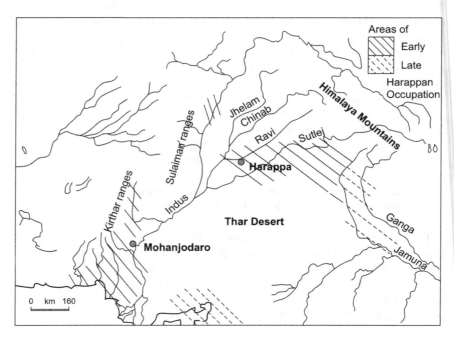

Figure 2.1 Sites of Indus Valley Civilisation (Harappa and Mohanjodaro)

This evidenced the existence of a cultivation system, which began to evolve to organise the food supply within the rural community and the surplus for the key urban centres. The Harappan civilisation was an urban settlement with two key townships, Mohanjodaro (located in the middle part of the Indus valley with an approximate elevation of 160m) and Harappa (located in the foothills of Siwaliks on the bank of Ravi, a tributary of Indus). These towns were well- planned settlements, which were configured in a rectangular shape with a matured drainage system. Both Mohanjodaro and Harappa were market centres, which facilitated the exchange of local commodities.

During the late Harappan civilisation (c. 600 BCE to 600 CE), new settlements were established in the middle and lower parts of the Ganga valley. They were organised around the notion of kingships (instead of communes), each of which had their individual service hinterlands. The territoriality of these kingships gradually evolved, established and organised in sixteen *Mahajanpadas* (kingdoms, state or province). A new set of trade-oriented townships was established as capitals. They also became administrative and political centres. An agricultural production system was developed in the vicinity of these townships, which were connected via road networks to ensure the continuous supply of food commodities from rural hinterlands. To fulfil the rising demand, an intensive cultivation of Rice in the middle and lower parts of the Ganga valley and Wheat in the North Western *Mahajan-padas* (Kuru, Sursa and Panchala in the Upper Ganga Valley) was practiced.

The teaching of Mahavir (Jainism) and Buddha (Buddhism) led the Indian society to transition towards practicing the principle of *karma* (work) and *shanti* (peace). Magadh (present-day Bihar) *Mahajanpada*, of which Patliputra (Patna) was the capital, was known for innovative farming practices during the 6th and 4th century BC due to the rising influence of vegetarian-diet-centred in Jain culture and non-violence-oriented Buddhist culture. By the end of the 1st century BCE, new chiefdoms and kingdoms were established in several parts of India. Chiefdoms of Chola in South India (part of Andhra Pradesh, Kerala and Tamil Nadu) and the chiefs and kings who ruled Western and Central India developed a systematic system for land tax collection and the generation of revenue from long-distance trade.

Empirical evidence from various sources indicates the widespread use of farm technology to assist in the cultivation of crops and dairy farming. These include:

• The use of iron-tipped ploughs to increase production especially in the upper and middle parts of the Ganga valley;
• The use of transplantation method of sowing rather than sprinkling to boost farm production in rice paddy;
• Irrigation through wells and tanks were started to increase crop production.

During the early historic period (200–100 BCE) when Harappan civilisation began to disintegrate, a new regime of capital and land accumulation started to emerge under the rural elites, called *Zamindars* (landlords). Granting of land to *Zamindars* and authority to collect taxes and revenues for the government became prevalent in the entire sub-continent (end of the Mauryan empire, emergence of Indo-Greek rules in the North West; Chola, Cheras and Pandyas in the South India and Satavahanas in the Deccan). The land was also granted to religious institutions to support the livelihood of Brahmins to develop Sanskrit inscription in South India. Parts of land particularly uncultivated land, which varied in size, were allocated to peasants. Agrarian society in India during the time of Chandragupta II (c. 375–415 CE) became more socially fragmented with structures built around kingships, castes and classes. This fractured social system created large regional variations in crop cultivation patterns, land tenancy and ownership. Nevertheless, meteorological observations to help improve the efficiency of land usage, construction of tanks and the development of new roads were the main technological changes of that period, which augmented agriculture production.

Arabs conquered Sindh in c. 712 AD and changed regional agricultural patterns in the Sindh area of the North Western part of the Indian subcontinent. This led to the beginning of a new era.

2.03.2 The rise of the Mughal empire (16th and 17th centuries)

The Mughal empire in the Indian sub-continent was established by the founder Babur's victory over Ibrahim Lodi, the last ruler of the Delhi Sultanate in the First Battle of Panipat (1526). Mughals, in general, adopted a non-intervention strategy to create a systematic, centralised and uniform rule through the empowerment of socio-ethnic groups such as the Marathas, the Rajputs, the Pashtuns, the Hindu Jats and the Sikhs. In the beginning, they tried to minimise interfering in the functioning of local societies and their way of life. There were numerous principalities and kingdoms which were operating in parallel across different parts of India including the Delhi Sultanate in the North (1206), the Gajapati rule in Orissa in the East (1435), the Sultanate of Golconda (1518) in the South and the Vijaynagra empire (14th to 16th century). Agriculture was largely practiced in isolation, but there is evidence to show interactions and understanding among these rulers to share new farm methods and techniques to improve the efficiency of agriculture practices. In particular, the regime of Akbar (1556–1605) was noticeable when land management and land use statistics were collected via systematic land surveys. Records were kept for each acre of land in each *suba* (province), which extended from Qandhar (the North Western Frontier) to Dhaka (Bay of Bengal) (Figure 2.2) in the Great Indo-Gangatic plains.

Figure 2.2 The geographic extent of Akbar's reign in 1605

A land revenue system was created at each administrative level from *suba* to *zila* (district) and even to *gaon* (village). Land ownership details were recorded for each *zamindar* and peasant. Cadastral mapping was done at the scale of 4 inch = 1.0 mile to maintain land records and to collect agricultural statistics at a village level. *Sazra* (map) and *Khasra* (a register in which land record was recorded) were written and meticulously maintained at a tehsil level (sub-division of district). The land tax and revenue collection system was developed by Todarmal, one of the *vazeers* (ministers) in the Akbar Government. The land management system was documented in *'Ain-i-Akbari'* (the vision document of agricultural reforms), which was written by Abu'lFazal (a historian in Akbar's court). The evolving land–labour relationship during the Mughal period was based on the division of labour and class-structure as discussed below.

Relationship between the state and Zamindars

A socio-economic hierarchy in the agrarian society was maintained by establishing the ordering from the *Raja* (king) to *Zamindars* (landlords) and then to *kisan* (peasant). Social and economic privileges were assigned to *Zamindars* by virtue of their superior status and ranking in the hierarchy. They occupied extensive personal lands (*milkiyat*), which were fortressed and armed with local contingents and a small unit of infantry. The division of land and the tenancy divided the society between 'have' and 'have not', which further reinforced a feudal system. This led to the initial development of quasi-federalism wherein *Zamindars* established a regional system within which market towns were created to control and command the commodity markets and labour dynamics.

Peasants and their relation with land

The name *raiyat* or *muzarian* was given to farmers who worked on a small piece of land allocated by *Zamindars*. This land was either granted to a farmer or leased at a nominal rate. The size of land leased/granted to peasants however varied regionally. The peasants of North India operated on an average land size of about 5 acres, so it could be practically manageable with a pair of bullocks and a plough (NCERT, Part II 2007). In Gujrat, the average size of a peasant's farm land was about 6 acres. In some cases, a rich *kissan* (peasant) owned a large piece of land (up to 10 acres). Such difference in land sizes created the class system even among peasants. Peasantry was latter stratified into three main classes, namely, the *Riyayati* – peasants given concession in revenue, the *Pahi-kasht* – peasants owning land in other villages, and the *Mauzrian* – peasants who were tenants in the village. This division of labour fractured the rural society, which till today is not able to unify as a single commune to raise awareness of their land ownership rights.

The land system was also reorganised in some areas, whereby forest lands were granted to *kisans*. They were required to clear the land and settled in the vicinity of forest. Villages either organically evolved in strategic locations or were established adjacent to forest. Farmers thus had access to forest resources such as honey, bees-wax, medicinal herbs, wild fruits and nuts. The gathering activity, often carried out by women, supplemented the household income of farmers. The agricultural production was also intensified whereby two crops were sown in the same field over a single year. Therefore, a new crop calendar was prepared which included three seasons: (i) the *rabi* (winter season, November to March) when Wheat, Bar-ley, Gram, Arhar, and Masoor were grown; (ii) the *zaid* (summer season, April to June) when vegetables, green pea, and fruits such as water melon were cultivated with irrigation; and (iii) the *kharif* (monsoon season, July to October) when rain-fed crops like Rice, Groundnut, Millets, Jowar, Bajara, Moogh were cultivated. Crop statistics were recorded as per the crop seasons during the Mughal period.

Improvement in farm technology

During the Mughal period, agricultural intensification and double cropping were developed due to the improvement in irrigation technology from *charas*, which was operated by human power (a bullock-operated *charas* was also used in some areas of the Indus valley), to *rahat* (Persian wheel), a device which was operated by a pair of bullocks (Figure 2.3 and 2.4). In Lahore plains (now in Pakistan) and in

Figure 2.3 Artistic expression of simple devices used for irrigation in the Mughal period: one-man operated *charas* and two-men operated *charas*

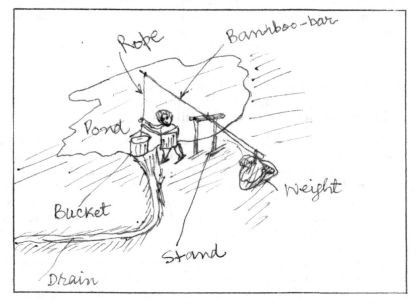

Figure 2.3 (Continued)

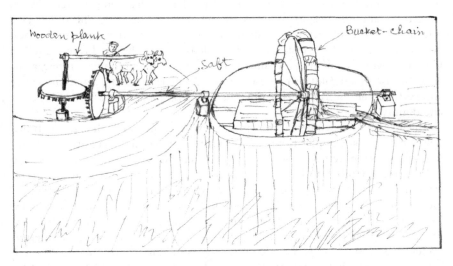

Figure 2.4 Artistic expression of oxen-operated *rahat* (Persian Wheel)

Delhi-Agra plains (presently called Western Uttar Pradesh), the Persian wheel was built with a chain of water buckets, which draws water from a well. It is operated with bullocks, which move the shaft in which a chain of buckets are connected (Figure 2.4). Such a device was particularly used to lift up water from wells in semi-arid areas of Sindh, Punjab and Ganga-Jamuna doab where the water table was 3 to 5 meters below the surface. It increased the production of Wheat, Sugarcane and Cotton during the dry winter *rabi* season. The rain-fed Rice was grown twice in the middle and Lower Ganga plains (the Bihar and Bengal provinces).

2.04 Colonial British era (19th till mid-20th century) with the beginning of modern phase of agriculture in independent India (1950–till date)

Agriculture under the British *Raj* had largely remained unchanged with the exception of plantation farming. Land and labour reforms, however, were introduced in the early 20th century but no significant restructuring of the agriculture sector occurred during the colonial period. The British inherited the *zamindari* system from the Mughal empire, which they adapted and retained to collect revenues and taxes. Regulatory reforms in the land management system were negligible despite the incessant struggle and relentless pain suffered by farmers under the exploitative regime.

Zamindars were not only allowed to control land but also authorised to implement laws, which changed the power dynamics. *Zamindars* managed to attain power and authority during the Mughal period, while continual increase in land rent impeded peasants' ability to grow the size of their landholdings. These class dynamics were further exacerbated during the East India Company reign when it fixed the amount of land tax that each *zamindar* had to pay. This didn't take into account the adverse impact of monsoon failure or other calamities. Local *Rajas* were also under pressure from the rule of paying the fixed revenue to the Company while simultaneously maintaining peace and tranquility among peasants. In case of a default or non-payment of *lagan* (land rent), *Zamindars* were stripped of their entitlements. Consequently, *Zamindars* lost their land, power and dignity.

The British Government introduced a few administrative changes in India, which had two key implications. First was the rapid commercialisation of farming, which promoted and incentivised the cultivation of industrial crops such as Sugarcane, Cotton and Jute. Second was the development of national infrastructure such as roads, rails and ports, which had provided more efficient means for transporting agriculture commodities nationally and internationally. This transport-led economic development in India has not only enabled mobilisation of agriculture commodities and resources but also created numerous trade-centred towns and strategic hubs such as military cantonments. With the beginning of the industrial revolution in Britain, the burgeoning demand for raw materials increased the pressure to grow more industrial crops in India. The demand for Cotton grew in England and its bulk export from India commenced when the Cotton Supply Association was founded in Britain in 1857. Soon after, Manchester Cotton Company was formed in 1859. This led to the mercantilist ideology of obtaining raw materials at a cheaper rate from India and then transforming into finished or semi-finished products to export to India and other colonies.

This initial stage of industrialisation in British India began to polarise power linked through trade and commerce in a few primary cities. The establishment and extension of railway networks, setting up of Cotton mills in Bombay (now Mumbai) to access cheap labour and raw Cotton, and the establishment of port infrastructure such docks, piers, ghats and maritime and shipping administrative services had laid the foundation of industrialisation of modern India. It rapidly changed the agrarian society and rural landscape. Agriculture commodities and resources were transported from rural areas to cities and then shipped to England for processing and manufacturing. The finished or semi-finished products were shipped back to India and were made available in the local markets. India became a key supplier of tea and other agriculture commodities to England and other global markets, but the benefits were not fully shared. Nonetheless, it led to agriculture growth in rural India and improved functional linkages with the key cities.

There is anecdotal evidence (Gopal and Srivastawa 2008) to suggest that Santhals, the tribes who lived in the Rajmahal hills, were enticed or forced to migrate as labourers to cultivate Cotton on cleared forest land in the West of Deccan (present day Central Maharashtra). The produce was then supplied to nearby mandies (markets), which were collection points of raw materials for cloth mills. The refined products were then exported from Calcutta port. Evidence also indicates that there were incidences of forced movement of tribal labourers from Orissa and Bengal provinces to work on tea plantations in North East India (Brahmaputra Valley) in the late 19th century (Goswami 1988: 159–172). Nevertheless, commercialisation of agriculture through linking it with industrial production systems created robust multi-modal transportation networks, which had integrated regional and remote areas with urban markets. They connected key plantation sites in rural India to intermodal port facilities or the manufacturing centres in cities. These functional trade linkages strengthened port-hinterland connectivity and helped develop port towns and harbour cities as new trade centres. But this connectivity also became the mechanism of resource drain from India to England and then later contributed to the civil disobedience movement and resistance for India's Independence.

2.05 Agriculture development during the 20th century and later

Agriculture development can be represented through changes in land use, mode of production and land productivity. With these changes, the Indian agriculture transitioned from one phase to another. Broadly, the agriculture in India can be divided into four phases. Each phase characterises different farming practices, land ownership and tenure systems, regulatory frameworks and market reforms. In this analysis, the data from 1891–2 and 2008–9 have been used to demarcate the

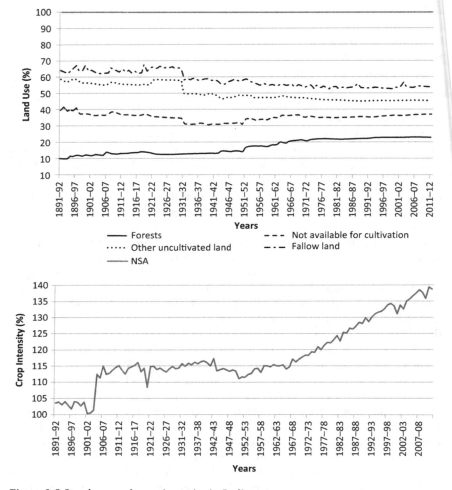

Figure 2.5 Land use and crop intensity in India

Source: 1. Summary of the Agricultural Statistics of British India 1891–92 to 1899–1900; 2. Agricultural Statistics of India 1900–1901 to 1904–05 Compiled by Director General of Commerce and Intelligence and printed at Office of the Superintendent of Government Printing India (1906); 3. Agricultural Statistics of India – General Summary (1904–05 to 1913–14) Vol-I, Department of Statistics, New Delhi (published in 1916); 4. Agricultural Statistics of India – General Summary (1911–12 to 1930–31) Vol-I, Department of Statistics, New Delhi; 5. Indian Agricultural Statistics, Vol-I, 1939–40 to 1942–43 (General Summary 1923–24 to 1942–43), Department of Statistics, New Delhi; 6. Indian Agricultural Statistics, Vol-II (Land utilisation Statistics- All India 1943–44 to 1949–50), Department of Statistics, New Delhi; 7. Land Use Statistics at A Glance 1999–2000 to 2012–13 (All India Tables 1950–51 to 2012–13), Directorate of Economics and Statistics, Department of Agriculture and Cooperation, Ministry of Agriculture, New Delhi transitioning of agricultural development in India. These phases are also separated through changes in land use and crop intensity, in addition to considering a range of other key parameters during the last 118 years (Figure 2.5). These phases include:

- the phase of colonial agrarian economy (1891–2 to 1949–50),
- the early planned phase (1950–1 to 1970–1),
- the Green Revolution phase (1972–3 to 1990–1) and
- the phase of economic liberalisation (after 1990–1).

Table 2.1 characterises the mode of production, technological regime, crop dominance and productivity levels to distinguish each of the phases. These phases are discussed as following.

2.05.1 *The colonial phase (1891–2 to 1949–50)*

The colonial phase of agricultural development is characterised by low share of Net Sown Area and Forest land, and low crop intensity (below 115 per cent). The

Table 2.1 Mode of production in different phases of Indian agriculture

Phase/System	Mode of production	Technological regime	Crop dominance	Productivity status
1. Colonial phase (traditional agriculture system before the Independence)	Animal draught ploughs, fodder food dominated agriculture, use of animal and human power in agriculture systems, completely determined by physical environment of land, use of indigenous seeds and organic manure because of dominance of animals.	Traditional means of irrigation. *Charas* and *dhakhi* operated by manpower and *rahak* operated by animals, irrigation by *dhakhi* was 0.10 ha/ day of 8 hr work and by *rahat* .30 ha/ day of 8 hr work. Canal irrigation in a few areas.	Rice in rainy season without irrigation, Wheat in winter with irrigation and Millets used for fodder such as Jowar, Bajra, Urad Gram Oilseeds.	Very low crop yield.

(*Continued*)

Table 2.1 (Continued)

Phase/System	Mode of production	Technological regime	Crop dominance	Productivity status
2. Early planned phase (Pre–Green Revolution agriculture system prior to the 1960s)	Animal draught plough, food grains dominated, researches in traditional means of land operations like land consolidation, seed–fertiliser determined by physical factors but emphasis on biophysical phenomena and expansion of agriculture activities.	Canal irrigation. Diesel–operated tube–well irrigation in few areas. Well with water–pump tube–well/ 2.0 ha/ day of 8 hrs work.	Wheat, Rice in Great Plains, Jowarbajra, Ragi, Maize in Karnataka, Cotton in Maharashtra, Rice dominated in coastal areas.	Low crop yield.
3. Phase of intensive agriculture (1960s–1980s)	Food grains dominated, intensive research on seed fertiliser technology and biophysical factors use of land. Small tractor for plough, animal use for transport of surplus products to market, tractor is considered as a multi–purpose tool for agriculture.	Electric power and tractor operated tube wells. Canal irrigation 2.5 ha, irrigation by tube–well 3.00ha/ day of 8 hrs work.	Food grains dominated: Wheat, Rice, Jowar, Bajra Gram, Cotton.	Increased fast to moderate to high crop yield.
4. Phase of economic liberalisation (1990s onward)	Commercial agriculture with food grains dominated, irrigation extensive and	Intensive tube–well operated irrigation. Canal irrigation. Use of	Food grains dominated but food grains are considered as commercial crops.	Much higher crop yield.

Phase/System	Mode of production	Technological regime	Crop dominance	Productivity status
	mechanisation in plough, transport and means of irrigation, contract farming in few areas, removal of labour and draught animal from agriculture.	modern water technology for irrigation, 2.0–3.0 ha/ tube–well/ day of 8 hrs work.	Increasing areas under vegetable crops and horticulture.	

traditional agricultural system prevalent during the colonial period was largely based on subsidence farming. Farming technology was rudimentary and primitive during this phase, which resulted in low productivity per unit of land or labour. There were two key classes in rural society, which constituted the rural society: the Landlords and landless labourers. Land ownership, rural assets and capital were accumulated in the hands of few *Zamindars* who held power and wealth. Labourers were largely from lower and backward castes who were either landless or worked on land to earn daily wages to sustain their livelihood. These labourers were also known as *bandwa-majdoor* (bonded labour) who worked in the field and served at homes of big landlords. However, this system varied across different parts of India, which consisted of several independent principalities. Some regions were more liberated, progressive and open for change than others. Nevertheless, the power-sharing mechanism largely remained similar, which was based on feudalism. During the colonial period, farming was largely subsistence and thus the productivity was very low. Crops were grown for household consumption or to feed animals. There was little surplus for the market.

2.05.2 *The early planned phase (1950–1 to 1970–1)*

The early planned phase considered agriculture as the key component of the national economy and employment generation. Economic policy in Post-Independence and early planned phase leaned towards protectionism and socialist model. The focus of key policies remained on import substitution, industrialisation under state control, strong state intervention in labour and financial markets, a large public sector and central planning.

The agricultural system started to change gradually after the Independence when numerous schemes and planned agrarian reforms were implemented to promote intensive and commercial farming (Table 2.1). It was this phase when the rural economy began to gain momentum through the wider adoption of farm technologies, generally referred to as the Green Revolution. The Land

Figure 2.6 The Upper Ganges canal irrigation system in Ganga-Jamuna doab

Consolidation Act was implemented in the state of Punjab (Haryana was part of Punjab) in the 1960s. The completion of the Bhakra-Nagal Project led to a wide-scale use of irrigation in the North Western region of India. The Upper Ganges Canal became the main feeder in water distribution system in the Western Uttar Pradesh. Canal irrigation was also the cheapest source of irrigation (see Figure 2.6).

This phase culminated with the intensive use of seed-fertiliser-irrigation technology during the mid-60s, which helped increase the farm productivity levels. The success of the Green Revolution was more pronounced in Northern India, which initially spilled-over from Punjab to its surrounding regions, but later the benefits of the Green Revolution percolated to other pockets across different parts of India.

2.05.3 *The phase of intensive agriculture (1970–1 to 1990–1)*

During the Green Revolution phase, the Net Sown Area (NSA) expanded significantly across different parts of India. Areas under forest however declined marginally during the planned phase of the economy, because of the significant conversion of waste land to NSA. Two key changes in land use occurred in this phase. First is the rapid expansion of farming area in previously non-farm land; second is the intensive use of existing farm land. Expansion of non-farm land under cultivation started when waste land was converted into NSA in the Great Plains of India and elsewhere (Figure 2.7).

Irrigation was paramount in the intensive use of finite land with restricted land potential. For example, during the medieval period when *dhakli* was the only means of irrigation, a farmer could irrigate 0.1 ha of crop land in an 8-hour working day on the field using one-person operated *dhakli*. With *rahat* technology, a farmer could irrigate 0.3 ha of crop land, whilst engine-operated tube-well enabled irrigation of 2.0 ha of crop land in a single day. Cropping intensity increased at an unprecedented rate of 120 per cent as modern means of irrigation and use of chemical fertilisers became widespread. Subsidies on fertilisers and High Yield Variety (HYV) seeds were provided to farmers to help increase food grain production per unit of land.

2.05.4 *The Liberalisation phase (1990–1 onward)*

Liberalisation simply means a reduction in government interventions, controls and restrictions in an economy. Liberalisation in India began in 1991 to promote partial or full privatisation, deregulation of markets, removal of trade barriers, free trade and open markets. Economic reforms were implemented to transform India into a market-oriented economy by expanding the role of private and foreign enterprises.

Liberalisation has its root in *classical liberalism* (see the work of John Locke, Thomas Malthus and David Ricardo), which advocated for civil libertarian ideology, economic freedom, and minimalist government intervention. It is an antithesis to socialist planning, where goods and services are produced directly for their use, as opposed to profit by businesses. Liberalisation is often associated with 'neo-liberalism', which is a modern resurrection of the ideology of *laissez-faire*.

During liberalisation, numerous agriculture policies, planning schemes and market reforms were introduced to deregulate commodity markets to enhance the competitiveness of open markets in India. These changes were partially driven by the specificities of increased knowledge-based agro-innovation, techno-institutional progress, and the construction of mega-scale transport and logistics infrastructure. However, agriculture is still a quasi-liberalised market which is

Figure 2.7 Reeds on the reclaimed waste land for cultivation

highly regulated to protect the local industries and farmers. The fear of full market liberalisation relates to the risk of transnational corporates crowding out local producers and service providers.

Technology substitution for labour was seen as a panacea for economic growth. The terms of trade in agricultural surplus production were reformed when fertiliser subsidies were removed and input costs driven by open markets were deregulated. Diversification of farm income and commercial cropping however started to occur in a market-led profit-driven farming, which added a new range of high-value crops. This resulted in increased profitability and farm productivity in more progressive regions while stagnation in others.

The Liberalisation phase is characterised by a substantial increase in agricultural productivity and growth, and rapid crop diversification. However, the share of the agriculture sector to GDP, as expected with increased industrialisation, decreased to about one-third during the late 1990s. At the time of economic liberalisation, the thresholds imposed by natural resource endowments (land and resources) were realised due to increased population pressure, burgeoning demand for food, competitive market conditions (increasing prices of agricultural products) and increased mobility of rural labour to urban labour markets (because of wage differentials and better job opportunities). The importance of food importation from low-cost production countries was mooted to tackle some of the challenges of food insecurity in India.

The changing production factor relationship as argued by Hicks (1932) strengthens capital over land and labour. Mechanisation of farms and intensive use of technology reduced the physical labour input and provided opportunities for farmers to seek employment in the non-farming sectors. But, it was not the case for farmers who had small landholdings, which restricted the use of technology, or for those who worked on farms as causal labourers. They were forced to find employment in other sectors with no former training, skills or knowledge. The subsequent creation of surplus capital increased the purchasing power of some farmers, which helped them accumulate farm assets and enabled further investment in new farm technology. Traditional methods of irrigation and ploughing were replaced with new technology to help increase agricultural productivity. Surplus capital also enabled some farmers to invest in non-agricultural activities either in farms or in a nearby town. This however widened the divide among farmer communities and intensified the coercive class struggle for power and control in economically depressed regions in India.

2.06 Organisational structures in Post-Independence India

India inherited the heavy administrative burden of the British bureaucratic system. Ironically it retained and unfortunately embraced most of the structural arrangement, top-down organisational systems and control mechanisms. Yet, in the 21st Century India, the structured public administrative reforms to eradicate red tape, incompetence and administrative inefficiency is heavily resisted.

The Ministry of Agriculture, Government of India is responsible for developing and implementing planning schemes and agriculture development programs. The multi-level administrative model of public administration is designed to prepare, plan and execute agriculture development schemes. The overarching goals of such agriculture plan and programs are to enhance agriculture production, growth and productivity through promoting greater labour force participation using the potential of modern farming technologies.

The Ministry has established industry boards and research institutions to assist in evidence-based planning frameworks and infrastructure support to enable crop diversification and intensification, commercialisation and farming efficiency while protecting land from the threats of environmental and anthropogenic degradation of land resources. Programs are specifically targeted to promote animal husbandry and dairying, fisheries, horticulture, and cultivation of cash crops such as oilseeds, vegetables and coconut.

Three main boards at the national level were established. The Ministry formed various commissions and corporations such as the Agriculture and Prices Commission, National Seed Cooperation, and National Fertilizer Cooperation to plan and execute programs to enhance agricultural productivity in India. The pivotal role of governmental institutions, namely, the Indian Council of Agriculture Research (ICAR) and International Crops Research Institute for Semi-Arid Tropics (ICRISAT) was widely recognised for their scientific contribution to agriculture development. Yet, there were failures, delays and inefficiencies in the *modus operandi* and thus opportunities for continuous improvements.

Agriculture and Processed Food Product Export Development Authority (APEDA) provides strategic direction and operational advice to trade key agricultural products in international commodity markets. The founding of APEDA provides impetus for growth of agricultural products and the associated processing. The authority assesses potential demand for food products in international markets. After the amendment of rules of APEDA in February 2005, the authority amended international trade terms by delineating Agri-Export Zones of India, which allowed each of the states to formulate state-specific export and import policies to promote international trade for their local agricultural produce. The APEDA has identified 60 agricultural products for processing and the exportation of those in the global marketplace (Appendix 2.1). The authority has adopted a two-pronged strategy to develop market centres for processing and distribution of agriculture surplus in specialised product categories and to enhance the diversification in agricultural commodities through increasing farm productivity levels.

Another major policy shift in government community programs occurred during the 11th five-year-plan period (2007–12), where the focus was centred on 'inclusive growth' and 'decentralised governance'. This was implemented through empowering a village-centred punchayati system – a micro-organisational structure which facilitates the management of local affairs and disputes within a village or in a village local network. Rastrya Krishi Vikas Yojana (RKVY, called National Agriculture Development Program) was implemented at a district level to strengthen the *Punchayat Raj* Institution. The Planning Commission (now NITI Aayog) developed and implemented small-area-level agricultural plans to accelerate agriculture production and productivity. This plan was promulgated by the National Development Council (NDC) on 29 May 2007. This district plan was subsequently integrated with agro-climatic regions, with the key goals

Appendix 2.1 Development of market centres for processing agriculture commodities

Agricultural products	State	District/Area
Pineapple	West Bengal	Darjeeling, Uttar Dinajpur, Coach Behar and Jalpaiguri
Gherkins	Karnataka	Tumkur, Bangalore Urban, Bangalore Rural, Hassan, Kolar, Chtradurga, Dharwad and Bagalkot
Lychee	Uttranchal	Udhamsingh Nagar, Nainital and Dehradun
Vegetables	Punjab	Fatahgarh Sahib, Patiala, Sangrur, Ropar and Ludhiana
Potatoes	Uttar Pradesh	Agra, Hathras, Farrukhabad, Kannoj, Meerut, Allgarh and Bagpat
Mangoes and Vegetables	Uttar Pradesh	Lucknow, Unnao, Hardoi, Sitapur and Barabanki
Potatoes	Punjab	Singhpura, Zirakpur (Patiala), RampuraPhul, Muktsar, Ludhiana, Jallandhar
Mangoes	Uttar Pradesh	Sahranpur, Muzaffarnagar, Bijnaur, Meerut, Baghpat, Bulandshar and Jyotifulenagar
Grapes and Grape Wines	Maharashtra	Nasik, Sangli, Pune, Satara, Ahmednagar and Sholapur
Mango Pulp and Fresh Vegetables	Andhra Pradesh	Chittor District
Pineapple	Tripura	Kumarghat, Manu, Melaghar, Matabari and Kakraban Blocks
Potatoes, Onion and Garlic	Madhya Pradesh	Malwa, Ujjain, Indore, Dewas, Dhar, Shajapur, Ratlam, Neemuch and Mandsaur
Mangoes	Maharashtra	Districts of Ratnagiri, Sindhudurg, Raigarh and Thane
Apples	Jammu and Kashmir	Districts of Srinagar, Baramula, Anantnag, Kupwara, Badgaum and Pulwama
Flowers	Tamil Nadu	Dharmapuri
Lychee	West Bengal	Districts of Murshidabad, Malda, 24 Pargana (N) and 24 Pargana (S)

(*Continued*)

Agricultural products	State	District/Area
Lychee	Bihar	Muzaffarpur, Samastipur, Hajipur, Vaishali, East and West Champaran, Bhagalpur, Begulsarai, Khagaria, Sitamarhi, Sarannd, Gopalganj
Kesar Mangoes	Maharashtra	Districts of Aurangabad, Jalna, Beed, Latur, Ahmednagar and Nasik
Walnut	Jammu and Kashmir	Kashmir Region–Baramuila, Anantnag, Pulwama, Budgam, Kupwara and Srinagar/Jammu Region–Doda, Poonch, Udhampur, Rajouri and Kathua
Flowers	Uttranchal	Districts of Dehradun, Pantnagar
Mangoes and Vegetables	Gujarat	Districts of Ahmedabad, Khaida, Anand, Vadodra, Surat, Navsari, Valsad, Bharuch and Narmada
Flowers	Maharashtra	Pune, Nasik, Kolhapur and Sangli
Potatoes	West Bengal	Districts of Hoogly, Burdwan, Midnapore (W), UdayNarayanpur and Howrah
Rose Onion	Karnataka	Bangalore (Urban), Bangalore (Rural), Kolar
Flowers	Karnataka	Bangalore (Urban), Bangalore (Rural), Kolar, Tumkur, Kodagu and Belgaum
Mangoes and Grapes	Andhra Pradesh	Districts of Ranga Reddy, Medak and parts of Mahaboobnagar Districts
Flowers (Orchids) and Cherry Pepper	Sikkim	East Sikkim
Ginger	Sikkim	North, East, South and West Sikkim
Apples	Himachal Pradesh	Shimla, Sirmour, Kullu, Mandi, Chamba and Kinnaur
Basmati Rice	Punjab	Districts of Gurdaspur, Amritsar, Kapurthala, Jalandhar, Hoshiarpur and Nawanshahar
Mangoes	Andhra Pradesh	Krishna District
Flowers	Tamil Nadu	Nilgiri District

Agricultural products	State	District/Area
Onion	Maharashtra	Districts of Nasik, Ahmednagar, Pune, Satara and Solapur
Ginger and Turmeric	Orissa	Kandhamal District
Vegetables	Jharkhand	Ranchi, Hazaribagh and Lohardaga
Seed Spices	Mahdya Pradesh	Guna, Mandsaur, Ujjain, Rajgarh, Ratlam, Shajapur and Neemuch
Basmati Rice	Uttranchal	Udham Singh Nagar, Nainital, Dehradun and Haridwar
Mangoes	West Bengal	Malda and Murshidabad
Vegetables	West Bengal	Nadia, Murshidabad and North 24 Parganas
Mangoes	Tamil Nadu	Districts of Madurai, Theni, Dindigul, Virudhunagar and Tirunelveli
Wheat	Madhya Pradesh	Three distinct and contiguous zones: Ujjain Zone comprising of Neermach, Ratlam, Mandsaur and Ujjain/ Indore Zone comprising of Indore, Dhar, Shajapur and Dewas/Bhopal Division, comprising of Sehore, Vidisha, Raisen, Hoshangabad, Harda, Narsinghpur and Bhopal
Horticulture Products	Kerala	Districts of Thrissur, Ernakulam, Kottayaam, Alappuzha, Pathanumthitta Kollam, Thiruvanthapuram, Idukki and Palakkod
Fresh and Processed Ginger	Assam	Kamrup, Nalbari, Barpeta, Darrang, Nagaon, Morigaon, Karbi–Anglong and North Cachar Districts
Basmati Rice	Uttar Pradesh	Districts of Bareilly, Shahajahanpur, Pilibhit. Rampur, Badaun, Bijnor, Moradabad, J. B Phulenagar, Saharanpur, Mujjafarnagar, Meerut, Bulandshahar, Ghaziabad
Medicinal and Aromatic Plants	Uttranchal	Districts of Uttarkashi, Chamoli, Pithoragarh, Dehradun and Nainital

(Continued)

Appendix 2.1 (Continued)

Agricultural products	State	District/Area
Dehydrated Onion	Gujarat	Districts of Bhavnagar, Surendranagar, Amreli, Rajkot, Junagadh and Jamnagar.
Gherkins	Andhra Pradesh	Districts of Mahboobnagar, Rangareddy, Medak, Karinagar, Warangal, Ananthpur and Nalgonda
Pomegranate	Maharashtra	Districts of Solapur, Sangli, Ahedabagar, Pune, Nasik, Osmanabad, Latur
Banana	Maharashtra	Jalgaon, Dhule, Nandurbar, Buldhana, Parbhanj, Hindoli, Nanded and Wardha
Oranges	Maharashtra	Nagpur and Amraoti
Lentil and Grams	Madhya Pradesh	Shivpuri, Guna, Vidisha, Raisen, Narsinghpura, Chhindwara
Oranges	Madhya Pradesh	Chhindwara, Hoshangabad, Betul
Cashew Nut	Tamil Nadu	Cuddalore, Thanjavur, Pudukottai and Sivaganga
Sesame Seeds	Gujarat	Amerali, Bhavnagar, Surendranagar, Rajkot, Jamnagar
Vanila	Karnataka	Districts of Dakshin Kannada, Uttara Kannada, Udupi, Shimoga, Kodagu, Chickamagalur
Darjeeling Tea	West Bengal	Darjeeling
Corainder	Rajasthan	Kota, Bundi, Baran, Jhalawar and Chittoor
Cumin	Rajasthan	Nagaur, Barmer, Jalore, Pali and Jodhpur
Medicinal Plant	Kerala	Wayanad, Mallapuram, Palakkad, Thrissur, Ernakulam, Idukki, Kollam, Pathanamittha, Thiruvananthaparam
Chilli	Andhra Pradesh	Guntur

Source: http://agricrop.nic.in/relatedsiteshtm

to enhance the efficient use of natural resources and technology to predominately support allied agricultural sub-sectors in rural India.

The Small Farmers Development Agency and the Marginal Farmers and Agriculture Labour Development were amalgamated to create the Integrated Rural

Development Programme (IRDP) during the fourth five-year plan (1969–74). The key functions of these institutions were to dispense subsidies and incentives to farmers for small irrigation or soil conservation projects. In 1999, it was again replaced by the Sanjaya Gandhi Gram Swarozgar Yojana (SGSY), which incorporated new initiatives to promote self-employment and micro-enterprise development schemes. Numerous schemes were implemented for the development of rural farm labour. These include:

1980: National Rural Employment program (NREP)
1983: Employment Assurance Scheme
1990: Jawahar Rozgar Yojana (Jawahar Employment Scheme)
2001: Smpurn Grameed Rozgar Yojana (Village Employment Scheme)
2004: National Commission on farmers which recommended quality of water, proper use of farm technology, adequate institutional credit, crop insurance and so on
2005: National Rural Employment Guarantee Act (NREGA, prioritisation of local needs for agriculture development)
2007: National Policy for Farmers (based on integrated well-being)

The Comprehensive District Agriculture Plan (C-DAP) was a flagship program which aimed at providing a basis for improving sustainable livelihood for farmers and landless labourers. One key objective of the plan was to deter rapid out-migration of the rural workforce to urban agglomerations for work. C-DAP is prepared by considering common elements of other district-level plans in order to integrate them into a broader umbrella as shown in Figure 2.8. The institutional structure in India is hierarchically structured into four levels ranging from the State to District through to a village Panchayat level. C-DAP formulated various schemes to support agricultural development at a grass-roots level through encouraging collaborative partnerships among various public organisations and stakeholders using local expertise.

2.07 Institutional credit flow to the agriculture sector

The premier institution for agriculture credit in India is the National Bank for Agriculture and Rural Development (NABARD), under which many credit organisations and institutions operate. One key feature of the liberalisation policy was a shift from a short-term to long-term flow of credit for agriculture projects. In India, the long-term agriculture credit had steadily increased from Rs 1.30 crores in 1950–1 to Rs 785 crores in 1990–1 during the early phases of economic development. As a result, the ratio of short-term, medium to long-term credit for agriculture reduced from 85:10:5 in 1960–1 to 71:18:11 in 1990–1, which indicates higher preference for larger collaborative and cooperative projects. According to the Economic Survey in India, the total credit for agriculture and rural-based projects amounted to Rs 4,253 crores at the beginning of the

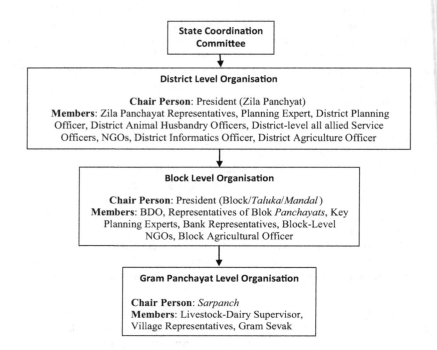

Figure 2.8 Integrated organisation of district plan and formation of planning units

Green Revolution in 1970–1, which increased to about Rs 20,65,618 crores in 2010–11.

A multi-agency approach to credit delivery system has also been adopted to promote open access to indirect credit for agriculture development through four major financial institutions:

1   Cooperatives provided credits to farmers, which increased from Rs 1,727 crores in 1990–1 to Rs 1,35,740 crores in 2006–7;
2   Commercial banks credited Rs 200 crores in 1990–1, which increased to Rs 86,732 crores in 2010–11;
3   Regional rural banks credited Rs 9 crores in 1990–1, which slightly decreased in 2012–13; and
4   Rural Electrification Corporation dispensed credits of about Rs 709 crores in 1990–1 which reached to Rs 39,275 crores in 2012–13.

The share of public investment to total capital formation in agriculture during the Green Revolution was 54 per cent in 1982–3. This is when there were better terms of trade offered by the Indian Government to the agriculture sector. They were offered in the form of subsidies on food, fertiliser, electricity and irrigation.

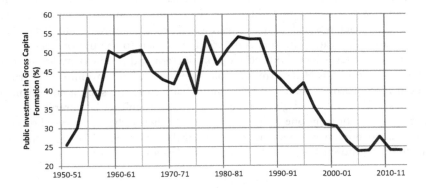

Figure 2.9 Share of gross capital formation in agriculture and allied sectors under public investment

Greater emphasis was on providing credits for farm inputs than farm assets (Mani 1996, Thomas and Mani 2015). During the subsequent periods of liberalisation, the share of private investment to capital formation increased, whilst the public investment in capital formation reduced substantially from 54 to 25 per cent during the Post- Liberalisation phase (Figure 2.9). This was one of the key objectives of the liberalisation policy.

2.08 Summary

The development of the contemporary agricultural landscape in India is the interplay of myriad evolutionary processes of change. The transitioning of agriculture development through various phases is fundamentally underpinned by socio-economic, techno-institutional and political changes. However, the operative forces which shaped the regional agriculture growth patterns varied across geographic space and over time. Indian agriculture undoubtedly is continually transitioning towards industrialisation and market-oriented commercialisation of farming, but the pace of change continues to be challenged by increased complexity of global production systems and the local inertia inhibiting behaviour change and technological innovation. Economic liberalisation and regulatory reforms have started to shape agriculture production landscape in India; nonetheless, increased global competitiveness in cross-border trade impedes the prospect of India entering into the global commodity markets.

The 'poly-cyclic' agriculture landscape in India is complicated in nature and complex in its structure. It emerged from a simple 'social ecosystem' prevalent in ancient times when Aryans assimilated with indigenous communities to formulate new socio-cultural norms and standards regulating and controlling the utilisation of land resources, to the 'administrative-heavy hierarchical feudal' system of land management during the medieval period when agriculture was practiced under closed-land management control, and then to the 'market'-based system.

Changes in farming technology – from the use of stone and wooden tools in the Harappan culture of the Indus Valley civilisation, to human/animal-operated hand-made machines such as the Persian wheel (*rahat*) and water lifter (*dhakali*) as a means of irrigation in medieval period, and then to the use of tractor-harvester technology – have boosted crop production and productivity levels. The wider adoption of modern farm technology, however, began to impact the rural labour force. Farmers shifted to other industrial sectors and sought employment in cities. This augmented geographic mobility of agriculture labourers from villages to towns or from one economic region to others either for survival or progress raised numerous concerns for policy-makers and planners regarding the virtue of the chosen trajectory for agriculture development in India.

3 Agricultural growth process

3.01 Introduction

This chapter examines the national- and state-level changes and emerging regional patterns in area, production and yield of food grains and other crops. Spatial variability in agriculture growth ratios is mapped across different phases of economic planning. Changes in crop area and crop yield are also measured to capture growth dynamics of agriculture change. Finally, agriculture growth, which is the proportionate change in the total volume of agricultural output over time, is measured using the agriculture growth ratio (crop area growth ratio, crop yield growth ratio) and further validated through the Incremental Input Output Ratio (IIOR). Incremental agricultural output reflects the changes in agricultural production components by measuring the absolute size of output increase within a specific span of time. Understanding the absolute and proportionate change of various components of agriculture output is critical to analysing the key trends, changes and dynamics in agriculture growth patterns in India.

3.02 Indian agriculture in the context of South Asia

Agriculture in India, despite the slow growth, has had significant advancements in the Post-Independence era. When India is compared with other countries in the Indian sub-continent, the statistics show signs of rapid growth and numerous episodes of productivity gains (Table 3.1). With a population density of 389 persons/ sq km in 2009, the growth of GDP in India in the year 2005–6 was higher (7.4 per cent) than Sri Lanka. However, the percentage of the agriculture sector to GDP is lower than Pakistan and Nepal, which affirms the positive impact of rapid urbanisation and industrial diversification with growing proportions of non-agricultural industries. The Gross Capital formation in India also attests the potential to grow the economy at a much higher rate (33 per cent of GDP) when compared to other South Asian countries.

Other trade and finance statistics are also noteworthy. The export of technology and manufactured goods contributed about 5 per cent of total exports in 2005. While the domestic credit is about 64 per cent of total GDP, which was

Table 3.1 Socio-economic development in South Asian low-income countries

Development indicators	Countries				
	Bangladesh	Nepal	India	Sri Lanka	Pakistan
(A) Basic indicators					
1. Density of population 2009 (person/sq.km)	1246	205	389	324	220
2. Population age composition 2010 (% of age 0–14)	31	36	31	24	37
3. Male life expectancy at birth (2010)	66	66	63	71	67
4. Adult literacy rate (%)	47	49	61	91	50
5. Population below national poverty line in rural (%)	53*	34.6**	30.2*	27**	35.9+
6. Gender parity ratio in primary and secondary school (2005)	103	93	89	102	75
7. Mortality rate under 5 years (per 1000)	73	74	74	14	99
8. HIV prevalence (% of population ages 15–49 2006)	0.1	0.5	0.9	0.1	0.1
9. Gross Domestic Product per capita % growth (2009–10)	4.4	2.7	8.3	7.2	2.1
(B) Economic Indicators					
10. Average annual growth of GDP (%) (2005–6)	5.6	2.7	7.4	4.8	5.4
11. Agricultural productivity per worker (base 2005 US$ value added) (2010)	948	—	3318	5238	2627
12. Value added as % of GDP (2009) in					
(a) Agriculture	10	33	18	13	22
(b) Industry	42	15	27	30	24
(c) Services	48	52	55	57	54
13. Household consumption expenditure 2009 (% of GDP)	77	81	56	64	80
14. Gross Capital Formation (% of GDP)	25	30	33	27	20
(C) Trade and Finances					
15. Manufactured export (% of merchandise export) (2005)	90	74	70	70	82
16. High technology export (% of manufactured export) (2005)	0	0	5	1	2
17. Foreign direct investment (US$ millions) (2005)	802	2	6598	272	2183

Development indicators	Countries				
	Bangladesh	Nepal	India	Sri Lanka	Pakistan
18. Official development assistance/aid (US$ per capita, 2003)	9	16	2	61	11
19. Domestic credit provided by banking sector (% of GDP, 2006)	58	—	64	44	42

N. B.: * The year 2000 *** for 2002–03, *** for 1995–96 and + for 1998–99

Source: World Development Reports 2008, 2012 and 2013, published by The World Bank, New York

the highest among the South Asian countries in 2006 (Table 3.1). The share of savings in Pakistan and Bangladesh is markedly small, which limits further investments. Furthermore, the difference between the investment and savings as a proportion of GDP in these countries is enormous. This means the prevalence of loan-based economy and the heavy reliance on international agencies such as the International Monetary Fund, multinational banks and inflow of remittance from overseas. This places these countries at a higher risk to global economic perturbations and thus more economically vulnerable.

From a labour market perspective, the share of agriculture-dependent work force (cultivators and agricultural labourers) declined but at a much slower rate. The share of agricultural-dependent work force to total working population has steadily reduced during the first development phase of 30 years by 2.9 per cent, from 69.42 per cent in 1951 to 66.42 per cent in 1981. There is further decrease of about 1.0 per cent per annum in agricultural labour force during the decade of 1991–2001. It is interesting to note a loss of about 20 per cent of agriculture workforce to other industry sectors during the first decade of this 21st century.

The rapid decrease in the share of agriculture in NDP and the concomitant out-migration of agricultural workforce to other more promising industries resulted in a net reduction of the NDP per farm worker, which declined by Rs 110 during the 1970s. Dandekar and Rath (1971) and Dantwala (1987) suggested an unprecedented occupational shift from primary to secondary and tertiary sectors. The problems of disguised unemployment and the stagnation of the agricultural sector are posing challenges associated with industrial trans-formation such as the requirement for skills upgrade and training. The use of technology is replacing old skills with a new set of skills. Non-agriculture sectors are well equipped and better placed in training their staff, but this would be a major challenge for the agriculture sector, which is not supported by any insti-tutional structure. It is therefore vital to track and monitor the scale, intensity and direction of occupational re-structuring and its associated implications on rural labour markets.

3.03 Collection of agriculture growth statistics

Data used in this research are collected from various sources, some of which are listed in Table 3.3. Goa, Daman and Diu, Sikkim, Chandigarh, Dadra and Nagar Haveli, Pondicherry, Lakshadweep, Andaman and Nicobar Islands and the state of Arunachal Pradesh in North-East India however were excluded because of the limited availability of comparable data. In addition, the districts where the share of urban population to total population is greater than 90 per cent or those which have a very low proportion of agriculture workforce were also excluded. These districts include Greater Mumbai (Maharastra), Channai (Tamilnadu), Kolkata (West Bengal), Hyderabad (Andhra Pradesh), Delhi State, The Dangs (Gujrat), Lahaul and Spiti (Himachal Pradesh) and Nilgiris (Tamil Nadu). This is also to avoid the noise or potential effects of outliers in the dataset. A total of 387

Table 3.2 Source of data

Attributes	Source
1. Normal annual rainfall	Indian Meteorological Department, Pune
2. Soil fertility rating	Some and Raichaudharuy cf. R.B.I. Bulletin, Bombay 1969
3. Country–level agriculture development statistics	Economic Survey, Gov. of India, New Delhi 2010–12
4. Land use statistics	Landuse Statistics – At a Glance (1999–2000 to 2013–14) DOE&S, Ministry of Agriculture, New Delhi
5. Net irrigated area	– Landuse Statistics – At a Glance (1999–2000 to 2013–14) DOE&S, Ministry of Agriculture, New Delhi
6. Production and acreage of crops	Agriculture Situation of India for different years
7. Farm harvest prices of crops	Agriculture Situation of India for different years
8. Use of chemical fertilisers	Fertilizer Statistics F.A.I., New Delhi
9. Machine tools	Indian Livestock Census, DOE&S Publication, GoI, New Delhi
10. Agriculture wage rates	Agriculture Wages in India, DOE&S Publication, Gov. of India, New Delhi
11. Statistics related to agriculture workers, literacy, urban population	Census of India, Primary Census Abstract, Final and Provisional Population Tables for 2001 and 2011
12. Statistical abstract and agricultural attributes	DOE&S Publication, GoI, New Delhi
13. Agricultural attributes and district–level crop statistics	important websites like: http://agricoop.nic.in/related sites/htm http://eands.dacnet.nic.in http://erdas.dacnet.nic.in

Abbreviations: R.B.I. = Reserve Bank of India, DOE&S = Directorate of Economics and Statistics, F.A.I. = Fertilize Association of India districts were included. Due to a few changes in census boundaries over the study period, this analysis has used 2001 census district boundaries as a base year and the changes in boundaries in previous years are either spilt or combined or integrated to make it compatible and comparable. Table 3.2 shows different sources of data that are obtained for this analysis.

Agricultural growth examined in this chapter is largely based on the national and state level agriculture statistics. In Chapter 4, areal patterns of agriculture growth are further interpreted at a district level, which represents a smaller-scale geographic unit for measuring and mapping the transformation of India agriculture systems.

3.04 Changes in agriculture growth attributes

In this section, three key attributes of an agriculture land system are examined. These include: the general land use, Net Sown Area (NSA) and Gross Cropped Area (GCA). NSA is the net sown area where crops are grown, whilst GCA is the gross sown area where double or multiple crops are cultivated across sessions. The changes in these attributes are examined across four broader planning phases since 1970–1. These include:

- the Green Revolution phase (1970–1 to 1979–80);
- Pre-Liberalisation phase (1980–1 to 1989–90);
- Liberalisation phase (1990–1 to 1999–2000); and
- Post-Liberalisation phase (2000–1 onwards).

The analysis begins by computing the constants and coefficient values of the best-fitted straight line equations to show the rate of change (indicated by slope *b*) and the degree of fluctuation in the actual trend of agriculture attributes over time (indicated by the Coefficient of Variation, CV) (see footnotes for more detail on Table 3.3). The results of the analysis of the average annual increase in the absolute size of agricultural production are presented in Table 3.3 and Figure 3.1. The results show the following changes in agriculture land use system in India.

1   There is an overall decrease in uncultivated land such as bush land, waste land and barren land after the planned economy phase (1950–1). The area reduced by 2,911 thousand ha during the first 20 years of the Pre-Green Revolution phase. It was 47 million ha in 1950–1, which decreased to 44.6 million ha in 1970–1. It further reduced to 41.3 million ha and 40.48 million ha during the Pre-Liberalisation and Liberalisation phase following the Green Revolution.

2   Fallow land is the land category, which is considered as a 'buffer' land between Net Sown Area and cultivable waste land. It delimits the net sown area and is generally used during the time when food demand increases drastically. The area under fallow land increased, but its use fluctuated across all the phases of agricultural development in India (Figure 3.1A).

Table 3.3 Statistical analysis of agricultural attributes during different phases of development

Phases of development	Area in million ha			Total food grains	Total pulses	Total oilseeds	Production in million tonnes	
	NSA	GCA	Crop intensity (%)				Total food grains	Total pulses
1	2	3	4	5	6	7	8	9
1970–1 to 1979–80, n = 10 (Green Revolution period)								
Avg	140.29	168.244	119.917	124.812	22.792	16.912	104.848	10.997
SD	1.993	3.978	1.661	3.149	1.016	0.529	10.993	1.347
CV (%)	1.421	2.365	1.385	2.523	4.458	3.128	10.485	12.252
Slope b	0.147*	0.918*	0.528*	0.573*	0.133*	0.067*	2.327	-0.026
1980–1 to 1989–90, n = 10 (Pre-Liberalisation period)								
Avg	140.613	176.817	125.752	126.809	23.082	19.436	140.844	12.159
SD	2.53	3.961	1.987	2.988	0.853	1.699	15.056	1.046
CV (%)	1.8	2.24	1.58	2.356	3.694	8.74	10.69	8.606
Slope b	-0.168*	0.655	0.615**	-0.285	-0.021	0.482	4.122	0.181
1990–1 to 1999–2000, n = 10 (Liberalisation period)								
Avg	142.354	187.526	131.732	123.618	22.706	25.63	184.069	13.43
SD	0.645	2.659	1.849	1.869	0.925	0.889	13.233	0.927
CV (%)	0.453	1.418	1.403	1.512	4.073	3.469	7.189	6.906
Slope b	-0.075*	0.726*	0.580*	-0.1	-0.138	0.038	3.939*	0.088
2000–1 to 2011–12, n = 12 (Post-Liberalisation period)								
Avg	140.104	190.705	136.1	122.179	22.877	25.517	213.457	14.211
SD	2.505	5.886	2.631	3.181	1.644	2.242	22.624	2.078
CV (%)	1.788	3.086	1.933	2.604	7.188	8.787	10.599	14.621
Slope b	0.152*	1.117	0.65	0.488**	0.352**	0.444	5.221**	0.485

* = at .01 significant level and ** = at .05 level

N.B.: 1. Foodgrains include paddy, wheat, jowar, bajra, maize,
2. Pulses include gram and tur (arhar), Moogh, masur, gram.
3. Oilseeds include groundnut, rapeseed and mustard and other six oilseeds.
4. Linear increase is calculated by fitting straight line equation in given date of time series as Y = a + bt where Y=value of agriculture attributes, t = time period,
a = origin of straight line and b= slope of line, i.e, average annual rate of change.

Abbreviations: NSA = Net Sown Area, GCA = Gross Cropped Area, Avg = average, SD = Standard Deviation, CV(%) = Coefficient of Variation = 100*(SD/avg).

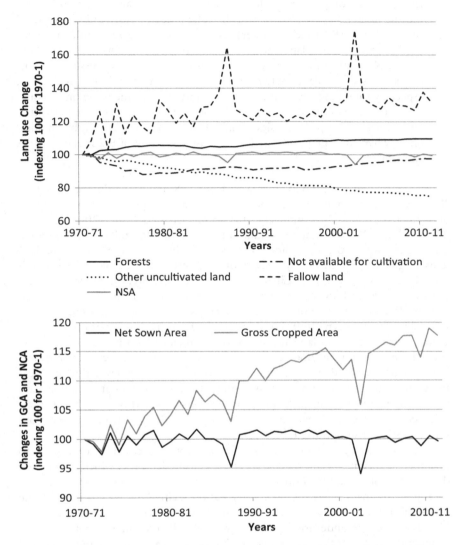

Figure 3.1 General land use patterns in different phases of agricultural development in India (1970–1 = 100 index number)

3   The Net Sown Area remained almost unchanged after the Green Revolution (1970–1). It covered approximately 140 million ha of land. The coefficient of variation for NSA has slightly increased from 1.42 per cent in the Green Revolution to 1.79 per cent in the Post- Liberalisation phase (Table 3.3). It means that there is not much growth in NSA. Relative growth in Gross Cropped Area (GCA), however, increased more rapidly, which indicates the

rising population pressure on limited land to increase land use intensity during the liberation phase (Figure 3.1B). The index of NSA and GCA (based on 1970–1 = 100 Index number) fell abruptly in the year 2003–4, whilst the increase in fallow land shows the potential impact of weather variability and El Nino effect on monsoon, which put farmers under pressure to grow crops in less fertile land. When the actual trend in agricultural production, especially total food grains and pulses, is plotted over time using linear equation method, as shown in cols. 8 and 9 of Table 3.3, it shows the best-fitted trend lines at 5.0 per cent significance level during the Post-Liberalisation phase when food grain production increased at a rate of 5.2 million tonnes annually.

Gross Cropped Area (GCA) increased from 168 million ha during the Green Revolution to 190 million ha in the Post-Liberalisation phase (between 2000–1 and 2011–12). The crop intensity, therefore, increased from 120 per cent to 136 per cent. GCA grew at an average annual rate of 0.92 million ha during the Green Revolution to 1.11 million ha in the Pre-Liberalisation phase (Table 3.2). This might suggest the likely impact of seed-fertiliser technology, which was introduced during the Post-Liberalisation phase. The area under food grains, pulses and oilseed however remained stagnant with minor fluctuation over this period. The area under potato and root crops expanded at an annual rate of 0.5 million ha between 1970–1 and 1989–90. This change affirms the increased crop diversification and land use intensity to enhance land productivity. However, the production of food grains such as Rice, Wheat, Maize, Ragi and Millets increased gradually throughout all phases of agriculture development. Areas under non-food crops and oilseeds during the Post-Liberalisation phase have marginally increased, which shows greater emphasis placed on growing market-oriented crops such as Sugarcane, Cotton, Jute and Mesta instead of staple crops for domestic consumption (Table 3.4).

At the beginning, the production of most crops increased as a response to planned expansion and intensification of agricultural land use, which culminated during the Green Revolution phase. With the introduction of seed-fertiliser packages, the main thrust of Green Revolution technology was to increase the production of cereals to reduce over-reliance on imports (Singh 1994: 27–32). However, the area under food grains grew slowly than the increase of total crop production. It means that the yield of such crops increased more rapidly than the increase in area, which indicates increased land productivity per unit.

The average annual production of food grains was 104.8 million tonnes during the Green Revolution and gradually reached 213 million tonnes during the Post-Liberalisation phase. Higher fluctuation in food grain production resembles the fluctuation in crop yields (Figure 3.2). However, the average annual rate of food grain production during different phases increased from 2.3 million tonnes in the Green Revolution to 5.22 million tonnes in the Post-Liberalisation phase.

The production of pulses also varies over time. The average annual production of pulses, for example, was 10 million tonnes but it varies more than 12 per cent from the average. It had shown negative trends (b= -0.026 million tonnes)

Table 3.4 Changes in area (A), production (P) and yield (Y) during the Liberalisation phase

Crops	2001-2			2008-9			in % (2001-2)		% (2008-9)		Change (%)		
	Area	Production	Yield	Area	Production	Yield	A	P	A	P	A	P	Y*
Rice	44.9	93.94	2079	45.54	99.18	2178	27.5	16.71	26.07	16.65	-1.43	-0.06	99
Wheat	26.34	72.77	2210	27.75	80.68	2907	16.13	12.95	15.89	13.54	-0.24	0.6	697
Jowar	9.8	7.56	771	7.53	7.25	962	6	1.35	4.31	1.22	-1.69	-0.13	191
Bajra	9.53	8.28	869	8.75	8.89	1015	5.84	1.47	5.01	1.49	-0.83	0.02	146
Maize	6.58	13.16	2000	8.17	19.73	2414	4.03	2.34	4.68	3.31	0.65	0.97	414
Total Cereals	97.15	195.71	1586	97.747	215.72	1895	59.51	34.82	55.97	36.22	-3.54	1.39	309
Gram	6.42	5.47	853	7.89	7.06	895	3.93	0.97	4.52	1.19	0.59	0.21	42
Arhar	3.33	2.26	679	3.38	2.27	671	2.04	0.4	1.93	0.38	-0.11	-0.02	-8
Lentil (Masoor)	1.47	0.97	664	1.38	0.95	693	0.9	0.17	0.79	0.16	-0.11	-0.01	29
Total Pulses	11.22	8.7	732	12.6504	10.27	753	6.87	1.55	7.24	1.73	0.37	0.18	21
Total Food Grains	108.37	204.41	1159	110.3974	226	1324	66.38	36.37	63.21	37.94	-3.17	1.57	165
Oilseeds	22.64	20.66	913	27.56	27.72	1006	13.87	3.68	15.78	4.65	1.91	0.98	93
Groundnut	6.24	7.03	1127	6.16	7.17	1163	3.82	1.25	3.53	1.2	-0.29	-0.05	36
Rapeseeds	5.07	5.08	1002	6.3	7.2	1143	3.11	0.9	3.61	1.21	0.5	0.3	141
Soya Bean	6.34	5.96	940	9.51	9.91	1041	3.88	1.06	5.45	1.66	1.56	0.6	101
Total Oilseeds	40.29	38.73	995	49.5316	51.99	1088	24.68	6.89	28.36	8.73	3.68	1.84	93
Cotton	9.13	10	186	9.41	22.28	403	5.59	1.78	5.39	3.74	-0.21	1.96	217
Jute	1.05	11.67	2008	0.9	10.37	2071	0.64	2.08	0.52	1.74	-0.13	-0.34	63
Total Fibres	10.18	21.67	1097	10.3076	32.64	1237	6.24	3.86	5.9	5.48	-0.33	1.62	140
Sugarcane	4.41	297.21	674	4.42	285.03	645	2.7	52.88	2.53	47.85	-0.17	-5.03	-29
Total	163.25	562.02	5084	174.652	595.66	5618	100	100	100	100	0		534

N.B.: *Change in Crop Yield is absolute yield difference in kg/ha

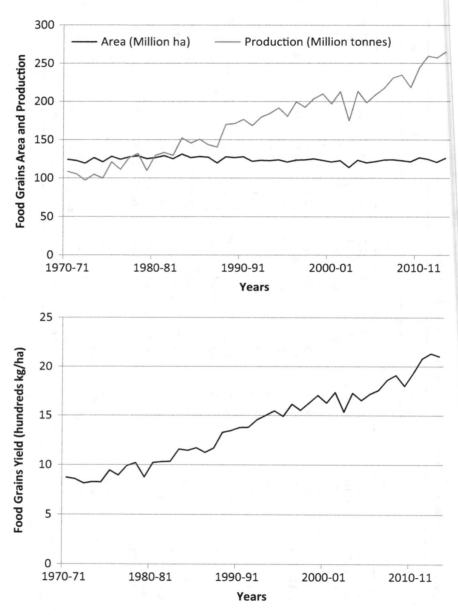

Figure 3.2 Area, production and yield of food grains across different phases of agricultural development in India

during the Green Revolution period, which reverted to positive (b= 0.485 million tonnes annually) during the Post-Liberalisation phase (Table 3.3).

The area under food grains increased marginally from 124 million ha to 126 million ha between 1970–1 and 2013–14. However, its share to total area reduced from 66 per cent to 63 per cent. Furthermore, the share of area under cereal crops also declined during the Post-Liberalisation phase (2001–2 to 2008–9). Areal share of Rice, for example, declined by 1.43 per cent (from 27.5 to 26.07 per cent), Wheat by 0.24 per cent (from 16.13 to 15.89 per cent), Jowar by 1.69 per cent (from 6.0 to 4.31 per cent) and Bajara by 0.53 per cent (5.84 to 5.01 per cent) (Table 3.4).

Area and production of Oilseeds, Soya Bean and Cotton increased in spite of gradual increase in their crop yields (Table 3.4). This growth in commercial crops might indicate a market-led production to fulfil the rising demand from globalised consumption of food in the urban and world commodity markets during the Post-Liberalisation phase. Interestingly, the area, production and yield of Sugarcane (a cash crop) all declined during this period. Sugarcane production declined by 5 per cent from 297 million tonnes in 2001–2 to 285 million tonnes in 2008–9. This in turn exerted an enormous pressure on domestic markets which relied on imports to fulfil the unmet domestic demand for raw sugar in sugar mills.

3.05 Net and gross irrigated area

3.05.1 *Source of irrigation*

Both Gross Cropped Area (GCA) of about 11.40 million ha (i.e., 6.98 per cent) and total crop production of 33.63 million tonnes (5.96 per cent) have increased during the eight years of the Post-Liberalisation phase (2000–1 to 2008–9). This is partly due to a large increase in net irrigated area and cropped area through crop intensification. There have been significant changes in the source of irrigation from the beginning of the planned economy when traditional means of irrigation such as human-operated (*Charas* and *Dhekli*) and oxen-operated water uplifter (locally called *Rahat*) (see Figures 2.3 and 2.4 in Chapter 2) were replaced by canal irrigation in the early period of planned agriculture.

Net irrigated area increased from 40.72 million ha in 1980–1 to 64.62 million ha in 2010–11 with an annual rate of 2.26 per cent. Water from rivers was effectively diverted to cultivated areas especially during the Green Revolution. The area under tube-well irrigation increased from 0.135 million ha (1960–1) to 29.108 million ha (2010–11). Tube-well irrigation was later operated by electric engines to lift ground water, and is now widely used in farms. Areas under other sources of irrigation such as canals, ponds and other traditional sources have registered no change throughout the planned period (Figure 3.3).

More than 40 per cent of the total irrigated area was covered by canal systems at the beginning of the Green Revolution. Tube-wells however became the main source of irrigation during the Post-Liberalisation phase whereby more than 45 per cent of total area (in 2010–11) was irrigated by tube-wells (Table 3.5). In the

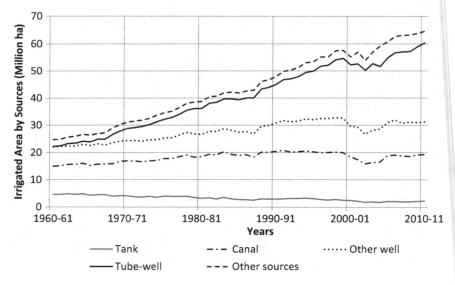

Figure 3.3 Area under different sources of irrigation in India

Table 3.5 Percentage share of irrigated area by different sources

Year	Canal	Tanks	Tube-wells	Other wells	Other sources
Pre–Green Revolution period					
1960–61	42.05	18.49	0.55	29.01	9.89
1961–62	42.2	18.53	1.04	28.51	9.72
1962–63	42.21	18.63	3.51	26.29	9.36
1963–64	42.58	17.76	3.97	26.1	9.59
1964–65	42.19	17.97	4.09	26.27	9.48
1965–66	41.6	16.16	4.91	27.94	9.39
1966–67	41.8	16.44	6.34	27.83	7.59
1967–68	41.35	16.52	7.77	25.74	8.63
1968–69	40.99	13.53	10.64	26.59	8.24
1969–70	41.74	13.44	12.38	24.63	7.8
Avg	**41.87**	**16.75**	**5.52**	**26.89**	**8.97**
Green Revolution period					
1970–71	41.28	13.22	14.34	23.88	7.29
1971–72	41.57	11.84	15.04	23.89	7.66
1972–73	40.82	11.37	16.94	23.78	7.08
1973–74	40.14	11.98	17.22	23.59	7.06
1974–75	40.09	10.51	19.53	22.68	7.19
1975–76	39.87	11.48	19.78	21.97	6.9
1976–77	39.43	11.1	21.14	21.78	6.54
1977–78	39.88	10.68	20.91	21.73	6.79
1978–79	39.8	10.34	21.44	21.73	6.68
1979–80	38.35	9.04	24.16	22.21	6.24
Avg	**40.12**	**11.16**	**19.05**	**22.72**	**6.94**

Year	Canal	Tanks	Tube-wells	Other wells	Other sources
Pre–Liberalisation period					
1980–81	39.49	8.22	24.62	21.08	6.59
1981–82	39.37	8.34	25.51	20.75	6.03
1982–83	39.78	7.22	26.47	21.08	5.46
1983–84	39.96	8.42	26.04	20.19	5.39
1984–85	38.62	7.17	27.44	20.95	5.83
1985–86	38.65	6.6	28.43	20.34	5.98
1986–87	38.75	6.29	28.89	20.02	6.05
1987–88	36.71	5.88	30.74	20.08	6.59
1988–89	37.06	6.49	29.72	20.58	6.15
1989–90	36.67	6.3	30.08	21.06	5.89
Avg	**38.51**	**7.09**	**27.79**	**20.61**	**6**
Liberalisation period					
1990–91	36.34	6.13	29.69	21.73	6.11
1991–92	35.68	6	30.42	21.8	6.11
1992–93	33.77	6.32	31.44	22.08	6.38
1993–94	33.38	6.17	31.9	21.85	6.69
1994–95	32.6	6.18	32.43	22.12	6.67
1995–96	32.06	5.84	33.54	22.07	6.49
1996–97	31.04	5.12	35.09	22.6	6.15
1997–98	31.51	4.7	35.65	22.52	5.63
1998–99	30.14	4.87	37.25	21.95	5.8
1999–00	30.31	4.41	38.31	21.9	5.06
Avg	**32.68**	**5.57**	**33.57**	**22.06**	**6.11**
Post–Liberalisation period					
2000–01	28.96	4.45	40.93	20.42	5.23
2001–02	26.7	3.84	40.83	20.98	7.65
2002–03	26.01	3.35	43.58	20.26	6.8
2003–04	25.23	3.36	43.03	20.85	7.53
2004–05	24.81	2.93	38.94	20.54	12.78
2005–06	27.38	3.43	39.23	20.13	9.83
2006–07	27.04	3.32	39.5	20.57	9.57
2007–08	26.45	3.12	41.74	19.07	9.62
2008–09	26.26	3.13	41.16	19.88	9.57
2009–10	26.65	3.32	43.82	18.61	7.61
2010–11	26.32	3.48	45.04	18.53	6.64
Avg	**26.53**	**3.43**	**41.62**	**19.98**	**8.44**

Great Plains of India, more than 80 per cent of Net Irrigated Area was irrigated by tube-wells. It was indispensable for farmers as it was not only the means of irrigation but also a source of water supply for domestic use.

3.05.2 *Agricultural growth – the general trend*

Agriculture growth is represented through three key parameters, including area, production and yield. Four key changes are discernible when a comparison of compounded growth of area, production and yield of principal crops in India from the Green Revolution phase of about 20 years (1967–8 to 1989–90) through to the Post-Liberalisation phase of 8 years (2001–2 to 2008–9) is undertaken. Each of these changes is discussed below.

1   The total crop area grew faster during the Post-Liberalisation phase (annual rate of 0.85 per cent) compared to the Green Revolution phase (annual rate of 0.26 per cent). The growth of crop area is mainly due to two reasons: first is the expansion of Net Sown Area, whereby non-agricultural land was converted into agriculture land; second is a rapid increase in crop intensity through the use of modern technology (i.e., seed-fertiliser-irrigation package).

2   The annual growth of crop production, however, marginally declined from 2.74 per cent in the Green Revolution phase to 2.53 per cent in the Post-Liberalisation phase. This is in spite of the growth in total crop area. The declining crop production is attributed to the slower growth in crop yield when compared to the growth in total crop area.

3   There is a notable shift from food grains to oilseeds and fibre crops. For example, the annual growth of area under Wheat (cereal) and Arhar (pulse) during the Green Revolution was 1.91 per cent and 1.52 per cent respectively. However, the growth of both crops fell to 0.66 per cent and 0.18 per cent during the Liberalisation phase. The growth of Millet yield also declined during the Post-Liberalisation as did the growth of Jowar (24.77 per cent) and Bajra (16.80 per cent). On the other hand, annual growth of the area under Oilseeds increased from 0.16 per cent to 2.61 per cent, whilst the area under fibre crops reduced by 0.31 per cent per year in the Post-Green Revolution, but then expanded by 0.16 per cent (Table 3.6).

4   The annual increase in Wheat yield was highest (3.15 per cent) during the Green Revolution and the Liberalisation phase. While the growth in yield of Rapeseed and Cotton was very high during the Post-Liberalisation phase. Such rapid growth in the production and yield of oilseeds and fibre crops is driven by commercial farming. Surprisingly, the growth in Cotton production has

Table 3.6 Annual compound growth (percent) of area (A), production (P) and yield (Y) during Green Revolution and Post-Liberalisation periods

Crops	Annual Growth during Green Revolution period (1967–8 to 1989–90)			Annual Growth during Post-Liberalisation period (2001–2 to 2008–9)		
	A	P	Y	A	P	Y
Rice	0.57	2.74	2.92	0.18	0.68	4.76
Wheat	1.91	5.14	3.15	0.66	1.3	31.54
Jowar	−0.68	1.31	2	−3.24	−0.53	−24.77
Bajra	−0.81	0.26	1.08	−1.06	0.89	−16.8
Maize	−0.1	1.15	1.26	2.75	5.19	20.7
Total Cereals	**0.18**	**2.95**	**2.35**	**0.08**	**1.22**	**19.48**
Gram	−0.75	−0.51	0.21	2.61	3.24	4.92
Arhar	1.52	2.08	0.55	0.18	0.03	−1.18

Crops	Annual Growth during Green Revolution period (1967–8 to 1989–90)			Annual Growth during Post-Liberalisation period (2001–2 to 2008–9)		
	A	P	Υ	A	P	Υ
Lentil (Masoor)	0.59	1.44	0.85	−0.79	−0.26	4.37
Total Pulses	0.28	0.78	0.57	1.51	2.1	2.87
Total Food Grains	0.2	2.74	2.2	0.23	1.26	14.24
Oilseeds	0.44	2.31	1.76	2.49	3.74	10.19
G Nut	0.29	1.45	1.16	−0.15	0.24	3.19
Rapeseeds	1.63	4.27	2.6	2.75	4.46	14.07
Soya Bean	−0.35	1.53	1.89	5.2	6.56	10.75
Total Oilseeds	0.16	2.15	1.51	2.61	3.75	9.35
Cotton	−0.34	2.18	2.54	0.37	10.53	116.67
Jute	0.05	1.89	1.57	−1.9	−1.47	3.14
Total Fibres	−0.31	2.07	2.28	0.16	5.25	12.76
S Cane	1.34	2.78	1.43	0.02	−0.52	−4.3
Total	0.26	2.74	2.02	0.85	0.73	10.5

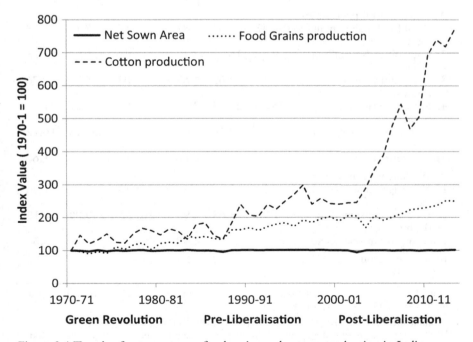

Figure 3.4 Trends of net sown area, food grains and cotton production in India

increased exponentially in comparison to the increase in food grain production and Net Sown Area during the Post-Liberalisation phase (Figure 3.4).

3.05.3 Incremental input-output ratio (IIOR)

Relative performance of production growth is calculated by the Incremental Input-Output Ratio (IIOR), which is the change in agricultural output per unit of change in inputs. IIOR has increased drastically to 2.15, but then slowed down in the later years during the Post-Liberalisation phase. This is in spite of the increase in area under irrigation as well as the higher use of fertiliser (Table 3.7). The rate of total inputs (in its real term) decreased from 4.42 per cent in the Post-Green Revolution to 3.5 per cent during the Post-Liberalisation phase. This indicates that the growth is subjected to the 'diminishing law of agricultural production returns', which shows a decrease in incremental

Table 3.7 Agricultural production growth and incremental input-output ratio (IIOR) in the Green Revolution and Post-Liberalisation periods

Items	Green Revolution period (20 years)			Post-Liberalisation period (12 years)		
	1970–1	1989–90	Annual growth	2001–2	2012–13	Annual growth
	P_0	P_1	r (%)[+]	P_0	P_1	r (%)[+]
A. Agricultural production						
1. Total food grains (million tonnes)	108.42	170.63	2.87	212.85	257.13	1.73
2. Total oilseeds* (million tonnes)	9.63	16.75	3.7	18.44	30.94	5.65
3. Groundnut (million tonnes)	6.11	8.09	1.62	7.03	4.7	–2.76
4. Sugarcane (million tonnes)	126.37	222.63	3.82	295.96	341.2	1.27
5. Fibres crops** (million bales)	10.95	19.76	4.02	20.84	61.15	16.12
Total production	–	–	**2.68**	–	–	**1.63**
B. Agricultural inputs						
1. Net irrigated area (million ha)	31.1	42	2.33	51.13	63.2	1.46
2. Fertiliser consumption (lakh tonnes)	1.98	115.68	2.92	167.98	249.09	0.15
Total input (in real terms)	–	–	**4.42**	–	–	**3.5**
Incremental input–output ratio (IIOR)	–	–	1.65	–	–	2.15

N.B.: * It includes nine oilseed crops, ** It includes cotton (in bales 170 kg of each), jute and mesta crops (in bales 180 kg of each)

+ Simple growth rate, r, is calculated as $r = \{100*(P1-P0)/P0\ t\}$, t = time period
IIOR = Ratio of growth of agricultural product to increase in inputs in a particular period of time.

output of a production when the amount of a single factor of production is incrementally increased, while the amounts of all other factors of production stay constant.

3.06 Agriculture growth dynamics

3.06.1 Era of planned development

The first three five-year plans have heavily invested in multi-purpose heavy industrial projects. Growing demand for raw materials for textile industries necessitated increased production of fibres and commercial crops such as Cotton, Jute, Mesta and Sugarcane. Consequently, the production of these crops grew faster than food grains. This shift, however, contributed to converting India to a net importer of cereals and pulses during the first phase of the planned economy (1950–1 to 1970–1).

Farming systems in India were re-organised and re-structured after the Independence to improve market efficiency and to enhance land productivity through various land reforms. Three major land reforms were implemented during the second and third five-year plans, including:

• Land re-distribution through land ceiling reform;
• Abolition of absentee landlordism; and
• Consolidation of landholdings (Bhalla 1988).

These structural reforms certainly contributed to increased food production and land productivity. Some of the changes were also driven by economic liberalisation policies including privatisation, deregulation and the reduction of trade barriers. In the early phase of agricultural development, the environmental conditions, particularly the availability of water and soil fertility for plant growth, were the dominating factors driving agricultural growth in India. They dictated the optimum conditions for sowing crops, crop mixing and crop rotation. Indian agriculture is still heavily 'monsoon-dependent' and the arrival and intensity of monsoon decide the farmers' fate. This was particularly critical in the third five-year plan. Irrigation was negligible in most parts of India and its effect on production growth was insignificant at that time. Irrigation is a key factor for productivity increase as Nath (1969) statistically established the correlation between the share of irrigated area and agricultural land productivity. However, this relationship was insignificant ($r=0.093$) during the Pre-Green Revolution phase. It could be attributed to the prevalence of irrigation infrastructure. Nonetheless, irrigation became the 'root-factor' for augmenting high agricultural growth coupled with a wide-scale use of HYVs seed-fertiliser technology, which came into practice at the beginning of the Green Revolution. Two notable features of production growth in the Pre-Green Revolution phase were:

1 expansion of Net Sown Area (NSA) and
2 changing cropping pattern.

The expansion of cultivation area to new non-cultivated land means changes in general land use. The expansion of agricultural land before the Green Revolution was examined by J. Singh (1971) who concluded that the share of waste land to total land is positively correlated with the rate of conversion especially during the 1950s That is, the higher the proportion of waste land, the greater the rate of land conversion. Cultivable waste land has drastically reduced from 16 per cent to 10 per cent in most parts of Rajasthan, Madhya Pradesh and the central and northern Uttar Pradesh, which had a significant share of cultivable waste land, well above the national average. Overall, a 6 per cent reduction of waste land was reported in the 15 years of the Pre-Green Revolution phase (1950–1 to 1965–6). Significant encroachment occurred in the fertile tracts in many states where irrigation and small-scale machine tool technology were readily available. For example, the *tarai* region of Uttar Pradesh (extending from Saharanpur to Gorakhpur along with the hills of Sivalik ranges of the Himalayas), which was largely marshland, bushland or wetlands before the Independence, was cleared and converted into arable land by the settlers who had migrated from Punjab and Sindh provinces (now in Pakistan) after the partition of India.

Wide-scale use of tractor as a machine tool had enabled both ploughing and irrigation of land. Consequently, the production and land productivity markedly increased in these areas of Uttar Pradesh. But the agricultural land expansion in the Chambal ravines of Madhya Pradesh and Rajasthan was restricted because of more primitive and small hand-operated traditional farming tools, which yielded insignificant increase in land productivity and the expansion of cultivable land. Other factors such as socio-economic status and land fertility also contributed to lower productivity levels (J. Singh 1974).

Cropping patterns during the Pre-Green Revolution had also changed. During the first two decades of agricultural development (1950–1 to 1970–1), an increase of about 34 million ha in the total cropped area of the country has been recorded, which, among other factors, was due to an increase in Net Sown Area and farming intensity. It has already been discussed that net sown area increased at a constant rate of about 10 thousand hectare per annum and the area sown more than once (which refers to farming intensity) at an annual rate of 4.8 thousand hectare in the 20 years of the Pre-Green Revolution phase. The agricultural statistics reveal that the farming intensity is positively correlated to the area under irrigation and its intensity. Irrigation intensity was 10.82 per cent in 1950–1 and 12.28 per cent in 1970–1.

Production price mechanism was another catalyst of change in cropping patterns. The substitution of traditionally grown crops with more remunerative crops resulted in production increases. In spite of rapid increase in areas under the food grains, India still had to rely on food imports during the first three five-year plan periods. The area under cash crops, especially Sugarcane and Cotton, grew slightly as these crops were relatively more remunerative compared to food grains. They are also raw materials for textile and sugar industries.

3.06.2 Impact of Green Revolution technology

Agricultural production in India increased during the 20 years of the Post-Green Revolution phase (1970–1 to 1989–90). The production growth of various crops however varied in response to increased farm inputs. For example, the production of total cereals rose to 158 million tonnes (1989–90) from 96.60 million tonnes (1970–1) at an annual compounded rate of 2.97 per cent. This record increase in cereal crops is partially attributed to the rapid increase in Wheat production, which increased by 15.82 million tonnes, from 23.83 to 49.65 million tonnes, at an annual rate of 5.64 per cent over two decades of the Post-Green Revolution. However, the Wheat production increased because of an increase in area under cultivation and yield per unit of land. Area under Wheat increased at a compounded rate of 2.41 per cent per annum, whilst yield grew at an annual rate of 3.15 per cent.

The production of other food grains and commercial crops however registered a moderate growth. For example, the production of Oilseed increased from 9.63 million tonnes to 16.75 million tonnes at an annual compounded rate of 1.56 per cent. Pulses, in contrast, recorded the lowest annual compound growth (i.e., only 0.65 per cent) in the Post-Green Revolution phase. Sugarcane production registered high growth (2.70 per cent per annum) because of continuing expansion of area under it at 1.58 per cent annually with a compounded growth of yield at 1.11 per cent per year during this phase. The other commercial crops, particularly fibres, also increased but at a moderate rate.

Area, production and yield of principal crops in India over two points of time (2001–2 and 2008–9) show a broader agreement with a priori expectation, and confirm growth during the Liberalisation and Post-Liberalisation phases of Indian agriculture. The agriculture growth patterns in the Post-Green Revolution phase characterise two key changes: the increasing dominance of Wheat and Sugarcane, and use of new farm technology. The first feature is related to the overall growth of crop production influenced by a rapid increase in production of two major crops in India, namely,

1   Wheat, a staple food grain in India, had to be imported during the Pre-Green Revolution phase at relatively higher prices. Farming technology during the Green Revolution had helped increase the yield per unit of land during fifth and sixth five-year plan periods. Consequently, the area under Wheat cultivation has increased by 2.41 per cent per annum.
2   Sugarcane, a commercial crop, is the backbone of rural industrialisation in India. Area under Sugarcane increased at an annual rate of 1.58 per cent between 1970–1 and 1989–90.

Increased production (or market) prices of Wheat and Sugarcane during the fifth five-year plan was the basis for higher yield and expansion of area under these crops. Hence, the farming of Wheat and Sugarcane rapidly diffused from Punjab to western Uttar Pradesh (the area of the Upper Ganga plains and Sivalik foothills of *terai* and swamps).

During the seventh five-year plan, Wheat was grown as a commercial crop in parts of India instead of food grain. The surplus production of Wheat was sold in markets or local mandies. Food Corporation of India has played a key role in facilitating the Wheat markets to be efficient and cost-effective both for sellers, intermediaries and consumers.

Higher production and productivity of Wheat crop were achieved by the introduction of modern farm technology. The use of HYVs seed-fertiliser in the irrigated fields also stimulated further growth in yield and area. In addition, the use of medium-sized tractor (15 HP) became an essential multi-purpose tool particularly for marginal and medium-sized landholders (2.0 to 5.0 hectares) who mostly use it for irrigation, sowing of seeds by seed drills, Wheat thrashing, levelling off of fields/farms and for spraying weedicides and pesticides (see Figures 3.5 and 3.6).

With the adoption of farm technologies, India was able to produce sufficient stock of Wheat and other food grains. India produced 1.58 million tonnes of Wheat, 2.28 million tonnes of Rice and 0.83 million tonnes of coarse grains in the marketing year of 2003–4, which increased to 2.8 million tonnes of Wheat, 3.11 million tonnes of Rice and 1.23 million tonnes of Coarse grains during 2013–14.

Availability of low-cost Wheat has an impact on food consumption habits even among rural populace. Evidence shows that the economically disadvantaged people who used to consume Jowar and Maize (cheaper food), especially in winter and the rainy season historically, have started to consume Wheat.

Figure 3.5 Thrashing of Wheat crop

Figure 3.6 Tractor-operated thrasher in the Wheat field

The expansion and intensification of land use because of lower costs of irrigation by canal systems and private tube-wells, availability of HYVs of Wheat seeds, subsidised chemical fertilisers (specially NPK) and low-interest rate loans for the purchase of small- and medium-sized tractors during the 20 years of Post-Green Revolution phase resulted in a rapid increase in the production and agricultural productivity, especially of cereals and oilseeds. Input and production costs were driving the changes in land use and cropping patterns during the Green Revolution.

Annual growth of all crops was recorded at 2.74 per cent during the Post-Green Revolution, which surprisingly was lower than the growth rate during the 20 years of the Pre-Green Revolution phase. This has been often termed as a part failure of the Green Revolution in India (J. Singh 1974). Union Minister of Agriculture Buta Singh highlighted the inadequate use of farm technology, which resulted in the lower growth rate during the Post-Green Revolution phase. This is in spite of increased inputs in its real terms at a rate of 4.1 per cent per annum over seven years (from 1976–7 to 1982–3) (B. Singh 1985).

Farm inputs have significantly increased in India. The Gross Irrigated Area increased at an annual rate of 5.6 per cent, irrigation pump sets (i.e., diesel and electric) at 8 to 9 per cent, area under HYVs at 7 per cent and the consumption of chemical fertilisers (specially NPK) at 11 per cent. Despite these positive changes, the annual rate of real agricultural output only increased by 2 per cent (i.e., about half of the input increase) during the period.

Agricultural growth in India varies spatially. It is therefore vital to devise and deploy area-specific policy interventions to improve yield and productivity. For instance, Pulses and Oilseeds production remained stagnant in spite of increased prices and market demand. Mohapatra (1982: 210–218) and Bhatia (1988: 17–18) also have acknowledged the shortcomings of the Green Revolution growth strategy, whereby they blamed the restricted use of seed-fertiliser technology for Wheat and Sugarcane farming to cause sporadic adoption in more developed parts of India. Bhatia (1988: 17–18) states that price mechanism is the key driver of input technology innovation adoption. He demonstrated that the costs of crop production and fertiliser significantly affected the growth of Wheat production in the early 1970s. Every 1 kg of nitrogen and 1 kilo of NPK fertiliser would help gain about 10 kg of additional Wheat (Bhatia 1988: 25).

NPK fertiliser was widely applied to enhance Wheat production with HYVs of Mexican Wheat seeds particularly in the irrigated areas of Punjab, Haryana and Uttar Pradesh in the early 1970s. Interestingly, the quantity of Wheat required an investment of 1 kg of NPK, which decreased from 3 kg (1970–1) to 2.27 kg (1991–2) because of the rapid increase in Wheat price in comparison to the increase in fertiliser costs, which was subsidised until 1991.

The second key feature of the Post-Liberalisation phase relates to changes in traditional farming practices in India, which were largely dictated by biophysical constraints. Intensive land use and commercial farming however helped farmers to grow crops with higher returns. Wheat and Sugarcane in the Upper Ganga plains, Grams in central Peninsular India and Cotton in Gujarat and Maharashtra all have shown radical land use changes where more diverse farming has been gradually replaced by monoculture farming with the dominance of a single crop. Whilst in other parts of India, there were opportunities for farmers to diversify cropping, from a single-crop monoculture to multiple crops farming. Dogra (1981) noted this shift from crop specialisation to crop diversification later during the Green Revolution phase (1962–5 to 1972–5).

3.06.3 Areal change in crop patterns

High physiographical diversity and agro-ecological conditions in India make a regional approach imperative to understand inter-state and inter-district variations in agriculture practices and cultivation regimes. India is predominately a food grains growing country. Over three-fourth of GCA is under food grains. Regional variations were mapped by the Agriculture Commission (1964), followed by Bhat and Learmonth (1968) in the late fifties, and later by Bhalla and Alagh (1979b: 57–139) in the late sixties; all concluded that by and large the cropping patterns in India were driven by agro-climatic conditions and soil fertility levels. For example, areas under humid climate – characterised by an annual rainfall of more than 100 cm, temperature ranging between 20° C to 40° C and high soil fertility, confined notably in the middle and lower parts of the Great Plains of India (Bihar and West Bengal states), the Brahmaputra valley (Assam), the coastal areas of deltas and plains (coastal Orissa, Andhra Pradesh, Tamil Nadu, Kerala and Maharashtra) – are predominately Rice-growing 'mono-culture' farming. On the other hand, Wheat-dominated areas include semi-arid climate particularly in Punjab, Haryana, and the western part of Uttar Pradesh, where cereal is grown with the help of irrigation supported by seed fertiliser technology. The arid zone of India that includes the state of Rajasthan and the central part of peninsular India (interior Maharashtra, Madhya Pradesh, Andhra Pradesh, Karnataka) are traditionally dominated by Jowar and Bajra.

The areas under Rice and Wheat increased from 42.17 and 23.46 million ha to 42.75 and 30.00 million ha. However, their shares to total production decreased by 7.1 and 1.1 per cent respectively during the Liberalisation and Post-Liberalisation phase. There seems to be a decreasing trend in the areas of Pulses (Arhar and Masoor) and Millets (Jowar and Bajra) (Table 3.8). Millet-dominated farming in Rajasthan and interior Maharashtra changed to WheatRice or Oilseed-dominated

Table 3.8 Changing crop pattern from Pre-Liberalisation (1989–90) to Post-Liberalisation (2012–13) periods in India

Crops	1989–90		2012–13		Change in area and percentage share	
	Area	*%*	*Area*	*%*	*Area*	*%*
Rice	42.17	26.499	42.75	19.404	0.58	−7.095
Wheat	23.46	14.742	30	13.617	6.54	−1.125
Jowar	14.95	9.394	6.21	2.819	−8.74	−6.576
Bajra	10.89	6.843	7.3	3.313	−3.59	−3.53
Maize	5.86	3.682	8.67	3.935	2.81	0.253
Gram	6.5	4.084	8.52	3.867	2.02	−0.217
Arhar	3.58	2.25	3.89	1.766	0.31	−0.484
Lentil (Masoor)	13.14	8.257	1.58	0.717	−11.56	−7.54
Oilseeds	0	0	26.48	12.019	26.48	12.019
G Nut	8.71	5.473	4.72	2.142	−3.99	−3.331
Rapeseeds	0	0	6.36	2.887	6.36	2.887
Cotton	7.33	4.606	11.98	5.438	4.65	0.832
Jute and Mesta	0.91	0.572	0.86	0.39	−0.05	−0.181
S Cane	3.41	2.143	5	2.269	1.59	0.127
Others	18.23	11.455	56	25.418	37.77	13.962
Total	**159.14**	100	**220.32**	100	61.18	

Table 3.9 State-wise crop pattern of 14 Crops during Post-Liberalisation (2008–9) (area in million ha)

	Rice	Wheat	Jowar	Bajra	Maize	Gram	Arhar	Masoor	Oilseeds	G Nut	Rapeseeds	Cotton	Jute/ Mesta	Sugarcane	Total
Andhra Pradesh	4.39		0.28	0.06	0.85	0.61	0.44		2.6	1.77	0	1.4	0.04	0.2	12.63
%	34.7		2.21	0.47	6.72	4.8	3.5		20.54	13.96		11.06	0.29	1.55	99.79
Assam	2.48	0.05						0.02	0.25		0.23		0.07	0.03	3.13
%	79.35	1.6						0.64	8.15		7.24		2.09	0.92	100
Bihar	3.5	2.16			0.64	0.06	0.03	0.16	0.14		0.09		0.15	0.11	7.03
%	49.76	30.68			9.1	0.87	0.4	2.27	1.96		1.21		2.15	1.59	100
Chattisgarh	3.73				0.24										3.97
%	93.96														100
Gujarat	0.75	1.09	0.17	0.7	0.5	0.18	0.27		2.98	1.91	0.29	2.35		0.22	11.42
%	6.57	9.55	1.52	6.16	4.38	1.53	2.33		26.13	16.7	2.57	20.61		1.94	100
Haryana	1.21	2.46	0.08	0.61		0.12			0.54		0.52	0.46		0.09	6.09
%	19.86	40.41	1.33	10.01		2.02			8.88		8.45	7.55		1.48	100
Himachal Pradesh		0.36			0.3										0.66
%		54.55			45.45										100
Jammu and Kashmir	0	0.28		0.02	0.32										0.62
%	0	44.95		2.89	51.61										99.45
Jharkhand	1.68	0.1			0.22	0	0.1								2.1
%	79.87	4.75			10.46	0	4.92								100
Karnataka	1.51	0.27	1.38	0.27	1.07	0.73	0.6		2.18	0.85		0.41		0.28	9.54
%	15.82	2.82	14.48	2.79	11.21	7.65	6.26		22.83	8.91		4.29		2.94	100
Kerala	0.23														0.23
%	100														100
Madhya Pradesh	1.68	3.79	0.48	0.18	0.84	2.84	0.32	0.53	6.49	0.2	0.71	0.62	0.07	0.07	18.75
%	8.96	20.19	2.57	0.93	4.48	15.15	1.71	2.83	34.61	1.07	3.8	3.33		0.38	100
Maharashtra	1.52	1.02	4.07	0.87	0.66	1.14	1.01		3.98	0.32	0	3.15	0.02	0.77	18.52
%	8.21	5.52	21.98	4.67	3.56	6.17	5.45		21.49	1.72		16.99	0.1	4.15	100
Meghalaya	0.02												0.01		0.03
%	70.42												29.58		100

Region															Total
Orissa	4.45	0.01				0.04	0.14		0.3	0.08			0.02	0.01	5.05
%	88.12	0.18				0.74	2.74		5.91	1.65			0.45	0.21	100
Punjab	2.74	3.53	0		0.15	0	0	0	0.06	0	0.3	0.53		0.08	7.38
%	37.11	47.75			2.03				0.81		4.06	7.14		1.1	100
Rajasthan		2.29	0.58	5.17	1.05	1.26	0	0.02	4.65	0.32	2.84	0.3			18.49
%		12.41	3.12	27.99	5.68	6.81		0.11	25.15	1.74	15.35	1.64			100
Tamil Nadu	0	1.93	0.26	0.06	0.29	0	0.03	0	0.59	0.49	0	0.11	0	0.31	4.06
%		47.49	6.37	1.4	7.14		0.72		14.41	12.06		2.82		7.6	100
Uttar Pradesh	6.03	9.51	0.19	0.8		0.55	0.32	0.52	1.35	0.1	0.88	0	0	2.08	22.33
%	27	42.59	0.86	3.58		2.48	1.41	2.33	6.03	0.43	3.96			9.33	99.99
Uttarakhand		0.4												0.11	0.51
%		78.81												21.19	100
West Bengal	5.94	0.31	0	0	0.09	0	0.02	0.05	0.7	0	0.41	0	0.59	0.02	8.13
%	73.02	3.77			1.11		0.27	0.61	8.65		5.07		7.28	0.22	100
All India	45.54	27.75	7.53	8.75	8.17	7.89	3.38	1.38	27.56	6.16	6.3	9.41	0.9	4.42	165.14
%	27.58	16.81	4.56	5.3	4.95	4.78	2.05	0.84	16.69	3.73	3.81	5.7	0.55	2.67	100

farming due to rapid expansion of irrigated area with completion of the Indira Gandhi canal (Table 3.9).

3.06.4 Changes in crop yield

There has been a significant increase in crop yield especially after the Green Revolution, although crop yield levels are still relatively low compared to world standards. Yields of cereals increased remarkably after the Green Revolution. For example, Rice yield increased from 1,637 kg/ha (1989–90) to 2,079 kg/ha (2001–2). The rate of increase, however, reduced during the Post-Liberalisation phase. Likewise, the yield of Bajra increased by 59 per cent from 544 kg/ha to 869 kg/ha during the Post-Green Revolution phase. Its growth, however, slowed down after the Liberalisation phase. Yield of Arhar (pulse) declined marginally in the Post-Revolution phase but increased subsequently by 14.3 per cent during the Post-Liberalisation phase (2001–2 to 2012–13). On the whole, industrial crops (i.e., Cotton, Jute and Mesta) and Oilseeds (i.e., Mustard Seeds, Rapeseeds and Soya Beans) yields have all increased significantly in the Post-Liberalisation phase (Table 3.10).

Table 3.10 Changes in crop yield (kg/ha) from Pre-Liberalisation to Post- Liberalisation period in India

Crops	Crop yield			Change 1989–90 to 2001–2		Change 2001–2 to 2012–13	
	1989–90	*2001–2*	*2012–13*	*absolute*	*%*	*absolute*	*%*
Rice	1637	2079	2462	442	27	383	18.42
Wheat	2121	2210	3117	89	4.2	907	41.04
Jowar	774	771	850	−3	−0.39	79	10.25
Bajra	544	869	1198	325	59.74	329	37.86
Maize	1343	2000	2566	657	48.92	566	28.3
Gram	678	853	1036	175	25.81	183	21.45
Arhar	741	679	776	−62	−8.37	97	14.29
Lentil (Masoor)	445	664	797	219	49.21	133	20.03
Oilseeds	727	913	1168	186	25.58	255	27.93
Groundnut	929	1127	995	198	21.31	−132	−11.71
Rapeseeds	826	1002	1262	176	21.31	260	25.95
Soya Bean	–	940	1353	–	–	413	43.94
Cotton	252	190	486	−62	−24.6	296	155.79
Jute and Mesta	2393	2008	2281	−385	−16.09	273	13.6
Sugarcane	62100	67370	68254	5270	8.48	884	1.31

Source: Crop yield data were compiled from the tables provided by the Department of Economics and Statistics, Ministry of Agriculture, New Delhi, See: http://dacnet.nic.in/ends/latest_2006.htm downloaded on 25.10 2013

Table 3.11 State-wise crop yield of 14 crops in the Post-Liberalisation period (2008–9) (crop yield in kg/ha; sugar cane qu/ha)

States	Rice	Wheat	Jowar	Bajra	Maize	Gram	Arhar	Masoor	Oilseeds	G Nut	Rapeseeds	Cotton	Jute/Mesta	Sugar cane
Andhra Pradesh	3246		1563	1017	4873	1412	456		842	880		434	1435	78469
Assam	1614	1090						512	542		543		1856	38451
Bihar	1599	2043			2676	925	1178	785	999		959		1455	44324
Chattisgarh	1176					831								
Gujarat	1744	2377	1195	1365	1481	1011	989		1345	1395	1136	507		70181
Haryana	2726	4390	506	1769		1041			1723		1738	694		57000
Himachal Pradesh		1520			2273									
Jammu and Kashmir		1735		592	2005									
Jharkhand	2031	1541			1407		616							
Karnataka	2511	918	1179	703	2833	552	528		556	589		360		83018
Kerala	2519													
Madhya Pradesh	927	1723	1193	1373	1361	981	804	505	1075	1140	1034	233		42199
Maharashtra	1501	1483	881	765	2382	677	600		857	1116		257	260	78969
Meghalaya													1170	
Orissa	1529		629			662	860		604	1156			918	59833
Punjab	4022	4462			3404				1276	1670	1222	737		57654
Rajasthan		3175	577	828	1736	779		869	1114		1234	408		
Tamil Nadu	2683		827	1483	4389		608		1782	1989		279		106197
Uttar Pradesh	2171	3002	1010	1609	1499	1014	914	883	865	705	1123			52326
Uttarakhand		2003												52243
West Bengal	2533	2490			3782	1037		652	828		764		2422	93085
All India	2178	2907	962	1015	2414	895	671	693	1006	1163	1143	403	2071	64553

Crop yield during the Post-Liberalisation phase shows two notable regional changes. These include:

1   A regional shift in the impact of seed-fertiliser technology was seen in the Upper Ganges Plain (Punjab-Haryana-Uttar Pradesh) during the Green Revolution phase. The impact was initially confined to Rice and Wheat growing areas. During the Post-Liberalisation phase, the impact expanded to coastal plains of West Bengal and Eastern Ghats (Andhra Pradesh and Tamil Nadu), where Rice yield increased remarkably to 2683 kg/ha in Tamil Nadu and 2533 kg/ha in West Bengal.
2   Higher crop yields of Oilseeds and Groundnut were recorded in the sandy loam soil-dominated arid climate of Punjab and Rajasthan and in the semi-arid central part of Tamil Nadu. In Tamil Nadu, Oilseeds and Groundnut crop yields increased to 1782 kg/ha and 1989 kg/ha respectively (Table 3.11). High Sugarcane yield was also reported in Tamil Nadu in 2008–9.

The area under Millets (Jowar and Bajra) however has declined after the Liberalisation, although the yield per unit of land of these crops increased. Rajasthan and Haryana are key Millets-growing areas, and there has been no regional shift during the Liberalisation or Post- Liberalisation phase.

Yields of almost all crops, except for Arhar (pulse), increased after the economic reforms during the Liberalisation phase. Punjab and Rajasthan were high-performing states in achieving high yield of Oilseeds and fibre crops in the Post-Green Revolution phase. Tamil Nadu however also increased yield of Oilseeds, Cotton, Jute and Groundnut in the Post-Liberalisation phase. The reasons for these states to generate high production and productivity include:

*   Increased demand for cash crops, which are regionally grown in specific areas (e.g. Oilseeds in Punjab-Haryana-Rajasthan; Cotton in Maharashtra, Gujarat and Punjab; Jute in West Bengal, Bihar and Assam; and Groundnut in Rajasthan and Gujarat). Demand of such crops however increased nationwide, which incentivised farmers to change cropping patterns and increase inputs to attain greater return on investment;
*   Government intervention rather than market-led price mechanism regulated the purchase, sale and supply of these commodities across states, which aimed to protect small farmers from market uncertainty.

National Agriculture Cooperative Marketing Federation of India Ltd (NAFED) regulates the commodity supplies by procuring and regulating price. It is a government agency that organises marketing, processing and storage of agricultural commodities, distribution of agricultural inputs and regulation of import and export of agricultural commodities. NAFED has a turnover of Rs 5735 crores and procured 574,550 metric tonnes of Cotton during 2009–10. About 2.00 lakh metric tons of Mustard Seed was procured in 2005–6. It regulates prices of the agricultural products and operates the Public Distribution System (PDS).

Table 3.12 Procurement of agricultural products by NAFED under Price Support Scheme

Sl. no.	Commodity	Year	Support price (Rs/qu)	Quantity produced (metric tonnes)	Value (Rs lakhs)
1	Soya Bean	2005–6	1010	886	97.49
2	Groundnut	2005–6	1520	3,428	552.19
3	Sunflower Seed	2005–6	1550	24,278	4005.05
4	Mustard Seed	2005–6	1715	1,99,896	364,708.78
5	Sesamum	2005–6	1500	2,162	354.29
6	Gram	2005–6	1425	72,741	11305.23
7	Urad	2004–5	1410	2,113	310.65
8	Arhar	2002–3	1325	51	7
9	Masoor	2003–4	1525	3,946	632.52
10	Cotton	2008–9	2500	1,234,846	358,487.97

Source: http:www.nafed-india.com/objective.asp

Table 3.12 provides the support prices and quantity of some main crops procured by NAFED.

The trends in Cotton and Jute purchases through Cotton Corporation and Jute Corporation of India are notable during the Post-Liberalisation phase. Agricultural production diversified from food-grain-dominant farming of the Pre-Liberalisation phase to increasingly more commercialised production of crops such as Oilseeds, Cotton, Groundnut and Jute. Diversification and increase in the production of these crops are largely driven by market demand and better prices in domestic and international markets. Purchase of raw Cotton reached to 1,352.42 thousand bales in 2005–6, which increased to 8,939 thousand bales (of 170 kg each) in 2008–9. On the other hand, the purchase of raw Jute declined gradually from 483 thousand bales (of 180 kg each) in 2006–7 to 103 thousand bales in 2008–9. The cause of increase or decrease in the purchase of raw Cotton or Jute is the fluctuating demand for raw material. The confinement of Jute production in West Bengal also contributed to a decline in addition to the constantly falling demand for Jute.

3.07 Measurement of growth and growth components

3.07.1 Aggregation approach to measure agricultural growth

The elemental-decomposition technique considers agricultural output as the product of three production elements: area, yield and production price. However, there are other measurement frameworks, which apply other methods such as the additive decomposition analysis (Minhas and Vaidyanathan 1965); the multiplicative decomposition scheme of growth components, which predicts annual exponential rate of agricultural output growth (Bhalla and Alagh 1979b: 40–61); and the compound rate of aggregated agricultural output (Mohapatra 1982: 220–243). Similar approaches are applied to estimate the growth rate of area, production and yield of principal crops by the Department of Agriculture and Cooperation (Ministry of Agriculture 1991: Table 14.2).

3.07.1.1 Growth of aggregated output based on linear-trend equation

According to the additive growth model of Minhas and Vaidyanathan (1965), the observed increase in aggregate agricultural output has been decomposed into four components, which contribute to change in: (i) cultivated area, (ii) crop yield, (iii) cropping patterns and (iv) the interaction between the latter two components.

The model developed is based on the 'arithmetic law' of agricultural production growth rather than 'geometric law', which follows an exponential or compounded trend in production increase. Exponential and compounded trends are based on semi-logarithmic distribution of agricultural production increase over time. Exponential trend follows the form:

$$p_1 = p_0(e)^{rt}, \quad \ldots \qquad \ldots \qquad \ldots \qquad \ldots \tag{3.1}$$

where, p_1 = production of current year, p_0 = production of base year, r = annual rate per unit and t = number of years. Its linearised form is expressed as:

$$\text{Log}_e \, p_1 = \log_e p_0 + rt. \quad \ldots \qquad \ldots \qquad \ldots \tag{3.2}$$

On the other hand, compound growth is based on the formula below:

$$p_1 = p_0(1 + r)^t. \quad \ldots \qquad \ldots \qquad \ldots \tag{3.3}$$

It follows $\log p_1 = \log p_0 + \log (1 + r).t$ form of the distribution.

Note that the linear form of production increase follows as:

$$p_1 = p_0 + (p_0 r)t, \quad \ldots \qquad \ldots \qquad \ldots \tag{3.4}$$

where $r = [(p_1 - p_0)/p_0 t]$, and $(p_0 r)$ = annual absolute increase in the total size of production.

Empirical evidence suggests that agricultural production is subject to the law of diminishing return (Miller 1966); that is the production increases with a decreasing rate due to factors such as land capability constraints, changes in agro-ecological conditions, various levels of substitution rate of input factors, and local variation in food requirements. Thus, it is argued that production-increase follows arithmetic rather than a geometric progression. This was validated by fitting the straight line in the distribution of production of various crops and total food grains using 40 years of crop production data by the Department of Agriculture and Cooperation (Ministry of Agriculture 1991). The results of the analysis demonstrated that the growth of agriculture output was unlikely to follow a compounded as well as exponential trend. The inherent characteristics and weaknesses of these schemes of decomposition have also been tested by Bhalla and Alagh (1979a and 1979b: 40–41 and table 11), although they used the geometric progression method (i.e., exponential growth rate formula) to measure district-wise growth of agricultural output. Minhas and Vaidyanathan's model however has a better fit, which had applied linear models, as in Equation 3.4, to analyse the decomposed elements of agricultural output.

As the aggregated agricultural output is the product of three production components – namely, area, yield and production-prices – the crop yield (called growth determinant) would, therefore, have direct effect on changes in agricultural output over time. It should be noted that the incremental output is simply the difference of total output increase between two points of time $(O_1 - O_0)$. Total output, O, is defined as the aggregated production of various crops in money term formulated as $O = \Sigma a.y.p$ where a is area, y is yield and p is harvest price of a particular crop.

The growth of agricultural output refers to the proportionate change of output differentials for various crops over time because of the linearity of crop-production increase. Thus, the equation of agricultural growth rate, r, which is $r = (O_1 - O_0)/O_0$, as in Equation 3.4, is the result of the growth rates of various crop production. The output growth of a particular crop, r_i, is expressed as:

$$r_i = (a_{i1}.y_{i1}.P_{i0} - a_{i0}.y_{i0}.P_{i0})/a_{i0}.y_{i0}.P_{i0},$$
$$\text{or } r_i = [\{(a_{i1}/a_{i0}).(y_{i1}/y_{i0})\} - 1.0], \quad \ldots \quad \ldots \quad \ldots \quad (3.5)$$

where a_{i1} and a_{i0} are areas under ith crop for the current and the base years, y_{i1} and y_{i0} refer to the crop yield for the current and the base year respectively, and p_{i0} denotes prices per unit of production of ith crop. This equation of crop production growth (Equation 3.5) establishes the relationship among growth components that the growth rate of crop output is the product of two growth ratios: the growth ratio of crop area (a_{i1}/a_{i0}) and of the crop yield (y_{i1}/y_{i0}) with the subtraction of unit constant to determine the actual crop growth.

3.07.1.2 State level variation in agricultural growth ratio

State-wise variations in growth components (area, yield and production price) show significant spatial variability in India. Key features of production growth ratio of various crops in the country indicate that:

1 The production of Maize, Gram, Arhar and Cotton doubled during the Post- Liberalisation phase. Maize crop area growth ratio was noticeably high in Tamil Nadu (4.09), Maharastra (1.98), Andhra Pradesh (1.98) and Karnataka (1.84). It was also high in Gujarat for Wheat (2.32) and Jharkhand for Arhar (5.17). The crop growth of area under Cotton cultivation increased substantially in Gujarat (1.34) and Andhra Pradesh (1.26) (Table 3.13). This suggests that the geographical expansion of area under Maize and Gram contributed to accelerated agricultural growth process

Table 3.13 State-wise crop area growth ratio of 14 crops (2001–2 to 2008–9)

	Rice	Wheat	Jowar	Bajra	Maize	Gram	Arhar	Masoor	Oilseeds	G Nut	Rapeseeds	Cotton	Jute and Mesta	Sugarcane
Andhra Pradesh	1.15		0.44	0.66	1.98	2.09	1.05		1.07	1.05		1.26	0.46	0.89
Assam	0.98	0.72						1	0.82		0.84		0.93	0.95
Bihar	0.98	1.01			1.09	0.87	0.7		0.99		0.95		0.94	1.02
Chattisgarh	0.98					1.41		0.94						
Gujarat	1.11	2.32	0.97	0.75	1.13	3.5	0.81		1.05	1.01	1.18	1.34		1.23
Haryana	1.17	1.07	0.81	1.03		0.88			0.98		0.95	0.73		0.56
Himachal Pradesh		0.97			0.99									
Jammu and Kashmir	1.07	1.07		1.79	0.96									
Jharkhand	1.11	1.43			1.54		5.17							
Karnataka	1.07	1.03	0.77	1.27	1.84	1.52	1.24		1.25	1		0.67		0.69
Kerala	0.73		0.75											
Madhya Pradesh	0.95	1.02		1.1	0.99	1.11	1.04	1.06	1.16	0.91	1.4	1.16		1.76
Maharashtra	1.01	1.31	0.79	0.62	1.98	1.5	0.99		1.69	0.74		1.01	0.9	1.32
Meghalaya													0.84	
Orissa	0.99		0.89			1.25	1.07		0.9	1.39			0.75	1.08
Punjab	1.1	1.03			0.89				0.75			0.86		0.58
Rajasthan		1	0.95	1.01	1.03	1.3		1	1.49	1.34	0.54	0.59		
Tamil Nadu	0.94		0.81	0.44	4.09		0.49		0.75	0.74	1.54	0.6		0.97
Uttar Pradesh	0.99	1.03		0.95		0.66	0.81	0.83	1.09	0.86	1.04			1.02
Uttarakhand		1.05			0.86									0.82
West Bengal	0.98	0.71			3.03	0.43		0.71	1.17		0.94		0.9	0.88
All India	1.01	1.05	0.6	0.92	1.24	1.23	1.01	0.94	1.22	0.99	1.24	1.03	0.86	1

Table 3.14 State-wise crop yield growth ratio of 14 crops (2001–2 to 2008–9)

	Rice	Wheat	Jowar	Bajra	Maize	Gram	Arhar	Masoor	Oilseeds	G Nut	Rapeseeds	Cotton	Jute and Mesta	Sugarcane
Andhra Pradesh	1.09		1.58	1.31	1.43	1.11	1.02		1.27	1.19		1.51	0.94	0.95
Assam	1.06	0.92				0.97		0.97	1.07		1.08		1.08	1.03
Bihar	1.09	0.99			1.07		1.02	0.98	1.19		1.14		1.16	0.96
Chattisgarh	0.88					1.13								
Gujarat	1.12	0.98	1.29	1.02	0.74	1.82	1.76		1.05	1	0.96	3.07		0.99
Haryana	1.03	1.07	2.39	1.24		1.22			1.17		1.17	3.56		0.99
Himachal Pradesh		0.87			0.89									
Jammu and Kashmir	1.7	1.31		0.99	1.22									
Jharkhand		0.87					0.67							
Karnataka	1.1	1.2	1.54	1.31	0.94	0.94	1.73		0.95	0.86		2.11		1.02
Kerala	1.15				1.13									
Madhya Pradesh	0.97	1.06	1.32	1.08	0.69	1.04	0.98	1.05	1.31	1.02	1.14	1.88		1.09
Maharashtra	0.86	1.07	1.16	1.29	1.32	1.14	0.79		0.91	0.97		1.75	0.98	1.01
Meghalaya													1.14	
Orissa	0.96	1.09	1.09			1.02	1.33		1.43	1.17			1.07	1.02
Punjab	1.13	0.98			1.25				1.27		1.02	3.01		0.89
Rajasthan		1.14	1.39	1.11	1.19	1.03		0.96	1.11	1.36	1.17	4.34		
Tamil Nadu	0.84		0.95	1.21	2.72		0.95		1.06	1.06		0.95		1.05
Uttar Pradesh	1.03	1.09		1.42	0.92	1.04	0.79	1.1	1.03	0.84	1.13			0.9
Uttarakhand		1.04												0.87
West Bengal	1.01	1.12			1.46	1.22		1.24	1.01		1		1	1.09
All India	1.05	1.32	1.05	1.17	1.21	1.05	0.99	1.04	1.1	1.03	1.14	2.17	1.03	0.96

especially in the central parts of the Deccan Plateau of the semi-arid zone of the country. Similarly, Cotton contributed to agriculture growth in Rajasthan and Gujarat during the Post-Liberalisation period.

2   In general, the crop yield ratio of almost all crops in most states of India was over 1. This indicates that the crop yields of all principal crops were marginally increased almost uniformly across the country. However, a few states had significant increase in crop yield. For instance, Tamil Nadu and Andhra Pradesh had very high crop yield growth ratio for Maize; Gujrat and Orissa for Arhar pulse; and Rajasthan, Haryana, Punjab and Gujrat for Cotton (more than 3.00 ratio value) (Table 3.14). This means yield of Cotton crop increased three-fold especially in the semi-arid areas of North West India.

3   In many states, the area growth under cereals was relatively high, whilst in other states the yield growth of industrial crops remained high. In many states, there was a negative relationship between the increase in crop area and crop yield during the Post-Liberalisation phase. There were similar relationships between growth components during the Green Revolution when the regional pattern of growth started to change (Singh 1994: 41). Tamil Nadu and Andhra Pradesh of semi-arid climatic condition had high value of crop area growth ratio and yield growth ratio of Maize, whilst Gujrat had high growth ratio of crop area and crop yield of Cotton crop.

3.08 Agriculture and economic development

The conventional wisdom suggests that the share of the agriculture sector to total output declines with economic growth. The ratio of labour force employed in the agricultural sector to total employment also reduce as the economy diversifies and becomes more industrialised (World Development Report 1982: 40). The significance of agriculture and the associated sectoral shift towards the manufacturing and services sectors was a symptomatic of higher levels of economic development. However given the levels of regional disparities and income inequality there is an urgent need to re-examine the role and contribution of the agriculture sector to the national economy and the future this sector holds for the farming communities. It can be examined using four key parameters:

1   the Product Contribution, which indicates its contribution to GDP;
2   the Factors' Contribution, which reflects its contribution to the shift of surplus capital and labour force from the agricultural to non-agricultural sectors. Such shift is largely driven by higher income elasticity of non-agricultural products (due to their higher demand), higher incremental demand for capital especially in non-agricultural sectors of the economy, and lower Incremental Capital-Output Ratio (ICOR) in agriculture than non-agricultural industries. It could also mean higher productivity of farmers to invest surplus money in non-agricultural activities instead on their own farms (Ingersent and Ghatak 1984: 43–46);

3   Market Contribution, which represents surplus agricultural products supplied to domestic or global markets. This led to the rapid emergence of
market towns (mandi), which acted as the collection points for surplus food
commodities; and

4   the Foreign Exchange Contribution, which provides exportable food products of international value to help earn foreign currency.

Using the Kuznet's (1964) model, the contribution of the agriculture sector
to Gross Domestic Product (GDP) is explained below. In general, the contribution of agricultural product to GDP is a function of two main attributes of
the economy: i) magnitude and ii) the rate of growth of the agricultural sector.
The relationship between agriculture magnitude to GDP growth (Pa.ra/dP)
and change in the magnitude of GDP of agriculture sector (Pa.ra) is often non-
linear because:

$$Pa.ra/dP = (1.0 + Pn.rn/Pa.ra)^{-1} \quad \ldots \quad \ldots \quad \ldots \quad (3.6)$$

Where Pa and Pn are the magnitude of the agriculture and non-agriculture sectors' GDP respectively, ra and rn are the growth rate of the agriculture and non-
agriculture sectors and dP is the annual change in total GDP. The simplification
of the above equation for its reciprocal form shows its linearity as

$$(Pa.ra/dP)^{-1} = 1.0 + Pn.rn (Pa.ra)^{-1} \quad \ldots \quad \ldots \quad \ldots \quad (3.7)$$

This relationship thus follows a 'reciprocity law' of agricultural contribution to
the rate of economic growth. Best-fit curve follows the reciprocity law when data
capturing 63 years (1950–1 to 2013–14) of agricultural contribution (Pa.ra/d
GDP) are plotted against the change in the magnitude of the agricultural sector
(Pa.ra) (Figure 3.7). It shows that the agricultural sector has significant increase
in its magnitude and growth despite the slowly shrinking contribution to the
GDP particularly after the Green Revolution.

There is an increase in the magnitude of agriculture sector of about Rs
816,390 crores during the planned economic period of 63 years. Its contribution
increased from Rs 83,158 crores (1950–1) to Rs 800,548 crores (2013–14).
However, it grew at an average annual rate of 3.1 per cent, which is far lower
than the average annual growth of total GNP. This shows that there is a gradual
decline in the share of agricultural to total GNP from nearly 60 per cent in the
beginning of the planned economy phase in 1950–1 to 52.5 per cent in 1971–2.
It further reduced to 35 per cent in 1990–1 and then to 24.2 per cent in 2003–4
and further reduced to 16.27 per cent in 2013–14 (Table 3.15, Figures 3.8a
and b). Such trends are expected to occur with economic development when the
share of agricultural declined in comparison to other sectors of the economy such
as services sectors. Similar trends were noted in other countries, for example,
Poland when its economy went through major economic reforms (Zegar and
Florianczyk 2003).

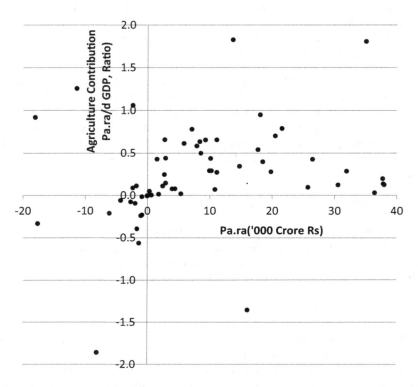

Figure 3.7 Contribution of the agriculture sector to economic growth (Pa.ra/d GDP) subject to change in GNP of agriculture sector

The annual growth rate of the agricultural sector also showed significant yearly fluctuation over the last few decades. For example, in the year 1965–6, agriculture had -10.23 per cent annual growth due to the vagaries of monsoon, but it had a positive growth in the year 1967–8 with a record growth of 14.32 per cent. During the second phase of economic growth, and the introduction of Green Revolution technology led to moderate agricultural growth (2.84 per cent) although the degree of variability was still relatively high (CV = 242.68 percent). This variability in agricultural growth however was insignificant during the Liberalisation phase. Cropping practices were diversified and farming was commercialised in many regions in India, which in turn increased overall agricultural productivity (CV = 124.25 percent) with higher annual growth return of 3.15 per cent (Figure 3.8). Annual growth therefore has been heavily dependent on weather conditions and the reliability of monsoon.

Table 3.15 Contribution of agricultural sector to the Indian economy

Years	Total GDP (Rs crores)	GDP–agriculture (Rs crores)	Share of agriculture sector to GDP (%)	Growth rate Agriculture GDP (unit)	d GDP (Rs crores)	Pa.ra (Rs crores)	Pa.ra/d GDP (Ratio)
1	2	3	4	5	6	7	8
1950–1	139912	83154	59.43307	0	0	0	0
1951–2	143399	84620	59.01017	0.01763	3487	1491.845	0.427831
1952–3	147544	87269	59.14778	0.031305	4145	2731.926	0.65909
1953–4	156590	93841	59.92784	0.075307	9046	7066.92	0.78122
1954–5	163126	96632	59.23764	0.029742	6536	2874.009	0.43972
1955–6	167535	95559	57.03823	-0.0111	4409	-1061.09	-0.24066
1956–7	177006	101061	57.09467	0.057577	9471	5818.789	0.61438
1957–8	174756	98619	56.4324	-0.02416	-2250	-2382.99	1.059108
1958–9	187925	106374	56.6045	0.078636	13169	8364.822	0.63519
1959–60	191717	105486	55.02172	-0.00835	3792	-880.587	-0.23222
1960–1	205196	112848	54.99522	0.069791	13479	7875.803	0.584302
1961–2	211287	113147	53.55133	0.00265	6091	299.7922	0.049219
1962–3	215601	111423	51.68019	-0.01524	4314	-1697.73	-0.39354
1963–4	226577	114056	50.33874	0.023631	10976	2695.22	0.245556
1964–5	243472	124236	51.02681	0.089254	16895	11088.61	0.656325
1965–6	234394	111530	47.58228	-0.10227	-9078	-11406.5	1.256501
1966–7	236846	110131	46.49899	-0.01254	2452	-1381.45	-0.5634
1967–8	255843	125907	49.2126	0.143248	18997	18035.87	0.949406
1968–9	262687	125864	47.91406	-0.00034	6844	-42.9853	-0.00628
1969–70	279791	133874	47.84786	0.06364	17104	8519.757	0.498115
1970–1	293933	142581	48.50709	0.065039	14142	9273.293	0.655727
Mean	205482.7	108486.3	53.71924	0.027307	7334.333	3203.967	0.384552
1971–2	266688	140142	52.54905	-0.01711	-27245	-2397.28	0.08799
1972–3	295752	133699	45.20646	-0.04597	29064	-6146.78	-0.21149
1973–4	329950	142988	43.33626	0.069477	34198	9934.371	0.290496
1974–5	314009	141185	44.96209	-0.01261	-15941	-1780.27	0.111678

(Continued)

Table 3.15 (Continued)

Years	Total GDP (Rs crores)	GDP-agriculture (Rs crores)	Share of agriculture sector to GDP (%)	Growth rate Agriculture GDP (unit)	d GDP (Rs crores)	Pa.ra (Rs crores)	Pa.ra/d GDP (Ratio)
1975-6	343173	159337	46.43052	0.128569	29164	20485.78	0.702434
1976-7	347530	150766	43.38215	-0.05379	4357	-8109.95	-1.86136
1977-8	343464	165410	48.15934	0.097131	-4066	16066.38	-1.35678
1978-9	394335	169248	42.91985	0.023203	50871	3927.053	0.077196
1979-80	374640	148663	39.68156	-0.12163	-19695	-18081.3	0.918067
1980-1	401970	167770	41.73695	0.128526	27330	21562.74	0.788977
1981-2	425168	177341	41.71081	0.057048	23198	10117.01	0.436116
1982-3	436577	177300	40.61139	-0.00023	11409	-40.9905	-0.00359
1983-4	469293	193508	41.23394	0.091416	32716	17689.67	0.540704
1984-5	489206	196353	40.13708	0.014702	19913	2886.828	0.144972
1985-6	511058	198740	38.88795	0.012157	21852	2416.018	0.110563
1986-7	532021	196735	36.9788	-0.01009	20963	-1984.77	-0.09468
1987-8	551409	227095	41.18449	0.154319	19388	35045.13	1.807568
1988-89	607207	231389	38.1071	0.018908	55798	4375.193	0.078411
1989-90	648108	242012	37.34131	0.04591	40901	11110.7	0.271649
1990-1	683670	239253	34.99539	-0.0114	35562	-2727.55	-0.0767
Mean	438261.4	179946.7	41.97762	0.028427	19486.85	5717.398	0.138111
1992-3	691143	252205	36.491	0.054135	7473	13653.16	1.826998
1993-4	726375	262059	36.07765	0.039071	35232	10239.01	0.290617
1994-5	769265	276049	35.88477	0.053385	42890	14736.86	0.343597
1995-6	824816	275153	33.35932	-0.00325	55551	-893.092	-0.01608
1996-7	886961	299461	33.76259	0.088344	62145	26455.46	0.425705
1997-8	959359	295051	30.75501	-0.01473	72398	-4345.06	-0.06002
1998-9	1005946	312485	31.06379	0.059088	46587	18464.14	0.396337
1999-2000	1137185	314252	27.6342	0.005655	131239	1776.992	0.01354
2000-01	1186438	314589	26.51542	0.001072	49253	337.3614	0.00685
2001-2	1257636	333271	26.4998	0.059385	71198	19791.44	0.277977
2002-3	1310471	314578	24.00496	-0.05609	52835	-17644.5	-0.33396

2003-4	1422479	343806	24.1695	0.092912	112008	31943.63	0.285191
Mean	**1014840**	**299413.3**	**30.51817**	**0.031582**	**61567.42**	**9542.948**	**0.288064**
2004-5	2629198	565426	21.50565	0.064432	1206719	36431.53	0.030191
2005-6	2877284	594487	20.66139	0.051397	248086	30554.64	0.123161
2006-7	3149149	619190	19.66214	0.041553	271865	25729.5	0.094641
2007-8	3451829	655080	18.97777	0.057963	302680	37970.29	0.125447
2008-9	3664388	655689	17.89355	0.00093	212559	609.5662	0.002868
2009-10	3966408	660987	16.66462	0.00808	302020	5340.808	0.017684
2010-11	4293586	717814	16.71829	0.085973	327178	61712.58	0.18621
2011-12	4573328	753832	16.48323	0.050177	279742	37825.29	0.135215
2012-13	4728776	764510	16.16719	0.014165	155448	10829.25	0.069665
2013-14*	4920183	800548	16.2707	0.047139	191407	37736.78	0.197155
Mean	**3825413**	**678756.3**	**18.10045**	**0.042181**	**349770.4**	**28474.02**	**0.098465**

N.B.: * Provisional

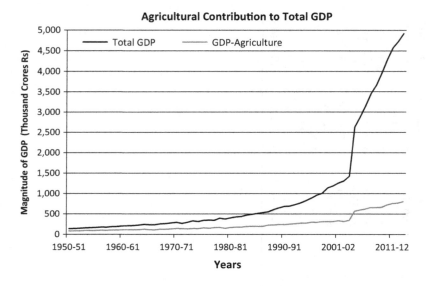

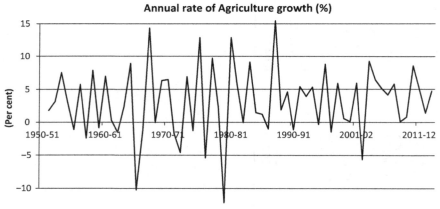

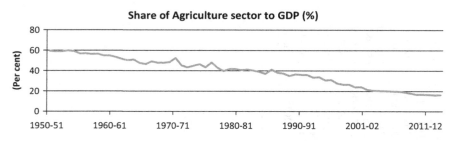

Figure 3.8 Contribution of the agriculture sector, share to the total GDP and the annual rate of agriculture growth over time

3.09 Summary

Chapter 3 examined the emerging trends and regional patterns in area, production and yield of food grains and other crops. State-wise variability in agriculture growth ratios was mapped for the Post-Liberalisation phase of economic planning. Changes in crop area and crop yield were also measured to capture growth dynamics of agriculture change. Net Sown Area and Gross Cropped Area are two major components of land use dynamics which have shaped crop production in India. Overall, the area under food grains decreased from 66 to 63 per cent (i.e., 3.17 per cent) during the Post-Liberalisation period (2001–12 to 2008–9). Annual growth of crop production declined marginally from 2.74 per cent in the Green Revolution to 2.53 per cent in the Post-Libralisation phase. This could be linked to the improper use of chemical fertilisers and the excessive use of land beyond the threshold set out by the biophysical conditions of land. There was evidence of crop diversification in some areas whilst the prevalence of monoculture in others through crop specialisation. Areas under horticulture crops and fruit cultivation have increased.

Changing crop area and crop yield show agriculture growth dynamics in subsistence-dominated farming in India. The geographic 'expansion' of agriculture has remained slow in most parts of India especially after the Green Revolution. Areas under waste land and fallow land have decreased, which has resulted in a gain in Net Sown Area. Agriculture technology and institutional structure influence crop yield, while agro-ecological and weather conditions tend to affect the scale and type of crop production. In addition, crop-production increase was also associated with higher land use intensity. Intensification of non-farm activities associated with farm production such as dairying, poultry, and piggery have helped increase the farm-household (farm-HH) income. Crop diversification and shift to crops with higher returns such as vegetables and fruits have increased agriculture production.

The impact of Green Revolution technology on farm production began to gradually diminish over time. Increasing IIOR over time from 1.65 to 2.15 after the Green Revolution shows this tendency. The average annual rate of input intensification in its real terms decelerated by 1.92 per cent from 4.42 per cent during the Green Revolution to 3.5 per cent in the Post-Liberalisation phase. This further reiterates the diminishing impact of the Green Revolution on agriculture production. In addition, the average rate of agriculture production also decreased by 1.05 per cent from 2.68 to 1.63 per cent during the same period. The deceleration of input intensification had occurred due to increasing burden of labour force on agriculture practices. However, the traditional technology was gradually replaced with advanced agriculture technology during the Post-Liberalisation phase. Such unprofitable and unfettered agriculture in areas of low land potential arrested the growth process. The analysis of the absolute and proportionate growth of various components of agriculture outputs captured the key trends, changes and spatial dynamics in agriculture growth patterns in India.

4 Agriculture growth and regional change

4.01 Introduction

Chapter 4 examines the nature and characteristics of agriculture growth patterns and regional change in India. During the 11th five-year plan period (2006–7 to 2011–12), the average annual agricultural growth was 4.0 per cent, which reduced to about 2.0 per cent in the first three years of the 12th five-year plan period (2012–13 to 2014–15) (Vijayshankar 2016). This decline in agriculture growth is seen as a policy concern, which requires urgent policy intervention and planning strategy to boost growth. This chapter, thus, examines the agricultural growth trends, identifies the key growth determinants and demarcates areas of growth concentration.

4.02 General trends in agricultural growth

Agriculture growth in India varies across different planning phases. The first detailed regional growth analysis was attempted by Nath (1969) using state-wise data for the Pre-Green Revolution phase, which covered about 13 years of the first three five-year plans from 1952–3 to 1964–5. He estimated the average annual agricultural growth of 3.42 per cent for India during that period. The states of Punjab (presently Punjab and Haryana), Gujarat, Madras (presently Tamil Nadu) and Mysore (now Karnataka) had high growth rates of 5.56, 5.42, 4.91 and 4.06 per cent respectively. Punjab and Gujarat recorded an average annual agricultural growth of more than 5 per cent due to increased farm production per unit of land. This resulted due to two main reasons: application of modern farming techniques and crop substitution. Gujarat had experienced the highest rate of agriculture productivity increase (4.52 per cent) because of the replacement of less productive Jowar and Bajra by more productive crops such as Groundnut and Cotton. Cultivated area under Groundnut increased on an average of 15.4 per cent per annum during this phase. Similarly, Millets were replaced by Cotton and Sugarcane in Punjab. Nath's study concluded that the rapid urbanisation and intensive use of modern agricultural inputs (i.e., irrigation facilities, services of HYV seed supply and use of chemical fertiliser) were the key drivers of this rapid agricultural growth.

Dogra (1981) investigated the regional imbalances in agricultural growth between 1962–5 and 1972–5 using district-level crop data. His study found that the rapid agricultural growth of about 4.5 per cent per annum was largely confined to one-fifth of the country (19 per cent area covered by 48 districts). The average annual growth of agriculture production was 2.15 per cent, which was relatively quite low at world standards and even lower than the growth rate estimated by Nath. However, the conclusions drawn by dogra (1981) were comparable to the findings of Bhalla and Tyagi (1989: Tables 4.4 and 4.5, 115), which noted higher agricultural growth during the Pre-Green Revolution in Haryana, Punjab and the Upper Ganga–Jamuna doab (more than 5.0 per cent annually).

Two key studies, namely Bhalla and Tyagi (1989) and Singh (1994), were conducted using the district-level data to analyse regional agricultural growth patterns during the Green Revolution and Post-Green Revolution phase. Both studies have examined the changing regional structures of agriculture growth over a period of 20 years. Aggregate value-added agricultural outputs – considering area, yield and harvest price of agricultural products of each crop – was calculated using base-year constant prices of products. An analysis of agricultural growth by Planning Commission was based on a comparison between the Pre-Green Revolution and Green-Revolution phase (1962–5 to 1980–3), while the analysis undertaken by Singh (1994) compared the data for the Green Revolution and Post-Green Revolution periods (1969–72 to 1988–9). The salient characteristics of regional disparities in output growth are discussed as follows.

4.03 Average annual agricultural output growth

Agriculture production, growth and productivity had formed a spatially clustered pattern, which was further intensified before and after the Green Revolution. For example, high production growth of all crops (more than 5 per cent annually) was associated with a large increase in land productivity (i.e., production per unit of land), which increased to Rs 793/ha during the early 1960s to Rs 1789/ha during the early 1980s. This positive relationship between growth and land productivity indicates areal concentration of agriculture growth in high-performing regions in India. Bhalla and Tyagi (1989: 110–133) also noted this positive relationship between the high output growth (6.43 per cent) and productivity increase (4.62 per cent annually) during the same period.

Most parts of the Punjab region (Punjab and Haryana and the Jammu Plains of Jammu and Kashmir) and a few districts of the Ganga-Jamuna doab had experienced high agriculture growth coupled with high productivity during the 1960s. Wheat and Rice were the dominating crops of this region. Later, a few districts in Gujarat surrounding the Bombay-Ahmadabad industrial region and Vidarba–the interior Maharastra were added to the category of high agricultural growth during the Green Revolution decade of the 1970s.

During the Post-Green Revolution phase of the 1980s, most areas in Punjab, Haryana and Western Uttar Pradesh, which had very high agriculture growth during the Green Revolution, sustained the high growth rate, which latter gradually diffused to the adjacent *Terai* and middle Ganga plains of Uttar Pradesh (Figure 4.1). Coastal areas of Orissa and Andhra Pradesh and the Malabar coastal

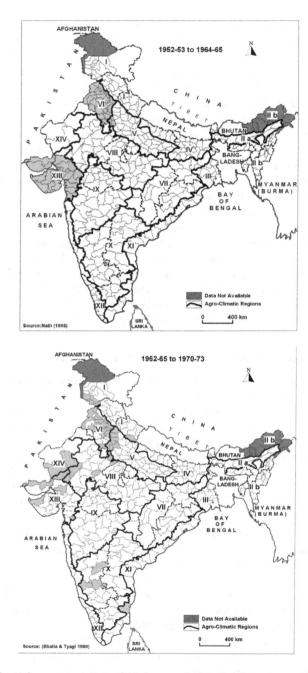

Figure 4.1 Spatial concentration of high growth (above 5 percent annual average agricultural output growth) during planned economic development

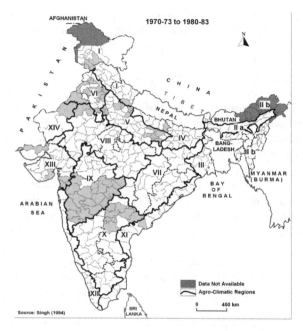

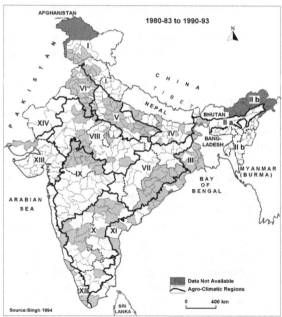

Figure 4.1 (Continued)

plain were also included in the high growth category during the same period. The interior Karnataka and Malwa plateau of Madhya Pradesh had also experienced high growth. Good fertile soil and high rainfall contributed to high growth in the coastal areas while the use of chemical fertilisers and irrigation contributed to growth in the semi-arid regions of the Great Plains of India. The areas having more than 5.0 per cent annual growth across different periods have expanded mostly in the Great Plains and coastal plains of India (Figure 4.1).

The national average annual growth of output increased marginally from 2.15 (during the 1960s) to 2.67 per cent (during the 1970s) and then to 3.03 per cent (during the 1980s). However, this increase varies significantly between districts. There is substantial inter-district variation with the degree of 125 per cent. Pithoragrah district in Uttar Pradesh had the highest annual growth rate of 116 per cent whilst Sehore district in Madhya Pradesh had the lowest -9.15 per cent in the 1970s. This was marginally reduced to 87 per cent in the 1980s, ranging from 75.87 (North Arcot district of Tamil Nadu) to -11.735 (Palghat district of Kerala) (Singh 1994: 46–54).

During the period of economic liberalisation, a number of economic reforms and policy changes in the agriculture sector were implemented, which have had notable impact on the regional agriculture structure in India. These include:

1   The preliminary introduction of market-oriented economy intended to promote commercial farming and cultivation of cash crops remained confined to few more progressive areas;
2   The rapid rise in prices of agricultural products in response to burgeoning market demand led to escalating inter-district variation in agricultural growth; and
3   Change in crop patterns as the result of changing relative prices of crops had some impact on agricultural growth.

Aggregate data of 46 crops for the base year starting with the Post-Liberalisation phase (2000–1) and the year (2006–7) using multiplier of area, yield and harvesting price of crops (as defined by Equation 3.4 in Chapter 3) indicate discernible regional change. The average annual output growth of each district was calculated by using a simple growth formula (Equation 3.5 in Chapter 3).

The real average annual growth of agricultural production was 1.95 per cent of the total output of 443,238 million rupees in 2000–1 at a constant price to 4950,878 million rupees in 2006–7. The Ministry of Agriculture, India reported 2.5 per cent growth during the decade 2000–1 to 2010–11. However, the national average of prices considered growth (at current price) to be 10.33 per cent, higher than the national average of real growth which is about 4.33 per cent. Such deviation was due to the impact of commodity price increase during the Post-Liberalisation phase. Surprisingly, there had been a marginal decrease of about 1.18 million ha in Gross Cultivated Area during the six years of the Post-Liberalisation phase. This means that there was no increase in cultivated area during this phase. The Net Sown Area however had slightly decreased from

141 million ha in 2000–1 to 140 million ha in 2012–13. This indicates that there were significant changes in cropping intensity, crop combination and yield to achieve this real product growth.

Such changes in crop cultivation have been witnessed even in tribal-dominated areas which practiced subsistence farming in the high-altitude zone (3,000–7,000 m) of Lahaul-Spiti in Himachal Himalayas. The food grains including Potato have reduced their share of total cropping area, while Orchard cultivation such as Apple expanded phenomenally accounting for one-third share of the cultivated area in the district (Thakur and Sharma 2010). In another area of subsistence economy in the central part of Deccan Plateau in the state of Madhya Pradesh, rapid agricultural growth can be attributed to increase in areal extent of commercial crops such as Oilseeds and Pulses. Area under Oilseeds have increased five times and Pulses have grown two-times. This has accelerated the agriculture growth in the state (Shri 2012).

4.04 Area and yield of various crops

Agriculture growth impulses are basically dependent on two key attributes: change in crop area and crop yield. The total cropped area increased from 155 million ha to 188 million ha in India during the Post-Liberalisation phase (2000–1 to 2012–13). However, there has been a gradual shift in crop area from cereals to vegetables and commercial crops as the areal share under cereals decreased from 61.43 to 53.83 per cent, while the area under vegetables and commercial crops increased from 21.71 to 29.26 per cent during the same period. On the other hand, there was a significant increase in yield in almost all crops, except Safflower (-10.98 per cent), Sunflower (-12.23 per cent), Sugarcane (-15.59 per cent) Niger seeds (-10.21 per cent), Garlic (-22.24 per cent) and Sanhamp (-15.51 per cent) (Table 4.1).

In spite of a decrease in the share of area-coverage especially under Rice, Wheat and Millets, these cereals continued to increase their yield. For example, Rice yield increased from 1,901 kg/ha (2000–1) to 2,462 kg/ha (2012–13), whilst Jowar yield increased from 764 kg/ha (2000–1) to 850 kg/ha (2006–7). Bajara yield increased from 688 kg/ha to 1,198 kg/ha and grew by 74 per cent. The yield of Cotton also markedly increased by 155 per cent during the same period. Yield of pulses and vegetable crops had high increase (Table -4.1). Overall, the crop production increased over this period, which in turn helped to increase agriculture growth. However, Tamil Nadu has been an area of low agricultural growth since 2000–1 and is identified as a region which had not met the growth target prior to the Liberalisation phase (Agrawal and Gisselquist 1999).

4.05 Regional agriculture growth patterns

In this section, districts are classified into eight categories (seven in the map clubbing negative growth into one) on the basis of annual agriculture growth to

Table 4.1 Changes in area and yield of various crops in India

Crops	Area (in million ha)				Change in areal share	Yield (kg/ha)		Change in yield	
	Total 2000-1	%	Total 2012-13	%	%	2000-1	2012-13	Total change (kg/ha)	%
Food Grains									
Rice	42.05	26.97	42.62	22.67	-4.3	1901	2462	561	29.51
Wheat	25.11	16.11	30	15.96	-0.15	2708	3118	410	15.14
Jowar	10.05	6.45	6.21	3.3	-3.14	764	850	86	11.26
Bajra	10.05	6.45	7.3	3.88	-2.56	688	1198	510	74.13
Maize	6.37	4.09	8.67	4.61	0.52	1822	2566	744	40.83
Ragi*.	1.41	0.91	3.87	2.06	1.15	1250	1348	98	7.84
Barley*	0.73	0.47	2.56	1.36	0.9	2828	3149	321	11.35
Pulses									
Gram	5.21	3.34	8.52	4.53	1.19	744	1036	292	39.25
Arhar	3.77	2.42	3.89	2.07	-0.35	618	776	158	25.57
Urad*	2.41	1.55	2.58	1.37	-0.18	1020	1320	300	29.41
Moong*	2.82	1.81	3.03	1.61	-0.19	1085	1254	169	15.58
Masoor	0.94	0.6	1.42	0.76	0.15	619	797	178	28.76
Horse Gram*	0.68	0.43	0.59	0.31	-0.12	615	785	170	27.64
Other Kharif Pulses*	1.32	0.84	2.36	1.26	0.41	1020	1630	610	59.8
Other Rabi Pulses*	0.99	0.64	1.14	0.61	-0.03	1203	1503	300	24.94
Groundnut	6.55	4.2	6.75	3.59	-0.61	977	995	18	1.84
Sesamum*	1.6	1.02	1.48	0.79	-0.24	711	824	113	15.89
Vegetables									
Potato*	1.02	0.65	1.2	0.64	-0.01	2664	2770	106	3.98
Tapioca*	0.25	0.16	1.26	0.67	0.51	980	1138	157	16.11
Onion*	0.28	0.18	1.35	0.72	0.54	2177	2734	556	25.57

Sweet Potato*	0.06	0.04	0.58	0.31	0.27	909	1144	234	25.82
Peas and Beans*	0.4	0.26	1.46	0.78	0.52	154	166	13	8.23
Commercial									
Rapeseed and Mustard	3.97	2.55	6.36	3.38	0.84	936	1262	326	34.83
Linseed*	0.48	0.31	1.39	0.74	0.43	93	102	9	9.62
Castor Seed*	1.09	0.7	2.68	1.43	0.73	102	105	3	2.4
Safflower*	0.45	0.29	1.64	0.87	0.58	37	33	-4	-10.98
Coconut*	1.4	0.9	1.81	0.96	0.06	572	852	280	48.98
Sunflower*	1	0.64	2.12	1.13	0.48	605	531	-74	-12.23
Cotton	8.06	5.17	11.98	6.37	1.2	190	486	296	155.79
Mesta	0.15	0.1	0.87	0.46	0.37	421	499	79	18.7
Chilli*	0.72	0.46	0.98	0.52	0.06	207	256	49	23.51
Turmeric*	0.17	0.11	0.69	0.37	0.26	431	521	90	20.81
Aracanut*	0.28	0.18	0.38	0.2	0.03	69	77	9	12.57
Coriander*	0.35	0.22	0.64	0.34	0.12	60	72	11	18.84
Sugarcane (Gurh)	4.21	2.7	5.78	3.07	0.38	16766	14153	-2613	-15.59
Banana*	0.29	0.19	0.37	0.2	0.01	2163	2678	514	23.76
Tobacco*	0.22	0.14	0.34	0.18	0.04	121	158	38	31.3
Niger Seed*	0.46	0.3	0.41	0.22	-0.08	31	27	-3	-10.21
Jute	0.81	0.52	0.87	0.46	-0.06	1868	2281	413	22.11
Dry Ginger*	0.05	0.03	0.08	0.04	0.01	485	576	91	18.83
Garlic*	0.05	0.03	0.09	0.05	0.01	392	305	-87	-22.24
Soya Bean	6.3	4.04	8.02	4.27	0.23	116	130	14	12.17
Sanhamp*	0.04	0.02	0.14	0.07	0.05	159	135	-25	-15.51
Moth*	1.01	0.65	1.2	0.64	0	11	19	8	71.46
Black Pepper*	0.21	0.14	0.25	0.13	0	20	27	7	32.39
Cardamom*	0.06	0.04	0.07	0.04	0	13	20	7	49.23
All Crops	155.91	100	187.99	100	0	-	-	-	-

N.B.: *The yield of crops under star mostly the vegetables and commercial crops are estimated from the statistics of Area, Production and Yield at district level for 2000–1 and 2006–7 enable the identification of spatial growth patterns in India. Key observations are discussed as follows:

1   *Very high agricultural growth region* (above 8 per cent), which consists of 103 districts and represents a large share of area coverage under commercial crops (above 27 per cent). This region also contributes to more than 75 per cent share of commercial crops to total agricultural commercial output (Table 4.2). These districts represent: most parts of Rajasthan including Aravalli hills and Malwa plateau of Madhya Pradesh and other arid areas including Saurashtra region of Gujarat; the central part of Chattisgarh under humid climate; hilly and mountainous areas of Uttarkhand, Himachal and Jammu, Shiwalik hills of high altitudes; and the hill areas of the North Eastern region (Figure 4.2).

Increased share of the output of commercial crops was the main cause of rapid growth in agriculture production during the Post-Liberalisation phase. However, growth in Rajasthan and Malwa plateau during the Post-Liberalisation phase was largely driven by changes in food- grains-dominated production, especially in cereals and pulses. For example, Millets, Jowar, and Bajra were often replaced by Wheat and Gram in Rajasthan and Malwa plateau. But in the hills and mountain districts of Uttarkhand and Himachal, there was a shift from food grains to orchard farming. The changing pattern of high growth areas in the hills of North Eastern India also started to take shape in the Khasi-Jaintia hills of Meghalaya (change in jhum to broom cultivation), the Lushai hills of Mizoram (Bamboo plantation and commercial beans) and the Patkai hills of Nagaland (changes in Bun cultivation in fruit and beekeeping and piggery culture).

2   The Green Revolution technology-dominated region consists of Punjab and Western parts of Uttar Pradesh plains including the Lower Ganga Valley. Some parts of this region have low to moderate annual agricultural growth (ranging from 2 to 6 per cent), despite attempts to increase crop intensity (165 per cent recorded in 2006–7). Sugarcane cultivation in Punjab and Uttar Pradesh plains gained momentum due to rapid demand and increased prices for Sugarcane products such as *gurh* and sugar. This provided the impetus to increase farm productivity during the Post-Liberalisation phase, nevertheless the growth continued to remain stagnant.

3   Regional negative growth in agricultural output was recorded in the central part of Deccan Plateau, including interior Tamil Nadu and Karnataka. Cotton is grown as a commercial crop in the Deccan trap. Other crops include Mango, Grapes, Oranges and Citrus fruits.

The major share of foreign direct investment (FDI) was largely concentrated in the city-market region. The food processing industries were also established in urban centres such as Mumbai, Chennai, Hyderabad and Bengaluru to gain closer proximity to the market and improve access to logistics infrastructure. Agriculture growth stabilised in some areas during the Post-Liberalisation phase,

Table 4.2 Share of area and output of food grains and commercial crops (2006–07) by agricultural growth (2000–1 to 2006–7) categories

Annual growth rate		No. of districts	Food grains crops				Commercial crops			
	%		Total area (in 000 ha)	%	Total output Rs (in millions)	%	Total area (in 000 ha)	%	Total output Rs (in millions)	%
Very High	>10	50	14951	72.3	7,974	30.79	5727	27.7	17,924	69.21
	10–8	53	16783	74.83	12,630	41.58	5645	25.17	17,743	58.42
High	8–6	42	10266	74.52	14,234	42.23	3511	25.48	19,473	57.77
	6–4	67	22483	77.07	36,148	46.48	6691	22.93	41,623	53.52
Low	4–2	64	21013	77.78	33,276	24.58	6004	22.22	1,02,103	75.42
	2–0	53	17856	79.99	33,434	35.02	4466	20.01	62,041	64.98
Negative	2	20	5930	79.09	16,368	50.42	1567	20.91	16,097	49.58
	–(2 >)	37	15038	79.78	18,302	53.49	3812	20.22	15,913	46.51

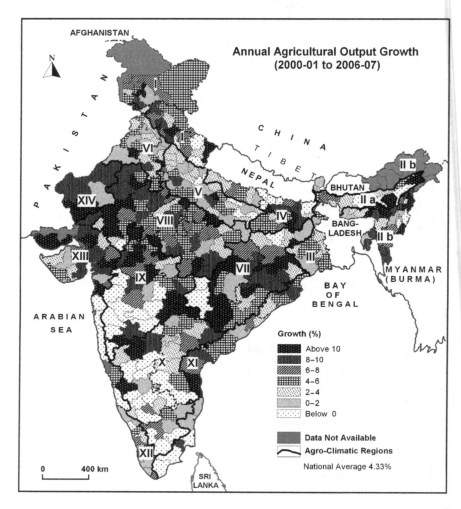

Figure 4.2 Annual agricultural growth at a constant price (2000–1 to 2006–7)
(National Average = 4.33%)

which were fuelled by a multitude of factors. It could be the non-inclusion of
these crops in the calculation of agricultural growth, or the rapid urbanisation,
expansion in urban infrastructure and industries, commercialisation and corporatisation of farming, rising demand of agricultural and non-agricultural commodities in large cities, and flow of rural capital and labour to nearby towns could have
contributed to the sluggish growth of agriculture output.

In the initial stage of agriculture growth in the hinterland of metropolitan centres especially in South India, the technological innovations in farming associated

with the Green Revolution were spatially diffused by these centres. The spill-over effects of large metropolitan urban economies had them act as a key trade/demand hub for circulating and then distributing surplus agricultural commodities to regional markets. These cities act as commodity markets – mass consumption centres which control and regulate the flow of agricultural commodities. This is equally valid for both food grains and commercial crops. Cotton, for example, was the key cash crop and raw material for textile industries, which were largely co-located in the hinterland of Bombay-Pune urban agglomeration (Singh 1994: 50–52).

Farm technologies were more widely adopted along the key transport corridors such as Bombay-Pune transport corridor in Maharashtra. Thus, the form of agriculture growth pattern was not merely concentric around the city-regional of mega-cities but also linear along the key transport corridors and trade routes.

Similarly, some areas of the Punjab region that previously had reported very high growth prior to liberalisation have also undergone very low growth. Cotton and Wheat were the dominating crops, which drove the initial growth propulsion in the region. After the implementation of new economic policies, rapid urbanisation has proven to be a strong impetus for spatio-functional integration of non-agricultural activities with rural–urban markets. Allied farm activities such as dairy, poultry and agro-businesses were preferred options for farmers to help generate higher income in comparison to cultivating traditional crops. Consequently, food grain cultivation became a subsidiary source of household income in the Punjab–Haryana region.

Cultivation of commercial crops transformed the agriculture landscape through 'contract farming'. This propensity for commercial farming has been further accentuated by government schemes. For example, Punjab Food Grains Corporation started a program in 2002 which provided tax concession and reduction of farmers' levies on market fees as well as on rural development charges from 2.0 to only 0.25 per cent. These incentives accelerated farm commercialisation, which in turn boosted transfer and wider adoption of farm technology to enhance land productivity. In Punjab, Tomato yield increased three-fold and Chilli and Potato yields also improved dramatically.

Further, profile of Pepsi, a product of Punjab Agro-Industries Corporation Ltd with the partnership of Punjab Agricultural University, is well recognised in the global market. Its raw material is supplied through contractors who are direct farmers. They diffuse new farm technology adoption to encourage other non-participating farmers to be part of integrated global supply chains. However, the agricultural growth in Punjab during the Post-Liberalisation period remained sluggish (Figure 4.2). Likewise, it is difficult to speculate the reasons for negative growth in Tamil Nadu even in the Pre-Liberalisation phase (1990s), in spite of the substantial deficit of food grains for domestic consumption. Agarawal and Gisselquist (1999: 1–4) have alluded to agro-climatic factors such as temperature and precipitation as contributors to negative growth in Tamil Nadu.

The annual agricultural growth in India varies from a maximum of 14.69 per cent in the Adilabad district of Andhra Pradesh to -14.64 per cent in the Ratnagiri district of Maharastra. The range between the two is 29.43 per cent. Both districts represent different types of environmental conditions (CV = 130.97 per cent). Since the mid-1970s, particularly during the Green Revolution, regional inequalities in agricultural growth started to escalate. This tendency continued unabated till the Post-Liberalisation phase. Growth of secondary and tertiary sectors increased more rapidly than the agricultural sector, which resulted in greater regional industrial diversity in rural India.

A regional contrast in rural landscape driven by the Green Revolution-oriented growth strategy started to emerge in the North Western part of India during the Post-Liberalisation phase. Areas of and adjacent to highly fertile *bhawar* and *tarai* tracts of Shiwaliks, called the Punjab plains, witnessed high to very high agriculture growth in the Pre-Liberalisation phase, which in subsequent phases either stabilised or declined during the Post-Liberalisation. A reduction in the share of area coverage and continual decline in the proportion of commercial crops to total output may be linked to low growth, despite the phenomenal growth of contract farming as a mode of production (Figure 4.3 A and B).

Regional disparity in agriculture growth in this region reduced when adjoining hill areas in the Agro-climatic Zone I such as the Himalayan zone of Kumaon, Garhwal, Himachal and Jammu hills on the Northern side of Punjab plains and the Aravalli hills (a part of Agro-climatic zone VIII) and the arid region of Rajasthan plains (Zone XIV), located in the Southern surroundings of Punjab plains, registered high agriculture growth during the Post-Liberalisation phase (Figure 4.3 C).

Flat topography and high soil fertility in the Great Plain of India led to changes in crop diversity and intensive use of land. High population pressure and rapid urbanisation fuelled further changes in land use and farming practices in rural areas. Key changes that have shaped agriculture in India are discussed below.

1   Decreasing share of area under commercial crops restricted agriculture growth in the Great Plain during the last decade. This region is still dominated by the cultivation of food grains. However, contract farming to grow commercial crops is increasingly becoming popular among medium-to-large-sized farmers. Areal share of food grains has shown a decline with the rise of other high-value crops in this region, which diminishes agriculture growth (Figure 4.4 A).

2   Increasing the share of output of commercial crops seemed to exert positive effects on agricultural growth during the Post-Liberalisation phase. Most districts of the Great Plains have increased the share of output of commercial crops to total agriculture output. The widespread cultivation of commercial crops, both in terms of area and production, has been the key driver of rapid agriculture growth in India. Few districts in central parts of Bihar plains however showed a decline in the share of commercial crop output, which in turn resulted in very low to negative growth in agricultural output. High demand for food grains to fulfil the basic household needs in a densely populated area might be linked to practicing subsistence farming (Figure 4.4B).

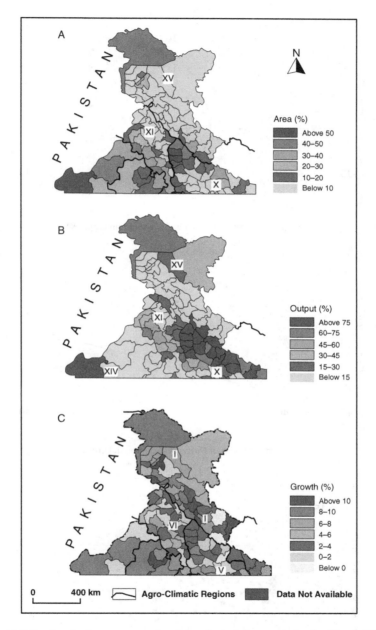

Figure 4.3 Regional contrast emerging in agricultural growth in the North Western part of India: (A) Area coverage under commercial crops, (B) Output pattern of commercial crops (2006–7) and (C) Annual average agriculture growth (2000–1 to 2012–13)

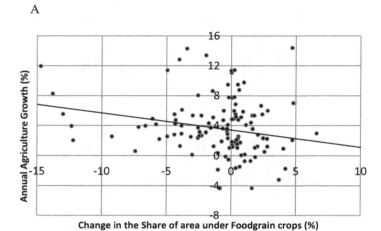

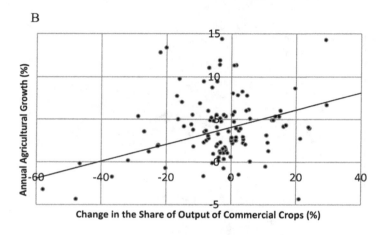

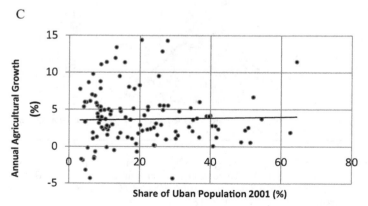

Figure 4.4 Agricultural growth and its determinants: (A) Growth versus change in the area under food grain crops, (B) Growth versus changes in the share of commercial output and (C) Growth versus urbanisation in the most gentle sloping Great Plains of India (N = 121 districts)

3   The share of urban population to total population has little impact on agricultural growth in the Great Plains (Figure 4.4 C). This means growth is not linked with the market forces as the regional settlement system is yet to be matured. However, there might be localized impact in the vicinity of larger city regions, which tend to create demand-driven production in their respective hinterlands. It could also be linked to price variability and demand volatility.

4.06 Commodity price and agricultural growth

The new economic policies and regulatory reforms have increased minimum prices for food grains, subsidised food, fuel and electricity, helped reduced phone bills in rural areas and reduced interest rates for farmers. The key purpose of these incentives was to encourage farmers to increase farm productivity and overall production. Increased market demand and prices of agricultural commodities increased profitability for some farmers but may have not simultaneously increased the scale of production at the same rate. Increasing market price of agricultural products in competitive and globalised commodity markets when inflation was driven by supply shortfalls of agricultural products remained a planning challenge for productivity enhancement and effective economic policy-making in India (Acharya 2012).

Price policy mechanism for agriculture commodities is driven by two key considerations: *first* is the market assessment of agricultural products as tradable commodities in terms of demand and consumption of food in urban areas (i.e., related to wholesale pricing policy); *second* is the relative pricing of products to regulate farm practices and crop cultivation patterns.

Undoubtedly, there has been an increase in the wholesale price index of food grains and other food commodities in the deregulated market during the Post-Liberalisation phase. The price index of pulses, for instance, showed remarkable growth in the last 12 years of the Post-Liberalisation phase from 1997–8 to 2009–10. Pulses such as Masoor, Urd and Moong had a very high rise in the wholesale price index. Masoor has grown by 290 index number (from 176 to 467), Urd by 284 (from 175.3 to 460.0) and Moong by 254 (from 165.7 to 420.0) considering the base year 1993–4 = 100 (Table 4.3). However, the increase in the wholesale price of cereals did not equally respond to that of other crops. This increase in wholesale price index brought a positive change in agricultural growth and generated additional income for farmers.

However, the relative pricing of agricultural products provided the incentives to farmers to alter cropping patterns as farmers intend to maximise profit from farm by sowing more profitable commercial crops. As shown in Table 4.4, the relative price of Jowar, Bajra and Ragi were much lower in 2006–7 in comparison to commercial crops. They tend to be two to three times higher than food grains. This incentivised farmers to shift to cultivating commercial crops and to maintain growth in areas of marginal growth rate in the country.

Table 4.3 Trends in wholesale price index of food grains (base year: 1993–4 = 100)

Commodity	Weight	1997–8	1998–9	1999–2000	2000–1	2001–2	2002–3	2003–4	2004–5	2005–6	2006–7	2007–8	2008–9	2009–10 (P)
1	2	3	4	5	6	7	8	9	10	11	12	13	14	15
(I) All Commodities	100	132.8	140.7	145.3	155.7	161.3	166.8	175.9	187.3	195.6	206.2	215.7	233.9	242.7
(a) Primary Articles	22.03	139.4	156.2	158	162.5	168.4	174	181.5	188.1	193.6	208.7	224.4	247.3	273.6
(b) Fuel, Power and Lubricants	14.23	143.8	148.5	162	208.1	226.7	239.2	254.5	280.2	306.8	323.9	327	351.4	343.1
(c) Manufactured Products	63.75	128	133.6	137.2	141.7	144.3	148.1	156.5	166.3	171.4	179	187.8	203.1	209.6
(II) Food Grains	5.01	139.3	152	176.4	173.8	172.4	174.3	176.3	177.5	187	206	215.5	234.1	270.5
(a) Cereals	4.41	138.4	150.9	177.8	173	170.1	173.5	176.3	177.9	185.8	199.4	211.7	230.5	261.7
1 Rice	2.45	134.3	146.2	171.3	167.5	167	166	168.8	168.2	174.5	179.6	191.7	213	243.7
2 Wheat	1.38	138.1	151.8	174.7	176.6	175.3	175.7	181.4	184.1	191.5	216.5	225.7	239.6	264.7
3 Jowar	0.22	172.3	191.1	240.6	199.7	182.4	218.7	218.8	233.4	244.5	272	309.4	331.7	379.6
4 Bajra	0.11	143.4	156.6	201.2	184	151.3	190.3	178.6	183	210.8	227.6	235.7	251.7	327.1
5 Maize	0.19	148.5	154.4	193.6	178.9	171.5	189.5	181.2	187.9	205	224.9	235.7	256	291.8
6 Barley	0.03	166.3	151.7	199.2	174.3	160.2	193.8	179.5	188.6	205.3	220.8	228.8	243.6	240.5
7 Ragi	0.03	138.4	152.4	178.7	182.1	158	174.3	197	184.5	186.8	205.6	227	247.7	325.3
(b) Pulses	0.6	145.9	160.1	166.1	179.6	189.2	180.6	176.6	174.4	194.9	254.2	243.1	259.8	334.3
8 Gram	0.22	124.6	110.9	115.4	139.2	170.3	149.7	142.5	137.1	157	208.7	189.9	209.3	206
9 Arhar	0.13	136.2	186.2	176.3	150.3	142.6	157.5	172.8	179.3	170.8	182	207.4	228.5	250.2
10 Moong	0.11	164.7	181.2	180.6	186.9	205.6	208	195.9	187.4	219.2	303	267.3	286.7	420.2
11 Masoor	0.04	176.6	202.6	216	206.8	203.9	214.1	233.4	234.7	242.8	254	319	394.9	467.2
12 Urad	0.1	175.3	197.3	234	295.7	273.9	239.8	217.4	216.3	270.4	403.8	336.8	338.5	459.5
(III) Sugar, Khandsari and Gur	3.93	134.4	153.5	156	153.2	146.1	134.6	139.3	163.3	178.8	179.8	155.2	168.7	242.4
13 Sugar	3.62	133.8	135.4	137.4	142.6	135.4	123.5	124.4	148.1	164	164.9	142.7	160.4	233.2

14 Khandsari	0.17	133.5	144.7	137.3	137.3	145.3	133.2	130.3	164.1	197.8	203.5	169	199.2	274.6
15 Gur	0.06	126.1	130.3	129.9	129.1	137.8	128.2	122	172.9	192.5	185.3	170.3	205.1	282.2
Food Articles	15.4	141.4	159.4	165.5	170.5	176.1	179.2	181.5	186.3	195.3	210.5	222	239.8	274.9
Non–Food Articles	6.14	137.5	151.8	143	146.5	152.9	165.4	186.3	187.6	179.1	188.2	211.9	235.8	244.6

N.B.: (P) Provisional

Source: Office of the Economic Adviser, Ministry of Commerce & Industry, New Delhi

Table 4.4 Relative prices of different crop products in India

Crops	Price 2000–1		Price 2006–7		Change in
	Rs/qu	Relative price	Rs/qu	Relative price	Relative price
Food Grains					
Rice	612	100	825	100	0
Wheat	621	101.396	814	98.609	−2.79
Jowar	376	61.436	368	44.569	−16.87
Bajra	368	60.125	492	59.566	−0.56
Maize	446	72.911	614	74.347	1.44
Ragi	251	40.998	308	37.349	−3.65
Barley	302	49.29	295	35.762	−13.53
Pulses					
Gram	1489	243.245	1544	187.102	−56.14
Arhar	1441	235.296	1408	170.567	−64.73
Urad	2387	389.735	1074	130.126	−259.61
Moong	2042	333.507	1100	133.315	−200.19
Masoor	1314	214.54	3742	453.44	238.9
Horse Gram	1539	251.315	1517	183.836	−67.48
Other Kharif Pulse	1453	237.365	2455	297.47	60.11
Other Rabi Pulse	1263	206.265	2300	278.714	72.45
Groundnut	1238	202.247	1493	180.876	−21.37
Sesamum	1744	284.86	1259	152.555	−132.3
Vegetables					
Potato	308	50.353	465	56.354	6
Tapioca	46	7.53	529	64.066	56.54
Onion	200	32.661	533	64.61	31.95
Sweet Potato	380	62.116	577	69.921	7.81
Peas and Beans	1409	230.136	1670	202.37	−27.77
Commercial					
Rapeseed and Mustard	1062	173.479	1544	187.095	13.62
Linseed	1082	176.748	886	107.325	−69.42
Castor Seed	759	123.883	582	70.559	−53.32
Safflower	4965	810.848	5983	725.05	−85.8
Coconut					
Sunflower	562	91.818	630	76.323	−15.49
Cotton (Lint)	1530	249.864	915	110.836	−139.03
Mesta	261	42.643	261	31.639	−11
Chilli	2302	375.965	2096	253.976	−121.99
Turmeric	1211	197.822	1226	148.529	−49.29
Aracanut	841	137.337	11535	1397.796	1260.46
Coriander	2814	459.538	3845	465.932	6.39
Sugarcane (Gurh)	1871	305.53	2864	347.115	41.59
Banana	903	147.525	2115	256.263	108.74
Tobacco	1378	224.97	2233	270.654	45.68
Niger Seed	420	68.586	426	51.676	−16.91
Jute	259	42.243	179	21.715	−20.53
Dry Ginger	708	115.688	3000	363.54	247.85
Garlic	9587	1565.552	12765	1546.844	

Crops	Price 2000–1		Price 2006–7		Change in
	Rs/qu	Relative price	Rs/qu	Relative price	Relative price
Soya Bean	3391	553.741	4461	540.54	–3920.11
Sanhamp	482	78.669	565	68.472	–496.57
Moth	1582	258.316	1817	220.128	–1596.41
Black Pepper	23450	3829.484	31721	3843.938	15.454
Cardamom	112558	18381.524	176279	21361.473	2979.579

NB: Rice price =100 for calculation of Relative prices

In further analysis, the effect of commodity prices is isolated by computing the deviation of scatteredness between price-propelled growth (Y) and constant price growth (X) with 1:1 ratio (when Y = X). It follows as: Y = 9.05 + 1.199X. As shown in Figure 4.5, this relationship confirms that:

1   There is about 9.05 per cent flat increase in agriculture growth in all districts because of increased price-effect during the Post-Liberalisation phase, and
2   The rate of price-propelled growth compared to the real term growth is about 19.9 per cent because the rate difference between two straight lines is 0.199 (1.199 – 1.00).

4.07 Agriculture growth in agro-climatic regions

In this section, agricultural growth patterns are explained using agro-climatic regions as an analytical unit. It is widely recognised that the land potential in India is largely driven by the variability in agro-climatic conditions. Agriculture productivity levels are thus heavily dependent on biophysical properties of land.

Here, two key measures are employed to explain agriculture growth: the range and growth concentration. Range is simply the difference between the highest and lowest value, whilst growth concentration measures the distribution through using a Quartile Distribution System (QDS). Values are categorised into three groups: one-fourth, a half (median) and three-fourths.

The Great Plains of India (Ganga–Brahmaputra plains) have moderate to below average growth (2 to 4 per cent annually) with negative skewness coefficients in areas such as Assam plains (-0.4), Lower Ganga plain (-0.2) and Middle Ganga plain (-1.2). These regions however show transitioning towards high growth. However, the Upper Ganga plain and Punjab plains are 'growth stagnant' as they had positive value of coefficient of skewness during the Post-Liberalisation phase (Table 4.5 and Figure 4.6). It is to be noted that the Lower Ganga (Bengal) Plain has the lowest range of growth rate varying from 6.65 per cent (Hawrah) to 0.07 per cent (Midnapur) with 3.71 per cent mean value of growth. Three crops of Rice are planted in a year across this region, which has increased uniformity in agricultural growth patterns. In the stagnant growth region of Punjab-Haryana, the farm-HH economy has started to change more rapidly from the goal of 'production enhancement' to

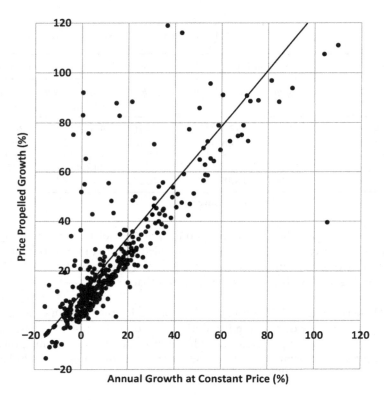

Figure 4.5 Constant production price and propelled price for agriculture growth

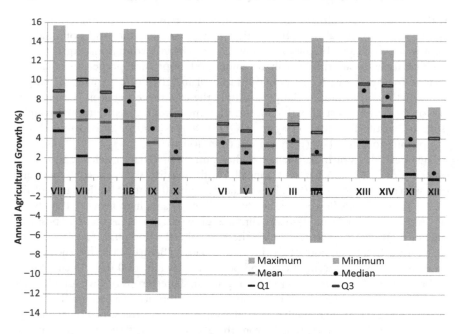

Figure 4.6 Agricultural growth dispersion across agro-climatic regions

Table 4.5 Distributional characteristics of annual agricultural growth of different agro-climatic regions

Agro-climatic regions		No. of dist.	Agricultural growth (in %) at constant price during 2000–1 to 2006–7								
			Mean	Median	Maximum	Minimum	SD	CV%	Q1	Q3	Skewness
I	Western Himalaya	34	5.66	6.87	14.92	-14.29	5.3744	94.89	4.13	8.77	-1.7472
IIA	North East – Assam Plains	11	2.38	2.66	14.39	-6.68	5.8184	244.87	-1.18	4.65	-0.4817
IIB	North East – Hills and Mts	30	5.75	7.84	15.32	-10.88	5.5039	95.76	1.3	9.28	-0.8216
III	Lower Ganga Plains	12	3.71	3.88	6.65	0.07	2.0487	55.16	2.22	5.47	-0.2434
IV	Middle Ganga Plains	30	3.28	4.59	11.38	-6.84	5.787	176.56	1.09	6.97	-1.2436
V	Upper Ganga Plains	39	3.25	2.55	11.42	-1.64	3.0863	94.92	1.5	4.78	1.1574
VI	Punjab Plains	25	4.41	3.59	14.44	0.17	4.0976	92.99	1.25	5.51	1.4798
VII	Eastern Plateau	25	5.91	6.81	14.77	-13.95	6.4869	109.77	2.19	10.06	-1.1718
VIII	Central Plateau	48	6.66	6.36	15.69	-4.05	3.6158	54.3	4.77	8.9	0.0104
IX	Western Plateau	33	3.58	5.02	14.71	-11.77	8.6845	242.76	-4.6	10.13	-0.5203
X	Southern Plateau	39	1.94	2.66	14.8	-12.42	6.5396	336.8	-2.48	6.43	-0.1164
XI	East Coast	20	3.31	3.99	14.69	-6.45	4.919	148.49	0.39	6.23	0.1372
XII	West Coast	17	-0.12	0.5	7.24	-9.65	6.2254	5294.59	-0.17	4.06	-1.3124
XIII	The Gujarat	20	7.36	9	13.48	0.96	3.7165	50.47	3.66	9.67	-0.2445
XIV	The Thar	4	7.44	8.34	12.9	0.18	5.2956	71.18	6.3	9.49	-0.9831
XV	The Islands	–	–								–

creation of 'non-agricultural activities' at farms. This shift has generated additional income for farmers but has reduced overall agriculture growth.

The highly fertile coastal regions of India experienced high to very high average annual agricultural growth (6–7 per cent). The Western Coastal Region (XII) of the Malabar-Konkan coast is an exception where the growth rate was recorded close to zero with moderate intra-regional variation (± 10 per cent). This might be due to paddy-dominated farming that increases production and, consequently, crop growth. Rice is also considered as a commercial crop in this region, which has provided further impetus to growth (Figure 4.6 and Table 4.5). In addition, the cumulative impact of urbanisation has also been a catalyst in boosting agricultural production in the region.

A much higher range of spatial dispersion of agriculture growth was recorded in the mountain and hill regions of India where the signs of progressive growth, especially in the hill region in the foreland of the Deccan (agro-climatic regions VII, VIII and IX), can be detected. This is because the median growth rate was higher than the mean growth, which shows the agriculture performance.

4.08 Farm size and road infrastructure

Farm size and road infrastructure are two key factors *inter alia* that have significant impact on agricultural growth and productivity in India. But, the scale of their impact varies across different regions in India. Farm size, in terms of landholding, limits the scale of farm operation and therefore it is a significant barrier to achieving economies of scale. Resource-poor farmers with marginal landholdings (less than 1 ha of operational land) tend to have limited choices except to engage in subsistence farming over commercial farming. Consequently, farmers remained less competitive in a deregulated market compared to farmers with a larger farm operation who produce agriculture products for the market. Farmers with marginal landholdings are unable to produce food surplus, which they could sell in the market to raise their household income. Ironically, these farms constitute two-thirds of the total farms in India but contribute much less to the total agriculture output (about one-third of the total production) (Randhawa and Sundaram 1990). This distribution and income disparities have been a common challenge in most countries within South Asia. India is no exception to this challenge.

Farmers are therefore left with little choice except that of using a significant proportion of their land to grow grain crops instead of cultivating high-value commercial crops to generate food surplus. Transport infrastructure and market have no impact on these small farm owners because of the disadvantages associated with subsistence farming. They add no value to the production or distribution as food is locally produced and consumed. Instead, they are vulnerable to high uncertainties associated with weather fluctuations, severe land degradation due to intensive land use and market risks (market price fluctuation of agricultural products and input costs) (Sundaram 2007). Consequently, agricultural land use and aggregated outputs at a village/district level remain largely food grains-dominated. Even after the economic liberalisation, the commercialisation of crop production using market-driven large scale farming practices is largely restricted to few districts in India (Singh and Chhetri 2013). This has been a key reason that contributed to the stagnation of agriculture growth in India.

Development of road infrastructure is a prerequisite for a growing market economy. There are a number of advantages in building robust rural infrastructure and resilient transportation chains. These include:

- Increasing road connectivity between farms and the market, which enables farmers to produce as per market demand through contract farming;
- Decrease in farm-gate production prices with lower transport costs;
- Reduction in farm input costs (e.g. equipment, tools and fertiliser);
- Frequent movement of farm labour to non-farm to perform non-agricultural activities at a farm or in the nearby towns (Hine and Riverson 1984); and
- Better integration of rural economies with metropolitan markets.

Hine modelled the effect of transport costs on the volume of agricultural commodities transported and sold in urban markets using a producer surplus equilibrium (i.e., surplus farm products which are sold to market). He found that road infrastructure-led growth increases farm-gate commodity prices from P1 to P2 and reduces input costs from the marginal cost curve MC-I to MC-II with an increase in the volume of agricultural commodities transported to market from Q1 to Q2 (c.f. Francisco and Routray 1992) (Figure 4.7). The diagram given in Figure 4.7 illustrates *a* and *b* areas, which show additional benefits for farmers due to increased farm gate prices from P1 to P2; whilst areas *c* and *d* show benefits of reduced input costs (as MC curve shifts from MC-I to MC-II). The value of *e* shows the benefits from the combined effect of both factors (Figure 4.7). Collectively, the area under *a, b, c, d* and *e* represents the total benefits which are generated from improvement in road connectivity of rural areas to urban markets.

At the time of economic reforms, two key changes have affected agricultural growth and farm productivity. *First* is the elimination of subsidies and the government support which hampered competitiveness and disadvantaged resource-poor farmers. It adversely affected farm productivity of marginal farm landholders; they could not sustain the continuous supply of basic food commodities for their own families. *Second* is the limitation of innovative farming and adaptation of modern techniques, which would compel disadvantaged farmers with small and marginal landholdings to adopt cooperative farming, which required a collaborative management of common farm assets. Agricultural Institutions like ICAR, to some extent, assisted farmers by providing agriculture extension services. However, rural road is considered as common infrastructure through which productivity levels can be enhanced to maximise farm growth.

4.09 Rural road, market efficiency and food supply

There has been significant expansion of road infrastructure in rural India over the last few decades. Surfaced road in India has extended from a total length of 1,091 thousand km (332 km/1000 square km) in 1991 to 1,420 thousand

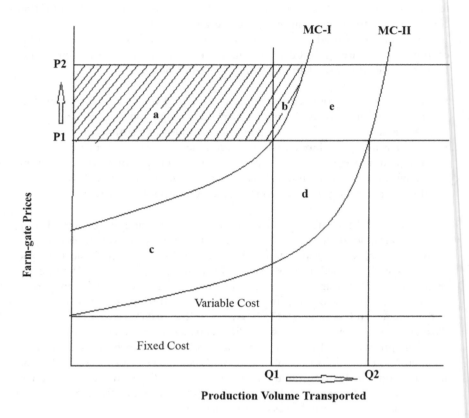

Figure 4.7 Production volume and farm-gate price (MC = Marginal Costs)

km (432 km/1000 sq km) in 2002. Better road connectivity between farms and urban and rural markets has improved the processing of farm commodities, increased rural market efficiency by maintaining the balance between supply and demand, increased profit margins and farm-based household income, enhanced farm productivity and supported rural cottage industries. Three empirical case studies are presented below to demonstrate how improvements in road infra-structure in India has delivered a range of benefits for farmers and helped improve market efficiency.

Case-I: Maize-growing farmers in Ahamadnagar district of Maharashtara

An empirical study on the market efficiency and supply of *kharif* Maize to nearby market centres was recently conducted by Navadkar et al. (2012). Their study selected 90 Maize growers from a broad range of landholdings. Ahamadnagar district is largely a Maize-producing area in Maharastara, where about two-thirds of the total Maize production is consumed as a food item. This study was conducted in 2008–9 when *kharif* Maize was considered as a cash crop and about 20 per cent of its production was supplied to market.

Effects of rural road infrastructure on market efficiency and producers' profit were traced by analysing the linkages between Maize growers/producers and the market. The study shows that an improvement in a marketing system through the conversion of gravel roads to bitumen 'pucca' roads has improved rural road connectivity. An improved transport network within the district has increased the connectedness between farms and the markets where Maize is supplied. There are three key sources of efficiency gains. *First* is the reduction in the commission paid to agents or intermediaries who were part of the distribution channels. So there was an overall improvement in the efficiency of supply chains. *Second* is the cost savings from parking charges and transport costs due to the substantial reduction in lead time. *Third* is the reduction in waste, which helped make the Maize supply chain more lean and responsive to market demand.

Case-II: *Rabi vegetables as cash crops in the Tinsukia district of the upper Assam plains*

This case study is based on a field survey, which was conducted in 2009–10 involving 461 rural farm households who partially grow vegetables and supply them to nearby market centres, often referred to as Chapakwa. This case study area is located in the Tinsukhia district, which is part of the Upper Brahmaputra river valley near the foothills of Arunachal Himalayas. Biophysical conditions in this district are highly suitable for crop cultivation due to high soil fertility and the required amount of moisture in newly formed alluvial plain. Cereals, vegetables and fruits are predominately grown without irrigation. These crops are supplied to Chapakwa throughout the year. The key question investigated in this case study was to ascertain whether the location of farms from this town influences the farm-gate prices of farm commodities and affects the quantity of commodities supplied to the market.

Two villages, which were located at different distances from the market centre (Case-I the farthest village 16.8 km from Chapakwa and Case-II the nearer village of 3.9 km distance), were chosen as case studies. The data were collected using survey questionnaires in the year 2010–11. Farm-HHs were requested to participate in the survey. The impact of transportation costs and market prices were calculated to measure their effects on the size of commodity supply (Figure 4.8).

The findings show that farm-gate prices of supplied agriculture commodities tend to have direct influence on the quantity of products sold at the market. Farm-gate prices are often influenced by transportation cost, which was found to be a key element in classical land use models such as von Thunen's cost-efficient transport system. The service frequency and responsiveness have increased the average farm gate prices of cereals and vegetables, which in turn, provide greater economic return to farmers if they increase the supply of agricultural

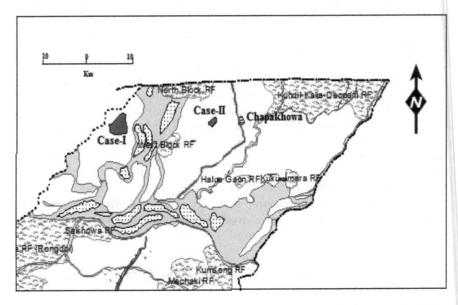

Figure 4.8 Case-I (Ghahpur, the farthest) and Case-II (Borgorah, the nearest) villages in the Northern part of the Tinsukia district (courtesy: Talukdar 2013)

commodities. Farm location and transport costs are the key drivers, which are likely to affect the total market surplus in the Northern part of the Tinsukhia district (Talukdar 2013).

The results indicate that an increase in the farm-gate price is more likely to increase the quantity supplied to the market. It could be either due to an improvement in transport mode or increase in market price of agricultural commodities. This provides convenience and incentives to farmers. For instance, an increase of farm-gate price from Rs 786/qu to Rs 886/qu of cereals and vegetables at the Case-I village (Ghahpur) resulted in an increase in the market supply from 67.4 qu/HH/Yr to 132 qu/HH/Yr (the difference of Case-I with Case-II, see Table 4.6 and Figure 4.9A). It also raised the producers' surplus from Rs 30,398/HH to Rs 39,125/HH, a net increase of Rs 8,727/HH. Thus, the farm-gate prices tend to exert a significant impact of the investment return to farmers if they sell their produce at the market.

In addition, a reduction in input costs would also add to additional increases in producers' surplus. Farmers operating at a farm closer to the market (Case-II) had lower input costs (as evidenced due to a marginal cost line shift from Case-I to Case-II), which increased the supply to Chapakwa market from 67.4 qu/HH to 98.22 qu/HH per year with a 46 per cent increase in surplus and a net gain of Rs 135,997/HH per year (Table 4.6, Figure 4.9B).

Table 4.6 Attributes related to transport costs and market prices of farm products in the Tinsukia District

Sl. no.	Items	Units	Amount (Case-I, 16.83km)	(Case-II 3.88km)
	A. Quantities			
1	Farm production Case–I	Q_1 (qu/hh)	67.4	98.22
2	Farm production Case–II	Q_2 (qu/hh)	–	132.00
3	Farm–HH consumption	Qh	12.43	12.43
4	Production supplied to market	Qm = (Q – Qh)	50.32	82.44
	B. Costs			
5	Fixed costs	Cx (Rs/hh)	209.5	209.5
6	Variable costs at market centre excluding transport charges	Cv (Rs/hh)	337	337.0
7	Transport rate per unit of product supplied to market	Tr (Rs/qu)	39	52.00
8	Variable input costs at farm gate	Cf = (Cv + Tr) (Rs/qu)	376	389.00
	C. Distance attribute			
9	Location of farm from the road side	Km	16.83	3.88
	D. Prices			
10	Price of unit product supplied to market at initial level	Pm_1 (Rs/qu)	825	825
11	Price of unit product supplied to market at increased price level	Pm_2 (Rs/qu)	925	925
12	Farm–gate price of unit product supplied initially p_1	$P_1 = (Pm_1 – Tr)$ (Rs/qu)	786	773
13	Farm–gate price of unit product supplied at higher price when market price increases	$P_2 = (Pm_2 – Tr)$ (Rs/qu)	886	873
	E. Constant and coefficients of marginal cost lines			
14	Initial price level of fixed costs	a' (Rs/qu)	165	165
15	Initial price level of variable costs	a (Rs/qu)	320	200
16	Rate of change in variable costs	B	0.308	0.308
	F. Effects and producer surplus/ gain			
17	% increase in output supplied at same price p_1 for Case–I	100 * (Q_1 – Qh)/Qh	442.24	–
18	% increase in output supplied at same price p_1 for Case–II	100 * (Q_2 – Qh)/Qh	–	961.95

(*Continued*)

Table 4.6 (Continued)

Sl. no.	Items	Units	Amount	
			(Case-I, 16.83km)	(Case-II 3.88km)
19	% increase in output price	$100 * (P_2 - P_1)/P_1$	12.72	–
20	Total producer surplus at initial price $P_1 = [(Q_1 - Qh) * P_1] - [1/2(Q_1 - Qh) * (P_1 - a)]$	(Rs/hh)	30,398	–
21	Total producer surplus gain due to price rise from p_1 to $P_2 = [(Q_1 - Qh) * (P_2 - P_1)] + [1/2(Q_3 - Q_1) * (P_2 - P_1)]$	(Rs/hh)	8,727	–
22	% increase in producer surplus due to price rise from p_1 to p_2 Row 22 = (Row 21/Row 20) * 100	%	28.71	–
23	% increase of additional supply of products to market due to reduction of transport cost from Case–I to II	%	46	–
24	Producer net gain = $[(Q_4 - Qh) * (P_2 - P_1)] + [(Q_4 - Q_3) * P_1]$	(Rs/hh)	135,997	–

Source:Talukdar 2013,

N.B. :Farm-HH Survey conducted during September 2010 to March 2011

Case-III: the revival of the village khadi industry

The ancient art of weaving in rural India is at the verge of extinction despite its significance in generating local employment or its role in India's struggle for freedom against the British Rule. It has evolved as the 'Khadi Cottage Industry', which was supported through government incentives and subsidies to farmers. Despite the effort, the cottage industry is barely surviving due to the changing consumer behaviour and preferences for international brands, which provide durability, contemporary designs and modern-day fashion driven by the brand-conscious world of consumerism. In addition to changing consumer taste for more contemporary western-oriented fashion for clothing, the labour force working in the cottage industry started to shift to other industrial sectors of the economy.

Recent government rural tourism initiatives provided new opportunities to rural artisans to use their craftsmanship to remain competitive in the national and global market place (Jain 2013). Engagement of craftsmen in tourism, government-sponsored or supported training and entrepreneurial skilling of labour, and

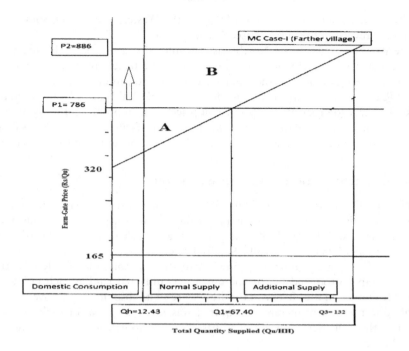

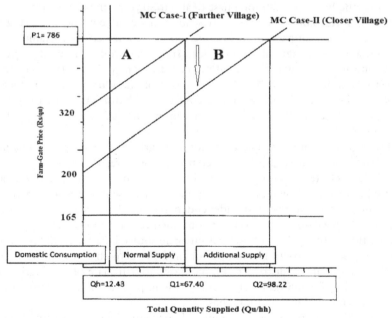

Figure 4.9 Increasing producer's surplus with (A) increasing farm-gate process and (B) the reduction of input costs

the burgeoning demand for cotton/linen in the Western world contributed to the recent revival of the village-based khadi industry.

The bamboo-crafts of the North Eastern Hills, the doll-making, leather tanning, pottery and metal works of Uttar Pradesh, the bangle-making, traditional jewellery-making of Gujarat, the embroidery of Kolkata, and the miniature painting of Rajasthan are the main hand-made products of rural India, which started to make their way to urban and global market places. The improvement in the transportation chains is one of the contributing factors that facilitated the seamless flow of rural farm products to small-scale industrial production and then to the market.

4.10 Concentration of agriculture output

Bhalla and Tyagi (1989) and Singh (1994) calculated district-wise agriculture output of major crops at constant prices during the early 1960s, 1970s and 1980s. Bhalla and Tyagi (1989) adopted the approach of incremental output between two points of time, whilst Singh (1994) measured the concentration of agricultural output by computing one-fourth share of total magnitude of agricultural output produced by the share of total cultivated land at each point of time. He compared the change in the areal share to its absolute degree over time. Areal concentration of incremental output was first calculated for each district and then these districts were classified based on one-fourth share of total incremental output.

During the Pre-Liberalisation phase of about 30 years, the results of the impact of the Green Revolution became more spatially discernible in India. The regional disparities in agriculture output became more pronounced. For example, one-fourth share of total agriculture output in India was produced by 18.70 million ha of cultivated land, which is 13.34 per cent to total cultivated land covered by 38 districts in the early 1970s. The areal extent of one-fourth output reduced to 11.58 per cent to total cultivated land covered by 37 districts in the early 1980s and again reduced to 9.77 per cent representing only 27 districts (Singh 1994: 46; Table 2.11).

This infers to an increased concentration of agricultural output in India up to the 1980s. There was a growing concern in terms of rapid agriculture development in few selected districts while the rest of the country exhibited dismal agriculture performance, giving rise to a significant increase in regional disparities in agricultural growth in the Post-Independence India. Ironically, the spatial concentration of total agriculture output continued to escalate even after economic liberalisation in India. Agricultural output again showed higher spatial concentration with just 13 districts accounting for 6.92 per cent share of cultivated land in 2000–1 and only 10 districts resulting in one-fourth share of total agricultural output. Table 4.7 shows the marginal increase in production at a constant price after the economic Liberalisation phase.

Another method for measuring regional concentration of agricultural output is the 'rank- size rule', which shows an inter-district output variation. It measures the degree of primacy in the output distribution. The higher the coefficient values of rank-size rule (q), the larger is the inter-district variation and, thus, the higher the concentration. Using this rule for district-wise output data for the last five decades (since the 1970s), there are three key characteristics which succinctly reflect the distribution patterns. These are listed below:

1   The value of q increases from 0.31 in the early 1970s to 0.42 in 2006–7 as shown in Table 4.7 and in Figure 4.10. This shows that the total agriculture output is gradually concentrated in a few districts. In other words, a handful of districts have generated a larger sum of total agriculture output. These districts are often those where crops are grown for the market rather than for domestic consumption and where the use of technology is widely prevalent to help enhance land productivity per unit of area.

2   The total production value of the highest ranked district has increased over time from Rs 195 crores in the early 1970s to Rs 373 crores in the early 1990s, to Rs 15,600 crores in the early 2000s and then culminated to Rs 17,600 crores in 2006–7. There is a growing gap in output of the ranked districts between the Green Revolution and Post-Liberalisation. This could be associated with regional variations of crop harvest prices from 1969–72 to 2000–1.

3   If the output concentration is retained over time in the same areas, that would infer increased concentration of agricultural growth patterns. Bhalla and Tyagi (1989: 167–193) found that one-fourth share of incremental output in India during the Green Revolution phase (1962–65 to 1980–3) is concentrated in few districts of the Upper part of Great Plains (most of

Table 4.7 Percentage share of cultivated land and number of districts included 1/4th share of total agricultural output of India index

Years	Total aggregate output (million Rs)	1/4th share of total output (million Rs)	No. of districts sharing 1/4th output	% share of cultivated land covered under these districts	Output value of the First-Rank district (Rs)	Degree of concavity (q) under rank-size rule*
1969–72	131,100	32,775	38	13.342	1.96E + 09	−0.311
1979–82	161,324	40,331	37	11.581	2.57E + 09	−0.38156
1988–90	200,440	50,110	27	9.773	3.73E + 09	−0.40052
2000–1	4,432,383	1,108,095	13	6.923	1.56E + 11	−0.41223
2006–7	4,950,878	1,237,719	11	5.212	1.76E + 11	−0.42127

N.B.: Total agricultural output is based on 15 major crops. It is cultivated at constant harvest price (1969–72) for 1969–72, 1979–82 and 1988–90, while the figures of total agricultural output for the years 2000–01 and 2006–07 are based on 46 crops with constant price of 2000–01.

* Rank size rule is formulated as Production size for a particular district rank r is Pr = P1 (r) −q where P1 is production size of rank first district and q refers to degree of concavity of production curve.

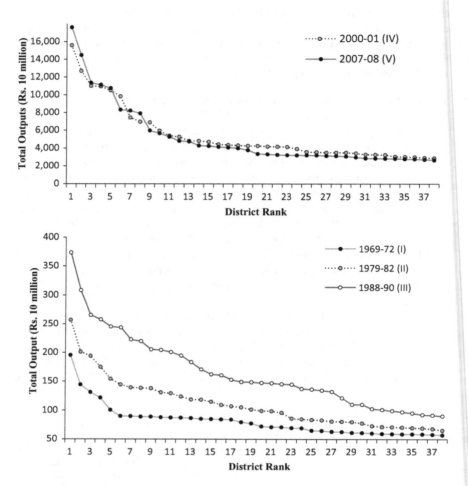

Figure 4.10 Agricultural output of districts ordered by their ranks

the districts from Punjab and Haryana states and the Western part of Uttar Pradesh). These districts of high-output concentration were also the areas of high agricultural growth. This could be attributed to a multitude of factors including an incremental increase in modern farm inputs. For example, the districts in this region account for 24.5 per cent of incremental irrigated land, 21.7 per cent share of incremental fertiliser consumption and 29.65 per cent share of incremental number of tractors for a period of 18 years. During the Post-Liberalisation phase, the areas of incremental output shifted to Haryana and Ganga-Jamuna doab to *tarai* areas of Uttar Pradesh and South Arcot of Tamilnadu.

4.11 Summary

Agriculture growth is largely driven by two key changes in agricultural production systems: the change in crop area and crop yield. Undoubtedly, the total cropping area in India has increased significantly during the Post-Liberalisation Phase (2000–1 to 2012–13); however, there has been a gradual shift in the concentration of the areal share of food grains towards non-food grain crops especially commercial crops. This happened due to their higher relative prices and increasing food demand not only in India but also in the global market. Such areal shift in the cropping pattern is indicative of improved linkages between farm products and market.

Regional processes of agricultural growth are still largely governed by the biophysical factors of land and the use of farm technology. Agriculture growth first began in Punjab-Haryana and Gujrat in the Pre-Green Revolution phase, then shifted to the Maharastra–Karnataka region of central Deccan in the Post-Green Revolution phase and later percolated to the coastal areas of deltaic narrow plains and interior Deccan in the Pre-Liberalisation phase. During the Post- Liberalisation phase, the agriculture growth began to permeate to the hills of the North-East, Siwaliks, Himachal Himalayas and foreland plateaus of Deccan (Malwa-Bundelkhand-Banghelkhand and Chotanagpur) including the Thar. Interestingly, the areas of high growth in the Interior Deccan during the Pre-Liberalisation phase experienced lower growth after the economic liberalisation.

Effects of rural road networks and increased relative prices of commercial crops have shaped the agriculture production growth from a 'production-oriented' to a 'profitability-oriented' growth model. Improved transportation has enabled better integration of rural economies with metropolitan markets, reduced transportation and inventory-holding costs and enhanced overall efficiency of commodity supply chains. The development of 'quadrilateral' road national networks had also accelerated agriculture growth by overcoming the physiographic constraints of land. Consequently, higher growth rate was recorded in the physically challenging terrain of the parts of Madhya Pradesh, Jharkhand, North East Hill regions, and the hills of Himachal Pradesh, Uttrakhand and Jammu and Kashmir.

Development of rural road networks has connected farm to market by reducing transport costs and by increasing the prices of farm products. This in turn helped increase farm efficiency. Emerging new market centres (called mandies) have also added market efficiency in the commodity chains, which again reduced the marketing and distribution costs and taxes on farm products. Relaxation of the terms of trade of agricultural products, emergence of horticulture and cash crops in cropping pattern, and profit-making 'contract farming', which linked agriculture to market, are major changes in the mode of agricultural practices which have added a new dimension to agricultural production systems in India.

5   Regional dimensions of land and labour productivity

5.01 Introduction

Agricultural production in India is still largely driven by biophysical character-istics of land and hence the regional variability in agricultural productivity is essentially a reflection of the differences in land potential or capacity. Agriculture productivity refers to the production per unit of its factors, namely the land (e.g. soil fertility, moisture and temperature), labour (e.g. costs and skills) and technol-ogy (often defined in monetary terms). Productivity is generally viewed as 'crop yield' or aggregated production of all crops per unit of land, referred to as 'land productivity'. Productivity is also measured in terms of production produced by a unit of a factor of labour or capital, called the 'labour productivity' and 'capital productivity' respectively.

In this chapter, land and labour productivity are first conceptualised and then measured. Regional patterns of land and labour productivity are mapped to exhibit key areas of strategic importance or concerns. A generic view of produc-tivity is adopted to identify the key regional variability to differentiate areas of high or low productivity with a particular focus on the impact of liberalisation policy.

Regional differences in productivity levels are also being measured across dif-ferent agro-climatic regions to examine whether the land potential makes any dif-ference in terms of production return per unit. An optimal productivity–growth relationship is ascertained to enable the development of a geo-targeted invest-ment strategy to enhance productivity levels.

5.02 Formulating the agriculture productivity

In this analysis, agricultural productivity is presented as a synonymous to land productivity that is defined as the total agricultural output per unit of cultivated area. Various concepts and measures of productivity have been developed for dif-ferent purposes, notwithstanding they all represent different ways of measuring output relative to agricultural production factors (Cuadrado-Roura et al. 2000). Since market price of agricultural products is a key driver of agricultural output, the economists thus consider three elements of agriculture, namely area, yield and price of crops, to measure the total output in monetary value. Aggregation of output of each crop was considered by many researchers such as Bhalla and Tyagi (1989), and Singh and Zoramkhuma (2015) who have assessed total agricultural output as:

$$O = \Sigma (A_i.Y_i.P_i) \quad \ldots \quad \ldots \tag{5.1}$$

Agricultural productivity (land productivity is inter-changeably used because agricultural production factors are inherently related to land conditions) is simply the output per unit of cultivated land as:

$$Y_A = (O/A) \quad \ldots \quad \ldots \tag{5.2}$$

Further, labour productivity refers to output per worker (a cultivator or labourer) engaged in agricultural activities as labour dominates in agricultural production processes. It may be mathematically written as:

$$Y_L = (O/L) \quad \ldots \quad \ldots \tag{5.3}$$

where, Y_A = agricultural productivity per unit area, Y_L = labour productivity per worker, A_i = area of ith Crop, Y_i = yield of ith Crop, P_i = harvest price of ith Crop, O = total agricultural output in monetary term and L = labour engaged in agriculture.

5.03 Agricultural productivity – the general contours

Agricultural productivity is analysed using district wide statistics on area, yield and prices of 42 crops, which include both food grains and commercial crops. Results show that agricultural productivity levels in India are relatively low when compared to countries of a similar level of economic development. The average yield of cereals, for instance, was 5,095 kg/ha in China, which was more than double to that of India, which was 2,417 kg/ha in 2003–5. The share of irrigated area to arable land was also low (32.7 per cent) in India in comparison to China. The use of nitrogen fertiliser in India was much lower (107 kg/ha) than China, which used about four times more chemical fertilisers (395 kg/ha) in the same period of time.

Despite the lower agriculture performance of India, there has been noticeable increase of about 50 per cent in the area under commercial crops. It increased from 31 million ha (2000–1) to 49 million ha (2012–13), while the output increased by 14.88 per cent. There are two principal reasons for this change: *first* is an increase in crop yield per unit of land and *second* is a rapid increase in prices of commercial crops.

Higher relative price of commercial crops has increased productivity because of better linkages between production choices and market demand. Area under food grains has increased marginally during the Post-Liberalisation phase. The

Table 5.1 Area, output and productivity of food grains and commercial crops in India during the Post-Liberalisation period

Sl. no.	Items	2000–1	2012–13
1	Total cultivated area under food grains (million ha)	124.07	138.83
2	Total cultivated area under commercial crops (million ha)	31.83	49.16
3	Areal share of food grains (%)	78.29	73.85
4	Areal share of commercial crops (%)	21.71	29.26
5	Output of food grain crops (%)	58.77	43.67*
6	Output of commercial crops (%)	41.44	56.32*
7	Average productivity of food grains (1000 Rs/ha)	12.57	23.42*
8	Average productivity of commercial crops (1000 Rs/ha)	127.86	471.68*

N.B.: 1. * Starred figures are based on 2006-7 data.
2. Output of non-commercial and commercial crops has been calculated at constant (2000-01) price for the year 2006-7 and average productivity is simply the aggregation of crop output per unit of cultivated area.

output of commercial crops rose from 41 per cent to 56 per cent. Average land productivity, therefore, rose much faster during the Post- Liberalisation phase (Table 5.1). The main reason behind the abrupt hike in the average productivity of commercial crops is the rapid increase in crop prices.

5.03.1 Land productivity levels (Y_A)

Land productivity is simply defined as the total crop output per ha of cultivated land. Land productivity in India was largely affected by differences in land potential, which is heavily dependent on biophysical characteristics of land. It was particularly a key driver of agriculture productivity prior to the Green Revolution. Productivity in some areas was however enhanced by the use of yield-augmented technology such as irrigation and use of HYV seeds. Recent changes in agriculture output, crop diversification and technology improvements have however resulted in greater regional variation in land productivity (Dayal 1984, Singh 1994, Singh and Chhetri 2011), which needs urgent attention to help examine the issues associated with regional inequality, resource allocation and the diffusion of agricultural innovation.

The spatial variability in land productivity increased after the economic liberalisation when market forces begin to influence commodity prices. Studies such as Bhalla and Tyagi (1989), Dayal (1984), Singh (1994) found higher productivity levels in the fertile alluvial soils of the Great Plains and Coastal Deltaic Plains prior to the implementation of liberalisation policy. Such areas of high productivity (Rs 60,000/ha and above) have now started to contiguously expand outward to incorporate the *Tarai* areas along the foothills of the Himalaya (Ambala to Kheri-Lakhimpur), few districts in Krishna Delta, large parts of Cauvery Delta in the South and the Cotton-growing districts linked to the Bombay-Ahmadabad textile industry. Commercial farming might be the key reason for the spill-over effect of high productivity whereby food grains are replaced by Sugarcane in the *Tarai* region and Jowar-Bajra by Cotton and Groundnut in the Gujarat-Maharashtra plains.

Two main regional changes can be discernible in land productivity in India. *First* is the emergence of a few districts in the central part of Deccan Plateau, which earlier held low levels of productivity, that have transitioned to moderate levels of productivity. *Second* is that districts which held very high levels of land productivity have notable spill-over effects on their neighbouring districts after the Green Revolution (Singh 1994: 57–67).

During the Post-Liberalisation phase, the areas of high productivity expanded in the hills of North Eastern States. Most parts of Manipur as well as areas of South Mizoram and central parts of Meghalaya gained productivity increases to the highest level (above Rs 70,000). The expansion of cultivable area and increase in yield of horticulture crops were primary drivers of this rapid increase in the productivity level. Furthermore, the hills of Uttarakhand and Himachal Pradesh including the Kashmir Himalayas also were categorised under the high-productivity zone in 2006–7 (Figure 5.1). Oilseed cultivation in river valleys and fruit gardening on the hill-slopes of Himalayas were largely shaping the agricultural practices and performance in these areas.

In contrast, most districts within the Central Deccan Plateau had minor changes in productivity levels except for the Gujrat Plains, Central Madhya Pradesh and Aravali Hills of Rajasthan. The land productivity in these areas rose from very low to moderate during the six years of the Post-Liberalisation phase. Most districts in Orissa, Jharkhand and Chattisgarh (the part of Chotanagpur plateau) remained at levels of low to extremely low productivity (Figure 5.1). The deregulation and liberalisation reforms have thus made insignificant impact in these districts of low land productivity. Most of these districts are also the areas of high economic deprivation and remoteness from the key urban centres, major amenities and foci of agriculture technological innovation and change in India.

There was a significant shift in the level of productivity from low-productivity districts to higher levels in few strategic regions during the Post-Liberalisation phase. The total number of districts under the category of extremely low productivity reduced to 41 in 2006–7 when compared to 128 in 2000–1. In addition, there was an increase in the number of districts in the categories of high and extremely high productivity, which recorded an average increase of 12 per cent.

Nonetheless, the levels of land productivity continue to remain low in parts of Rajasthan, Orissa and Madhya Pradesh, except for a marginal increase after 2000–1. Movement of districts from very low to low and moderate productivity took place in the foreland of Deccan (Figure 5.1). The number of districts in extremely high-productivity classes from 132,537 Rs/ha (2000–1) to 148,665 Rs/ha (2006–7) increased from 33 to 48 (Table 5.2). The increase in average productivity was recorded at 45 per cent; it increased from 27,580 Rs/ha in

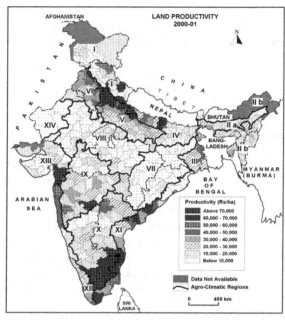

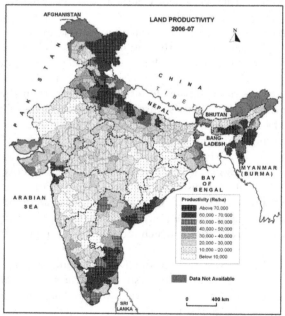

Figure 5.1 Land productivity patterns (2000–1 and 2006–7)

Table 5.2 Change in average land productivity during the Post-Liberalisation period

Productivity class (Rs/ha)	Average productivity (Rs/ha)				Number of districts		
	2000–1	2006–7	Change Total	%	2000–1	2006–7	Changes (in Nos.)
Extremely high (above 70,000)	132,537	148,665	16,128	12.17	33	48	15
Exceptionally high (70,000–60,000)	66,137	62,606	–3,526	–5.34	5	13	8
Very high (60,000–50,000)	55,194	54,312	–882	–1.6	12	16	4
High (50,000–40,000)	44,154	43,986	–168	–0.01	13	26	13
Medium (40,000–30,000)	35,048	34,833	–215	–0.01	27	42	15
Low (30,000–20,000)	25,033	24,508	–525	–0.021	49	81	32
Very low (20,000–10,000)	14,160	15,030	870	6.14	119	119	0
Extremely low (10,000–below)	6,621	7,824	1,203	18.17	128	41	–87
Average	**27,606**	**48,579**	**12,471**	**45.17**	**386**	**386**	–

2000–01 to 40,077 Rs/ha in 2006–07 within a period of six years of economic reforms.

Overall, there was a geographic expansion of classes of high to very high productivity, whereby a number of new districts attained high-productivity levels. There was an overall increase in average land productivity across all categories. However, some areas grew faster than others, which resulted in wider regional disparities in land productivity. Some of these changes were driven by physiographical properties of land whilst others were fuelled by technology and market forces.

The relationship between agricultural productivity and the share of commercial crops output to total output is highly correlated both in 2000–1 and 2006–7. In general, increased proportion of area under commercial crops tends to increase agricultural productivity (Table 5.3). The graph below shows the distribution of districts on an equal share of area under commercial crops for both periods. Equitable distribution follows a diagonal path in the graph, which represents the unit ratio of 1:1 (Figure 5.2). The above section of the graph shows higher dispersion and the bottom section shows lower dispersion in the distribution of area share and output share. It is evident that most districts in India which had lower percentage share of area under the commercial crops had increased faster in the area under commercial crops. Rapid growth of output of commercial crops, thus, has increased agricultural productivity.

Table 5.3 Percentage share of area and output of commercial crops and changes in their various categories of level productivity

| Productivity class (Rs/ha) | % Share of commercial crops of their | | | | | |
| | Area (%) | | | Output (%) | | |
	2000–1	2006–7	Change %	2000–1	2006–7	Changes %
Extremely high (above 70,000)	25.34	27.34	2	85.95	83.46	–2.49
Exceptionally high (70,000–60,000)	25.98	17.37	–8.61	71.83	72.89	1.06
Very high (60,000–50,000)	12.64	18.48	5.84	69.09	67.74	1.35
High (50,000–40,000)	14.72	20.13	5.41	69.6	67.18	–2.42
Medium (40,000–30,000)	16.45	19.62	3.17	53.83	55.45	1.62
Low (30,000–20,000)	70.83	23.66	2.83	50.46	54.37	3.91
Very low (20,000–10,000)	20.54	70.88	0.34	34.84	50.79	15.95
Extremely low (10,000–below)	14.77	11.38	–3.39	23.71	30.08	6.37
Average	**18.91**	**19.85**	**0.95**	**57.41**	**60.24**	**3.17**

A few districts, however, do exhibit slower growth in area under commercial crops, but most have higher growth in output of these crops. This could be due to the effect of increasing production of high-value crops (Figure 5.2A and B). It means that farmers have greater return to switch from food grains to commercial crops. Furthermore, higher returns from commercial farming promoted greater variety in crop cultivation. For example, many districts in the Punjab plains, despite the high degree of commercialisation, didn't escalate to the category of extremely high productivity, whilst the districts in Gujarat plains and coastal areas of Godavari and Cavery deltas have substantially increased land productivity. At the national level, the degree of distribution of areal share under commercial crops was significantly higher (with R^2 value of 0.594) than the share of output of commercial crops during the Liberalisation period (Figure 5.2). It has diversified the productivity patterns during the Post-Liberalisation phase when the area under commercial crops is grown and their production prices increased simultaneously. This may not necessarily correspond to high-productivity areas. The reasons of high diversity in agricultural productivity are discussed below:

1   The expansion of area under commercial crops, especially the Coconut production in Malabar and Konkan coasts, Sugarcane in West Uttar Pradesh (Upper Ganga-Jamuna *doab* and Rohilkhand) and Groundnut in Gujarat and Cotton in Interior Maharashtra and Punjab, has resulted in higher diversity in agricultural productivity (Nag 2010).

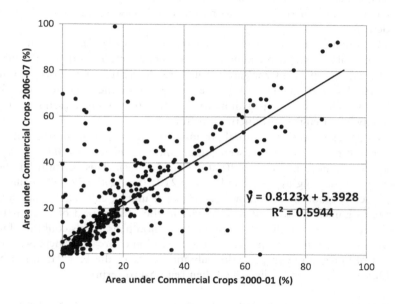

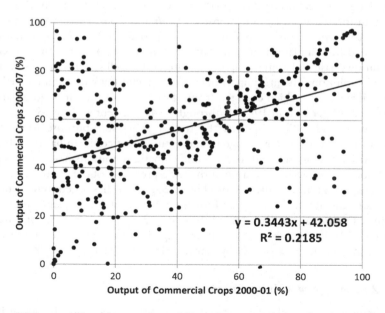

Figure 5.2 Increase in the area share (A) and output share of commercial crops (B) during the Post-Liberalisation phase

2   The relative pricing of commercial crops varies significantly across different parts of India partially due to regional and seasonal variability in market demand.

3   The proximity to market (i.e., cities) has strategically placed few districts in locational advantage in comparison to others. Farms located near the market generated surplus at farm-gate and incurred lower transport costs than those situated further out. This advantage made farm production much more competitive. However, the proximity to market in turn has increased spatial variability in agriculture productivity in India.

4   At a national level, agricultural productivity and output of commercial crops per unit of cultivated area were significantly correlated (r = 0.6845) at the advent of liberalisation in 2000–1 (Figure 5.3). This relationship however was not highly correlated (r = 0.218) during the Post-Liberalisation phase. The output of commercial crops per unit of cultivated area contributed significantly to land productivity in the early period of liberalisation, but it weakened during the Post-Liberalisation phase. This could be due to increased variety of crops grown, the expansion of area and increase in output of horticulture crops in the hills and valleys of the Himalayan foothills. Output of such crops diversified their regional pattern.

Irrigation is critical to enhancing land productivity and changed crop patterns. Irrigation technology has rapidly evolved in India. It has been technologically transformed from labour-intensive *Dhekli* and *Charas* systems in semi-arid regions of Upper Ganga and Punjab plains and in interior Karnataka, Maharashtra and Malwa plateau to animal-drawn *Rahat* system during the Pre-Green Revolution phase and then to engine-operated tube-well systems as a result of the Green Revolution. The first impact of irrigation technology was an increase in the total irrigated area, which changed from 18 per cent of total food grain area in 1950–1 to 29 per cent in 1980–1, through to 45 per cent in 2004–5.

Binswanger (1978) recognised the tractor as a multi-purpose tool. It has proven to be a catalyst for change in agriculture practices in India. Punjab-Haryana and Uttar Pradesh plains of semi-arid climatic conditions have had a significant boost in productivity because of the widespread use of the tractor in farming and transporting agriculture goods (Figure 5.4). This has an equivalent impact in the arid climate of Rajasthan and the humid areas of Assam plains. Increasing income of marginal and larger-size landholders realised the benefits of buying a tractor of 20HP, which is used for tillage, irrigation and transportation of surplus agricultural products to the nearby market (Singh and Sharma 2007).

5.03.2 Labour productivity (output per worker)

Labour productivity, which is defined as the output per work, has been influenced by a myriad of factors which have produced significant spatial variability in rural India. Here we link labour productivity with the levels of urbanisation and

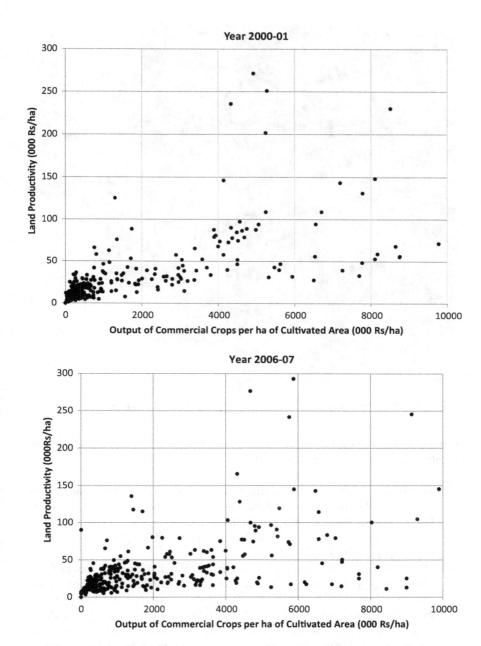

Figure 5.3 Relationship of land productivity with output of commercial crops per unit of cultivated area for the year 2000–1 and 2006–7

Figure 5.4 Tractor-trolley used for transporting agricultural produce

variations in agriculture performance and productivity levels. Key spatial patterns of labour productivity are highlighted as follows:

- Very high to high labour productivity is exhibited in Punjab-Haryana plains. Labour productivity however diminishes towards Avadh (Central) plains of Uttar Pradesh. Low labour productivity predominately prevailed in Bihar Plains, which has been a source of labour supply to high-performing areas in various parts of India.
- Other areas of low labour productivity include: (i) most parts of Chotanagpur plateau, and the tribal-dominated districts of Chhattisgarh, Jharkhand and Orissa; (ii) most districts of Rajasthan including the Aravali hills; and (iii) the central sub-humid districts of interior Andhra-Karnataka region. The labour productivity in these districts largely remained unchanged over the period. However, the area under low labour productivity increased during the Post-Liberalisation phase. It expanded further from Chotanagpur to Madhya Pradesh and Eastern Uttar Pradesh, whilst the areas in interior Karnataka extended into interior Maharashtra.

- Few districts of low labour productivity in Gujarat in 2000–1, which bordered Rajasthan and Central Madhya Pradesh, have significantly improved (Figure 5.5). These districts, previously categorised as low productive areas have been now transformed into highly productive areas. This could be partly due to the sectoral shift of workers from farming to non-farming, which in turn has resulted in an increase in labour productivity (a denominator in labour productivity Equation 5.3).
- Low labour productivity for the year 2006–7 is reported in the entire Chota Nagpur Plateau including Chattisgarh, Jharkhand and hills of Orissa. Socioeconomic deprivation, low levels of urbanisation and predominance of informal and unorganised rural markets might have contributed to a lower level of land and labour productivity. Contrary to this are the districts of high land and labour productivity, which are located in the deltaic East Coast, including tropical semi-humid interior Tamil Nadu. These districts have improved labour productivity despite the intensive Rice-dominating farming, which requires intensive use of labour to reap and to harvest crops. Besides Rice, value added crops such as vegetables, Coconut and other horticulture crops, especially in interior Tamil Nadu, have been gaining importance, which might have a positive impact on land and labour productivity.
- The districts of low labour productivity coincide with those of very high labour intensity (agricultural labour per ha of cultivated area), particularly in the Bihar plains and most districts of Chotanagpur plateau (Figure 5.6). This region typically employs primitive farming techniques, practices subsistence farming and is characterised by high population density and unemployment. On the other hand, mountain areas of Himachal and Uttaranchal of Central Himalayas of the dry-cold hills and the hills of interior Tamilnadu of tropical wet lands of South India have tremendous increase in labour productivity in spite of high population pressure on limited cultivable land. Labour productivity is high in these areas of low labour intensity (Table 5.4).

5.04 Inter-regional productivity differences

Overall, land productivity increased from Rs 28,361/ha to Rs 37,956/ha (10.48 per cent increase per annum), whilst labour productivity increased from Rs 27,424/worker to Rs 30,844/worker (6.14 per cent per annum). For instance, in the Great Plains of India, the land productivity differences between Gujarat plains and Thar dry region has been the highest. It was Rs 63,627/ha in 2000–1, which reduced to Rs 54,811/ha in 2006–7. Likewise, labour productivity was the highest in Punjab plains and the lowest in the Thar dry region in 2000–1. Inter-regional difference between them also reduced during the Post-Liberalisation phase due to increased labour productivity in the Thar dry region (Table 5.5). Despite substantial increase in land and labour productivity in India, there is significant variability within and between regions.

Highly urbanised regions, namely, the Gujarat plains and the Western Plateau (the hinterland of the Mumbai city-region) have lower level of labour productivity.

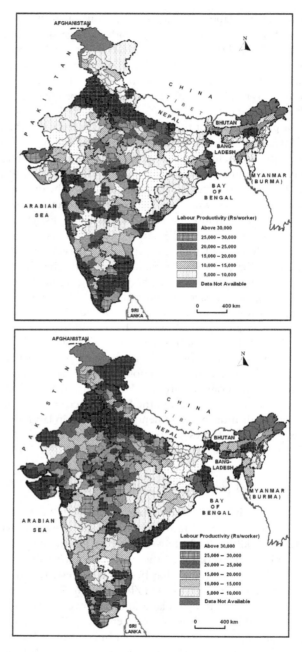

Figure 5.5 Pattern of labour productivity (2000–1 and 2006–7)

Table 5.4 Bi-variate frequency distribution of labour intensity (persons/sq km) with labour productivity (Rs/worker) in 2001

Labour productivity (Rs/ worker)	Labour intensity (persons/sq km)						
	Above 250	205–200	200–150	150–100	100–50	50–0	Total
Very high (Above 30,000)	2	13	12	22	36	5	90
High (30,000–25,000)	0	4	6	2	6	1	19
Moderately high (25,000–20,000)	1	3	10	5	13	1	33
Moderately low (20,000–15,000)	0	0	9	11	15	1	36
Low (15,000–10,000)	3	3	7	22	19	0	54
Very low (10,000–5,000)	16	6	17	22	32	5	98
Extremely low (5,000 below)	21	4	6	16	5	4	56
Total	**43**	**33**	**67**	**100**	**126**	**17**	**386**

N.B.: The districts belonging to the states of Sikkim, Tripura and Mizoram were not included in the present classification due to non-availability of land use statistics.

The Western Coast has also experienced a decline in labour productivity. Higher mobility of farm labour to non-farm work, which is often deemed better paid, could have resulted in higher labour productivity. Interestingly, the labour productivity in more rugged hills and vulnerable mountain regions of the West and North-East Himalayas (I and IIb) and the Western Dry Region (XIV) have improved. In particular, the North Eastern Hills (II b) have the highest increase in land productivity (251 per cent) as well as in labour productivity (157 per cent). A notable change in agriculture in the Post-Liberalisation phase is the rapid increase in productivity in low- productivity regions whilst a marginal increase in high-productivity regions. This phenomenon has increased the gap between high- and low-productivity regions and, thus, changed the spatial labour mobility dynamics in rural India.

Land productivity in the West mountain region of the Uttarakhand, Himachal Pradesh and Jammu and Kashmir Himalayas increased faster than other regions, decreasing inter-regional differences across almost all agro-climatic regions except in the Western Plateau region of the interior Maharashtra. However, the regional gap in land productivity between the Mumbai-based region of Western Plateau (IX) and

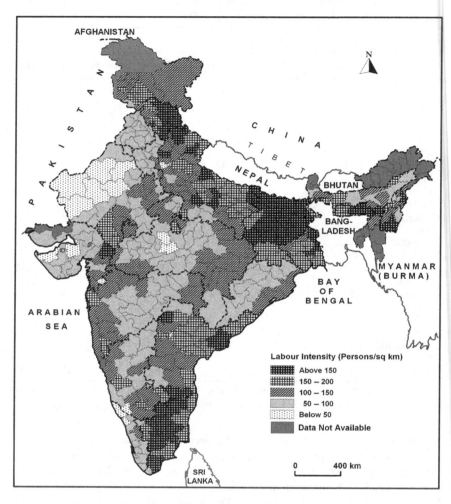

Figure 5.6 Labour intensity in agriculture in 2001

horticulture-based hill areas of the North-East (IIb) has reduced due to the rapid increase in land productivity in the North Eastern Hills Region. It has also reduced the regional gap in districts within the contiguous Assam plains (Table 5.6).

To recapitulate, during the Post-Liberalisation phase of agriculture development in India, inter-regional differences in labour productivity have reduced as a result of increasing productivity levels in low-productivity areas. Cultivation of high value crops including fruits and vegetables in the vicinity of urban markets has increased labour productivity in the Bengal plain, which reduced regional differences in labour productivity with the adjoining Middle Ganga Region. Both of

Table 5.5 Change in the levels of average land and labour productivities in different agro-climatic regions

Agro-climatic region	Land productivity (Rs/ha)		Change		Labour productivity (Rs/worker)		Change	
	2000–1	2006–7	Total	%	2000–1	2006–7	Total	%
I Western Himalaya (N = 34)	22778	70849	48071	211.036	25580	39693	14113	55.172
IIa North East – Assam Plains (N = 11)	16221	31338	15116	93.188	18393	18427	33	0.182
IIb North East – Hills and Mts (N = 30)	14824	52102	37278	251.463	8965	23081	14116	157.458
III Lower Ganga Plains (N = 12)	30114	36274	6161	20.458	25732	29484	3752	14.58
IV Middle Ganga Plains (N = 30)	24205	27670	3465	14.314	16913	16223	-690	-4.081
V Upper Ganga Plains (N = 39)	57136	66896	9760	17.081	63576	64566	990	1.557
VI Punjab Plains (N = 25)	37514	36311	-1202	-3.205	80489	68623	-11866	-14.742
VII Eastern Plateau (N = 25)	6408	9014	2606	40.661	7067	6999	-68	-0.957
VIII Central Plateau (N = 48)	8575	16537	7962	92.843	12431	20842	8410	67.656
IX Western Plateau (N = 33)	18345	15271	-3074	-16.756	22222	18330	-3892	-17.514
X Southern Plateau (N = 39)	37025	48221	11196	30.238	25930	24313	-1617	-6.236
XI East Coast (N = 20)	45117	51767	6649	14.738	25404	25734	329	1.297
XII West Coast (N = 17)	38632	38356	-276	-0.713	47104	37652	-9453	-20.067
XIII The Gujarat (N = 20)	66076	61774	-4302	-6.511	24990	46957	21966	87.901
XIV The Thar (N = 4)	2449	6963	4513	184.288	6568	21733	15165	230.871
XV The Islands	–	–	–	–	–	–	–	–
Average	28361	37956	9595	62.875	27424	30844	3419	36.872

N. B.:1. Agricultural output figures for the year 2000–01 and 2006–07 were calculated at price constant (2000–01) values to make affectless price productivity figures

2. District wise agricultural workforce to calculate labour productivity for the year 2006–07 were estimated by extrapolating decadal growth of agricultural workforce during 1991–2000.

3. Land productivity refers to total agricultural output per ha of cultivated area (O/A) and labour productivity is output per agricultural worker (O/L).

Table 5.6 Inter-regional differences in land productivity and labour productivity and changes in land productivity (Rs/ha)

Agro-climatic zone		I	IIa	IIb	III	IV	V	VI	VII	VIII	IX	X	XI	XII	XIII	XIV
I	2001	0														
	2006	0														
	Changes %	0														
II a	2001	6557	0													
	2006	39511	0													
	Changes %	503	0													
II b	2001	7954	1397	0												
	2006	18746	-20765	0												
	Changes %	136	-1587	0												
III	2001	-7335	-13892	-15289	0											
	2006	34575	-4937	15828	0											
	Changes %	-571	-64	-204	0											
IV	2001	-1427	-7984	-9381	5909	0										
	2006	43179	3668	24433	8604	0										
	Changes %	-3126	-146	-360	46	0										
V	2001	-34358	-40915	-42312	-27023	-32931	0									
	2006	3953	-35558	-14793	-30621	-39226	0									
	Changes %	-112	-13	-65	13	19	0									
VI	2001	-14736	-21292	-22689	-7400	-13309	19622	0								
	2006	34537	-4974	15791	-37	-8642	30584	0								
	Changes %	-334	-77	-170	-99	-35	56	0								
VII	2001	16370	9813	8416	23706	17797	50728	31106	0							
	2006	61835	22324	43089	27261	18656	57882	27298	0							
	Changes %	278	127	412	15	5	14	-12	0							
VIII	2001	14203	7646	6249	21538	15630	48561	28938	-2167	0						
	2006	54312	14801	35565	19737	11133	50359	19774	-7523	0						

Changes %	282	94	469	−8	−29	4	−32	247	0					
2001 IX	4433	−2124	−3520	11769	5860	38791	19169	−11937	−9769	0				
2006	55578	16067	36831	21003	12399	51625	21040	−6257	1266	0				
Changes %	1154	−857	−1146	78	112	33	10	−48	−113	0				
2001 X	−14247	−20804	−22200	−6911	−12820	20111	489	−30617	−28449	−18680				
2006	22628	−16883	3882	−11946	−20551	18675	−11909	−39207	−31683	−32949				
Changes %	−259	−19	−117	73	60	−7	−2536	28	11	76	0			
2001 XI	−22339	−28896	−30293	−15004	−20912	12019	−7603	−38709	−36542	−26772	−8092	0		
2006	19082	−20429	336	−15493	−24097	15129	−15455	−42753	−35230	−36496	−3546	0		
Changes %	−185	−29	−101	3	15	26	103	10	−4	36	−56	0		
2001 XII	−15853	−22410	−23807	−8518	−14426	18505	−1118	−32223	−30056	−20287	−1607	6486	0	
2006	32493	−7018	13747	−2082	−10686	28540	−2044	−29342	−21819	−23085	9865	13411	0	
Changes %	−305	−69	−158	−76	−26	54	83	−9	−27	14	−714	107	0	
2001 XIII	−43298	−49855	−51252	−35962	−41871	−8940	−28562	−59668	−57501	−47731	−29051	−20959	−27445	0
2006	9075	−30436	−9672	−25500	−34104	5122	−25463	−52760	−45237	−46503	−13554	−10007	−23418	0
Changes %	−121	−39	−81	−29	−19	−157	−11	−12	−21	−3	−53	−52	−15	0
2001 XIV	20329	13772	12375	27665	21756	54687	35065	3959	6126	15896	34576	42668	36182	63627	0
2006	63886	24375	45140	29312	20707	59933	29349	2051	9575	8309	41258	44804	31393	54812	0
Changes %	214	77	265	6	−5	10	−16	−48	56	−48	19	5	−13	−14	0

(*Continued*)

Table 5.6 (Continued)

Agro-climatic zone		I	IIa	IIb	III	IV	V	VI	VII	VIII	IX	X	XI	XII	XIII	XIV
Labour productivity (Rs/ worker)																
2001	I	0														
2006		0														
Changes %		0														
2001	II a	7187	0													
2006		21266	0													
Changes %		196	0													
2001	II b	16615	9428	0												
2006		16612	-4655	0												
Changes %		0	-149	0												
2001	III	-152	-7339	-16767	0											
2006		10209	-11057	-6403	0											
Changes %		-6800	51	-62	0											
2001	IV	8667	1480	-7948	8819	0										
2006		23470	2204	6858	13261	0										
Changes %		171	49	-186	50	0										
2001	V	-37996	-45183	-54611	-37843	-46663	0									
2006		-24873	-46139	-41484	-35082	-48343	0									
Changes %		-35	2	-24	-7	4	0									
2001	VI	-54909	-62096	-71524	-54757	-63576	-16913	0								
2006		-28930	-50196	-45542	-39139	-52400	-4057	0								
Changes %		-47	-19	-36	-29	-18	-76	0								
2001	VII	18513	11326	1898	18665	9846	56509	73422	0							
2006		32693	11427	16082	22485	9224	57566	61624	0							
Changes %		77	1	747	20	-6	2	-16	0							
2001	VIII	13149	5962	-3466	13301	4482	51145	68058	-5364	0						
2006		18851	-2415	2240	8642	-4619	43724	47781	-13842	0						

Changes %	43	−141	−165	−35	−203	−15	−30	158	0						
2001 IX	3358	−3829	−13257	3510	−5309	41353	58266	−15155	−9791	0					
2006	21363	96	4751	11154	−2107	46235	50293	−11331	2511	0					
Changes %	536	−103	−136	218	−60	12	−14	−25	−126	0					
2001 X	−350	−7537	−16965	−198	−9017	37646	54559	−18863	−13499	−3707	0				
2006	15380	−5886	−1231	5171	−8090	40253	44310	−17313	−3471	−5982	0				
Changes %	−4496	−22	−93	−2718	−10	7	−19	−8	−74	61	0				
2001 XI	176	−7011	−16439	328	−8491	38171	55085	−18337	−12973	−3182	525	0			
2006	13959	−7307	−2653	3750	−9511	38832	42889	−18734	−4892	−7403	−1421	0			
Changes %	7849	4	−84	1043	12	2	−22	2	133	−370	0				
2001 XII	−21524	−28711	−38139	−21372	−30191	16471	33384	−40037	−24882	−21175	−21700	0			
2006	2041	−19225	−14570	−8168	−21429	26914	30971	−30652	−16810	−19321	−13339	−11918	0		
Changes %	−109	−33	−62	−62	−29	63	−7	−23	−52	−45	0				
2001 XIII	590	−6597	−16025	742	−8077	38586	55499	−17923	−12559	−2768	940	414	22114	0	
2006	−7264	−28530	−23875	−17473	−30734	17609	21666	−39957	−26115	−28626	−22644	−21223	−9305	0	
Changes %	−1332	332	49	−2454	281	−54	−61	123	108	934	−5225	−142	0		
2001 XIV	19011	11825	2397	19164	10345	57007	73920	499	5863	15654	19361	18836	40536	18422	0
2006	17960	−3306	1348	7751	−5510	42833	46890	−14734	−891	−3403	2580	4001	15919	25224	0
Changes %	−6	−128	−44	−60	−153	−25	−37	−3055	−115	−87	−79	−61	37	0	

N. B.: Regional gap in productivity is measured by calculating productivity differences between two regions for 2000–01 and 2006–07 as $G_{01} = (R_i - R_{i+1})$, $G_{06} = (R_i - R_{i+1})$ and proportionate Change in regional gaps over time during 2001 to 2006 $= 100(G_{06} - G_{01})/G_{01}$, where G_{01} and G_{06} are regional gap between ith region and next to Region R_i (R_{i+1}) for 2001 and for 2006 respectively.

these emerged as high-productivity regions. However, the rate of increase in labour productivity was recorded higher in Bengal plains than middle Ganga Region that reduced productivity differences between them. Overall, inter-regional differences in land and labour productivity in India is largely driven by the differences in physiographical characteristics (e.g. slope, aspect, relative relief and soil fertility) and agro-climatic conditions (e.g. temperature, rainfall and potential evapotranspiration). However, these inter-regional differences in productivity levels in recent years are accelerated due to the effect of high increase of productivity in low-productivity areas, technological advancement and integrated rural–urban market. Whether these inter-regional differences in land and labour productivity converge or diverge during the Post-Liberalisation phase is yet to be examined.

5.05 Agricultural growth and productivity

Agriculture growth and productivity are often interrelated and interdependent. Nevertheless, this relationship and interdependency could vary in space and time. Vardooren's 'law of inverse relationship between growth and productivity' however explains that the growth often occurs more rapidly in areas of low land productivity. Applying this law in the context of agricultural systems in India, the areas of low productivity, that is, the under-developed agricultural regions of the central India – starting from Rajasthan-Gujarat in the West to Orissa in the East, would be expected to grow much faster than areas of high productivity. An examination of growth patterns of districts by their productivity and the growth trends shows that there are a large number of districts that have exhibited a fit to this hypothesis of high growth rate and low productivity (Figure 5.7). Findings therefore confirm the validity of Vardooren's law of inverse relationship (Table 5.7). This might mean that the low-productivity areas would eventually

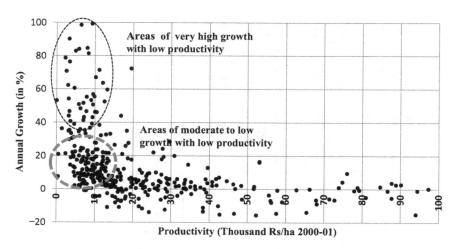

Figure 5.7 Productivity-growth relationship

Table 5.7 Land productivity versus agricultural growth in India

Land productivity 2000–1 (Rs/ha)	Annual growth (%) (2000–1 to 2006–7)							
	Above 10	10-8	8-6	6-4	4-2	2-0	Negative 0-(-2)	Total
Extremely high (above 70,000)	3	1		2	8	6	14	34
Exceptionally high (70,000–60,000)							5	5
Very high (60,000–50,000)	3					1	8	12
High (50,000–40,000)			2	2	4	1	4	13
Medium (40,000–30,000)	3			4	4	7	9	27
Low (30,000–20,000)	6	5	3	8	8	7	12	49
Very low (20,000–10,000)	51	7	10	12	10	7	20	117
Extremely low (10,000–below)	95	7	6	8	7	4	3	130
Total	161	20	21	36	41	33	75	387

be able to catch up with high-performing areas whereby the regional disparities would start to dissipate with the continuation of growth process within a regional economic system.

5.06 Summary

This chapter examined the scale and characteristics of regional variability in land and labour productivity in India. Impacts of production factors like bio-physical properties of farm land, labour involved in farming and capital (in the form of technology) invested in agricultural activities were assessed in terms of their contributions to enhancing agriculture productivity. Since agriculture production processes are linked with market forces, the crop price has become an important factor of land productivity. There has been significant change in land productivity (output per unit of cultivated land). Land productivity levels were first increased in fertile soils of the Great Plains and Coastal Deltaic areas during the Pre-Liberalisation phase and then percolated through to the Himalayan foothills, Mumbai-Ahamdabad Cotton and Groundnut areas of Gujrat and Maharastra and the Meghalaya-Manipur hills of the North Eastern region after the Liberalisation phase. Although the increasing share of output of commercial crops augmented land productivity regional differences before liberalisation, the land intensification and expansion of commercialisation in the other parts of

India such as hill areas of the North East have kept agriculture more productive and market oriented.

Labour productivity (output per person of agriculture work force) is also a vital indicator of agriculture performance and workforce participation. In the condition of an unlimited supply of labour, increasing labour pressure on land increases labour intensity (agriculture workers per unit of cultivated land), which in turn diminishes labour productivity due to increasing labour burden on agricultural practices. Therefore, regional patterns of labour productivity remained unchanged during the Post-Liberalisation phase (2000–1 to 2006–7). The areas of low labour intensity like North Western parts of the Great Plains, Jammu through to Uttrakhand hills of the Western Himalayas and Kathibad-Kuchh of Gujrat have improved productivity levels. Overall, the inter-regional productivity gaps were reduced (10 per cent in land productivity and 6.1 per cent in labour productivity) over time during the Post-Liberalisation period when productivity levels increased in low-productivity areas such as Rajasthan of the West, Himachal and Uttrakhand mountains of the North and most of hill districts of the North East region.

Productivity and growth have shown an inverse relationship whereby the areas of low productivity are those which exhibited higher growth. The districts of foreland Deccan (from Malwa to Chatanagpur through Bundelkhand and Banghalkhand) manifested low productivity–high growth; whilst the districts in North Western parts of Great Plains (most areas of Punjab to Western Uttar Pradesh) and the South Deccan (Madras interior), which had higher level of productivity prior to liberalisation, have shown moderate to low growth in agriculture. These changes in productivity–growth relationship started to reduce regional gaps in productivity levels.

6 Regional convergence in agricultural productivity

6.01 Introduction

This chapter rejuvenates the traditional debates on regional economic development models. Should development be equitably dispersed or should it be concentrated in few high-performing growth areas to achieve high-efficiency standards? Development theorists have created myriad development models to predict the geographic propagation of economic growth process, though none unabled to predict a perfect growth trajectory that would ideally generate an equitable spatial economic system. The concept of growth is also being challenged epistemologically to define its fundamental meaning, scope and theoretical foundation.

The preceding chapter examined the scale of regional disparity in agriculture growth and productivity, which have marginally reduced due to increased productivity levels in low- productivity areas in the Post-Liberalisation phase. Since the agro-ecological conditions of land are largely invariant, would productivity be more likely to respond to technological change or market conditions? Do these centripetal and centrifugal forces cause regional growth dynamics to converge or diverge? Did liberalisation and deregulation of the India economy accelerate greater convergence in growth diffusion in a globalised market place? These debates are, thus, presented in this chapter so as to reignite the regional development arguments to help revisit contemporary development approaches and models to evaluate regional agriculture performance in India.

Most economic development models have focused on industrial or services-led economic growth. Only a few studies have examined agriculture as a catalyst for regional economic growth. Recent globalisation of farming and the emerging importance of the market to shaping agriculture production systems have raised academic interest in examining the relevance of economic development models in the context of globalised agriculture production systems. The diffused and sporadic adoption of farming technology in high-performing areas has indeed contributed to the rapid increase in regional inequality in agriculture productivity. The interspersed spatial markets in rural India have also intensified the embedded agricultural productivity and land use patterns (Visser 1980, 1982).

This chapter, therefore, focuses on the key debates on the impact of economic liberalisation on convergence or divergence processes in India. This chapter begins with the key conceptual debates on regional convergence or divergence as a way of assessing agriculture development. It is followed by methods and techniques that allow measuring its scale and intensity, linking up agricultural productivity with land potential. It concludes with a summary of findings.

6.02 Beta convergence hypothesis – convergence or divergence argument

Traditional regional economic development models such as Rostow's stages of growth, input-output models, growth poles and core-periphery have investigated the regional economic growth dynamics. From a policy perspective, it is important to investigate whether 'an uneven distribution of agriculture growth and productivity is undesirable', or whether 'there should be policy intervention to mitigate the increasing spatial disparity in growth patterns'. Agriculture, if not controlled, regulated and planned, can be spontaneous in response to initial resource endowments. For example, land potential provides competitive advantages to more fertile, productive and high-capacity land, which in turn accelerate growth to occur and concentrate. The relationship between productivity and economic development was examined with the premise that low-productivity areas within the national context eventually catch up with high-productivity areas through spill-over effects of technology, labour or capital.

The relevance of regional growth models is particularly critical for agriculture development as it is an instrument with the potential to permeate agriculture growth in regional and rural areas (Chhetri et al. 2008). Earlier theories in regional science and economic geography were founded on similar premises to those of cluster theory. For example, Perroux (1950) and Friedmann (1966) developed the 'growth pole theory', which is grounded in the diffusionist paradigm, where a growth pole is conceived as a rapidly expanding node of propulsive industry with strong industry linkages to generate multiplier effects and facilitate rapid innovation. The core-periphery model was extended to include regions traversing through a spectrum of economic growth. These regions include: the core, upward transitional and downward transitional regions (further sub-divided into resource frontiers and special problem regions) (Friedmann 1966: 40–44).

Agglomeration economies are achieved when firms benefit from locating near each other. Co-location enable firms to achieve economies of scale and network effects. The intellectual antecedents of agglomeration theory date back at least to 1890–1920 when Alfred Marshall introduced the term 'externalities' of specialised industrial locales. Marshall identified the 'agglomeration externalities', which he explained using four major principles. These include: i) access to specialised labour, ii) access to specialised inputs, iii) access to technology spill-overs and iv) access to greater demand. The agglomeration theory was first documented in 1948 by Hoover, who explained agglomeration as a process of creating space relations and forming a boundary. Such boundaries enable firms to produce spatial linkages that, in turn, generate agglomeration effects. Agglomeration economies also create core-periphery structure where the core represents a city and periphery relates to its hinterland. Interconnectivity and interdependence of core-periphery create a functional region which facilitates the movement of goods, services, technology and labour (Chhetri et al. 2014).

From a theoretical perspective, it questions the fundamental premise of endogenous regional economic growth theories such as those of Friedmann (1966) and Perroux (1950), who have argued that economic growth at a certain point starts to percolate through to less developed areas as the capital/labour and technology becomes more mobile. Myrdal (1957) however contradicts the equilibrium theory and noted the perpetuated polarised regional structure with substantial sustained regional differences in economic growth. Myrdal's (1957) critics also accentuated the strengthening of cores and weakening of periphery through backwash effects, creating a widening gap between rich and poor regions, resulting in increased regional inequality. More recent theories however accepted the significance of agglomeration, and recognised the clustered pattern of economic growth as an inherent characteristic of space economy. The perspective that argues for monopolistic competition and increasing returns, as opposed to constant returns-perfect competition, has gained popularity. This new genre, often referred to as 'New Economic Geography' (NEG), was able to explain where and why employment or economic activities cluster and how growth of economic agglomerations is sustained.

In the global context, the classical work of Bernard and Jones (1995), Blomstrom and Wolff (1989), McCunn and Huffman (1999) and many more conclude that the technological differences and capital accumulation contribute to the convergence in agricultural productivity. This is, however, debatable in the context of India where the diffusion and adoption of farming technology, capital and labour from one region or more is evident across the country. The issue of regional inequality of agricultural productivity levels is of particular importance in the deregulated efficiency-driven argument, which supports the beta-convergence hypothesis to explain the productivity patterns in emerging competitive markets in India.

In a globalised economic world, the economic growth of the under-developed countries has been relatively higher than developed countries. These two ends of the spectrum are transitioning through different changes of economic development, thus they have different growth potential and growth trajectories. The growth is also affected by the diminishing rate of return in developed economies. The tendency of 'catch-up' growth of under-developed countries is more likely to minimise inter-country economic gap. Arguably, all economies should converge in terms of per capita income. In the process of growth, two terms are used: sigma-convergence (or σ-convergence), which refers to a reduction in the dispersion of per capita income over time; and beta-convergence (β-convergence), when the partial correlation between growth in income over time and its initial level is negative (Barro and Sala-i-Martin 1992, Mankiw et al. 1992, and Sala-i-Martin 1996). In other words, β-convergence hypothesis states that the growth rate in per capita income is inversely related to initial level of per capita income.

In the distribution of growth of countries versus per capita income, the income coefficient called beta becomes negative. It is the state of growth convergence. In the context of a country, the inter-state or inter-district variations are examined to measure the dispersion of per capita income. It is a neoclassical growth paradigm that analyses inter-state variability to estimate regional economic growth convergence rate. A statistically significant negative beta-coefficient indicates a high degree of convergence across the country. If the beta-coefficient is significantly positive, it suggests that there is a greater divergence in economic growth in per capita income. Diminishing return of growth is a major operative force behind the process of growth convergence.

Regional convergence is a process through which the gap between the developed and under-developed areas decreases. In other words, poor or deprived regions grow faster than their richer counterparts and the entire nation starts to converge towards a regional parity (Somra and Singh 2010, Thakur 2007). The convergence-divergence hypothesis of income and economic growth relationship was tested in the Indian context by Rao et al. (1999). They conclude that the divergence in per capita income had taken place across the states during the period from 1960–1 to 1994–5 when the economy was in its progressive mode and the main emphasis was the development of the agricultural sector. This means that the differences in inter-state per capita income declined over time till the late 1990s.

While this finding is interesting, it contradicts the findings reported by Mathur (2003), who analysed the GDP statistics of 48 years of data (1950–1 to 1998–9). His study applied coefficient of variation (CV) and computed beta-coefficients for different sectors of the economy over time and concluded that the inter-state variation in the primary sector of the economy (agriculture and allied activities) increased from 33 to 41 per cent after the Green Revolution (1980–1 to 1995–6). High-income states showed signs of convergence while low-income states were in the stage of absolute regional divergence especially during the period from 1960–61 to 1994–95. This means the high-income states converged and low-income states diversified growth with an increasing regional gap in agriculture growth patterns.

A substantial decline in agricultural growth especially in areas of Green Revolution (North Western parts of the country) was noted during the Post-Green Revolution phase of the 1980s. Average annual growth of farm output in Punjab declined quite substantially from 7.91 per cent (during the 1960s and 1970s) to 3.92 per cent (during the 1980s), whilst in Haryana it also reduced from 5.73 per cent to 3.31 per cent. Similarly, Western Uttar Pradesh (Ganga-Jamuna doab and Rohilkhand) experienced a reduction in agriculture output from 5.04 per cent to 3.22 per cent (Bhalla 1988, Thakur 1987).

A pioneer work on regional inequalities in India was undertaken by Mohapatra (1982: 172–218) who found the evidence of increased intra-regional economic inequalities but their (intra-regional) rate of increase is slower than the rate of inter-regional inequalities in agriculture productivity. Studies under the leadership of Moonis Reza (such as Chattopadhyaya and Raza 1975, Raza 1981, Raza and Kundu 1975, Raza et al. 1975) have examined the regional dimensions of economic and agricultural development in India. Their studies have found the significant impact of modern farming techniques such as irrigation and HYV seeds in diversifying farming practices that in turn have resulted in rising regional inequalities in agricultural growth. Other factors such as natural, historical, economic, socio-demographic, institutional and entrepreneurial tend to play a vital role in shaping spatial variability in agriculture performance.

The 'Sasakawa Global 2000' project, which was implemented to strengthen Green Revolution technology in Africa, made it clear that the benefits of Green Revolution technology are under serious doubt. It was found to be less effective in tackling Africa's food crisis (Groniger, undated). The failure of Green Revolution in many countries of the world was also acknowledged and addressed by the Food and Agriculture Organisation (FAO). They suggested the 'Save and Grow' strategy to cope with food insecurity. FAO advocated for practice of 'conservation agriculture' to help retain soil nutritional properties, minimum use of chemical fertiliser, better integration of precision irrigation, pest management and the use of seed-fertiliser technology. The agency also emphasises an 'ecosystem approach' to crop cultivation rather than a 'profit-boost' approach to agriculture development.

Agricultural productivity is often subject to the '*law of diminishing return*' in agriculture growth. Regional convergence of productivity growth is to be viewed in relation to land potential, which is the key driver of regional growth processes. In this context, an agro-ecological model for assessing agricultural production potential was developed to take into account the biophysical parameters of land (Grosjean and Messerli 1988) (Figure 6.1). Planning Commission also realised the importance of land potential mapping, and suggested to integrate agro-ecological and later agro-climatic attributes as a part of agriculture growth strategy for sustainable agriculture practices (Alagh 1989).

Regional convergence of agricultural productivity has five key limitations that underpin the regional convergence hypothesis.

1   Agriculture in India is labour intensive. Farming in India has long been suffering from low productivity, disguised rural unemployment and mass-migration of farm labour to non-farm activities. Further expansion of farming is also limited due to high population pressure on limited cultivable land, which restricts the convergence process.

2   The growth per capita agricultural output is less suitable to test the regional convergence hypothesis in the context of Indian agriculture. Instead, agricultural productivity change over time (that is output per unit cultivated area) is applied, which is a function of land potential.

3   The *economies of agglomeration* as a result of the implementation of liberalisation policies in India had created acute intra-regional variability in agricultural productivity. The economic convergence hypothesis therefore may not be able to produce good results for agricultural productivity change due to an increase in inter-state variation in agricultural growth. Beta-convergence thus may not exhibit (Somasekharan et al. 2011). There is a chance that sigma-convergence (intra-regional dispersion) may underpin the growing Indian regional agriculture economy.

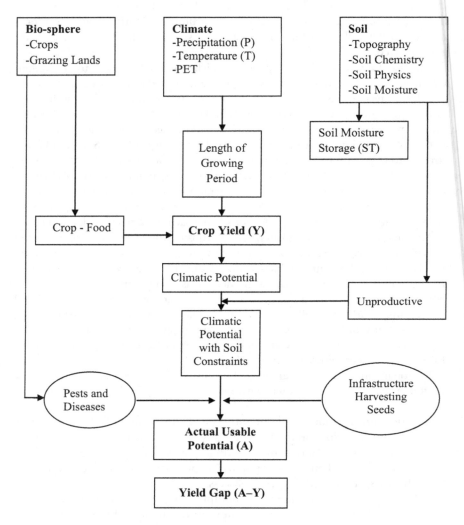

Figure 6.1 Land potential assessment framework

4   Regional inequalities in agricultural productivity in India are a function of land conditions and production potentials. Inter-regional disparities are often examined by adopting the frame of agro-climatic regions, which are homogeneous units with uniform physiographic characteristics.

5   It is assumed that there is no or insignificant change in production potential over a shorter period of time due to the invariant and stable biophysical properties of farm land. Production potential is associated with 'hidden' capacity of land and is assessed by calculating the difference between maximum and existing productivity levels called 'productivity gap' or 'yield gap' (Figure 6.1).

6.03 Potential productivity and productivity gap

The term 'potential productivity' is defined *as the maximum expected crop yield*. It is also referred to as the 'front-line crop yield' by Mathur and Gupta (1985) and Prasad et al. (1987), 'growth potential' by Singh (2007) and 'potential productivity' by Singh (2012). It (in its output term) or potential yield (in physical term) has been an essential parameter to assess 'crop yield-gap', which is the difference between existing yield (Y) and potential yield (A) (Kumar 1986, Varadarajan 1986).

Potential crop yield is implicitly controlled by the biophysical environment of land (e.g. rainfall, temperature, soil type and available soil moisture), also referred to as 'yield stimulating factors'. While on the other hand, technology and use of labour (as inputs, X) increase the crop yield by converting potential yield into actual output. A, Y and X are, therefore, essential parameters to establish the condition of diminishing marginal return to input factors. Therefore, agricultural efficiency (Y/A) is yield-gap dependent rather than technology-dependent (Bhatia 1967). That is, the greater the available production potential (i.e., productivity gap), the higher is its efficient use (agricultural efficiency) and *vice-versa*. Production gaps, thus, increase productivity levels and resource utilisation.

6.03.1 Yield potential function

Agricultural production functions are generally based on two sets of parametric relationships: a set of crop-yield potential, which is dependent on land; and a set of variables which are related to inputs including technology, capital and labour (say X). Most economic models of agriculture production function do not consider land potential as a parameter of agricultural output. Agriculture output is the product of productive capacity of yield potential, which is fundamentally dependent on the biophysical potential of land, termed here as maximum expected yield (A), and potential resistance, which diminishes subject to intensification of yield-enhancing factors.

Modelling of maximum expected crop yield is indeed a matter of debate as it depends upon various disciplinary perspectives. However, soil fertility and agro-ecological factors of land are vital in the measurement of total capacity of land in terms of its level of maximum genetic or expected yield (Prasad et al. 1987). Schemes, such as 'lab to land' programs and 'field trials', were fundamentally developed by the Indian Council of Agriculture Research to identify the key land potential parameters of agriculture productivity.

Theoretically, the size of productivity gap per unit of land $(A - Y)$ is subject to $A > Y$; its proportionate share to actual yield $[(A - Y)/Y]$ that measures the degree of its potential resistance $[(A - Y)/Y]$. It ranges from zero to unity; its higher values mean high resistance (see Figure 6.2). They are the key structural components of productivity potential. Production function $Y(X)$ is, therefore, estimated by considering the productivity gap $(A - Y)$. It is a proportion of variation in yield potential per unit supply/application of yield factor (X) from its maximum level, A/X, to the minimum of $[(A - Y)/X]$ as:

$$(A - Y) = B \left[(A/Y) - \{(A - Y)/X\} \right],$$

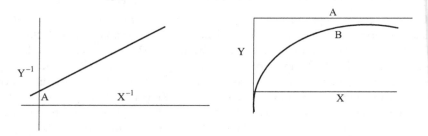

Figure 6.2 Yield function and its forms

where B is proportionality constant that shows maximum response of yield attainable from the use of X. Simplification of algebraic form of above equation for Y^{-1} yields

$$Y^{-1} = A^{-1} + (B/A) X^{-1},$$

and then

$$Y(X) = A [1.00 + B X^{-1}]^{-1} \text{ subject to}$$

1   X and Y are non-negative variables, and
2   A and B are greater than zero and are constants.

The 'unity-constant' attached to the denominator of yield function does not affect Y in its initial phase of input application. At later phases of input intensification when X tends to reach infinity, BX^{-1} becomes very small, then unity constant controls yield curve to be parallel to A. Thus, 'asymptotic divergence' in yield curve may be seen in later phases of intensive production.

Linear form of the function follows 'the reciprocity law of diminishing return to scale' in which parametric ratio (B/A) indicates the rate of change in yield function. Phases of the use of yield potential and enhancement of technology are discussed separately (Singh 2000). More details about the yield speculation through this function have been provided in Singh et al. (2006).

Due to the symptotic divergence in the yield function, the whole process of agricultural productivity is controlled by yield gaps. The validity of beta-convergence hypothesis of productivity increase may be tested with the use of 'productivity gap', *vis-à-vis* 'productivity increase over time' in productivity distribution.

Potential productivity (A), agriculture efficiency (Y/A), productivity gap
(A – Y) and productivity increase (Y06 – Y01): a regional comparison

Most areas of Himalayan foothills, *tarai* areas of moist soils in the Great Plains, and the Deltaic plains of East Coast including Tamil Nadu Interior have exhibited higher agriculture efficiency levels. This is because of the high potential productivity in areas of high land potentials, except for a few patches in the North Eastern region (Figure 6.3 A and B). Potential productivity of land is high in most of the humid *tarai* longitudinal belt located between foothills of Arunachal Himalayas and Brahmaputra River (Northern plains of Upper Assam), narrow plains of Surma Valley between Meghalaya plateau and Lusai hills and subsiding Himalayan hills and mountainous areas of Mizoram due to favourable biophysical conditions. Nevertheless, its agriculture efficiency is low as the land is not efficiently utilised to its full potential. This could be partly due to traditional methods employed for Rice cultivation, but it is yet to be proven through reliable crop statistics.

In this context, some of the key arguments are tested to establish relationships between productivity increase and the contextual factors. As shown in Figure 6.4, productivity gap tends to decrease with productivity increase, which further shows that the areas of higher productivity increase are often those which have lower productivity gaps. It suggests that the actual production is almost achieved in terms of land potential. Areas of Rajasthan, hills of the North Eastern region and foothills of the Western Himalayas are good examples of very high increase in productivity during the Post-Liberalisation phase (Figure 6.4).

If the efficient use of potential productivity of land (or yield) and yield gaps are examined for each of the crops, Wheat reported the lowest yield gap (755 kg/ha), which indicates the most efficient use of land potential. Likewise, potential crop yields of Sugarcane, Jute and Moong are also used efficiently (Table 6.1). These crops also have high-productivity levels and are cultivated in well-developed parts of India. Groundnut-growing areas of Gujarat, Onion- producing areas of interior Maharashtra, Wheat-producing states of Punjab and Haryana and Jute-growing areas of West Bengal have reached the level of high crop productivity. This is because of lower yield gaps. Yield of pulses is yet to harness the potential productivity of land in areas of current practice. The land potentials for these crops are underutilised, which shows the opportunity for further growth. Despite the greater emphasis on high value commercial crops, the area-specific yield strategy of pulses has yet to be successfully implemented.

If the districts are ordered and ranked according to the values of potential productivity (A) and existing productivity (Y), few areas have very high level of potential productivity, which is illustrated through the concave shaped curve. It indicates the distribution by rank, in a decreasing order of size. There is a large variability in productivity levels in areas where the potential productivity is high. Productivity gaps are large in areas of high and moderate levels of potential productivity (Figure 6.5). Productivity gaps also diminish as the level of potential productivity reduces.

There are studies that have explained the reasons for high variability in areas of high potential yield. This might be attributed to the variegated use of technology. Large farm operators have the capacity and resources to increase the intensity of technology use to optimise their crop output. Size of landholdings, socio-economic conditions and adoption of new farm technologies are the most notable factors affecting agricultural productivity levels in high potential productivity areas. Farmers with high income elasticity and better connectivity to market within the close vicinity of urban centres are able to enhance high potential yield

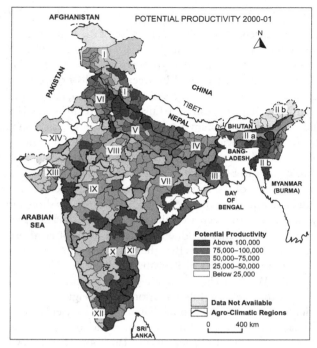

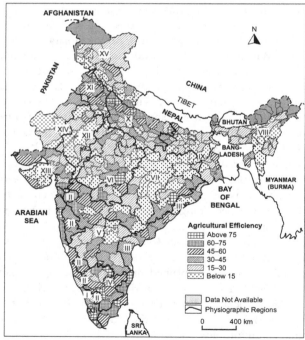

Figure 6.3 Potential productivity (A in Rs/ha) and agricultural efficiency (Y/A in percent) in 2000–01

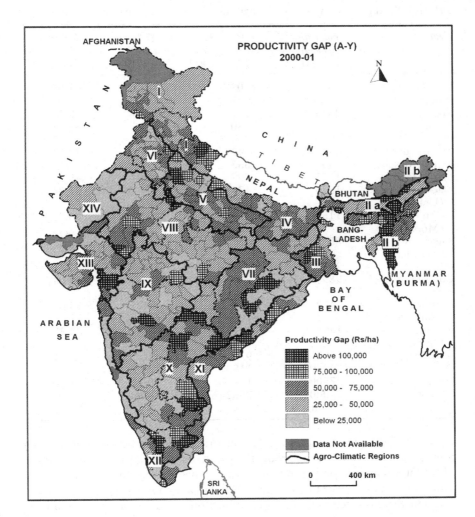

Figure 6.4 Productivity gaps (A – Y)

and productivity levels (Bhalla and Tyagi 1989). To conclude, the areas which have high land potential tend to increase efficiency in farming while boosting productivity through reducing productivity gap (i.e., efficient use of hidden capacity of land).

6.04 Intra-regional convergence

Inter- or intra-regional convergence/divergence is subject to two forces: centrifugal and centrifugal forces. There are forces, often referred to as centripetal forces, which minimise inter-regional gaps in agriculture productivity over time. Whilst other forces, called centripital forces, tend to exacerbate the divergence of

Table 6.1 Yield gap (A – Y) and its efficient use (Y/A) of principal crops in India

Crops	Potential yield (A) (kg/ha)	Average actual yield (Y) (kg/ha)	Yield gaps (A–Y) (kg/ha)	Efficient use of potential (Y/A) (%)
Rice	4891	2037	2854	41.65
Wheat	3429	2674	755	77.98
Maize	4554	1921	2633	42.18
Jowar	2435	780	1655	32.03
Bajra	1928	844	1084	43.77
Arhar (Tur)	1469	642	827	43.7
Lentil (Masoor)	1448	653	795	45.1
Bengal Gram	1771	797	974	45
Black Gram (Urad)	1375	431	944	31.34
Green Gram (Moong)	1151	354	797	30.75
Sugarcane (tons/ha)	85	65	20	76.47
Jute	2678	2215	463	82.71
Cotton (kg lint/ha)	989	396	593	40.04
Sunflower	1472	524	948	35.6
Groundnut	1690	1036	654	61.3
Rapeseed and Mustard	1298	1043	255	80.35
Soya Bean	1592	976	616	61.31
Onion	32289	11830	20459	36.64
Potato	27500	17453	10047	63.46
Coconut	27000 (nuts/ha)	7032 (nuts/ha)	19968	26.05

areas and create greater separation between rich and poor areas. Inter-regional convergence occurs when the productivity differences between regions diminish whilst intra-regional convergence is the state when the productivity differences within the region reduce to create greater internal homogeneity.

Productivity is often assumed to be a function of agro-ecological conditions, which determine the production capacity of land for farming. Regional analysis of agriculture productivity, therefore, should measure spatial variability in production potential. Intra-regional productivity variation is also vital to the development of regional structure of agriculture as it minimises internal variability within agro-climatic region. The agricultural productivity gap between its maximum expected and actual levels (A–Y) is used as a surrogate measure to represent the process of regional growth convergence.

Sigma-convergence is a concept that shows how intensive use of technology (or input) influences and reduces the unevenness of productivity within the region over a period of time. The sigma-convergence hypothesis can be tested through changes in the coefficient of variation and range of productivity distribution over time, which shows the levels of dispersion. Increased use of modern

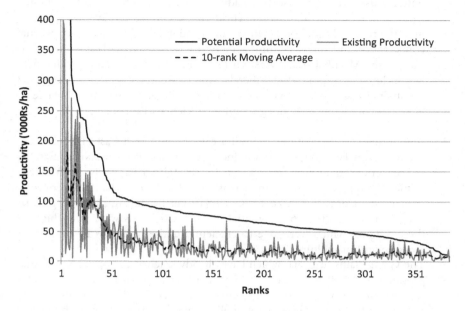

Figure 6.5 Trends of potential and existing productivity ordered by district rank

farm technology enhances crop yield per unit of land and, thus, increased output levels, but increases the degree of unevenness in productivity pattern (Singh and Sharma 2007). However, this hypothesis is yet to be tested in terms of agricultural productivity levels in India. It is particularly vital to evaluate the impact of Liberalisation policies in creating regional inequality in aggregated farm outputs across a geographic space. A statistical analysis has been carried out on regional productivity data and the following observations are derived.

1   There is evidence of regional restructuring of agriculture as a consequence of market-oriented reforms in the Liberalisation phase in the 1990s. For example, the land productivity in most parts of the Great Plains of India has increased along with decreased variability within the agro-climatic regions. It is inferred from the decline in coefficient of variation. An exception is North-East Assam, where the variability within the region has increased significantly.

In the Greater Ganga plains, which extend from the lower plains of Kolkata hinterland to upper parts of Uttar Pradesh plains, the regional variability decreased to a great extent. Although, a region of low urbanisation but marked by the rapid growth of new emerging towns in rural areas during the time of economic liberalisation might be linked to increase uniformity in productivity levels. These market towns acted as catalysts in diffusing new farm technology (i.e., irrigation equipment and seed-fertilisers) to their

hinterlands. They also absorbed additional farm labour in non-farm industries in rural or peri-urban areas. These centripetal forces have helped minimise the regional variation in agriculture productivity, thus creating regional
convergence and internal homogeneity. Even in metropolitan hinterlands
such as the Mumbai-based Western Plateau region where land productivity
has declined during the Post-Liberalisation phase, the coefficient of regional
variability in land productivity significantly declined from 95 to 37 per cent,
but at the moderate level of agricultural efficiency (Table 6.2).

2   Agricultural productivity in the hill areas of the North East (IIb) and the
Western Himalayan region has also increased in relative terms. North Eastern
hills experienced an increase of about Rs 35,108 per ha, whilst the Western
Himalayan region witnessed an increase of Rs 48,071 per ha (211 per cent).
It increased from Rs 22,778 to Rs 70,849 per ha during the high growth
period in India (2001–6). Potential productivity levels were fairly high in
these regions, which were able to efficiently utilise resources by expanding
areas under horticulture crops.

3   The Great Plains of India, which have already reached the optimal potential
productivity levels through the efficient use of modern technologies, have
reported very low increase in agricultural productivity. The changes in average productivity levels however spatially vary from 20 per cent in the Lower
Ganga plains (III) to – 3.2 per cent in the Punjab plains during the seven
years from 2000–01 to 2006–07. Growing urban economies in metropolitan cities might have contributed in slowing down the rate of productivity
increase. This might be attributed *firstly* to rural labour migrating to the
growing number of new towns; *secondly* to the shift in resources from agriculture to allied activities, which marginalised the rate of agricultural productivity increase at farm; and *thirdly* to the saturation of the maximum land
potential by reaching the biophysical limit to growth (Table 6.2).

4   In the Western Coastal region and Gujarat plains (Regions XII and XIII),
productivity change is marginal or even negative in some instances. These
regions have harnessed the full potential productivity. The agricultural efficiency has also exceeded above 50 per cent, which shows the areas exhibiting
the diminishing marginal returns. In the dry Thar region (XIV), the productivity levels have rapidly increased (184 per cent) from a low of Rs 2,449 to
Rs 6,977 per ha. There is also a reduction in the degree of unevenness in its
distribution (CV = -38 per cent) during the seven years of increased growth.

5   The Southern Plateau region (including interior Tamil Nadu, Karnataka and
South Andhra plateau) however has a different growth pattern where agricultural productivity increase was relatively moderate (43.7 per cent). The
region exhausted 33 per cent of its production potential. But there is an
increase in the level of regional variability (difference of CV = 50 percent).
In spite of the rapid urban growth of Bengaluru, Hyderabad and Chennai,
there is slower growth in the number and size of rural towns, which might
have resulted in stagnation in productivity increase.

Table 6.2 Statistical analysis of intra-regional dimensions of land productivity in different agro-climatic zones

| | | Land productivity (Rs./ha) (Y) | | Productivity change | | Crop intensity 2006–7 | Potential productivity (A) | Productivity gap (A – Y) | Ag efficiency (Y/A) |
		2000–1	2006–7	Total	%	%	(Rs./ha)	(Rs./ha)	%
I	**Western Himalaya (N = 34)**								
	Min	5552	17018	11466	206.52	100	36085	27955	6.89
	Max	271321	791547	520226	191.74	206.5	308475	101465	87.96
	Range	265769	774529	508761	191.43	107	272390	73510	81
	Mean	22778	70849	48071	211.04	143.43	75277	52499	30.26
	SD	47425	132194	84769	178.74	35.89	48214	16534	18.2
	CV %	208	187	–22	–10.38	25.02	64	31	60.15
IIa	**North East – Assam Plains (N = 11)**								
	Min	7089	10039	2950	41.61	0	54437	43117	1.24
	Max	30969	117485	86516	279.36	196.11	767683	754494	33.45
	Range	23880	107446	83566	349.95	196	713246	711377	32
	Mean	16221	31338	15116	93.19	133.68	224060	207839	7.24
	SD	7066	30235	23169	327.88	50.87	264070	266900	11.44
	CV %	44	96	53	121.48	38.05	118	128	158.01
IIb	**North East – Hills and Mts (N = 30)**								
	Min	7402	8132	730	9.87	0	12000	3585	2.12
	Max	30858	104675	73817	239.22	158.74	701080	686201	70.73
	Range	23456	96543	73087	311.59	159	689080	682616	69
	Mean	16155	51262	35108	217.32	62.51	155544	139389	10.39
	SD	7026	26849	19822	282.11	64.67	211192	209159	20.14
	CV %	43	52	9	20.42	103.45	136	150	193.9
III	**Lower Ganga Plains (N = 12)**								
	Min	13180	24031	10851	82.33	115.68	77531	42688	8.81
	Max	48380	49539	1159	2.4	242.96	235068	214358	51.02
	Range	35200	25508	–9691	–27.53	127	157537	171670	42
	Mean	30114	36274	6161	20.46	188.25	105574	75461	28.52

(Continued)

Table 6.2 (Continued)

	Land productivity (Rs/ha) (Y)		Productivity change		Crop intensity 2006–7	Potential productivity (A)	Productivity gap (A − Y)	Ag efficiency (Y/A)
	2000–1	2006–7	Total	%	%	(Rs/ha)	(Rs/ha)	%
SD	10800	8670	−2130	−19.72	37.37	42122	45781	13.32
CV %	36	24	−12	−33.36	19.85	40	61	46.69
IV Middle Ganga Plains (N = 30)								
Min	7350	11102	3752	51.05	110.51	52375	12923	9.85
Max	146100	165466	19366	13.26	165.24	234243	88143	85.11
Range	138751	154364	15614	11.25	55	181868	75220	75
Mean	24205	27670	3465	14.31	138.94	79146	54941	30.58
SD	28269	29773	1504	5.32	15.03	32179	13725	17.74
CV %	117	108	−9	−7.87	10.81	41	25	58.01
V Upper Ganga Plains (N = 39)								
Min	8764	15384	6620	75.53	118.01	47838	16233	13.13
Max	301396	355669	54273	18.01	189.24	465600	204689	93.92
Range	292632	340285	47654	16.28	71	417761	188457	81
Mean	57136	66896	9760	17.08	156.08	120527	63390	47.41
SD	70507	82608	12101	17.16	15.52	86768	36134	20.28
CV %	123	123	0	0.07	9.95	72	57	42.78
VI Punjab Plains (N = 25)								
Min	3119	11593	8474	271.73	112.92	34642	4014	5.58
Max	108649	114236	5587	5.14	202.55	191560	82911	94.44
Range	105530	102643	−2887	−2.74	90	156918	78897	89
Mean	37514	36311	−1202	−3.21	178.6	83280	45766	45.05
SD	22160	20478	−1682	−7.59	20.6	30251	18696	18.88
CV %	59	56	−3	−4.53	11.53	36	41	41.92

VII	**Eastern Plateau (N = 25)**								
	Min	3089	4476	1387	44.91	101.26	12991	2807	2.75
	Max	24257	17540	-6717	-27.69	168.05	215685	209754	81.85
	Range	21168	13064	-8104	-38.28	67	202695	206947	79
	Mean	6408	9014	2606	40.66	129.28	57530	51122	11.14
	SD	4335	2669	-1665	-38.42	21.24	45681	46187	18.77
	CV %	68	30	-38	-56.22	16.43	79	90	168.53
VIII	**Central Plateau (N = 48)**								
	Min	1042	6382	5340	512.37	107.46	12578	4737	1.65
	Max	21499	49000	27501	127.92	165.03	297753	292853	80.53
	Range	20456	42618	22162	108.34	58	285175	288116	79
	Mean	8575	17198	8622	100.54	136.63	56439	47863	15.19
	SD	4377	7307	2930	66.93	13.82	41618	42271	15.58
	CV %	51	42	-9	-16.76	10.12	74	88	102.53
IX	**Western Plateau (N = 33)**								
	Min	3151	5689	2538	80.52	88.07	25156	8269	9.26
	Max	94019	28729	-65289	-69.44	177.15	165166	132594	73.59
	Range	90867	23041	-67827	-74.64	89	140010	124325	64
	Mean	18345	15271	-3074	-16.76	126.65	57117	38772	32.12
	SD	17515	5642	-11872	-67.78	24.62	30944	23287	18.46
	CV %	95	37	-59	-61.3	19.44	54	60	57.47
X	**Southern Plateau (N = 39)**								
	Min	7305	5282	-2022	-27.69	0	25000	4049	5.93
	Max	230191	528219	298027	129.47	161.51	462713	435265	90.76
	Range	222887	522936	300050	134.62	162	437713	431216	85
	Mean	38179	54862	16683	43.7	114.97	114099	75920	33.46
	SD	44648	91460	46812	104.85	23.43	106362	93069	22.49
	CV %	117	167	50	42.56	20.38	93	123	67.2
XI	**East Coast (N = 20)**								
	Min	6126	7753	1627	26.55	100.91	17527	7743	7.86
	Max	143427	145302	1876	1.31	187.37	285175	187853	89.51

(*Continued*)

Table 6.2 (Continued)

	Land productivity (Rs/ha) (Y)		Productivity change		Crop intensity 2006–7	Potential productivity (A)	Productivity gap (A – Y)	Ag efficiency (Y/A)
	2000–1	2006–7	Total	%	%	(Rs/ha)	(Rs/ha)	%
Range	137301	137550	249	0.18	86	267648	180111	82
Mean	45117	51767	6649	14.74	139.58	102646	57529	43.95
SD	35990	39079	3088	8.58	28.57	62336	40171	22.32
CV %	80	75	–4	–5.37	20.47	61	70	50.79
XII West Coast (N = 17)								
Min	15378	18400	3022	19.65	84.87	26806	1914	25.07
Max	125055	135493	10438	8.35	185.99	195684	88575	94.67
Range	109677	117092	7415	6.76	101	168878	86661	70
Mean	38632	38356	–276	–0.71	128.94	72158	33526	53.54
SD	26650	29868	3218	12.08	25.65	46102	28524	22.93
CV %	69	78	9	12.88	19.89	64	85	42.83
XIII The Gujarat (N = 20)								
Min	2217	11576	9358	422.05	107.23	24125	8150	4.09
Max	549003	369961	–179041	–32.61	144.2	557152	185039	98.54
Range	546785	358386	–188399	–34.46	37	533027	176889	94
Mean	66076	61774	–4302	–6.51	120.67	117751	51674	56.12
SD	143794	89739	–54056	–37.59	11.84	159304	44444	26.27
CV %	218	145	–72	–33.25	9.81	135	86	46.82
XIV Western Dry Thar (N = 4)								
Min	1366	3430	2065	151.17	105.97	8248	6882	8.34
Max	3582	10447	6865	191.66	115.21	30105	27593	25.18
Range	2216	7017	4801	216.61	9	21857	20711	17
Mean	2449	6963	4513	184.29	110.69	19125	16676	12.81
SD	908	2977	2069	227.85	3.9	9761	9584	7.69
CV %	37	43	6	15.32	3.53	51	57	60.09
XV The Islands	—	—	—	—	—	—	—	—

6.05 Regional convergence or divergence in productivity increase

A 'regional fixed effects' model which traces the effect of land potential on productivity change within the fixed agro-climatic conditions of each region is applied to examine the regional convergence in agricultural productivity. The key assumption is that the larger the productivity gap (Ai–Pi) between productivity potential and actual productivity (the term Pi is used for existing productivity hereafter instead of Y), the greater is the magnitude of productivity increase $(P_{06}-P_{01})$. It has been written in the form of natural logarithmic system because of asymptotic divergence of the use of potential land productivity as described in section 6.03. The real form of relationship is written as

$$\ln Pi_{06} - \ln Pi_{01} = \acute{\alpha} + \beta \ (\ln Ai - \ln Pi) + ei \quad \ldots \quad \ldots \qquad \ldots (6.1)$$

There are three parameters in the above equation, which show the effects of land potential and technology on productivity increase. They are:

1   $\acute{\alpha}$ shows the origin of productivity increase when $\acute{\alpha} = 0$, there is no effect of production potentials ($\ln Ai - \ln Pi$) or technology. If $\acute{\alpha}$ is positive, the effect of technological and anthropogenic factors is significant; while a negative $\acute{\alpha}$ shows no technological effects but production potentials determine production increase. The higher the value of positive $\acute{\alpha}$, the greater is the effect of technological factors and *vice versa*.
2   β indicates the rate of productivity increase subject to the use of land potential. The higher value of β coefficient indicates the effect of potential productivity factors on productivity increase.
3   Term ei shows the standard error in the distribution of productivity increase. It shows its degree of unevenness. Higher values of ei mean greater the degree of unevenness, which represents increased divergence in productivity increase. Lower ei values, on the other land, show regional convergence.

The results show that there are many agro-climatic regions, which display substantial spatial variability in productivity increase. There are two types of group that show distinct patterns of productivity increase. The *first* group includes regions which have made exhaustive use of land potential. It includes the entire Indo-Gangetic and Coastal plains, which converged at a lower level of productivity increase. The *second* group of regions incorporates hills and mountains as displayed at the North-East corner of graph, which forms a dispersed pattern indicating divergence in productivity increase subject to rapid use of productivity gaps (Figure 6.6). Productivity increase has diverged at a rate of 0.631 times with the use of per unit of land potentials in India as a whole. Regional convergence is displayed in detail by calculating beta-coefficients for each region (Table 6.3).

The rate of productivity increase has been relatively high ($\beta = 1.0816$) in the Mumbai-based Western Plateau Region (IX). Farm productivity is well aligned with land potential, thus farmers, upon saturating the land potential, started to change cropping patterns and seeking additional income from other forms of employment. Consequently, areas within this region have high divergence levels (SE = 0.1788 at 1 percent significance level). On the other hand, the apple gardening in the Western Himalayan Region and vegetable farming in lesser Himalayas have also exhibited regional divergence with further increment in the rate of productivity increase, although with limited use of farm technology.

High productivity increases in the North Eastern Hills Region (IIb) is achieved by harnessing the full land potentials with an intensive use of modern horticulture techniques, especially on the valley slopes. Technology-driven commercial crop farming has positive effects on land productivity in Rice-dominated Assam plains in the North East (IIa), which in turn reduces the gap between developed and under-developed areas. This shows a tendency towards regional convergence in productivity increase within the broader region.

More fertile parts of Dry Thar (XIV) and Gujarat (XIII) have both shown productivity increases. Farmers in Gujarat have maximised land potential to increase the rate of productivity (β = 0.779) though with limited application of modern technologies. While in the Dry Thar Region, farmers have widely used seed-fertiliser technology to increase the rate of productivity increase but without considering the need for crop diversification.

The Punjab plains of India (VI) has experienced a high rate of productivity increase (β = .64631) with intensive use of farm technology. Rapid growth of non-agricultural and allied farm activities and the emergence of rural growth centres have driven the productivity in this region. It is also the home of the Green Revolution, which also propelled regional growth throughout the region. Contrary to it, the use of land potentials (called productivity gap) and increased intensity of labour use have helped expedite the processes of productivity increase in Lower Ganga plains (III) as indicated by a β coefficient of 0.207 (Table 6.3). Intensive Rice and vegetable cultivation and the growing allied farm activities such as poultry and fishery added to agricultural productivity increase in the Kolkata region.

The inter-regional variability in India has resulted in an outward flow of farm technology from high-performing regions such as Punjab-Haryana to highly fertile lower Ganges of Bihar-Bengal. This spatial diffusion of farm innovation started to spill over from early adopters of technology to areas that lagged behind. There is also a phenomenon of inverse flow of unskilled farm labour from Bihar and Eastern Uttar Pradesh to Punjab and Haryana. Wheat farming in the Northern Plain has been mechanised while the paddy-growing areas of Bengal and Bihar still remain labour intensive for undertaking manual paddy transplantation, weeding and harvesting of crops. This inter-regional flow of labour and technology might minimise inter-regional disparities in productivity increase to enable regional convergence of economic systems to occur in the Great Plains of India.

In the context of the beta-convergence model, the findings show mixed results, which indicate the absence of a single dominating spatial pattern in Indian agriculture systems. Productivity increase has accelerated in regions which were capable of harnessing the land potential (productivity gap). A significant beta-divergence

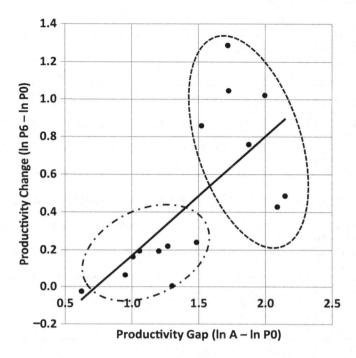

Figure 6.6 Productivity change (2000–1 to 2005–6) versus productivity gaps

Table 6.3 Analysis of productivity increase regressed against productivity gap for different agro-climatic regions

	Agro-climatic region	Parameters					
		ά	β	R	R²	SE (e)	t-Value
I	Western Himalaya (N = 34)	–0.17143	0.84853	0.51789	0.26821	0.24777	3.42469*
IIa	North East – Assam Plains (N = 11)	0.64879	–0.07576	0.17292	0.0299	0.14383	–0.52671
IIb	North East – Hills and Mts (N = 30)	0.77851	0.15525	0.26509	0.07027	0.10672	1.45476**
III	Lower Ganga Plains (N = 12)	–0.0425	0.20728	0.4888	0.23893	0.11699	1.77182
IV	Middle Ganga Plains (N = 30)	–0.65057	0.59994	0.67905	0.46111	0.12257	4.89477*
V	Upper Ganga Plains (N = 39)	0.01241	0.17201	0.55775	0.31109	0.04208	4.08754*

(*Continued*)

Table 6.3 (Continued)

	Agro-climatic region	Parameters					
		ά	β	R	R²	SE (e)	t-Value
VI	Punjab Plains (N = 25)	−0.55107	0.64631	0.74101	0.5491	0.12212	5.29232*
VII	Eastern Plateau (N = 25)	−0.05636	0.23183	0.43132	0.18604	0.10111	2.29277**
VIII	Central Plateau (N = 48)	0.10261	0.3501	0.5924	0.35094	0.0702	4.98712*
IX	Western Plateau (N = 33)	−1.40162	1.0816	0.73578	0.54138	0.1788	6.04929*
X	Southern Plateau (N = 39)	−0.02531	0.18247	0.23509	0.05527	0.12403	1.47122
XI	East Coast (N = 20)	−0.12497	0.28596	0.50366	0.25367	0.11561	2.4735**
XII	West Coast (N = 17)	−0.15252	0.20416	0.20769	0.04313	0.24828	0.8223
XIII	The Gujarat (N = 20)	−0.32801	0.77958	0.79929	0.63886	0.13815	5.64291*
XIV	Western Dry Thar (N = 4)	0.94685	0.03777	0.17224	0.02967	0.15276	0.24727
XV	The Islands	–	–	–	–	–	

N.B.: *significant at 1 percent and ** significant at 5 percent

value (63 per cent) indicates a satisfactory performance of productivity increase. The regions located in the Western Himalayan Highlands and North Eastern Hill areas accelerated the rate of productivity increase relative to the other regions. The difference in the rate of productivity increase in hills and mountain regions is more than Rs 25,000/ha. In contrast, the lowest difference in productivity increase (below Rs 5000/ha) is noted in the Greater Plains (lower, middle and upper Ganges Valley areas, III, IV and V) and the Foreland Deccan (Eastern and Central Plateau regions, VII and VIII).

The highest rate of regional convergence occurs in regions between the Middle Ganga and Eastern Plateau regions where a minimum difference of Rs 859/ha in productivity increase was calculated (Table 6.4). It shows the potential effect of spatial contiguity and regional convergence when productivity of Jharkhand and Madhya Pradesh were increased through transferring agricultural technology from the nearby Ganga Plains of intensive cultivation to the hilly areas of the Eastern Plateau. Further, Punjab and Western Uttar Pradesh Plain also have a minimum gap in the rate of productivity increase during the Post-Liberalisation phase (Below Rs 5000/ha) compared to the Dry Thar Region (XIV). It might mean a possible transfer of farm technology and innovation from the Punjab-Haryana plains to the nearby Thar areas in dry Rajasthan. It shows the spatial spill-over and proximity effects of high-performing regions to spatially contiguous regions of lower productivity. Productivity growth started to converge in these high-productivity regions.

6.06 Conditions for productivity increase

Agriculture productivity is also subject to technological intensification (reflected in crop intensity) and the construction of rural infrastructure such as rural roads and market facilities. The farming practices and technological adoption in India have the following changes in the production system.

1 Farming in India is largely operated on small landholdings by resource-poor farmers. They are about two-thirds of total farms and contribute one-third of total agriculture production (Randhawa and Sundaram 1990). Farm-size is a key determinant of cropping pattern, crop yield, technology use and commercialisation. Most farms have a high proportion of land allocated to the production of food grains. A large portion of total food production is usually consumed domestically. Short of market surplus and small-scale sub-sistence farming in India put farmers under high uncertainty of weather and increased risk of output price fluctuation (Sundaram 2007).

Punjab and Haryana implemented land reforms such as a land-consolidation scheme (locally called *Chak-bandi*) in the Pre-Green Revolution period, which has proven to help increase farm operational efficiency and productivity per unit of land. This became a key catalyst for the Green Revolution in the 1970s. Despite the rapid growth in farm production, there were notable inequalities in farm income even within the high-performing regions in India.

The size of landholding is a key determinant of regional disparity in land produc-tivity and farm income. Increasing landholding size tends to increase the share of farm income and improve land productivity. More than 50 per cent of landholdings are of medium size (3–8 ha) in Punjab, which accounts for more than 60 per cent of total Net Sown Area. It is economical for farmers to use agricultural technology due to the scale economies. In contrast, three-fourths of the landholdings (about 76.65 per cent) are of marginal (less than 1.0 ha) size in Bihar.

Farmers are neither able to use modern farm machines nor commercialise farming. Resource utilisation in India is therefore strained due to high popula-tion pressure per unit of land, which poses insurmountable challenges for the agriculture-dominated Indian economy. A very small percentage of farmers have landholdings of large size (above 8 ha), which allows them to commercialise farming to generate food surplus for the market (Table 6.5). Thus, the benefits of market reforms are confined to bigger farmers. They therefore have the com-petitive advantage and are first to innovate. This inequitable land distribution will further accelerate economic inequality with the rising population pressure on limited cultivable land under a rigid lineage system of inheritance, which leads to sub-division of land. This creates circularity effects and the vicious circle of economic disadvantage for farmers operating on small and medium-sized farms.

2 Increased population pressure in India since the Independence has exerted further stress on farmers to increase food production per unit of land or input. An annual average of 2.11 per cent was added to country's population,

Table 6.4 Inter-regional differences in the speed of productivity increase during the Post- Liberalisation period of fast-economic growth (2000–1 to 2006–7) (figures in Rs/ha)

	I	IIa	IIb	III	IV	V	VI	VII	VIII	IX	X	XI	XII	XIII	XIV	XV
I	0	32954	12963	41910	44606	38311	49273	45465	39448	51144	31388	41421	48346	52373	43557	–
IIa		0	-19991	8956	11652	5357	16319	12511	6494	18190	-1566	8467	15392	19418	10603	–
IIb			0	28947	31643	25348	36310	32502	26486	38182	18425	28458	35383	39410	30594	–
III				0	2696	-3599	7363	3555	-2462	9234	-10522	-489	6436	10463	1647	–
IV					0	-6295	4667	859	-5157	6538	-13218	-3185	3740	7767	-1049	–
V						0	10962	7154	1137	12833	-6923	3110	10035	14062	5246	–
VI							0	-3808	-9824	1871	-17885	-7852	-927	3100	-5716	–
VII								0	-6017	5679	-14077	-4044	2881	6908	-1908	–
VIII									0	11696	-8061	1973	8898	12924	4109	–
IX										0	-19757	-9723	-2798	1228	-7587	–
X											0	10033	16958	20985	12169	–
XI												0	6925	10952	2136	–
XII													0	4026	-4789	–
XIII														0	-8815	–
XIV															0	–
XV																0

Categories of Inter Regional Productivity Deferential: 1. extremely large regional gap (above Rs. 40, 000/ha) Western Himalayan Region; 2. Large regional gap (Rs. 40000–25000/ha) North-Eastern Hill Region; 3. Moderate Regional gap (Rs. 25000–10000/ha); 4. Marginal Regional Gap (Rs. 10000–5000/ha); 5. Low Gaps (Below Rs. 5000/ha)

Nomenclature: I = Western Himalaya, IIa = North East- Assam Plains, IIb = North East- Hills and Mrts, III = Lower Ganga plains, IV = Middle Ganga plains, V = Upper Ganga plains, VI = Punjab plains, VII = Eastern Plateau, VIII = Central Plateau, IX = Western Plateau, X = Souther Plateau, XI = East Coast, XII = West Coast, XIII = The Gujarat, XIV = Western Dry Thar; XV = The Islands which resulted in an increase of 169 million from 849 to 1,210 million during the 1990s and 2000s (1991–2011). About 83 million of the total population lived in rural areas in 2011.

Despite the rapid population growth in the Post-Independence era, there has been a net decrease in the total main agricultural work force. It declined from 185 (1991) to 167 million (2001) and then to 104.46 million (2011). Outward rural-to-urban migration of labour force has caused a substantial decrease in the agricultural labourer/cultivator ratio, which decreased from 0.67 to 0.61 during the 1990s. Uneconomical farming on small pieces of land with the use of traditional and rudimentary farming methods force a large number of landless and marginal farmers to migrate to urban areas for work. These unskilled workers were largely employed in the informal sectors of urban labour market. It added to the swelling pool of urban poor, which were concentrated in large metropolitan cities in India.

3   Traditional means of farming are yet to be modernised in India. Most farming methods are still rudimentary and inefficient. However, there has been a 24 per cent decline in the number of wooden and iron ploughs and in animal-drawn carts. The use of tractors and diesel/electric pump sets increased by 31 per cent and 58 per cent respectively during the Liberalisation phase (1990–1 to 2006–7). Net irrigated area also increased (22.58 per cent), as did the use of fertiliser (62.12 per cent) in this period. These changes have not strongly responded to government policies, which promoted the greater use of technology adoption. Average crop yield increased by 27.54 per cent with an increase of 43.57 per cent in the index of non-food grain production. However, the average yield of food grains and commercial crops in India is still much lower than that of China, which has intensified the use of technology while having similar land and labour conditions (Table 6.6).

4   Expansion of education and adoption of new communication systems are commonly accepted antecedents of high agricultural productivity. Literacy rate in rural India (based on NSS 55th and 64th round) was 56 per cent, which increased to 67 per cent during the Post-Liberalisation phase (1999–2000 to 2007–8). Rural female literacy rate however remained relatively higher (50.38 per cent) than rural male literacy (34.22 per cent) according to the 2011 Census. The lowest rural literacy rate (42 per cent) was recorded in Bihar and the highest (91 per cent) in Mizoram in 1999–2000 as per data collected by NSS. Bihar is still lagging behind in literacy. The state had a 56 per cent literacy rate with very low Gross Enrolment Ratio (19.9 per cent) at secondary and higher secondary education levels in 2007–8. Such regional disparities in education attainment potentially create different value perceptions of technology. This in turn prohibits the adoption in innovative farming methods. Arguably, it might lead to varying degree of agricultural productivity driven by differences in economic, demographic and socio-institutional structures in India.

5   The attitude of Indian farmers towards modernisation of farming is often regarded as traditional, conservative and monolithic. The Indian farming system is initially based on the subsistence farming model, which prioritises

Table 6.5 Percentage share of area operated under major landholding sizes (2000–1)

State/UT	Marginal size (below 1.0ha)	Small (1.01– 2.0 ha)	Semi-medium (3.0–4.0 ha)	Medium (4.0–8.0ha)	Large (above 8.0ha)
Andhra Pradesh	21.56	24.76	26.35	19.83	7.5
Arunachal Pradesh	21.56	24.76	26.35	19.83	7.5
Assam	21.29	23.47	30.76	16.02	8.48
Bihar	43.09	19.21	22.88	12.76	2.07
Chhattisgarh	14.86	19.49	26.33	27	12.31
Goa	31.48	14.81	14.81	14.81	22.22
Gujarat	7.01	18.58	29.38	33.85	11.18
Haryana	8.93	11.89	22	34.08	23.13
Himachal Pradesh	21.56	24.76	26.35	19.83	7.5
Jammu and Kashmir	21.56	24.76	26.35	19.83	7.5
Jharkhand	21.56	24.76	26.35	19.83	7.5
Karnataka	21.56	24.76	26.35	19.83	7.5
Kerala	56.28	19.12	12.17	5.42	7.14
Madhya Pradesh	21.56	24.76	26.35	19.83	7.5
Maharashtra	21.56	24.76	26.35	19.83	7.5
Manipur	21.56	24.76	26.35	19.83	7.5
Meghalaya	21.56	24.76	26.35	19.83	7.5
Mizoram	23.66	38.71	31.18	6.45	1.08
Nagaland	0.19	1.05	6.88	40.11	51.86
Orissa	21.56	24.76	26.35	19.83	7.5
Punjab	1.94	6.02	21.78	43.04	27.25
Rajasthan	21.56	24.76	26.35	19.83	7.5
Sikkim	21.56	24.76	26.35	19.83	7.5
Tamil Nadu	30.97	24.56	22.25	15.69	6.53
Tripura	46.67	27.78	15.93	3.33	5.93
Uttrakhand	28.83	26.22	25.15	15.66	4.27
Uttar Pradesh	36.97	24.28	21.72	14.35	2.69
West Bengal	21.56	24.76	26.35	19.83	7.5
Total	21.56	24.76	26.35	19.83	7.5

Source: Agriculture Census of India

fulfilling the basic family needs over the market. Farming is traditionally a means of food production for family and village. Food surplus is largely regulated locally through the exchange mechanism operating within the village market.

The value of market-led farming has not yet been fully realised after the Independence. The commodity market in India is hierarchically structured into multiple tiers whereby farms are linked with local, district and state-level market systems. Commodities prices are often regulated by the government at the state-level market. There are however some changes in the household income in rural India. A study conducted in the Upper Brahmaputra valley shows that about

40 per cent of Farm-HH income is contributed by crop production and the remaining 60 per cent is generated from income through allied and non-farm activities. Increased crop diversification, growth in the share of high value crops, expansion of allied activities like dairying, piggery, and poultry, and emergence of agro-processing and non-agricultural activities are now adding a significant proportion of HH income (Talukdar 2013).

6.06.1 *Agriculture productivity distance decay and the effect of metropolitan economies*

Spatial disparity in agricultural productivity within the region is largely due to the variability in the diffusion of technological innovation. Urban centres and transport networks often play a vital role in regulating the spatial diffusion of technological innovation in farms. Two key findings related to the impact of urban centres on regional convergence include:

1   the Lower Ganga plains of West Bengal show a partial divergence with a rate of productivity increase, $\beta = 0.207$ wherein the Kolkata metropolitan economy influences the spatial dynamics of agricultural productivity in its surrounding hinterland; and
2   the Punjab-Haryana plains where an inherent impact of Delhi metropolitan area is readily noticeable on the diversity of crops and productivity change ($\beta = 0.646$).

As noted earlier, these two agro-climatic regions in India have undergone a convergence in productivity increase over time. The reasons for such convergence in regional processes are different, which are captured in the following two case study examples.

Table 6.6 Annual average yield of food grains and commercial crops at the time of implementation of economic reforms (figures in kg/ha)

Crops	India	China	World
Wheat	2569	3787	2565
Rice	2848	6186	3757
Coarse Grains	982	4358	2678
Maize	1540	4867	4050
Pulses	1540	4867	4050
Groundnut	1059	2686	1318
Sugarcane	71040	64159	63266
Tea	1776	697	1158
Coffee	741	–	538
Tobacco Leaves	1442	1845	1616
Jute	1827	2522	1757

N.B.: Figures are of three years average (1995-06 to 1997)

Source: Food and Agriculture Organisation Year Book 1997.

Case study-1: regional economy of Lower Ganga Valley

Kolkata-centred agriculture hinterland has a relatively slow response to agricultural revolution in India. The hinterland consists of areas starting from Hawrah and Barddhman through to North of Kolkata. The role of Kolkata's city economy in transforming its hinterland to market-based farming is rather weak. A rural–urban divide in the agriculture landscape is spatially explicit, which shows discrete demarcation between rural and urban spheres instead of a transitioning zone.

This is demonstrated through the case study of Nadia. The district of Nadia is located in the outskirt of North Kolkata, which has enormous agricultural potential for the development of agro-based food processing industries. These allied industries have proven to be essential in the transitioning of the rural economy to a more city-based integrated economy. This district however is still predominantly rural. More than three-fourths of the population (77.4 per cent as per 2001 Census) live in rural areas in Nadia.

Nevertheless, Nadia district has very high population density (1,316 persons/sq km), which exerts intense population pressure on limited land resources. This area is also weakly connected with the city economy, so it is not functionally diverse and economically linked. This is substantiated from the distance-decay gradient of economic change from Kolkata and its hinterland, which has shown a sharp decline. This has resulted in lower levels of agricultural productivity in the Kolkata hinterland despite being one of the leading metropolitan city-regions in India.

Case study-2: expanding effects of Delhi metropolitan

The spatial organisation of Delhi-centred agriculture hinterland is more dynamic, robust and transformative. Delhi and its surrounding hinterland are rapidly growing due to higher responsiveness to technological change, market and innovations. Significant growth of satellite towns and the rapid emergence of new towns have created a web of agriculture markets, supported by dense road networks, for farmers to efficiently trade their commodities within the metropolitan market. This has also provided employment opportunities for the rural labour force to shift from the primary (especially agricultural) to secondary and tertiary sectors. This regional restructuring has transformed the agriculture landscape in peri-urban hinterland into a mass-produced built environment which has functional interdependencies with the Delhi metropolitan region (see Figures 6.7 and 6.8).

Agriculture productivity is equitably distributed throughout the region, thus the growth has shown the signs of intra-regional convergence. Rapid industrialisation of farm operations, globalisation of farm production, expansion of rural infrastructure, housing boom and decentralised employment structure have transformed traditional subsistence farming into profit-oriented commercial farming. This has empowered farmers to reach not only the Delhi metropolitan market but also global commodity markets.

Figure 6.7 Apartments under construction in rural–urban fringe of the national capital region

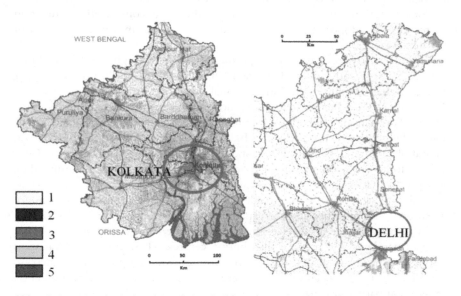

Abbreviations: 1 = Agricultural Land, 2 = Build up Areas, 3 = Forest Cover, 4 = Coastal Low Lying Areas and 5 = Water Bodies

Source: Land Use Land Cover Atlas of India (Based on Multi-temoral Satellite Data of 2005–06), National Remote Sensing Centre, ISRO, Dept. of Space, Govt. of India, Hyderabad, 2011.

Figure 6.8 Changing land-use patterns around two large metropolitan economies (Kolkata and Delhi)

6.07 Summary

This chapter presented the theoretical basis of the regional convergence/divergence thesis. It developed a methodological framework to test and validate the key premises of the thesis using the measure of agriculture productivity increase in India. The regional patterns of potential productivity are found to be similar to those exhibited by agricultural efficiency and productivity gap (between potential and existing productivities). It confirms the fact that agriculture efficiency and productivity gap are influenced by the potential productivity of land.

Agricultural productivity and growth are not only determined by the variability in the agro-ecological characteristics of land, but also affected by the ability of each region to harness the potential of farm technology, innovation and skilled labour. Spatial diffusion of technological innovation and seasonal movement of labour force were found to drive the regional convergence in agricultural performance, which has been instrumental in reducing the gap between high- productivity and low-productivity areas. Agriculture growth, which is shaped by land potential, is also subject to the diminishing law of return. Agriculture production increase in India is, therefore, subject to fixed and region-specific potential production (biophysical crop productivity of land in its agro-ecological term or maximum expected crop production in its economic term). However, the conditions production is fixed and invariant within the limit of land potential; the regional variation in productivity increase is, therefore, considered as a function of technology adoption and transfer and labour spatial movement in areas of labour shortages.

Regional variation in agriculture productivity is much higher (CV = 123 percent in 2000–1 and remained the same in 2006–7) in the Punjab and Upper Ganga plains. However, the intra-regional variation within the Lower Ganga Plains (Bihar-West Bengal Region) as shown by there productivity gap is much higher. This is in spite of highly fertile humid soil, which escalates the land potential to help increase productivity. High values of beta-coefficient for Punjab, Gujrat plains and Himachal-Uttrakhand indicate the regional convergence. Centripetal forces are stronger in high-productivity regions which are surrounded by low-productivity regions. This indicates the presence of spill-over effects onto the neighbouring regions. The trickle down process is fuelled by complementary allied non-farm activities and the expansion of infrastructure in rural India. The regional convergence is also accelerated due to the rapid emergence of market towns (mandies), which act as distribution centres. These towns in rural areas also absorb farm labour. However, agriculture growth and productivity increase are driven by both beta and sigma convergence, which tend to operate differently in different parts of India.

7 Hierarchically nested agriculture regions of India

7.01 Introduction

This chapter develops a methodological framework to delineate spatially integrated hierarchically nested agriculture regions in India. The identification of homogenous agriculture regions is a vital tool for agro-economic and rural planning. It is important to understand the reason for adopting the regional approach to examine the dynamics of agricultural economy. Does *geography* matter in shaping agriculture performance and regional productivity? If the country has uniformity in terms of resource distribution, would there be any need for geography or will geography become irrelevant? Geography matters because areas exhibit deeply rooted regional variations in their physiographical, sociological, economical and institutional characteristics.

Furthermore, agriculture is a 'space-consuming' and now a 'market-oriented' activity, which operates within the biophysical constraints of space. These constraints shape the nature, intensity and characteristics of farming practices. They also contribute to the creation of regions, which structure the space into uniform areas of similar agriculture characteristics. As policy-makers, it is important to ensure that agriculture is optimally practiced in the most efficient and effective manner to harness the full potential of factors of production. It is equally vital to establish an equitable and balanced agriculture growth approach to help create prosperity and high living standards.

New changes in market-based technology-led agriculture have started to occur in rural India. Agriculture is increasingly becoming 'process-driven' in order to adjust to market forces. This shift indicates a transitioning of agricultural economies in the context from Ricardian's model of agricultural systems with biophysical capacity constraint towards Thunen's model of spatially organised market-based regional structure of agricultural system. The reconstruction of agriculture regions based on formal criteria to a more functional definition is now needed to organise farming around farm-based markets wherein transport infrastructure and retail distribution networks become the key catalyst of change.

This chapter, therefore, examines the ontological basis of delineating regional boundaries of different agricultural systems, assesses the procedures and criteria required to delimit the agricultural regions to maximise differences in agriculture performance and finally identifies the way agricultural regions are structured and organised hierarchically in India.

7.02 Agriculture regionalisation

The root of regionalisation of human-environment interactions dates back to 1915 when Ellsworth Huntington developed a methodology for mapping the spatiality of human civilisation and habitation within the constraints imposed by the physical environment. He argued that climatic conditions play a critical role in shaping the rise and fall of human civilisations (Huntington 1915). Earlier attempts had led to the ideology of *environmental determinism*, which has had an immense impact on the development of geographical thought. Twenty-five years later, Griffith Taylor (1940) extended this concept and interpreted the impact of environmental conditions in analysing the rate of population and economic growth in Australia.

Whittlesey (1936), however, for the first time, developed a systematic methodology for demarcating climatic regions and regional variability in agricultural practices globally. This led to the development of the school of determinism, which identified human behaviour and settlement choices to be largely shaped by environmental conditions.

The classical theories of agriculture also recognised the pivotal role of environmental factors in producing regional differences in agricultural productivity. For example, Ricardian theory of economic rent delineates different agricultural zones, which were based on the land suitability and environmental conditions. The same concept of economic rent was later presented diagrammatically by McCarty and Lindburg (1967) who recognised the limitations imposed by biophysical factors (e.g. precipitation and temperature) in producing the optimal conditions for farming. Thuenen's location theory, however, emphasised the importance of markets in shaping land use patterns and agriculture practices (Hall 1966). Using the concept of *isotropic* surface, which assumed homogeneity in physical and socio-economic conditions, he argued that agricultural production is location-dependent in terms of its relative positioning to the market. Thus, the economic rent diminishes with distance from the market and land in peripheral zones increasingly becomes less productive. The economic rent changes in relation to market influence, distance and transportation costs.

Agricultural regionalisation of India was carried out largely using the biophysical attributes of land. The regional formation of agriculture systems however remained a contentious issue from the early 1940s until the 1950s. George Kuriyan, M.B. Pithawalla and K.S. Ahmed are among the pioneers in developing new methods for regionalisation. The debate concluded with an agreement that agriculture regions are to be delineated primarily on the basis of universally accepted biophysical parameters of land. Although, it was emphasised that region formation is not merely a classificatory procedure, but also a complex process of creating and constantly evolving regional identity and character, as Kuriyan (1942) argued.

In 1954, the key derivatives from land relief were used as a basis of the 'division' of the Indian sub-continent, which was carried out by Spate and Learmonth

(1967: 407–423). Similar rules were applied in the subsequent work by Misra (1970) and then by Singh (1971). It was realised that the agriculture regional boundaries generated using various classificatory schemes were not coterminous to those of administrative boundaries, which were the base of regional and rural planning in India. To overcome the difficulties involving the use of non-overlapping boundaries for regional planning, the Regional Survey Unit of the Indian Statistical Institute developed a new approach for the identification of regional personality of agriculture land use systems, which has integrated common district boundaries with physiographic regions (Bhat and Das 1968). Subsequent work by Bhat and Learmonth (1968) further incorporated agricultural growth and crop productivity with physiographic characteristics to demarcate new agriculture regions. Most of these approaches used district as a unit of analysis to classify areas into more homogenous agricultural regions.

7.03 Agriculture regions in India

India is a large country (3,287,263 sq km). It is twice as large as Libya or Iran in its areal extent. It is situated to the North of Equator between 8^0 4' to 37^0 6' N latitudes and 68^0 7' to 97^0 25' E longitudes. India's climate is significantly affected by the Inter Tropical Convergence Zone (ITCZ). It is also characterised by a variety of physiographical and climatic conditions, which in turn make India's agricultural practices much more diverse. Since the Indian agricultural systems are heavily influenced by regional variations in agro-ecological conditions, arguably it is prudential to use a regional frame for rural planning to improve agriculture practices to help align production with markets.

Determining the suitability of physiographic criteria of land as a basis of defining agricultural regions has been long debated in India. Due to a large areal extent and diversified climatic settings, researchers from the beginning of the planned economy phase have acknowledged the need for a more stable regional framework based on formal physical and climatic parameters that underpin the formation of agriculture regions. On the basis of physiographic and agricultural attributes, Nath (1954) prepared a regional frame, which divides India into 61 resource development regions. He considered it as a second order taxonomy of regional divisions for natural resource development when agriculture was conceived as a part of the natural system. The Planning Commission considered this approach useful for planning a balanced regional development despite its deterministic approach to building regional taxonomy.

In the initial phase of planned economy, Agriculture Commission (1964) developed a set of guidelines for defining crop regions in India, which also incorporated the boundaries of physiographic regions. Pal (1961, 1963) and Rao and Bhat (1964) adopted various 'physio-economic' criteria of economic regionalisation. Sen Gupta (1968: 101–106) suggested a criteria-based classification for the identification of multiple tiers of regions. He used climatic conditions (rainfall and evapo-transpiration) at a macro-level, topographic attributes at a meso-level and crop combination at a micro-level. Sdasyuk (1968: 15–26) applied a quantitative method for economic regionalisation, which was useful for examining regional dimensions of Indian agriculture. Chatterjee (1964), who worked at the NATMO, identified the physiographic regions, which were based on more 'stable' regions. This scheme of physiographic regions was used as a foundation for regional planning (Regional Survey Unit 1967) to prepare land use plans for India (Bhat and Das 1968).

During the Post-Green Revolution phase, India confronted a new set of challenges. High agricultural growth was restricted in a few pockets of the country whilst other areas were substantially lagging behind in agriculture development. The Government of India, thus, recommended a review of existing planning frameworks used for agricultural development and growth with a particular focus on 'area-specific' re-organisation of agricultural development programs. The task was assigned to the Planning Commission, under the supervision of Y. K. Alagh. Agro-Climatic Regional Planning (ACRP) has been developed for implementing agricultural and rural development programs in tune with a region-specific approach using the guidelines set out by the Planning Commission in 1988. The ACRP identified 15 macro agro-climatic regions and 73 meso-regions (Figure 7.1). They were delineated using climatic (e.g. temperature, rainfall, potential evapotranspiration, soil types) and agricultural characteristics (e.g. crop system, production and productivity).

After the implementation of 73rd and 74th Schedules in the Indian Constitution, many administrative powers, including the rural land use planning and economic development, were transferred to village-Panchayats as one of the key components of the decentralisation strategy. District-level agricultural plans were prepared using the same criteria. It was the first time in the history of planned economy of the country to explicitly adopt a regional approach to organising and structuring agricultural systems in India. Rural activities and allied-agricultural activities such as animal husbandry, poultry, aquaculture, horticulture, and vegetable and fruit cultivation were included for the preparation of district agricultural plans under one umbrella of agricultural development (Alagh 1989). The agro-climatic regions are listed in Table 7.1 with a slight modification of Region II: Eastern Himalaya, which is divided into two sub-regions. Names are modified as per the context but number of districts in each region remains the same (Basu and Guha 1996).

During the phase of economic liberalisation, India's networks of communication, transportation and trade were expanded. A shift towards market-oriented economy started to operate at a village level. The availability and use of farming technology intensified, which provided the incentives to farmers to change cropping patterns – from cultivation of grains to commercial farming of high-return crops such as Sugarcane, fruits and vegetables. There were options for farmers to work in allied agricultural activities to perform off-farm activities either at a village or at the nearby town. The benefits of these new rural–urban linkages include increased interdependencies and diversified rural economies. A new scheme of regionalisation has thus been developed by National Sample Survey Organisation (NSSO) in its 66th round of Economic Surveys, which included additional parameters such

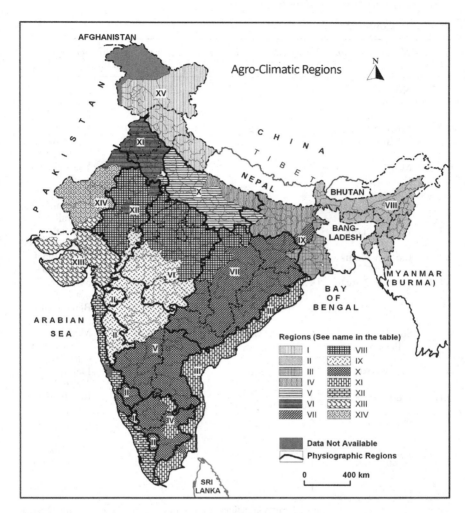

Figure 7.1 Agro-climatic and physiographic regions of India

Source: Planning Commission, New Delhi.

Table 7.1 Agro-climatic regions and sub-regions

Sl. no.	Name of region	No. of sub-regions	No. of districts	Average annual rainfall (mm)	Soil types
I	Western Himalayas	4	34	165–2000	Mountain and sub–mountain skeletal
IIa	North–East Brahmaputra Plain	2	11	1500–3000	Alluvial

(*Continued*)

Table 7.1 (Continued)

Sl. no.	Name of region	No. of sub-regions	No. of districts	Average annual rainfall (mm)	Soil types
IIb	North–East Hills and Mountains	3	30	2000–3500	Brown and laterite
III	Lower Gangetic Plains	4	12	1500–2500	Red and yellow alluvial
IV	Middle Gangetic Plains	2	30	1200–1500	Yellow alluvial
V	Upper Gangetic Plains	3	39	700–1000	Alluvial and terai
VI	Punjab Plains	3	25	500–800	Alluvial, calcareous
VII	Eastern Plains	5	25	1000–1200	Deep–black and red
VIII	Central Plateau	14	48	500–900	Mixed red and black
IX	Western Plateau	4	33	500–1000	Black shallow, red loamy
X	Southern Plateau	6	39	600–900	Medium black, red loamy
XI	East Coasts	6	20	1000–1300	Deltaic alluvial
XII	West Coasts	4	17	2500–3500	Red loamy and lateritic
XIII	Gujarat Plains	7	20	500–1500	Grain brown, coastal alluvial
XIV	Western Dry Thar	1	4	200–350	Sandy desert
XV	Islands	1	–	1500–2000	Latritic loamy

Source: 1. Alagh, Y. K. (1989): Draft Guidelines for Planning at the Agro-Climatic Reginal Level, Planning commission, New Delhi. 2. Wadia, F. K. (1996): Agro-Climatic Regional Planning at Zonal Level, in Basu, D. N. and Guha, G. S. (eds): (Vol-I)- Concept and Application, Concept Publication, New Delhi: 85–134.

as labour force in different occupations, expenditure and employment status. This regionalisation scheme of NSSO divided India into 88 homogenous regions on the basis of topography, climate, soil fertility and the growing rural economies (Appendix 7.1).

The practical utility of regionalisation techniques as a policy or a planning tool, especially for fast growing economies, is to effectively integrate industrial-type production farming and market-oriented re-structuring of agricultural economy. Some argue that the stable agro-climatic regional frame, which was developed for rural and regional planning, is too formal and static to incorporate new changes in the market and technology. As the agricultural economy is dynamic and constantly changing in response to technology and market demand, the use of physiographic regions, though highly valuable, has numerous limitations in dealing with the functional aspects of rural agricultural economic systems. A new approach that integrates aspects of stable physiographic regions with dynamic economic functionalities (e.g. services) is now called for. This would provide new insights in unbundling the complexity of globally connected rural and agriculture economies. Agriculture typically has been constructed as a space of production. New thinking that considers agriculture as a part of global consumption space requires new approaches and methods to improve resource allocation and agriculture development planning.

This is not to undermine the importance of physiographic basis for planning agriculture development. It is rather an attempt to plan agriculture more effectively in the context of globalised competitive economic order, whereby regions are constantly changing and functionally linked and connected to the key consumption hubs. Arguably, a macro-regional frame of agricultural regionalisation can be developed on broader biophysical attributes of land, whilst the meso- and micro-regional frames could be shaped by economic functions and services that areas provide to their hinterlands. Agricultural practices are thus not only influenced by the biophysical and/or agro-climatic conditions of land but also affected by market forces, which have a strong bearing on food production at a farm level. This is what derives the type, scale and characteristics of food production (Figure 7.2 NSSO regions). With an increasing share of agro-industry, allied agricultural and non-agricultural activities performed at a farm or off-farm locations, the urgency of incorporating functional parameters in regionalisation techniques is now warranted to enhance the effectiveness of policy-making process.

The debate on the concept and methods of delineating agricultural regions and their spatial representation has gained significant momentum in recent years. Among others, the debate about the methodological basis of classifying areal units using either subjective or objective approach remained active. Topographic-based criteria, which have been typically used in the previous approaches, is based on creating regional *'personality'* rather than characterising agriculture systems quantitatively. Sdasukh's (1968) taxonomy of agricultural regions, Chatterjee's (1964) regional planning regions and Bhat and Das's (1968) land use plans are some of the examples that applied areal personality to define agro-economic regions. However, studies by Singh (1994: 152–182) have adopted objective-based criteria to delineate agricultural regions using a classificatory approach.

7.04 Building ontology of agriculture regions

Building of ontologies of agriculture regional systems should provide the solutions to two major methodological problems. *Firstly*, it should be able to tackle the scale problem that may arise due to Modified Area Unit Problem (MAUP). *Secondly*, it should be able to integrate the characteristics of agricultural systems and sub-systems within the regional frame. The questions on ontology dealing with a typical classificatory problem of grouping of areal units to generate optimal boundaries that maximise inter-regional differences whilst minimising intra-regional differences based on a set of criteria remain a methodological challenge.

The areal unit of observation, which is used in the identification of agriculture regions, is district. If India is considered as a whole, should district be an ideal areal unit of analysis to study regional similarities and differences in the distribution of a geographic phenomenon? Is it an ideal size of administrative unit to help plan regional agriculture development by linking lower level units such as tehsi/taluka to the province and then to the state-based national framework? The optimal unit of analysis has always been a contentious issue. Ideally, the finer the spatial granularity, the better is the robustness and reliability of results, though greater the complexity and redundancy. Most studies have used district as a spatial unit, which they considered suitable for public administration, service delivery, resource management and strategic planning (Bhalla and Alagh 1979b, Pal 1975). For instance, the natural regions identified by the Office of the Registrar General (Census of India, paper No. 2 of 1952); the regions of India demarcated by the 16th round, National Sample Survey (NSS), Government of India, 1950–1; the planning regions of India by Regional Survey Unit, Indian Statistical Institute, 1965; and Asok Mitra's scheme of socio-economic regions of India, 1968, all have been based on district- level geography. However, they all have adopted a division approach to regionalisation rather than the approach of grouping areal units.

The elements (e.g. attributes or properties) of any observation can be used to classify or group areal units into areal classes or regions (Bunge 1962). Thus, the identification of agriculture regions requires grouping of objects into classes on the basis of properties or relationships they have in common (Grigg 1965, 1967). Methodologically, the logic of creating a system of agriculture regions is to group objects on the basis of similarity between objects, called the *principle of association by similarity* or on the basis of relationship between connectivity of objects, called the *principle of association by contiguity*. This leads to two key components of this regionalisation technique: Classification and Division (Grigg 1965, Simpson 1961, Singh 1974). Classification of objects is a logical division of a geographic space where the objects share similar properties or establish relationships based on a set of spatial laws or rules. This logic is linked to Tobler's First Law of Geography, *everything is related to everything, but things that sit together are more similar that those that are far apart*. This determines the association between objects or phenomena by the rule of spatial contiguity by which space is divided into parts. There are three main regionalisation or classification techniques, which are commonly used to identify and demarcate boundaries to differentiate homogenous agriculture regions.

7.04.1 *the analytical approach*

The analytical approach allows partitioning of space into its constituent parts using a set of criteria. Examples of such approach include Koppen's climatic classification, Harbertson's system of natural regions and Whittlesey's agricultural regions of the world. They all applied routines that used a set of criteria-based rules to create regions.

In India, the key studies that have produced geographical regions include the work of Baker (1928), Chatterjee (1964), Misra (1970), Singh (1971: 33–34), Spate et al. (1967: 407–423) and Stamp (1928). They have adopted a classical approach of superimposing multiple overlays to generate geographic boundaries separating different natural regions using biophysical parameters. There is no consideration for administrative boundaries, which limits its wider adoption from a policy or planning perspective.

7.04.2: the synthetic approach

The synthetic approach adopts a classificatory procedure of grouping objects into a hierarchy of areal classes (objects) using a set of criteria. It is an iterative process of classifying objects into homogenous units, which are hierarchically structured on the basis of similarity (e.g. attributes of objects) and spatial contiguity (e.g. adjacency, proximity). Recent advances in computing have enabled iterating and solving long logical procedures of complicated equations. For instance, the application of multivariate statistical techniques such as (i) the factor analysis, which helps to reduce the multi-dimensionality of large datasets of regions (Berry 1961, 1964, 1965, Berry and Rao 1968, Pal 1968, 1975, Verma 1974), (ii) the hierarchical grouping function to keep areal units called Operational Taxonomic Units (OTUs) in order (Ward 1963, Zebler 1958, Zobler 1972), (iii) the cluster analyses, which are based on distance function (Park (1970) and (iv) the discriminating procedure of regionalisation developed by applying trigonometric polynomial analysis in search for an optimal and logical solution for a regionalisation problem (Amedeo 1969, Amedeo and Golledge 1975, Casetti 1964, 1966) are commonly applied algorithms. They are tailored and, thus, are referred to as purpose-based approach to regionalisation.

7.04.3 non-parametric model

The non-parametric modelling is a new approach to regionalisation by which the process of classification is simulated on the proximity of a multi-dimensional functional set. Key work on this approach is conducted at the Departments of Geography and Mathematics of the Facultes Universitaires Notre-Dame Dela Paix (F.U.N.D.P.) and the University of Namur, Belgium. This approach has opened a new horizon for functional partitioning of space by applying uniform density functions of transformation of multi-dimensional data set. Rasson et al. (1988, 1989) consider the rules that discriminate areas from each other are associated with the Poisson Process, which solves space-partition problems of voluminous multi-dimensional set of data.

Analytical approach to regionalisation typically imposes the image-built regional frame to search for the reality of phenomena. It is therefore far from reality, while synthetic (based on normal density function) and non-parametric (uniform density function) approaches assimilate areal objects into identifiable homogenous regions using spatial contiguity and phenomena proximity. In the assimilation process, regions with similar features are identified on the basis of internal assemblages of the key criteria of the observed phenomenon. Objects are differentiated on the basis of the taxonomic distance between two objects in the discriminant space. Casetti (1964: 30) describes the computation of non-parametric approach as:

> . . . when the centroids of the classes are chosen as representative points, the classification generated by the Discriminant iterations from an initial classification has a smaller within class variability that the initial classification. In turn, smaller variability corresponds to a smaller average distance among the points in the same classes.

Amedeo (1969: 27) described the contiguity criterion of regionalisation in the following manner.

> . . . the desirable outcome (of discriminating procedure) is to obtain that set of regions such that members (unclassified areal units) of the same region in the set are as similar as possible and members of different regions in the set are as dissimilar as possible. It is intuitively clear that the more homogeneous each region in the set is made, the more total distance (deviation) is lowered, and each region in the set becomes more recognizable.

The procedure of discriminating objects follows three major steps:

1   Generation of discriminant space from multi-dimensional partitioning problem, which is generating from the transformation of variables,
2   Spatial arrangement of areal units, which establishes spatial relationships of point units in the discriminant space, and
3   Fixation of limit on the level of spatial similarity index to check the quality of classification/regionalisation.

The key purpose of *step 1* is to standardise and normalise data which are often collected in different measurement scales (e.g. kilometre, percentage, and population density in person/sq km). This could be conducted using a range of techniques, which transform a set of variables into a standard scale such as z-scores. Most studies which are based on factor analytic approaches have applied normal density function to transform a set of variables to generate a discriminant space. Mean and variance free 'Z' score transformation of the original variables is the initial stage of discriminating procedure. However, linear or non-linear polynomial transformations could also be adopted to generate a discriminant space.

Step 2 measures the functional distance between two areal units and its ordering (Singh 1988: 9). These distances reflect the degree of spatial contiguity, which (King 1969, Sokal and Sneath 1963) are measured using a range of methods. It could be based on spatial adjacency or proximity or in simple terms the degree of neighborliness. Others such as the pioneer work of Berry (1961) have used factor analysis to generate this space based on characteristics or by calculating proportionate loss

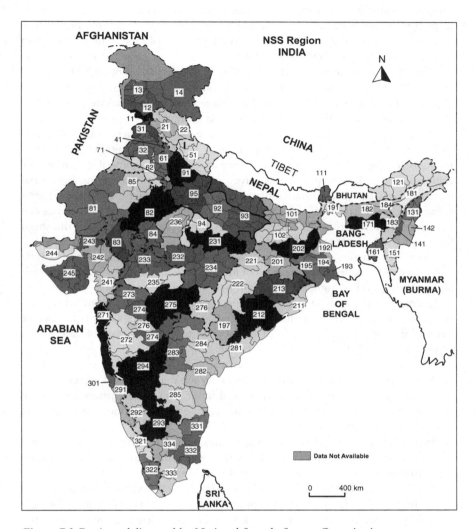

Figure 7.2 Regions delineated by National Sample Survey Organisation

N.B.: for names of regions, see Appendix 7.1.

of information of areal properties with each iteration in the assimilation process. Since discriminant procedure of regionalisation starts by assimilating areal units into broader classes, the degree of loss of information at each stage of computation becomes zero per cent (the case of complete detailed information). The loss of information increases gradually until the discriminating procedure becomes complete at its highest order (the case of complete generalisation), referred to as the 'uniform-universalisation' (Amedeo and Golledge 1975: 160–170).

The factor analytic approach, which is fundamentally correlation-based methods, is relatively less suitable for calculating the functional distance among areal

units especially for agricultural regionalisation of India. This is because of insignificant correlations between various variables representing agricultural production
systems. It is partly due to the effects of the Green Revolution, which brought in
significant changes in some parts but not in others, in relative terms. An alternative for factor analytic is the use of Euclidean distance function, which is based
on the Pythagorean Theorem. It is now a commonly used technique applied to
measure the nearness of points in the geometrical space (Casetti 1964: 6–10)
through which areas can be discriminated and grouped into classes.

The last but the most important step of the region-forming process is the optimal grouping of areal units (i.e., Operational Taxonomic Units, OTUs). Opti-
mality is achieved by minimising the degree of spatial contiguity of classification/
regionalisation. This step is a repetitive process that minimises the functional
distance from the main distance matrix based on its (functional distance) least
value. The reliability of regionalisation or grouping of area units into classes can
be tested by calculating the difference between classification and its threshold
limit. It fixes the level of areal similarities to create regional boundaries. The classification closer to its optimal limit is better with respect to given set of criteria
and hence, the smaller values of ratio of in-built class variability to total class variability correspond to higher level of homogeneity of the regions.

The main steps involved in the development of discriminant algorithm are presented to demonstrate its application in India. The main steps in the process for
determining the optimal solution of spatial contiguity to each level of assimilation
of observations/OTUs are explained below:

Step-1: Set the values of given attributes/variables, m, and observations/
OTUs, which form n.m dimensional input data matrix where i and j are
specific observations and k a specific variable with the condition i and j = 1,
2, 3, . . ., n and k = 1, 2, 3, . . ., m.

Step-2: Transform m dimensional attributes into a discriminant space through
a normal density function (Z scores) and generate a standardised data
matrix (Z-matrix of the same n.m dimensions).

Step-3: Compute Dij for all possible ij pairs of it observations and generate a
distance matrix (D-matrix) of n.m dimensions. D is taxonomic distance,
Dij, between OTUs i and j of k variables are calculated by applying the
Euclidean distance formula for m-dimensional space as:

$$D_{ij} = \left[\sum_{k=1}^{m} (X_{ik} - X_{jk})^2 \right]^{1/2} \qquad \ldots \qquad \ldots \qquad (7.1)$$

This formula can optimise an objective function of space partitioning (Ward
1963) and calculate a functional distance space to discriminate OTUs to delineate homogeneous regions (Park 1970). Later on, Monmonier (1972) applied
the same procedure using a linkage diagram, which is called taxonomic tree. The
formula is, therefore, adjusted to generate an algorithm of hierarchal clustering

using SPSS (Statistical Package for the Social Sciences). A new algorithm is written in SPSS to incorporate the assimilation or classification procedure as an iterative process to generate agricultural regions, which are hierarchically structured.

> *Step-4*: Find a minimum value of Dij in D-matrix, combine ith and jth observations of Dij minimum in Z-matrix by calculating means of their kth variables separately, and reduce dimension n.m of Step-2 to (n − 1).m through iteration.
>
> *Step-5*: If nm > 1.m go to Step- 3, if n.m = 1.m go to Step-6,
>
> *Step-6*: Write the value of Dij and its coordinates at each level of reduction.
>
> *Step-7*: Stop.

7.05 Spatial contiguity constraint and optimal regional partitioning

This section demonstrates the application of regionalisation method to generate agriculture regions using a set of 20 agricultural attributes. The spatial variance of various groups of OTUs is carefully adjusted to ensure the spatial contiguity of OTUs to delimit optimal agricultural regions. This procedure is implemented to a finite set of 348 OTUs using 20 dimensional attributes of agricultural characteristics.

Physiography of land plays an important role in shaping agriculture practices. It is therefore a vital consideration in the partitioning of geographical space based on biophysical characteristics of land. The key assumption is that the macro-agricultural regions are analogous to physiographic regions of the country. The total OTUs are classified by following the physiographic regional scheme at a macro-level namely, (A) the Coastal region, (B) the Deccan Plateau, (C) the Western Himalayas, (D) the Great Plains, and (E) the Rajasthan Plains. The newly generated regions are called Macro-Agricultural Regions. They are identified according to their levels of assimilation and degree of their similarities in physiographic characteristics and broadly agricultural attributes (see Figure 7.4).

Having run the computer program for an optimal solution to the ordering of spatial variance as discussed earlier, it is found that there are at least three basic concerns regarding the partitioning of contiguous areas and the formation of optimal agricultural planning regions which have to be dealt with while analysing the result of assimilation processes for various Macro-Agricultural Regions. The assimilation of OTUs and the formation of agricultural regions are subject to the levels of assimilation. The degree of spatial variance obtained within the emerging group consisting of similar OTUs and the stability of areal classes. There is a key feature in the assimilation procedure of agricultural attributes at the macro-level that the coastal region of India is physiographically as well as agriculturally different with the Deccan Plateau in the regional frame. In spite of a high degree of spatial variations between them (40.78 per cent at the level of variability); they are at the lowest level of 3.20 similarity index value when process of assimilation starts (see Figure 7.3).

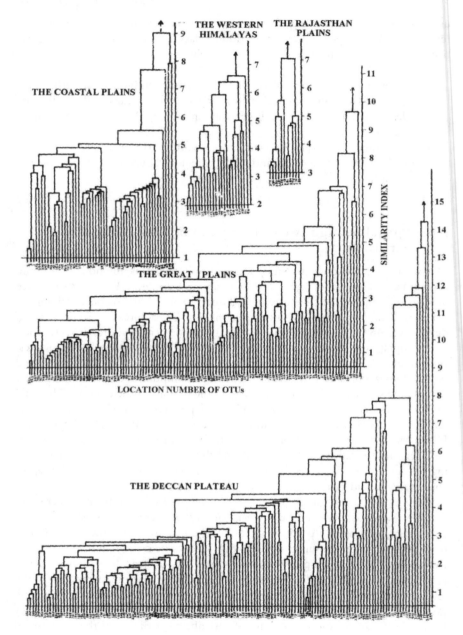

Figure 7.3 Dendrogram showing a hierarchically nested classification of agriculture regions of India

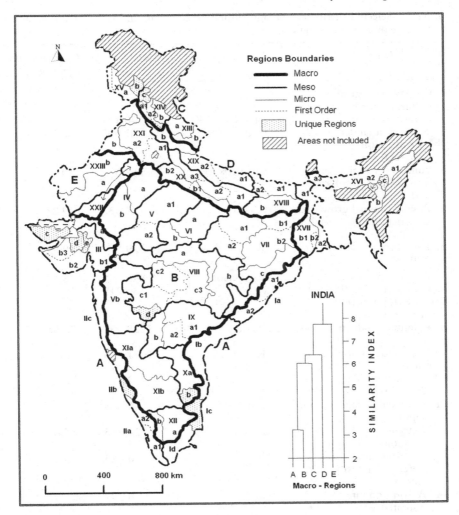

Figure 7.4 Agricultural planning regions of India

7.06 Identifying agricultural regions of India

The geographic boundaries of macro-agricultural regions are largely coterminous to the boundary of macro-natural regions as defined by climate and soil properties, which determine their shape and form. They are four broad regions, namely, (A) The Coastal region, (B) The Deccan Plateau, (C) The Western Himalayas, (D) The Great Plains. The technique of optimal partitioning is used for areal assimilation of OTUs to create groupings of similar OTUs on the basis of the degree of spatial variance (Amedeo and Golledge 1975). As listed in Table 7.2, the attributes related to agro-ecological, agricultural commodities, crop potential and

Table 7.2 Selected attributes for agricultural regionalisation, their definitions and coefficient of variations

Name of the attributes	Definitions	Mean	Coefficient of variation (%)
(a) Agro–ecological characteristics			
1. Moisture index	[(P – PE)/PE]	–0.151	–
2. Soil fertility index	Unit	61.908	15.26
(b) Production characteristics			
3. Annual per capita net availability of food grains 2013	(kg/Person)	182.5	130.04
4. Average annual growth rate of agricultural output 2001 to 2007	%	4.333	149.23
5. Land productivity (Y) 2006–7	(Rs/ha)	48,579	80.92
6. Labour productivity 2001	(Rs/Person)	30,844	98.37
7. Crop intensity 1988–90	%	134.219	19.6
© Growth potential characteristics			
8. Potential productivity index (A)	(Rs/ha)	3228.081	73.58
9. Magnitude of production potential (A – Y)	(Rs/ha)	1681.635	106.8
10. Production potential intensity (A/Y)	Ratio	2.578	58.3
11. Marginal product to labour input	Unit	3.688	240.48
12. Marginal product to technological input	Unit	22.515	417.88
13. Absorption rate of potential intensity w.r.t. labour	Unit	0.025	356
14. Absorption rate of potential intensity w.r.t. technology	Unit	0.292	506.51
(d) Organisational and technological characteristics			
15. Input of labour	(Rs/ha)	512.782	85.15
16. Input of non–land capital	(Rs/ha)	96.819	104.76
17. Extent of irrigation	%	35.584	75.76
18. Mechanisation	(Rs/ha)	155.31	145.98
19. Use of chemical fertiliser	(Rs/ha)	143.991	104.27
20. Average size of operational landholding	(NSA/Cultivator)	1.466	61.05

organisational and technological characteristics were used to demarcate agriculture regions in India. The key characteristics of these regions are described as follows.

1   The Coastal plains and the Deccan Plateau are the most diverse macro-agricultural regions in India, which account for more than 40 per cent of spatial variability in data. The Great Plains and Western Himalayan region are dissimilar to each other, in spite of being spatially continuous (Table 7.3). This is partly because of the physiographic differences between the two regions.
2   Meso- and Micro-agricultural regions in India are hierarchically structured, which are tiered due to the interplay of various factors. For example, the rapid adoption of seed-fertiliser technology in the Great Plains of India has diversified the agro-economic structure that in turn produced a large number of homogeneous regions, which differ from each other in the use of farm technology. These regions show different stages in the adoption of technological innovation in farm mechanisation and modernisation. The Peninsular Plateau regions also have many clusters at a meso- and micro-level, which is partly due to the differences in physiographical characteristics. For instance, four out of nine regions at a meso-level belong to the Peninsular Plateau, which are spatially contiguous yet holding distinctive characteristics to be deemed as separate regions on their own. In other words, they were not assimilated as a single group due to dissimilar characteristics despite of spatial adjacency to one and another.
3   Micro-agricultural regions are most dependent on the development of growth centres and mandi towns, which have strong bearing on agricultural growth and productivity and the development of rural road networks. Agricultural growth and productivity are, therefore, more responsive to techno-institutional changes rather than bounded by the physiographic characteristics of land at a micro-level.

Table 7.3 Assimilation process and groupings of the macro-agricultural regional units

Groups	Assimilation of macro-units	Within group D values	% of variance	
			Cumulative	Absolute
Prior to grouping	–	0	0	0
After I grouping	A/B	3.204	40.78	40.78
II grouping	AB/C	6.144	78.2	37.42
III grouping	ABC/D	6.551	82.82	4.62
Final grouping	ABCD	7.857	100	17.18

N.B.: 1. Final grouping is the stage of complete generality where total information's of the spatial are lost. For assimilation of the agricultural regional units, see inset of Figure 7.4.
2. For names of macro-regions, see Table 7.4.

Table 7.4 Nomenclature and hierarchy of agricultural planning regions with the degree of their spatial variation

Name of the regions	No. of OTUs	Assimilation levels		Within region variation	
		Mini	Maxi	Absolute	%
A. The Coastal Regions					
I. East Coast Plains					
a. Coromandal East	7	1.32	4.37	3.05	231.06
1. Utkal Plain	4	3.48	4.37	0.89	25.57
2. Andhra East Plain	3	1.32	1.64	0.32	24.24
b. Andhra Plains (Central Coast)	7	3.25	4.01	0.76	23.38
C. Madras Plains (Unique)	2	7.95	9.02	1.02	13.46
d. S. Tamilnadu Plain	3	3.1	3.31	0.21	6.77
II. Western Coastal Plains					
a. Malabar Coasts	11	2.13	4.12	1.99	93.43
1. South Kerela	7	2.27	4.12	1.85	81.5
2. North Kerela	4	2.13	3.31	1.18	55.4
b. Karnataka Coastal Plain (Unique)	1	0	4.55	4.55	–
c. Konkan Coastal Plain	5	2.16	2.99	0.83	38.42
III. The Gujarat Plains					
a. Panchamahal–Sabarkantha	3	3.27	4.43	1.16	35.47
b. Central Plains	11	2.63	3.21	0.58	22.05
1. Mehsana–Baroda Plain	6	3.03	3.21	0.18	5.94
2. Coastal Kathiabar	3	2.63	2.81	0.18	6.84
3. Interior Plain	2	0	3.27	3.27	–
c. Kutch Peninsula (Unique)	1	0	4.43	4.43	–
d. Sundernagar Plain (Unique)	1	0	7.65	7.65	–
e. Ahmedabad Plain	1	0	5.55	5.55	–
B. The Peninsular Plateau					
IV. Aravali Hills					
a. Eastern Rajasthan	6	2.32	4.2	1.88	81.03
b. Aravali Ranges	7	3.15	5.22	2.07	65.71
V. The Central Plateau					
a. N. W. Madhya Pradesh	21	1.25	2.28	1.03	82.4
1. Chambal Basin	13	1.42	2.28	0.86	60.56
2. Malwa Upland	8	1.25	1.68	0.43	34.4
b. Maharashtra Shayadri	9	1.24	1.7	0.46	37.1
VI. The Bundelkhand–Malwa Plateau					
a. Bundelkhand	8	1.05	1.91	0.86	81.9
b. East Malwa Plateau	5	1.32	2	0.68	51.51
VII. The Eastern Plateau					
a. Benghelkhand	7	3.4	5.51	2.11	62.06
1. The Sonpar Hills	4	3.4	4.81	0.41	12.06
2. The Maikal–Ramgar Hills	3	4.12	5.51	1.39	33.74
b. Chotanagpur Plateau	10	0.97	2.85	1.88	193.81
1. Hazaribagh Plateau	4	0.97	1.35	0.38	39.17
2. Ranchi Plateau	6	1.12	2.85	1.73	154.46
c. Orissa Hills	6	0.84	1.71	0.87	103.57

Name of the regions	No. of OTUs	Assimilation levels		Within region variation	
		Mini	Maxi	Absolute	%
VIII. The North Deccan					
a. The Narmada Valley	8	1.25	2.93	1.68	134.4
b. Baster Hills (including Mahanadi Basin)	4	2.3	3.29	0.99	43.04
c. Wardha Plateau	12	0.88	2.3	1.42	161.36
1. South Central Plateau	4	0.88	1.96	1.08	122.73
2. Ajanta Hills (N. Central)	4	1.58	2.3	0.72	45.56
3. Wardha Valley	4	1.52	1.93	0.41	26.97
d. Balaghat Range (Unique, Osmanabad)	1	0	2.52	2.52	–
IX. The Andhra Interior (Telengana)					
a. N. Telengana Upland	8	2.41	6.71	4.31	178.84
1. N. Andhra Upland	6	2.61	4.61	2	76.63
2. Hyderabad Hills	2	2.41	6.72	4.31	178.84
b. Karnataka East	3	2.91	4.78	1.87	64.26
X. The Rayalseema					
a. Chitor–Cudapah Upland	3	3.31	3.71	0.4	12.08
b. Javadi Hills (Unique)	1	0	14.26	14.26	–
XI. The South Deccan					
a. North Karnataka	7	1.92	3.23	1.31	68.23
b. South Karnataka	11	2.31	3.52	1.21	52.38
XII. The Tamilnadu Upland					
a. Middle Caveri Basin	4	3	5.66	2.66	88.67
b. Transitional Land of South Sahayadri–Nilgiri Hills	3	3.67	7.15	3.48	94.82
C. The Western Himalayas					
XIII. Uttar Pradesh Himalayas					
a. Garhwal Himalayas	3	2.94	3.56	0.62	21.08
b. Kumaom Himalayas	3	4.49	5.09	0.6	13.36
XIV. Himachal Himalayas					
a. Lesser Himalayas	8	1	3.56	2.56	256
1. Siwalik Foothills (Duns)	6	2.24	3.56	1.32	58.93
2. Main Valleys of Kulu, Mandi and Lahual	2	1	3.16	2.16	216
b. Central Himalayas	2	1.11	3.32	2.23	200
c. Sub–Himalayas Zone (Unique) (Upper Chinab Valley of Chamba)	1	0	6.58	6.58	–
XV. Jammu–Kashmir Valley					
a. Punch–Jammu Valley (Siwalik and Foothills)	5	2.84	4.04	1.2	42.25
b. Pirpanjal Ranges (Unique)	1	0	5.96	5.96	–
D. The Great Plains of India					
XVI. The Assam Plains					
a. Brahmaputra Valley	10	2.35	3.84	1.49	63.4
1. Upper Brahmaputra	3	2.64	3.84	1.2	45.45
2. Lower Brahmaputra	4	2.35	3.62	1.27	54.04

(*Continued*)

Table 7.4 (Continued)

Name of the regions	No. of OTUs	Assimilation levels		Within region variation	
		Mini	Maxi	Absolute	%
3. Tista Plain (N. Bengal Plain)	3	2.35	3.08	0.73	31.06
b. The Barak Valley (Kachhar)	2	0	4.65	4.65	–
c. Mikir Hills (Unique) (Karbi Anglong)	1	0	6.63	6.63	–
XVII. The Lower Ganga Plain					
a. Hoogli River Alluvial Plain	7	2.2	2.61	0.41	18.64
1. Upper Hoogli Plain	3	2.41	2.61	0.2	8.3
2. Lower Hoogli Plain	4	2.2	2.41	0.21	9.54
b. Central Bengal Plain	6	1.89	9.63	7.74	409.52
1. Rahar Plain	4	1.89	2.25	0.36	19.05
2. Calcutta Surroundings	2	7	9.63	2.63	37.57
XVIII. The Bihar Plains					
a. Trans Ganga Plains	13	1.13	2.32	1.19	105.31
1. Muzaffarpur–Saharsa Plain	10	1.14	2.32	1.18	103.51
2. Ghagra–Gandak Lower Doab	3	1.13	1.36	0.23	20.35
b. South Bihar Plains	9	1.15	2.23	1.08	93.91
XIX. The Bhawer Terai Plains					
a. Rohikhand Upper Ghagra Plains	11	1.14	2.36	1.22	107.02
1. Upper Sarda–Ghagra Doab	5	1.14	1.96	0.82	71.93
2. Ram Ganga Basin (Rohilkhand)	6	1.28	2.36	1.08	84.37
b. Haryana–Uttar Pradesh Bhawar (Foothills)	6	1.96	3.73	1.77	90.31
XX. The Central Ganga Plains					
a. Gomti Central Avadh Plains	15	0.78	1.53	0.75	96.15
1. Central Avadh Plain (E. U. P.)	6	0.93	1.19	0.26	27.96
2. Gomti Plians (C. U. P.)	5	1.19	1.69	0.5	42.02
3. Central Dry Zone	4	0.78	1.53	0.75	96.15
b. Lower Ganga–Jamuna Doab	9	1.16	1.9	0.74	63.8
1. Kanpur–Alahabad Doab	3	1.16	1.72	0.56	48.27
2. Agra Plain	6	1.33	1.9	0.6	45.11
XXI. The Punjab–Haryana–Western Uttar Pradesh Plains					
a. Central Punjab Plains	25	1.16	3.54	2.38	205.17
1. Delhi Surroundings	10	1.16	1.79	0.63	54.31
2. Punjab–Haryana Banghar	15	1.79	3.54	1.75	97.76
b. Border Lands of Punjab	2	2.41	6.94	4.53	187.97
E. The Rajasthan Plains					
XXII. The Rajasthan Bangar	5	3.53	5.01	1.48	41.93
XXIII. The Marusthali	6	3.27	5.57	2.3	70.36
a. Marusthali Central	3	3.27	3.37	0.1	3.06
b. Western Marusthali Border	3	3.37	5.57	0.2	59.35

Note: The Andaman and Nicobar, Lakshadweep and Maldive Islands form one separate agricultural planning region and can be placed in the last as meso-region number XXIV in the present scheme of regionalization. But it is not included in the present scheme because of non-availability of agricultural statistics.

7.07 Summary

Agriculture has been considered as a key mechanism for overall regional economic development, and continues to be a planning instrument for sustainable development and inclusive growth. Agricultural growth in India, however, has remained slow, sporadic and regionally unbalanced. More robust regionalisation techniques to demarcate functionally integrated regions are, therefore, vital for enhancing the effectiveness of regional and rural development plans.

An areal classification technique of regionalisation was applied on the principle of 'homogeneity of agricultural attributes between (inter) and within (intra) the delineated regions'. Uniform agricultural regions were formalised using a range of attributes related to agro-ecological, agricultural commodities, crop potential and organisational and technological characteristics, which formed the basis of identifying inter-regional agriculture homogeneity. Proximity of multi-dimensional set of agriculture attributes and spatial arrangement of areal units were kept as criteria for optimal partitioning of areal units to assimilate them to form regional boundaries at different levels.

The spatial variance of various groups of OTUs was adjusted to ensure the spatial contiguity of OTUs to delimit the generation of optimal agricultural regions. This procedure was implemented to a finite set of 348 OTUs using 20 dimensional attributes of agricultural characteristics. Procedure of assimilation as shown through dendrogram brings region formation process for creating hierarchically structured spatially tiered agricultural regions in India.

Broadly, five macro-regions were delineated following purely biophysical basis of agriculture regionalisation, assuming that topographical properties of land greatly impact on agriculture activities. They include: Deccan Plateau, Great Plains, Coastal plains, Western Himalayas and Rajasthan plains. Meso- and micro-agricultural regions in India are hierarchically structured, which are tiered due to the interplay of various factors. Micro-agricultural regions are most dependent on the development of growth centres and mandi towns, which have strong bearing on agricultural growth and productivity and the development of rural road networks. Agricultural growth and productivity are, therefore, more responsive to techno-institutional changes rather than bounded by the physiographic characteristics of land at a micro level.

Sl. no	State/U.T. (code)	NSS Region Code	Description	Composition of region (name of district)
(1)	(2)	(3)	(4)	(5)
1.	Andaman & Nicobar Islands (35)	351	Andaman & Nicobar Islands	All districts of Andaman and Nicobars
2.	Andhra Pradesh (28)	281	Coastal Northern	Srikakulam, Vizianagaram, East Godavari, West Godavari Visakhapatnam
3.		282	Coastal Southern	Krishna Guntur, Nellore Prakasam
4.		283	Inland North Western	Adilabad Nizamabad Medak, Hyderabad Rangareddi, Mahbubnagar
5.		284	Inland North Eastern	Karimnagar, Nalgonda, Warangal, Khammam
6.		285	Inland Southern	Cuddapah, Kurnool, Anantapur Chittoor
7.	Arunachal Pradesh (12)	121	Arunachal Pradesh	Tawang, Upper Siang, West Kameng, Dibang Valley, East Kameng, Lohit, Papum Pare, Changlang Lower Subansiri, Tirap, Upper Subansiri, Anjaw, West Siang, Kurungkumey, East Siang, Lower Dibang, Valley
8.	Assam (18)	181	Plains Eastern	Lakhimpur, Sibsagar, Dhemaji, Jorhat, Tinsukia Golaghat, ibrugarh
9.		182	Plains Western	Kokrajhar, Kamrup rural, Dhubri, Nalbari, Goalpara, Chirang, Bongaigaon, Baksa, Barpeta, Kamrup metro
10.		183	Cachar Plain	Karbi Anglong, Karimganj, North Cachar Hills, Hailakandi, Cachar
11.		184	Central Brahamputra Plains	Darrang, Sonitpur, Marigaon, Udalguri, Nagaon
12.	Bihar (10)	101	Northern	Champaran(W), Saharsa, Champaran(E), Darbhanga, Sheohar, Muzaffarpur, Sitamarhi, GopalganjMadhubani, Siwan, Supaul, Saran, Araria, Vaishali, Kishanganj, Samastipur, Purnia, Begusarai, Katihar, Khagaria, Madhepura,

Sl. no	State/U.T. (code)	NSS Region Code	Description	Composition of region (name of district)
13.		102	Central	Bhagalpur, Kaimur (Bhabua), Banka, Rohtas, Munger, Jehanabad, Lakhisarai, Aurangabad, Sheikhpura, Gaya, Nalanda, Nawada, Patna, Jamui, Bhojpur, Arwal, Buxar
14.	Chandigarh (04)	041	Chandigarh	Chandigarh
15.	Chhattisgarh (22)	221	Northern Chhattisgarh	Koriya, Surguja
16.		222	Mahanadi Basin	Jashpur, Rajnandgaon, Raigarh, Durg, Korba, Raipur, Janjgir-Champa, Mahasamund, Bilaspur, Dhamtari, Kawardha
17.		223	Southern Chhattisgarh	Kanker, Dantewada, Bastar
18.	Dadra& Nagar Haveli (26)	261	Dadra & Nagar Haveli	Dadra & Nagar Haveli
19.	Daman & Diu (25)	251	Daman & Diu	Diu and Daman
20.	Delhi (07)	071	Delhi	North West, Central, North, West, North East, South West, East, South, New Delhi
21	Goa (30)	301	Goa	North Goa, South Goa
22	Gujarat (24)	241	South Eastern	Panch Mahals, Surat, Dohad, The Dangs, Vadodara, Navsari, Narmada, Valsad, Bharuch
23		242	Plains Northern	Mahesana, Ahmedabad, Sabar Kantha, Anand, Gandhinagar, Kheda
24		243	Dry areas	Bans Kantha, Patan
25		244	Kachchh	Kachchh
26.		245	Saurashtra	Surendranagar, Junagadh, Rajkot, Amreli, Jamnagar, Bhavnagar, Porbandar
27.	Haryana (06)	061	Eastern	Panchkula, Sonipat, Ambala, Rohtak, Yamunanagar, Jhajjar, Kurukshetra, Gurgaon, Kaithal, Faridabad, Karnal, Mewat, Panipat
28.		062	Westernw	Jind, Bhiwani, Fatehabad, Mahendragarh, Sirsa, Rewari, Hisar
29.	Himachal Pradesh (02)	021	Central	Kangra, Hamirpur, Kullu, Una, Mandi

(Continued)

Sl. no	State/U.T. (code)	NSS Region Code	Description	Composition of region (name of district)
30.		022	Trans Himalayan& Southern	Chamba, Sirmaur, Lahul & Spiti, Shimla, Bilaspur, Kinnaur, Solan
31.	Jammu & Kashmir (01)	011	Mountainous	Jammu, Kathua
32.		012	Outer Hills	Doda, Punch, Udhampur, Rajauri
33.		013	Jhelam Valley	Kupwara, Badgam, Baramula, Pulwama, Srinagar, Anantnag
34		014	Ladakh	Leh (Ladakh), Kargil
35.	Jharkhand (20)	201	Ranchi Plateau	Garhwa, Singhbhum(W). Palamu, Singhbhum (E), Ranchi, Latehar, Lohardaga, Simdega, GumlaSaraikela Khareswan
36.		202	Hazaribagh Plateau	Chatra, Sahibganj, Hazaribag, Pakaur, Kodarma, Dumka, Giridih, Dhanbad, Deoghar, Bokaro, Godda, Jamtara
37.	Karnataka (29)	291	Coastal & Ghats	Uttara Kannada, Dakshina Kannada, Udupi
38.		292	Inland Eastern	Shimoga, Hassan, Chikmagalur, Kodagu
39.		293	Inland Southern	Tumkur, Mandya, Kolar, Mysore, Bangalore, Chamarajanagar, Bangalore (Rural)
40.		294	Inland Northern	Belgaum, Gadag, Bagalkot, Dharwad, Bijapur, Haveri, Gulbarga, Bellary, Bidar, Chitradurga, RaichurDavanagere, Koppal
41.	Kerala (32)	321	Northern	Kasaragod, Kozhikode, Kannur, Malappuram, Wayanad, Palakkad
42.		322	Southern	Thrissur, Alappuzha, Ernakulam, Pathanamthitta, Idukki,, Kollam, Kottayam, Thiruvananthapuram
43.	Lakshadweep (31)	311	Lakshadweep	Lakshadweep
44.	Madhya Pradesh (23)	231	Vindhya	Tikamgarh, Umaria, Chhatarpur, Shahdol, Panna, Sidhi, Satna, Anuppur, Rewa
45		232	Central	Sagar, Bhopal, Damoh, Sehore, Vidisha, Raisen

Sl. no	State/U.T. (code)	NSS Region Code	Description	Composition of region (name of district)
46.	Madhya Pradesh (23)	233	Malwa	Neemuch, Dewas, Mandsaur, Jhabua, Ratlam, Dhar, Ujjain, Indore, Shajapur, Rajgarh
47.		234	South	Katni, Mandla, Jabalpur, Chhindwara, Narsimhapur, Seoni, Dindori, Balaghat
48.		235	South Western	W. Nimar, Betul (Khargoan), Harda, Barwani, Hoshangabad, E. Nimar, Burhampur (Khandwa)
49.		236	Northern	Sheopur, Datia, Morena, Shivpuri, Bhind, Guna, Gwalior, Ashoknagar
50.	Maharashtra (27)	271	Coastal	Thane, Raigarh, Mumbai, Ratnagiri, Suburban, Sindhudurg, Mumbai
51.		272	Inland Western	Pune, Satara, Ahmadnagar, Kolhapur, Solapur, Sangli
52.		273	Inland Northern	Nandurbar, Jalgaon, Dhule, Nashik
53.		274	Inland Central	Nanded, Aurangabad, Hingoli, Bid, Parbhani, Latur, Jalna, Osmanabad
54.		275	Inland Eastern	Buldana, Wardha, Akola, Nagpur, Washim, Yavatmal, Amravati
55		276	Eastern	Bhandara, Gadchiroli, Gondiya, Chandrapur
56	Manipur (14)	141	Plains	Bishnupur, Imphal West, Thoubal, Imphal East
57.		142	Hills	Senapati, Ukhrul, Tamenglong, Chandel, Churachandpur
58.	Meghalaya (17)	171	Meghalaya	West Garo Hills, Ri Bhoi, East Garo Hills, East Khasi Hills, South Garo Hills, Jaintia Hills, West Khasi Hills
59.	Mizoram (15)	151	Mizoram	Mamit, Serchip, Kolasib, Lunglei, Aizwal, Lawngtlai, Champhai, Saiha
60.	Nagaland (13)	131	Nagaland	Mon, Kohima, Tuensang, Phek, Mokokchung, Kiphire, Zunheboto, Longleng, Wokha, Peren, Dimapur
61.	Orissa (21)	211	Coastal	Baleshwar, Jajapur, Bhadrak, Nayagarh, Kendrapara, Khordha, Jagatsinghapur, Puri, Cuttack

(*Continued*)

Appendix 7.1 (Continued)

Sl. no	State/U.T. (code)	NSS Region Code	Description	Composition of region (name of district)
62.		212	Southern	Ganjam, Nuapada, Gajapati, Kalahandi, Kandhamal, Rayagada(Phoolbani), Nabarangapur, Baudh, Koraput, Sonapur, Malkangiri,, Balangir
63.		213	Northern	Bargarh, Kendujhar, Jharsuguda, Mayurbhanj, Sambalpur, Dhenkanal, Debagarh, Anugul, Sundargarh
64.	Pondicherry (34)	341	Pondi- cherry	Yanam, Mahe Pondicherry Karaikal
65.	Punjab (03)	031	Northern	Gurdaspur, Hoshiarpur, Amritsar, Nawanshahr, Kapurthala, Rupnagar, Jalandhar, S.A.S. nagar (Mohali)
66.		032	Southern	Fatehgarh Sahib, Faridkot, Ludhiana, Bathinda, Moga, Mansa, Firozpur, Sangrur, Muktsar, Patiala
67	Rajasthan (08)	081	Western	Bikaner, Jalor, Jodhpur, Sirohi, Jaisalmer, Pali, Barmer
68		082	North- Eastern	Alwar, Dausa, Bharatpur, Jaipur, Dhaulpur, Ajmer, Karauli, Tonk, Sawai Madhopur, Bhilwara
69		083	Southern	Rajsamand, Dungarpur, Udaipur, Banswara,
70		084	South- Eastern	Bundi, Baran, Chittaurgarh, Jhalawar, Kota
71.		085	Northern	Ganganagar, Jhunjhunun, Hanumangarh, Sikar, Churu, Nagaur
72.	Sikkim (11)	111	Sikkim	North (Mongam), South (Nimachai), West (Gyalshing), East (Gangtok)
73.	Tamil Nadu (33)	331	Coastal Northern	Thiruvallur, Tiruvanamalai, Chennai, Viluppuram, Kancheepuram, Cuddalore, Vellore
74.		332	Coastal	Karur, Nagapattinam, Tiruchirappalli, Thiruvarur, Perambalur, Thanjavur, Ariyalur, Pudukkottai

Sl. no	State/U.T. (code)	NSS Region Code	Description	Composition of region (name of district)
75.		333	Southern	Dindigul, Ramanathapuram, Sivaganga, Toothukudi, Madurai, Tirunelveli, Theni, Kanniyakumari, Virudhunagar
76.		334	Inland	Dharmapuri, The Nilgiris, Salem, Coimbatore, Namakkal, Krishnagiri, Erode
77.	Tripura (16)	161	Tripura	West Tripura, Dhalai, South Tripura, North Tripura
78.	Uttarakhand (05)	051	Uttarakhand	Uttarkashi, Almora, Chamoli, Champawat, Rudraprayag, Nainital (P), Tehri Garhwal, Udham Singh, Dehradun (P), Nagar, Garhwal, Hardwar, Pithoragarh, Nainital (H), Bageshwar, Dehradun (H)
79.	Uttar Pradesh (09)	091	Northern Upper Ganga Plains	Saharanpur, J Phule Nagar, Muzaffarnagar, Meerut, Bijnor, Baghpat, Moradabad, Ghaziabad, Rampur, G. Buddha Nagar
80.		092	Central	Sitapur, Kanpur Dehat, Hardoi, Kanpur Nagar, Unnao, Fatehpur, Lucknow, Barabanki, Rae Bareli
81.		093	Eastern	Pratapgarh, Gorakhpur, Kaushambi, Kushinagar, Allahabad, Deoria, Faizabad, Azamgarh, Ambedkar Nag., Mau, Sultanpur, Ballia, Bahraich, Jaunpur, Shrawasti, Ghazipur, Balrampur, Chandauli, Gonda, Varanasi, Siddharthnagar, S.R.Nagar(Bhadohi), Basti, Mirzapur, S. Kabir Nagar, Sonbhadra, Maharajganj
82.		094	Southern	Jalaun, Mahoba, Jhansi, Banda, Lalitpur, Chitrakoot, Hamirpur

(*Continued*)

Appendix 7.1 (Continued)

Sl. no	State/U.T. (code)	NSS Region Code	Description	Composition of region (name of district)
83.		095	Southern Upper Ganga Plains	Bulandshahr, Bareilly, Aligarh, Pilibhit, Hathras, Shahjahanpur, Mathura, Kheri, Agra, Farrukhabad, Firozabad, Kannauj, Etah, Etawah, Mainpuri, Auraiya, Budaun
84	West Bengal (19)	191	Himalayan	Darjiling, Koch Bihar, Jalpaiguri
85.		192	Eastern Plains	Uttar Dinajpur. Murshidabad, Dakshin Dinajpur, Birbhum, Maldah
86		193	Southern Plains	North 24-Parganas, South 24-Parganas, Kolkata
87		194	Central Plains	Barddhaman, Howrah, Hugli
88		195	Western Plains	Bankura, Paschim Midnapur, Puruliya, Purba Midnapur

8   Agriculture growth models

8.01 Introduction

Agriculture growth is a relative change in agriculture output over time. It is different to agriculture productivity, which is a factor related output per unit of farm land. Most classical economic theories of growth such as theory of 'vicious circle' (Nurkse 1953, Singer 1949), 'growth pole' and 'big push' (Rodan 1943) were founded on the theoretical basis of 'capital accumulation' and demand-led growth. Most developing countries however struggle to substitute natural resources with labour and/or capital accumulation to stimulate economic growth during the early stages of economic development (Hayami 2001: 119–120). This has inhibited the ability of farmers to invest, innovate and improve the operational efficiency of farms. This in turn has led to labour-intensive farming and lower return to labour input.

This chapter begins with a discussion on the key methodological issues related to the assessment of agricultural growth. It defines the key concepts of agriculture growth and then identifies its major components. Finally, it examines the key drivers shaping the agriculture growth at a farm level where farm households are required to invest on farm assets and agriculture inputs. This chapter presents an empirical case study to demonstrate the development of agricultural growth model which simulates the impact of any change in an agriculture system and its performance.

8.02 Key theoretical debates and methodological challenges

Guided by the Keynesian theory of economic growth and development, the Harrod-Domar model explains that growth ($G = dY/Y$) is a positive function of saving rate ($S = S/Y$) and a negative function of marginal capital-output ratio ($ICOR = dX/dY$). Growth (G) thus can be mathematically expressed as $G = S/ICOR$. Growth is often low in low-income countries especially in agriculture-dependent economies because of the lower rate of saving (Hagen 1975). Income in most households in India is spent on buying the essential food commodities, thus the saving continues to remain low. While the saving rate might be correlated with the size of household income, nonetheless for majority of house-holds in India the net saving after the expenditure remains a key challenge.

After the liberalisation of the Indian economy, income for a few farmers started to increase because of the productivity gains from changing farming techniques and commercialisation. Additional income was also gained from employment in non-farm work in the rural labour market. This has marginally improved the ability of farmers to increase their savings. Government incentives, subsidies and schemes might have also contributed to raising additional income at farm. The Government of India initiated various schemes to raise capital in agriculture either by giving soft-loans through rural banking system or through subsidies on farm inputs such as fertiliser. Grants for strengthening irrigation were also provided along with initiatives to stabilise harvesting price mechanism for food products (Agricultural Price Commission).

The Indian Government started to deregulate foreign direct investment in select areas of the retail sector, which opened up access to domestic commod-ity markets and enabled linking producers of agricultural products to national/international markets. The retail sector in India has started to corporatise with the large domestics retail chains entered in the market. It was anticipated that market-led farm production would escalate the rate of capital accumulation and improve inter-industry linkages with urban markets. Although some of the retail corporates are vertically integrating the food supply chains to establish better control on the upstream of the supply chains by eliminating intermediar-ies. There is some evidence that income diversification in farms has occurred whereby farmers in addition to cultivation have begun to simultaneously engage in other economic pursuits such as dairy farming, piggery, poultry and fishery. Nonetheless, the capital growth and the rate of saving continue to remain slow in rural India despite the relentless efforts by farmers. Labour-intensiveness of agriculture and the inability of farmers to use modern farming techniques have largely affected the production levels that in turn establish the size of income. Ironically, unlimited supply of cheap rural labour has been a key factor in stabilis-ing the wage-rate at the lower end of the wage spectrum, which dumped down the labour market.

Systemic and organised attempts to raise savings from farm income are rare in rural India. This has thwarted the ability of farmers to innovate and improve operational efficiency of farming. The investment to establish and maintain farm infrastructure (as a sum of payment to hire labour and for purchase of farm tools) is limited to farmers with large landholdings and restricted to few high-perform-ing regions. Higher inflation and the resultant increases in food prices during the liberalisation in both urban and rural India have put the market under intense pressure to increase labour costs but have succeeded in increasing wages of farm workers marginally so as to maintain their basic living standards.

Given Ricardo's model of development, as wage rate is constant at W level and demand curve (i.e., assumed as marginal productivity of farm) is fixed at $D - D_0 K$ as shown in Figure 8.1, a total agriculture value product called agriculture out-put, PY, which is represented by an area $ADOL_0 = PY$, is equal to the sum of total

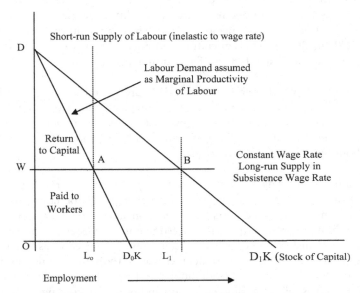

Abbreviations: Area (PY) ADOL$_0$ refers to total agriculture value product, ADW = total profit/ return to capital, WL = AWOL$_0$ = Total wage paid to workers and Profit Rate = (Y–WL)/K

Figure 8.1 Ricardo's labour demand and economic development model

wages paid to labour, AWOL$_0$ = WL and return to capital, K (i.e., total profit) represented by a triangle ADW. It works under the condition of short run supply of labour. As and when labour is increased at farm from L$_0$ to L$_1$ at a constant wage rate, W, with a capital stock of D$_1$K (instead of D$_0$K), marginal productivity increases from D – D$_0$K to D – D$_1$K. Under this condition, a total capital invested additionally at farm proportionately increases its return with a constant rate of profit as Profit rate = (Y – WL)/K, (c.f. Hayami 2001: 77–79) (Figure 8.1).

As Ricardo argued in his model of economic development (c.f. Hayami 2001), the profit increases disproportionately with the increase in capital investment at farm. This is because farming operates at a diminishing marginal return to capital (i.e., technology). So the rate of capital accumulation diminishes with further investment in agriculture infrastructure with long run equilibrium of constant wage-rate, the capital stock and labour employment.

In India, agricultural growth during the Liberalisation phase was basically dependent on two key dimensions: farmer's income, which is driven by farm production; and savings at farm, which is investment required to increase farm productivity. The key assumption is that the savings from a farm remains constant over time and the total saving for a farmer in the previous year is the potential investment in farming in the current year.

Capital accumulation and increased savings from farming are largely dependent on an increase in farm productivity through the intensive use of inputs (e.g. technological and labour) and quality of land where agriculture activities are performed (Malik 2005). The agricultural production function is, therefore, dependent on following three factors of agricultural production:

1   the biophysical (which refers to 'potential') production of land, which is often measured using maximum expected crop production (for more detail, see under a Potential Productivity in section 6.03 of Chapter 6),
2   the capital investment in the form of farm technology, and
3   the labour input and the set wage rate.

The optimum harnessing of agricultural land potential requires farmers to maximise farm outputs by either negotiating higher prices for farm products with buyers or minimising the costs of production factors or both. The total income from farm production minus the investment in farm assets, technological enhancement, labour hire and domestic consumption is referred to as 'total savings'. Other factors include the rate of depreciation of tools and techniques used by farmers, the size of operational landholdings and the investment on domestic consumption such as food, housing, education and others. According to Angle's law, the low-income households spent more of their share of income in fulfilling domestic requirements; thus they are likely to save less to invest in farm infrastructure. These factors are key inputs in building the agriculture growth function, which determines the growth in farm production.

8.03   Input-pulse response model and agriculture production function

The development of input pulse response model is dependent on two major input functions: i) the farm-level, which enables establishing relationships between inputs used and outputs produced from farm, where farmers use family members as 'farm labourers'; and ii) the saving from family income, which is then directed to enhancing farm technology to increase farm productivity levels.

Two main functions are used for building the input pulse response model, which include the 'agricultural production function' and the 'input pulse response function'. The first function is a transfer function, which estimates agricultural output in respect to input application; whilst the latter function estimates the agricultural inputs (e.g. technology and labour costs) and assets depreciation.

The agricultural production function is typically built using the biophysical parameters of land, techno-economic and labor factors. Previous research has built agriculture growth models using three key dimensions: (i) the biophysical attributes (Anbumozhi et al. 2003, Gorski and Gorska 2003), (ii) the physiological processes (such as photosynthesis, transportation respiration and assimilation of carbohydrate) (Aggarwal et al. 1994, Baker et al. 1972, DeWit et al. 1969, Kang et al. 2002 and 2003) and (iii) weather-crop yield modelling (Mall and

Singh 2000). Normalized Differential Vegetative Index (NDVI) was also used for the measurement of green leaf biomass growth of different crops (Kiniry et al. 2004, Manjunath and Potdar 2004, Shrestha and Naikaset 2003).

On the other hand, various models were developed to evaluate the effects of techno-economic and institutional factors on agricultural growth. These production functions include some classical models, for example, the exponential yield function (Spillman 1922 and 1933), the constant elasticity function (Douglas and Cobb 1928) or the neo-classical stochastic error-term crop yield functions to measure technological efficiency of crop output (Aigner et al. 1977, Subash et al. 2004).

The use of farm technology could also optimise the effects on biophysical attributes through improving or nourishing a better 'soil environment' with the use of seed-fertiliser techniques and farm machines. Such technological inputs are of two types:

1   Short-duration diffusive effects of a seed-fertiliser-irrigation technology package, which influences crop growth during crop season only, and
2   Long-duration constant effects of farm machines, irrigation equipment and farm tools, which have multi-purpose use for a relatively longer duration of about two years or more.

Farm machines and equipment are required to maintain healthy soil environment for crop growth. For example, a small tractor of 25HP is a multi-purpose tool, which is used for tillage of the land, operation of tube-well and transportation of farm products and input items (Johnston 1980). The lifecycle of such equipment is subject to maintenance, use-intensity and time-driven deterioration. Farm machines and tools are, therefore, common assets called infrastructure for agriculture at farms.

Farm labour is another important production factor (Singh 1994) in agriculture growth. At present, cheap available labour within or outside the labour markets in India is substituting for costly farm machines (Das 1984). Some workers work as casuals and are required on particular seasons, which are often outsourced from less developed regions in India. Some of them migrate from other states and work at farms for lower wages. The decision to hire farm labourers or use a farm technology as a replacement is dependent on a number of factors. These include the size of landholding, family size, income, HH types, perception of the benefits of technology and commercialisation potential, reliability of market demand, and socio-cultural traditions. These factors make the rural labour markets more complex and unpredictable.

8.04 Approaches to and assessment of agricultural production

If agricultural growth is a system of inputs to produce a unit output, then productivity is the system's output at a particular time (tn) from the time of its base year (to). Arguably, it is a function of technological investment and labour use over time. In order to model the effects of technological enhancement on farm outputs for each year, tn, an integrated production function based on two production factors (technological investment, Xdt and labour employed in the system, WLdt) need to be created. The key assumption is that the land condition could vary spatially but does not change significantly over time.

The farm production is subjected to the '*reciprocity law of diminishing marginal return*', under which agricultural output increases with a decreasing rate due to the effect of increased technology on hidden capacity of land (Singh 2000, 2002). The mathematical form of production function is as:

$$PYt = PA\,[1 + (B_1/CX) + (B_2/WL)]^{-1}, \ldots \qquad \ldots (8.1)$$

where Yt = agricultural production at a farm at particular time t, X = technological (capital) Input, L = investment on labour in farm activities, A = maximum expected output based on biophysical condition that refer to 'hidden capacity' of farm land (Singh 2006), P = market price per unit of farm production, C = factor price at market, W = labour wage rates, B_1 and B_2 are farm production efficiency coefficients based on land potential representing technology and labour in the production function.

Agricultural growth is the change in total output over time, which is measured by a given production function for each year. The base year savings at farm, t_0, is the base of investment at farm for the following years (Figure 8.2). There are two linkages created from farm income:

1 *The forward linkage*: Some share of income is invested in buying technological inputs such as seeds and fertiliser as additional (say incremental) input investment at farm (Idt) and additional hired labour for farm operations (Ldt) for planned years.
2 *The backward linkage*: Farm income is the result of the previous year's investments in the form of labour and technology applied at a farm (Lt_{n-1} and CXt_{n-1}).

Input demand at a farm is controlled by market prices of technological inputs and wage rate. Figure 8.2 illustrates the process through which agricultural growth respond when technological and/or labour input intensifies at a farm. The 'remainder method' of technological progress was used, which considers technological progress as one of the production factors in a production function (Hagen 1975: 250–258). However, accumulating effects of technological inputs at farm over time are measured by using the 'Input Pulse Response' technique. This technique calculates the amount and intensity of technological enhancement and the depreciation rate of farm assets over time. The formulation of input pulse response model is based on a method of 'compound depreciation' of technological assets used at farm, which is presented as:

$$CX_{tn} = (Idt + D_{tn})^*(1.00 - (r/100))^t \quad \ldots \qquad \ldots (8.2)$$

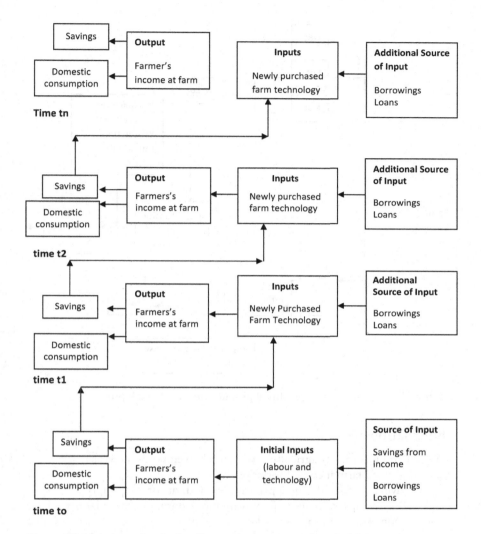

Figure 8.2 Mapping of agricultural growth process at a farm level

Where CX_{tn} = total depreciated technological investment, D_{tn} = depreciated assets investment for a particular time tn, Idt = additional input investment by the farmer through farm savings and borrowings from outside at a particular year dt, r = depreciation rate in percent, t = a particular point of time.

8.05 Agricultural productivity and growth parameters

The model parameters of agricultural growth and productivity are largely dependent on the functional chains associated with the forward and backward linkages of farm income and investments as shown in Figure 8.3.

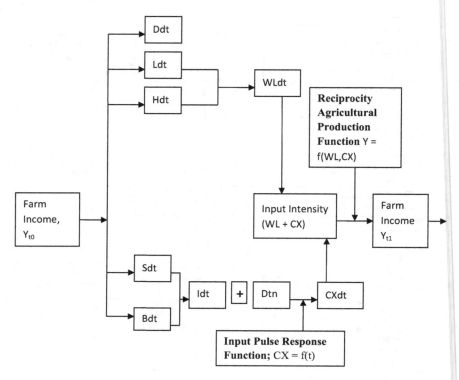

Figure 8.3 Computation of agricultural productivity and growth processes

Abbreviations:

Yt_0 = Farm income for agriculture (i.e., total revenue) in the year t_0

Yt_1 = Assessed farm income for the year t_1

Sdt = Savings at farm during a particular period, dt (dt = $(t_1 - t_0)$)

Bdt = Borrowings to intensify farm technology during a particular period, dt

Ddt = Domestic consumption of farm HHs involved in farm activities during a particular period, dt

Ldt = Domestic labour involved in farm activities during a particular period, dt

Hdt = Hired labour involved in farm activities during a particular period, dt

Dtn = Depreciated assets invested in the period n,

Idt = Additional input investment at farm for agriculture activities during a particular period, dt

WLdt = Total labour cost involved in cultivation at farm during a particular period, dt

CXdt = Total cost towards technology available at farm during a particular period, dt

Different parameters are incorporated at different stages of model building, which computes the growth patterns. The following parameters are used in the model:

1   The size of operational landholdings,
2   Current farm assets to represent technology and infrastructure maintained at farm for farming,
3   Crop production and the area under each crop are used to generate the output index for production function, and non-farm activities at farm to represent the diversification of farm activities,
4   Demographic structure of farm-HH to understand pattern of domestic consumption and available domestic labour for farm operations to enable computing labour input hired for farm operations,
5   Use of farm machines and tools to compute the depreciation rate of assets and technological input index,
6   Farm-HH income, savings and borrowings for agricultural intensification, and
7   Market prices of farm products and costs of technological assets and inputs and labour wages to compute agricultural output for planned years.

The data gathered to represent these variables are generated through village surveys. The sample surveys of farm-HHs at a village level were conducted to measure agriculture growth and productivity. The 'input pulse response' model was used to understand the requirements of farm assets owned by farm-HHs. The growth pattern were analysed by assessing the growth at different levels of input application through using production function as given above for different farm sizes. These include: large (above 8 ha), medium (2–4 ha) and small and marginal (below 2 ha). The parametric model is based on primary data obtained and results are interpreted in the proceeding sections.

8.05.1: key assumptions

There are a number of assumptions that underpin the development of the modelling framework. These include:

1   Market prices of agricultural production and labour wages are constant during the time considered for the period of growth assessment.
2   Depreciation rate of all technological assets is assumed 15 per cent each year in the area surveyed. But it is variable for different farm operational assets.
3   Total maintenance cost of assets is equal to total depreciation cost of agricultural equipment in the year.
4   Saving, S, is the difference between total annual revenue received from the farm (i.e., agricultural output, O) and total annual expenditure incurred for agriculture. Annual expenditures include the maintenance costs of equipment,

M; input used, I; labour wages, L; annual land rent paid to government and lease amount for private land, R, and farm-HH consumption, C. Thus, S= O – (M + I + L + R + C).

5   Farm-HH size affects directly and steadily on HH consumption.

6   Maintenance costs follow the rule of compound depreciation of technological enhancement in agriculture operations that are based on 'input pulse response' technique.

7   To assess the output of subsequent periods, t_n, for computation of simulated growth of agricultural, the production function is used. It follows the law of diminishing marginal return to agricultural productivity (Equation 8.1).

8   Agriculture growth (dY/Y) is a positive function of saving rate (S/Y), which is directly related to HH income from farm.

9   Since previous year saving is the investment for current year, farm-HHs spend savings in three ways: *first* to maintain assets, *second* to increase quality and quantity of technological inputs and *third* to intensify labour input for farm operations to optimise growth. In case of the savings are less than total depreciation of technological assets, farm-HHs will borrow money from credit agencies to enhance growth in farm operations.

8.06 Sample village

Salawa village is located in the outer periphery of Moradabad town in Rohilkhand administrative division in the Upper Ganga plains. It was selected as a sample for conducting agro-economic surveys. Agricultural land around the village' periphery is made of three types of soil: silty loam (old alluvial locally called *banghar*), clayey loam (new alluvial *khadar*) and sandy loam (sandy alluvial called *ratele*). Most farmers have 2 to 3 parcels of operational landholdings. Each one of these soil zones occupies a variety of farm sizes. Village farmers are progressive and have different sizes of landholdings. Sugarcane is a dominating crop. However, Wheat and Rice are also grown. Milk and milk products are vital sources of additional farm income. On account of high ground water table especially in areas of sandy loam and newly formed clayey loam, a 5 HP diesel engine is enough to run a tube-well, which is a cheaper source of irrigation.

There are 143 farms in the village, out of which 5 are landholdings of larger size (8 ha and above), 28 medium (2–4 ha) and 110 small and marginal size (below 2.0 ha). All farmers were surveyed in the months of December 2012 and July–August 2013. Winter and summer months were selected for survey to minimise any potential anomaly due to seasonal variability in weather and cropping behaviour. Data related to farm assets, technological and labour inputs used, farm-HH consumption and agricultural outputs were collected and compiled. Averages of agricultural attributes were computed at a farm level to analyse the effect of farm size on agriculture output and saving rates and to assess farm productivity and growth (Table 8.1).

Table 8.1 Farm assets, output, use of technology and labour and HH consumption in village Salawa (Moradabad District, Uttar Pradesh) in Upper Ganga Plains (surveyed in 2013).

Sl.	Agriculture attribute	Large-sized farm		Medium-sized farm		Small and marginal-sized farm	
1	Average farm size (ha)	8.1		2.24		0.61	
2	Dominance of crops	Sugarcane		Sugarcane		Wheat	
3	**Technological assets (Rs)**	Total	%	Total	%	Total	%
A	Tractor– trolley and machines (Rs)	8,00,000	70.36	5,00,000	76.1	–	–
B	Tube–well (Rs)	1,60,000	14.07	80,000	12.17	–	–
C	Bulls and bullukcart (Rs)	1,00,000	8.79	–	–	1,00,000	83.33
D	Harrow (Rs)	50,000	4.4	50,000	7.61	–	–
E	Thresher (Rs)	25,000	2.2	25,000	3.8	–	–
F	Other small farm equipment (Rs)	2,000	0.02	2,000	0.03	20,000	16.61
	Total	**11,37,000**	**100**	6,57,000	100	1,20,000	100
	Depreciation in assets @ 15% (Rs)	1,70,550		98,550		18,000	
	Depreciated assets (Rs)	9,66,450		5,58,450		1,02,000	
4	**Technological inputs annual**						
A	Diesel use for tractor and machines (Rs)	14,000	5.02	5,600	5.28	–	–
B	Fertiliser used (Rs)	20,000	7.17	8,000	7.55	8,000	4.35
C	Irrigation costs and electricity bills (Rs)	4,800	1.72	2,400	2.26	6,000	3.26
D	Labour: domestic (Rs)	1,20,000	43.04	60,000	56.6	1,20,000	65.22
E	Labour: hired (Rs)	1,20,000	43.04	30,000	28.3	50,000	27.8
F	Hired and domestic labour ratio	1:01		01:00.5		01:00.4	
	Annual total	**2,78,800**	**100**	**1,00,000**	**100**	**1,84,000**	**100**

(*Continued*)

Table 8.1 (Continued)

Sl.	Agriculture attribute	Large-sized farm		Medium-sized farm		Small and marginal-sized farm	
5	Land rents (Govt and lease) (Rs)	80,000		2,000		5000	
6	Annual output of farm crops (Rs)						
A	Sugarcane	9,00,000	84.5	2,70,000	90.6	9,000	9.67
B	Wheat	50,000	4.7	12,500	4.19	37,500	40.32
C	Jowar and Bajara	40,000	3.75	8,000	2.68	24,000	25.8
D	Rice	75,000	7.04	7,500	2.52	22,500	24.19
	Total (Rs)	10,65,000	100	2,98,000	100	93,000	100
7	Farm–HH size (persons)	8		4		4	
8	Annual HH consumption (Rs)						
a	Cereals and fruits	52,000	29.38	14,500	23.2	16,500	56.9
b	Cloths	50,000	28.25	10,000	16	5,000	17.24
c	Education	50,000	28.25	10,000	16	5,000	17.24
d	Transportation	20,000	11.3	5,000	8	2,000	6.9
E	Medicine	5,000	2.82	3,000	4.8	500	1.72
	Total (Rs)	1,77,000	100	62,500	100	29,000	100
	Per capita annual consumption (Rs)	22,125		15,625		7,250	
9	Land productivity (O/A) (Rs/ha)	1,31,481		1,33,035		1,52,959	
10	Labour productivity O – (M + I) Rs per worker	2,13,912		1,22,360		34,857	
11	Total Savings (Rs)	3,58,650		28,950		19,000	

8.06.01: farm tools and technological assets

Tractor and tube-well were two major technological innovations where most farm investment was made (more than four-fifths). They were also considered to be common farm infrastructure, which was collegially utilised for farm operations in large and medium-sized farms. Tractor is considered as a multi-purpose tool. It is widely used for pumping tube-well water, harrowing for plough fields, threshing Wheat crop and transporting Sugarcane to sugar mills. In some areas, tube-well is operated by diesel engine when the ground water is near the surface in the *khadar* areas of newly formed alluvial soils. Farmers who own small and marginal-sized farms do not have costly equipment such as tractors, harrows and others. But they hire them from other farmers during the farming session. Farmers continue to use traditional farm tools to plough farm fields and means of transportation such as rubber-tyre wheels or wooden-wheel bullockcarts (Figure 8.4 and 8.5). The Government of India initiated numerous schemes to provide credits to farmers for the purchase of tractors and other agriculture equipment through Prathama banks and cooperatives. Rural and commercial banks are also providing long-term credits and loans to farmers at a cheaper rate to invest in farm infrastructure.

8.06.02: *household consumption and expenditure*

Households owning farms of large and semi-medium size tend to spend annually about Rs 2.78 lakhs and 1.06 lakhs on technological and labour inputs respectively. About 86 per cent of total expenditure is spent on labour input. Labour cost is hence more expensive than technology input. Ratio of domestic

Figure 8.4 Buffalo-drawn cart with rubber-tyre wheels used for transporting agricultural goods to the local market

Figure 8.5 Rubber-tyred cart for local transportation of agriculture goods from field to home

labour with hired labour for farm operation is 1:1 in large farms. It however changes as farm size becomes smaller (Table 8.1). It is 1:0.5 in medium-sized farms and 1:0.42 in the small and marginal-sized farms. It means domestic labour is used in all farm sizes, but more intensively in small and marginal-sized farms.

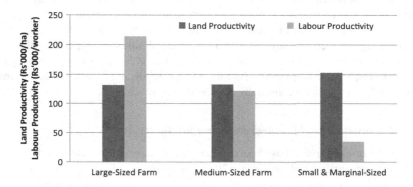

Figure 8.6 Land and labour productivity across different farm sizes

Cropping in this area is Sugarcane-dominated. It is a commercial and thus more remunerative crop. It occupies more or less three-fourths share of total land of large-sized farms. It however takes longer to grow Sugarcane. Its sowing session begins in March and harvested in December. Agro-ecological conditions are favorable for farming, which does not necessitate excessive use of fertiliser and irrigation. In addition, monsoon Rice and winter Wheat are also grown for domestic consumption and for the market.

In the village, per capita annual consumption is Rs 22,125 in households with large-sized farms, Rs 15,625 in medium-size and Rs 7,250 in small and marginal farms. Farmers with large- sized farms tend to earn more income, thus they have higher disposable income to spend on cloths and children's education. Expenditure on medicines is lower in rural areas, which could indicate inadequate access to health care amenities or potential lack of health awareness. It could also mean the dearth of lifestyle-oriented health conditions such as high obesity, diabetics and blood pressure. Consumption therefore is directly proportional to household income.

8.06.03: agriculture productivity and savings

Land productivity increases from Rs 1.30 lakhs per ha to Rs 1.52 per ha for large to marginal landholdings respectively. Large farms also have a higher labour productivity as compared to smaller and marginal farm sizes (Figure 8.6). Efficient use of modern farm tools, machines and technologies by HHs with larger farms enhance agriculture production and land productivity. While small to marginal farms apply rudimentary and primitive tools for farming, which results in lower agriculture output. Thus, there is no additional income from the sale of agricultural products as the smaller farmers are enabled to produce food surplus. Over-supply of family labour in rural areas to work at farms creates disguised unemployment that diminishes labour productivity. This is particularly problematic for farmers with small landholdings.

Household saving is the difference between the income and expenditure associated with farm operations, assets and expenditure on domestic consumption. It is often kept for farm investment for the next year as additional input to help increase agriculture output. Saving rate often diminishes exponentially with decreasing farm size. A highest annual saving of Rs 3.58 lakhs is reported by the HHs having large-sized farms of about 8.1 ha, whilst small and marginal farms with 0.61 ha of land save annually Rs 1,900 as farm savings.

8.06.04: assessment of farm-growth and productivity

Using the questionnaire-based survey data, a production function was developed to assess agricultural output for the 2013–14 assessment year, t_1. Total farm savings for the previous year (i.e., 2012–13), t_0, is an additional spending for the current assessment year and is spent on the maintenance of assets, capital inputs and labour to increase farm output. The parameters of production function however are sensitive to change in any input. Values of depreciated inputs especially related to technology (e.g. seed, fertiliser and irrigation) were placed in the production function. The constant and coefficients of the function, notated as PA, B_1 and B_2 (Equation 8.1) were calculated at a farm level. The parametric relationships of farm attributes indicate that:

- Increasing size of farms increases the coefficient of potential production for capital investment in technological input but it diminishes as labour input increases (Table 8.2). It is true to say that technology increases agricultural production at larger farms by allowing farm-HHs to increase the efficiency of farm operations. This cannot be concluded for small and medium-sized farms.
- Annual farm growth was higher (4.01 per cent) in larger farms but it is reported lower (only to 1.87 per cent) in small and marginal-sized farms. Households with small landholdings often use family workers and grow food grains largely for domestic consumption. Dairy farming is the main non-farm activity performed at farms to earn additional income.
- Small and marginal farms are more productive as they are intensively cultivated with higher land productivity (Rs 1,53,000/ha). But production increases slowly in these farms (1.87 per cent annually) so that the growth rate is lower. Due to the higher labour intensity, lower labour productivity is reported in small and marginal-sized farms.
- Further increase in inputs is not economically viable in small and marginal farms because of very high Incremental Input-Output Ratio (IIOR = 9.21). As a result, agriculture production grows slowly. Medium-sized farms (2–4 ha) are more likely to be receptive to higher technological inputs to help grow agriculture production. Low prices of farm products could also impact on farm productivity. The relative prices of food grains are often lower than more profitable commercial crops, which are 'consumer-driven' production. Consequently, larger farms focus more on the cultivation of

Table 8.2 Parameters of production function and assessment of growth and productivity during 2012–13 to 2013–14 in different farm sizes

Sl. no.	Items	Farm size		
		Large	Medium	Small and marginal
1	**Additional spendings (Rs) of savings and borrowings for**			
	Maintenance*	1,58,650	8,950	3,000
	Increase in technological inputs	1,00,000	10,000	10,000
	Labour increase	1,00,000	10,000	6,000
	Total	**3,58,650**	**28,950**	**19,000**
2	**Parameters of production function**			
	Total value of maximum expected biophysical output at farm (PA, Rs/ha)	18,09,354	5,33,934	1,64,950
	Total hidden capacity of farm for capital Investment (B_1) (Rs/ha)	64,541	9,685	6,094
	Total hidden capacity of farm for labour increase (B_2) (Rs/ha)	57,256	35,830	11,206
	Potential production coefficient for capital investment (B_1/CX)	0.46499	0.3725	0.2539
	Potential production coefficient for labour increase investment (B_2/WL)	0.1684	0.3583	0.4872
3	**Total farm output (Rs) and annual growth (%)**			
	Surveyed output (2012–13) (PYt_0)	10,65,000	2,98,000	93,000
	Assessed output by model (2013–14) (PYt_1)**	11,07,722	3,08,489	94,739
	Total increase in output**	42,722	10,489	1,739
	Annual output growth (%)**	4.011	3.52	1.87
4	**Incremental IIOR (dI/dO)**	4.681	1.906	9.21
5	**Farm land productivity (Rs/ha)**			
	Surveyed productivity for 2012–13	1,31,481	1,33,035	1,52,959
	Assessed productivity for 2013–14	1,36,756	1,37,718	1,55,310
	Change in land productivity (Rs/ha)	5,275	4,683	2,351
6	**Farm labour productivity (Rs/worker)**			
	Surveyed productivity for 2012–13	2,13,912	1,22,300	34,857
	Assessed productivity for 2013–14	1,84,930	92,494	29,869
	Change in labour productivity (Rs/worker)	28,982	29,806	4,988

N.B.: compilled by Authors

*= Maintenance costs is equal to share of additional spandings based on 15 percent depreciation rate on the major assets such as tractor and tubewell which have 20 years of life and determined by using Input Pulse Response function (Eqn.-8.2).

** = Assessed output is based on simulations made to use Production Function (Eqn.-8.1) which transfers inputs including additional ones (technological and labour) to agriculture output. Simulated growth from 2012-13 to 2013-14 and productivity for each year have been calculated by using assessed output.

commercial crops, which tend to produce greater surpluses for the market. Contract farming, which is demand-based farming, is often performed at large farms.

8.06.05: agriculture growth simulation in different farm sizes

Agriculture growth is simulated using input pulse response model. The depreciation in agriculture assets and production function to use additional inputs are determined based on savings of the previous year (i.e., 2012–13). The following key conclusions are drawn from the results:

- Potential production coefficient determines the rate of change in the hidden capacity of agricultural production based on biophysical capacity of land to ascertain the existing production when inputs are applied. This coefficient is higher for capital investment (technological) (0.464) in larger farms, which means that larger farms are relatively more capable of converting land capacity potential to increase total agriculture production. An increase of technological inputs is thus more profitable in larger farms. Potential production coefficient for labour input however is very low in these farms. Therefore, these farms use technological inputs and intensify farming methods and operations through changing the cropping pattern from food grains to commercial crops. Opposite to this, small and marginal-sized farms are labour-intensive and driven by traditional infrastructure to operate them.

- Agricultural output increases more rapidly in large-sized farms when farm inputs are increased. An annual growth of 4.68 per cent was simulated in these farms. Growth simulations, with additional capital inputs and labour input increase of Rs 1000 per ha, stimulate faster growth in medium-sized farms (Figure 8.7 A).

- Increases in land and labour productivity are often higher in large and medium-sized farms because of comparatively lower IIOR. Higher labour productivity indicates that they have higher capacity for absorbing additional labour in farm operations.

- Effects of changing agro-climatic conditions on agriculture growth are analysed by considering the maximum expected biophysical production available at farm (PA) as a variable in production function (Equation. 8.1). Simulated agriculture productivity (PYt_n) increases at a rate at which maximum expected biophysical production increases. PA works as numerator in the mathematical form of the production function (Equation 8.1). On account of operation of diminishing law of agriculture production activities at farm, simulated growth diminishes exponentially as biophysical production is increased at farm (Figure 8.8). This means that biophysical potential does not influence the growth processes.

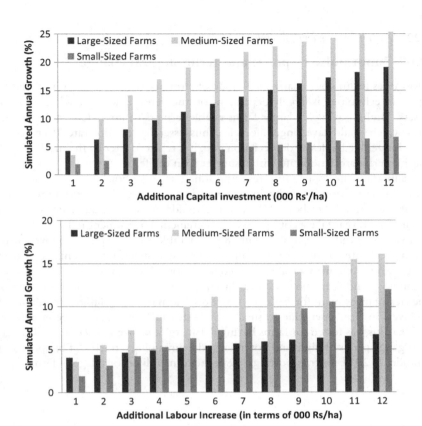

Figure 8.7 Simulated growth subject to additional technological investments and labour increase in production function

Figure 8.8 Simulated growth subject to increase in maximum expected biophysical production at farm

8.07 Input pulse response and technological change

How does technology change the mode of farm operations? Duration of change in farm technology is largely dependent on the depreciation rate of agricultural assets. Higher savings at larger farms enable farmers to upgrade farm technologies, which would have longer lifecycles, thus lesser depreciation rate. If a machine with longer life has lesser depreciation rate, it is replaced later by the machine that has higher depreciation rate with a shorter span of life.

Calibrating the input pulse response function (Equation 8.2) at 15 per cent annual depreciation rate with incremental investment of Rs 1,000 annually on assets and inputs for about 21 years, the trends of depreciated value of investment of each year take a concave shape. Incremental investment follows a kind of 'conversion trend' over time (Figure 8.9 and Table 8.3). Response to investment often accelerates technological change in its initial stage, but it diminishes over time with the maturity of the technological adoption. However, the adoption of technology and farm tools is slower in small and marginal-sized farms because of the lack of investment for replacing traditional farm tools and limited requirement to invest in farm assets due to small farm size, which makes it less economically viable. This was tested for farms having 8.1 ha of farm size located in the Ganga-Ramganga plains of high land potential and maintaining a tractor of big power of a model of 2011 for transporting Sugarcane to mandi or for tillage of farm.

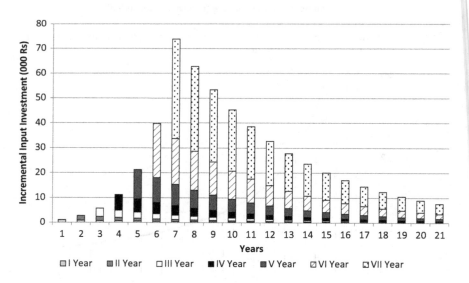

Figure 8.9 Input pulse response of Rs 1000 as additional input investment each year and depreciated value of old investment (at annual rate of 15 percent) each year in the time duration of 21 years

Table 8.3 Readily available calculator to calculate incremental input investment at depreciated rate of 15 percent annually

Years of investment	Initial investment	I year	II Year	III year	IV Year	V Year	VI Year	VII Year
1	1000	1000						
2	1000	850	1850					
3	1000	723	1573	3422				
4	1000	614	1337	2909	6331			
5	1000	522	1136	2472	5381	11712		
6	1000	444	966	2102	4574	9955	21667	
7	1000	377	821	1786	3888	8462	18417	40084
8	1000	321	698	1518	3305	7193	15654	34071
9	1000	272	593	1291	2809	6114	13306	28961
10	1000	232	504	1097	2388	5197	11310	24617
11	1000	197	428	932	2030	4417	9614	20924
12	1000	167	364	793	1725	3755	8172	17785
13	1000	142	310	674	1466	3191	6946	15118
14	1000	121	263	573	1246	2713	5904	12850
15	1000	103	224	487	1059	2306	5018	10923
16	1000	87	190	414	901	1960	4266	9284
17	1000	74	162	352	765	1666	3626	7892
18	1000	63	137	299	651	1416	3082	6708
19	1000	54	117	254	553	1204	2620	5702
20	1000	46	99	216	470	1023	2227	4846
21	1000	39	84	184	400	870	1893	4119

8.08 Summary

In this chapter, a robust agriculture growth model was developed by integrating two commonly used functions: the production and the input pulse function. The model simulated the effects of technology, labour and farm environment on agriculture growth. A case study of a village located in the Western part of Greater Ganga Plains was conducted to test model validity to assess agriculture growth across different sizes of farm.

Excessive supply of farm labour (especially the engagement of family labour) reduces labour productivity in small and medium-sized farms, which in turn creates disguised unemployment. IIOR is very high in small and medium-sized farms that arrest the growth process because of increased burden of farm labour on finite land supply. Consequently, unemployed or underemployed farm labourers migrate to urban labour markets for employment in non-farm activities. Unlimited supply of unskilled labour from rural areas is more likely to dump down wages in urban areas as the unskilled labourers from rural areas are often willing to accept lower wages to increase household income.

Land consolidation and cooperative farming have significant benefits for small and medium-sized farm owners to help innovate and accelerate growth process. Land consolidation and common farm infrastructure are created under cooperative farming schemes for small and medium farmers. Land consolidation is successfully completed in Punjab, Haryana and Uttar Pradesh and being implemented in other states through which smaller parcels are amalgamated into a larger farm to help improve operational efficiency and to achieve the economies of scale. Cooperative farming is widely practised in West Bengal where farms are predominately smaller in size.

Opportunities to increase agriculture growth and productivity is higher in medium-sized farms (2–4 ha) where the land potential supports further growth. These farms have the capacity to absorb additional labour in farm operations to help reach the full potential of land. Farmers often diversify crop patterns and apply modern technologies such as tractor and diesel engine to optimise farm production. Twenty per cent of total farms are medium-sized in India.

Growth is much more influenced by technological inputs. On account of the effect of the diminishing law of return in operation of agriculture, simulated agriculture growth tends to diminish over time. However, higher land potential (agro-climatic conditions) increases agriculture production and productivity at a constant rate, but it is less likely to influence agriculture growth.

Large-sized farms in the upper part of the Great Plains of India (Punjab, Haryana and Western Uttar Pradesh) are much more productive and market-driven. Larger farms use more powerful and high-capacity harvesters, tractors and thrashers to help increase farm productivity. Commercial cultivation of cash crops has helped farmers to generate surplus food production for the market. This has led to additional savings for farmers and thus further investment in farm to enhance production. The market-driven farm production thus has proven to be a successful strategy, which has helped many farmers to move out of subsistence farming and break the vicious circle of poverty.

9 Food production, consumption and insecurity

9.01 Introduction

Food insecurity is a major and a growing concern in the 21st century. Food is the basic necessity, which is fundamental to human survival. However, there are large segments of societies globally that struggle to fulfil the basic nutritional requirements. Globally, food production has been kept ahead of demand for the last few decades and now more food is produced to feed the world's population (Dyson 1996). In 2009/2001, 2250 Mt of grains was produced, which is approximately 325 kg annually per capita. But in spite of the food supply being so good and the successful maintenance of food production ahead of per capita globally, about 925 million people had to go to bed hungry in 2010 (Food and Agricultural Organisation 2010). Increase in production is not the only factor that secures the future of food supply.

Whether there is sufficient food to meet the daily dietary need of about 7 billion people on earth remains a public policy concern for many governments. There is no consensus on the amount of food that we need to produce to sustain and secure the supply of basic food commodities. From a geographical perspective, the fundamental question is whether the supply of food exists where it is most needed? This question necessitates a deeper investigation into the spatial mismatch between the areas of production and areas of consumption at a small area level. Food insecurity is fundamentally a spatial misalignment of demand and supply and the associated distribution networks.

In this chapter, the production of basic food grains is analysed to capture the national trends and changes in cropping patterns since the Independence of India. A district-level analysis is then carried out to enable mapping the scale of food production. The food availability in rural and remote India is of particular interest as farmers continue to change from growing the traditional crops largely for household consumption, to commercial crops for the market or for industrial production of processed food. Consumption patterns in rural and urban areas in India are also examined using National Sample Survey data, which highlight the key trends and changing consumption behaviour. The impact of changing consumption patterns are also investigated through the burgeoning demand for new genre of crops or for processed food such as breakfast cereals, which has not traditionally been part of the Indian dietary habits. The synthesis of production and consumption patterns help identify areas of food deficiency or surplus. This chapter thus generates evidence to help devise and deploy area-specific strategies to help mitigate challenges associated with malnutrition and undernourished population in food deficit areas or rising obesity in metropolitan cities.

9.02   Key trends in food grain production

Having compared the increase in the area under food grain crops, which include cereals (Rice, Jowar, Bajara, Ragi, Small Millers, Wheat, and Barley) and pulses (Gram, Tur and others) with the increase in population across different planning periods, it is concluded that there has been a relative increase in food grain production in India. The modernisation of farming and the demand led to significant changes in the types of crop and the areas where they were traditionally grown. It is not just the total production output that translates into securing a country's food requirements, but it is also essential to consider the changing patterns in agriculture practices that would potentially make places more vulnerable to the shortage of food.

The production share of total pulses declined from 18.6 per cent to 6.6 per cent and the Rice production share remained within the range from 37.8 to 45.9 per cent throughout the planned period (Figure 9.1A). Production of Pulses, Jowar, Bajara and Millets declined and were replaced by Wheat, which increased its share in terms of production from 13 per cent (1950–1) to an astounding 40 per cent (2013–14). This is one of the key reasons for the decline of Bajara and Pulses after the Green Revolution. The share of Maize production however has stabilised at its lowest level. Maize is also well-adaptive with local weather conditions, which makes it less vulnerable to the threats from climate change.

Areas under traditional crops in India have declined to the record level, which were supporting the daily food requirements particularly for the rural populace. The area under cereals was 97 million ha in 1950–1, which increased to 121 million ha in 2013–14, most of which were confined to Uttar Pradesh, Madhya Pradesh, Maharashtra and Rajasthan. Surprisingly, the area under food grains also declined from 127 million ha to 121 million ha (1990–1 to 2005–6) after the economic liberalisation and, then to 120 million ha in 2012–13 (Figure 9.1B). This is due to a significant decrease in the area of Jowar and Bajra, which reduced from 24.83 million ha to 17.97 million ha.

There are numerous causes for these changes in agricultural land use and production patterns including the rapid development of infrastructure and market systems, acceleration in metropolitan-driven urbanisation and changes in relative price of crops. Such market forces have increased the production of high-value crops demanded in larger megacities or in international markets. This in turn has resulted in less production of food grains. There are three main reasons behind the production change of food grain crops. These include:

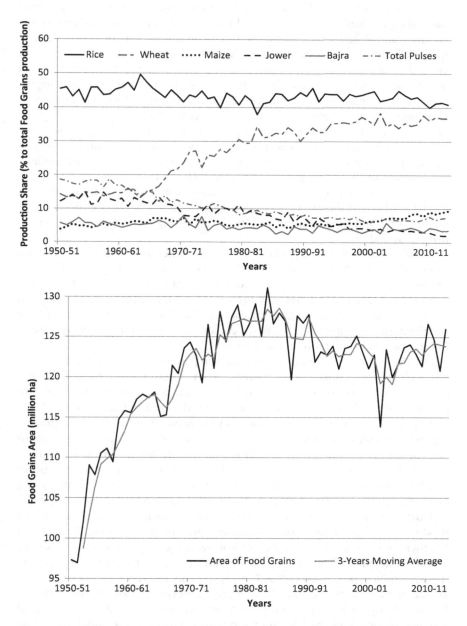

Figure 9.1 Share of the production of food grains to total grain production (A) and the area under food grains (B)

The first is the rapid increase in the total production of Rice and Wheat prior to the onset of economic liberalisation. Since then, the production of these crops has slightly reduced or at least stabilised to its current level. The total production of Jowar and Bajara, crops which are often consumed by poor people in rural India, fell sharply during the period of Liberalisation and later. Maize is the only grain that increased due to its growing commercial value. The production of pulses also stabilised after the Green Revolution (Figure 9.2). Interestingly, the production of pulses recovered from the earlier decline (0.814 million tonnes/year), which is almost equal to the rate of Rice production during the early phase of agricultural development. In subsequent planning phases, the production of pulses again lost its growth, which stumbled down to 0.106 million tonnes/year during the Green Revolution and reached to a record low level at 0.012 million tonnes/year in the Post-Liberalisation phase. However, it somewhat recovered with the production reaching at 0.644 million tonnes/year during 2007–08 to 2013–14 (see Table 9.1). These shortages of pulses, which are the key daily intake for the Indian population, resulted in importing these crops from overseas markets at higher prices.

The second is the impact of monsoon-related weather uncertainty and the application of seed-fertiliser technology on the growth of food grain production. One of the key issues with the Indian agriculture system in the past is the fluctuation in food production, which has now been more stabilised. Part of the fluctuation can be attributed to the uncertainty associated with the monsoon weather. The sustained use of rudimentary farming techniques in 21st century India also led to lower production and farm productivity.

The *third* is the cereals-based consumption patterns in rural India. However, rapid changes in consumption pattern, from traditional staple-food culture (the dominance of food grains with home-made food) to the flourishing of popular fast food culture in urban areas, have changed the food basket. More variety of food grains is now supplied and consumed in urban areas. Emerging popular culture (eating-out) and availability of the variety of food items has reduced per capita cereal consumption. Vegetables and meat substituted cereals. Increasing consumption inequalities and changing eating habits are also influencing the food production and processing landscapes of India. Rural poor are much more dependent on their own produced traditional food, while and the majority of urban people have started consuming more meat-based products. Rice and Wheat-based foods are often preferred in the Central and Southern Indian states, while on the contrary, the majority of people in the Eastern and North East Indian states prefer to eat non-vegetarian food. As the per capita expenditure on food in urban India increases, so does the overall demand for processed food (Re-emerging World Advisory Services 2012). Rapidly changing food consumption habits are, therefore, shaping the food production practices, which cause food distribution issues and longer *food mileage* in India.

Production of Jowar and Bajra has significantly fluctuated in response to their production growth (Table 9.1). The rate of the production of pulses slowly

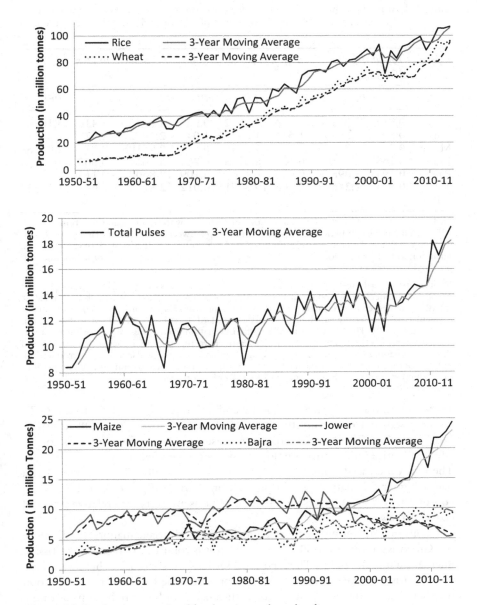

Figure 9.2 Production trends of food grains and total pulses

decreased over time until the Post-Liberalisation phase, and then increased in subsequent periods. The degree of fluctuation per unit of production-increase, however, rose from 12.25 in the initial phase of agricultural development (1950–1 to 1969–70) to 19.35 in the Green Revolution phase (1970–1 to

Table 9.1 Annual production increase (PI, in million tonnes/year) and degree of production fluctuation (PF) in different phases of agricultural development in India

Crops	19950–1 to 1969–70		1970–1 to 1989–90		1990–1 to 2006–7		2007–8 to 2013–14	
	PI	PF	PI	PF	PI	PF	PI	PF
Rice	0.914	2.93136	1.506	2.7012	0.963	4.3349	1.4102	3.1036
Wheat	0.542	2.58266	1.616	1.64292	1.045	2.50722	2.477	3.03431
Maize	0.203	1.00089	0.11	1.2985	0.416	2.05105	0.77	2.4226
Jower	0.168	4.5916	0.173	5.03654	0.284	4.0616	−0.363	–
Bajra	0.194	5.09533	−0.007	–	0.109	12.8609	−0.113	–
Total Pulses	0.814	12.24695	0.106	19.34916	0.012	72.5154	0.644	1.63037

N.B.: The concept of Production Fluctuation (PF) is linked with the annual Production Increase (PI) within a particular period. So the production gap between actual and moving average production of a particular point of time was calculated to measure the degree of PF of various crops. Such concept of Production Fluctuation would help in testing the premise of increasing crop production increases its fluctuation over time and vice versa.

Definitions: Annual Production Increase (PI) of different crops is calculated by using slope 'b' of simple line connecting two points first and last in production trend as referred to b = $(Pa1\text{-}Pa0)/(t1\text{-}t0)$. The degree of Production Fluctuation per unit of production increase over time (PF) is calculated by using the variability formula as standard deviation (called standard fluctuation, SF) per unit of PI. The Square Root of Standard Deviation from the 3- years moving average is formulated as SF=$\{\Sigma(Pa\text{-}Pm)^2/n\}^{1/2}$, where Pa refers to the quantity of actual production and Pm = the quantity of 3- years moving average production of particular foodgrain crop and n= number of time unit, that is year in present case. The degree of Production Fluctuation per unit of production increase (PF) is defined as PF= (SF/PI) for n years.

1989–90) and then to 72.51 in the Liberalisation phase (1990–91 to 2006–7). It decreased to 1.63 during the Post-Liberalisation phase (2007–08 to 2013–14) (Table 9.1). This is in spite of the increased prices as shown in the rise of the wholesale price index of total pulses during the time of economic liberalisation. The index increased from 145 in 1997–8 to 254 in 2006–7. Jowar and Bajara had a higher fluctuation rate in production than Rice production because of constant threat from adverse weather conditions and very low relative prices of coarse cereals.

Traditional manuring, such as animal dung and green manure used before the Green Revolution (1950–1 to 1970–1), was robust in mitigating the risk of fluctuation in food grains. The seed-fertiliser-based technology, which was introduced during the Green Revolution, has proven to be less resilient to monsoon weather. The production of food grains thus had a lot less variability prior to the Green Revolution. Crop-price-dependent production of the Post-Liberalisation phase had the most fluctuating trends in food grain production because of the market demand uncertainty. Production of Maize however has the least fluctuation compared to other crops in India. This is because Maize is traditionally the staple food for poor and disadvantaged people and those farmers who grow Maize for their domestic consumption.

The timely setting or delay of monsoon in India causes delay in the sowing session, which often leads to either severe drought or flooding. The production of food grains, therefore, is heavily dependent on rainfall received during the monsoon season. Monsoon-associated risk however has been mitigated through the use of irrigation and ground water; nonetheless most parts of India still remain under the risk of monsoon. Two empirical studies were conducted to show the impact of monsoon on crop production in India. One was conducted by O'Hare (1997) to correlate trends of rainfall and production in Rice-growing areas in India. Another by Singh et al. (2011) has shown the adverse impact of monsoon rainfall on food grain production by isolating the effects of Green Revolution technology by taking 7-years moving averages of various food grain crops production. These studies conclude that the change in the amount of monsoon rainfall is positively correlated to the fluctuations of food grain production. Fluctuation in production of food grains, for example, is significantly correlated with rainfall intensity ($r = 0.75$). It could mean that the monsoon failure in a particular year carries a high risk in causing crop failure in India.

9.03 Per capita net availability of food in India

From a per capita term, the national statistics are misnomer as they are absolute rather than relative indicators. These measures don't account for population per unit or in other words population pressure on land. Food grains production increased by 120 million tonnes from 50.82 to 170.47 million tonnes in 50 years from 1950–1 to 1989–90, however the extra production was largely consumed by 483 million people (361 million in 1951 to 844 million in 1991 and 1028 million in 2001) who were added to the total population in India.

Interestingly, per capita net availability of food grains was higher (548.0 gram/day) at the beginning of the 20th century (1905–6). However, it significantly declined to 132 gram/day at the time of India's Independence (1945–6) or immediately after World War II. There were severe food shortages in many regions during the British rule in India. Bulk export of food grains from India to England and other British colonies might have contributed to this level of severity of food shortages. World War I and II would have also fuelled food crisis in India during those periods.

The trends in net availability of food grains in Post-Independence India fluctuate significantly. There was slight improvement when net availability of food grains increased from 395 grams/day in 1951 to 469 gram/day in 1961. It remained relatively constant in the 1960s, but declined slightly in the 1970s. It stabilised during the sixth and seventh five-year plans. The sluggish growth in net availability of food grains in India was largely attributed to rapid population growth, which grew geometrically whilst food grains production increased arithmetically (Figure 9.3). This posited several planning challenges and policy concerns.

Further analysis indicates that the net food grains availability per capita was slightly improved in cereals from 334 gram/day in 1951 to 494 gram/day

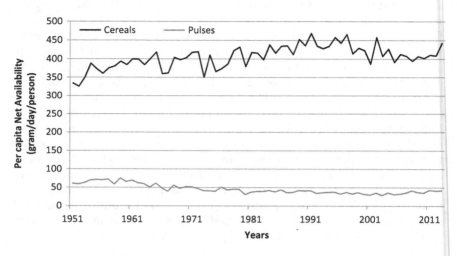

Figure 9.3 Per capita net availability of food grains (1951 to 2013)

in 2002. But a rapid decline of 30 gram/day in pulses (excluding gram) was recorded. It was 60.7 gram/day in the early 1950s, which reduced to 29 gram/day in early 2000s. These trends in food grains availability denote the likely impact of the Green Revolution technologies, which had variegated impacts on the production of different crops. The per capita net availability of pulses is substantially lower (38.1 gram/day) than the balanced diet recommended by Indian Council of Medical Research for adults having vegetarian diet (65.0 gram/day). In the first decade of the 21st century the population of India touched the 1,110 million or 1.11 billion mark. Since 2001, about 110 million additional people are to be fed in India. The unfulfilled basic food requirements of populace and the sluggish growth in per capita net food grains availability has had raised numerous food insecurity concerns for strategic planners to ensure continuous supply of sufficient food for an ever-increasing population in India.

9.04 Approaches to food distribution in India

Food security, in simple terms, is the continuity of food supply with access to food by all sections of the population (Adamowicz 1988). According to Adamowicz, there are two approaches to food security. These include the demand-based and consumption-based approaches. However, regional approach of food requirement is also important. In the following section, the three key food distribution mechanisms are discussed.

9.04.1 Public distribution system (PDS) approach

The demand-based approach to food distribution focuses on fulfilling the food consumption requirements, which vary significantly between different sections (e.g. rural–urban and poor–rich) and across regions in India. Rising income inequality and changing consumption habits underpin consumption behaviour of increasingly gloablised Indian society. For example, the gap in the average spending (or income) in urban India in 1999–2000 between the richest and poorest in the 10th percentile is about 12 times. This figure increased to 15 times in the year 2011–12.

In rural India, this ratio is slightly lower, but increasingly becoming more alarming. It increased from 7 to 9 times during the same period after the economic liberalisation (Sunday Times of India 2013). Although the growing hiatus between rich and poor is not a major concern *per se*, providing better access to food for disadvantaged sections is seen as a major challenge. Having greater accessibility to food for the rich is not a problem, as long as it is not a hurdle for the disadvantaged to have access to basic food. This thus far has remained a 'wicked problem' globally, and a common approach to tackling this issue of inequality to access to food is now required.

The demand-based approach was adopted by the Indian Government after the Independence to administer and manage an efficient, fair, just and centralised model. The model has established a public system of food procurement, storage and distribution to institutionalise a fair and just system of food distribution to protect the interests of the economically disadvantaged society. The Government of India established a Public Distribution System (PDS), which administers a vast network of retail outlets for supplying basic food commodities at a subsidised rate to low-income households. PDS is also a government-operated or regulated logistics conduit, which manages a network of producers, wholesalers and retailers involved in food supply chains. This agency also regulates price-setting mechanisms to control market-led inflation in the commodity market.

PDS is an old concept first introduced before World War II during the colonial period to help eliminate the threats of famines and epidemics. During the British India, ration cards were issued to low-income families in selected cities and towns, which were at a higher risk of chronic food shortages. During the five-year plan periods, the Indian Government continued this scheme but with major modifications. Public distribution of food grains was essentially city based in the first five-year-plan period. Later on, it was extended to rural areas to establish a proper network of food grain distribution. The fair price shops (the lowest-level retail outlets) were extended about three times during the second five-year plan from 18,000 in 1951 to 51,000 in 1961.

In 1965, the creation of two agencies, Agriculture Price Commission (APC) and Food Corporation of India (FCI), consolidated the position of PDS to regulate food supply with the key objective to provide food grains and other essential commodities to vulnerable sections of Indian society at a reasonable price while simultaneously competing in the open commodity market. With this mission, PDS spread to around 1,750 Development Blocks under the Punchayti Raj System. PDS has largely contained black marketing of food in the open market system because of the mechanism of monitoring and analysis prices at the Block level.

As per the Planning Commission Guidelines, the households under the poverty line were identified to provide them access to subsidised food. In 1995–6, it was decided that families below the poverty line (BPL) need at least 10kg food per family each month. Later on a 'Transitory Allocation' of surplus food of 103 lakh tonnes was earmarked to the states for distribution. Families above the poverty line (APL) were also given subsidised food under this allocation. Two rates were fixed for these two sections of society: food purchase price was Rs 9.00 per kg of Wheat for APL families and Rs 4.50 per kg of Wheat for BPL families in 2000. Though, there were some differences in the quality of food. For effective implementation of food grain distribution, this scheme was changed with Food Security Act passed by the Parliament in 2013 under which prices of food, identification of beneficiaries, the nature of centre-state relations and food coupon systems were under consideration to make the scheme more effective.

9.04.2 Need-based approach

The need-based approach to food distribution refers to a system of meeting the daily minimum nutritional requirements of food. Recommended nutritional standards are often used to calculate minimum food intake per person to maintain a healthy life. Arguably, if the food grain production growth is higher than growth in consumption, the likelihood of food insecurity would be minimised. Some of the additional food requirements however could be imported from countries that are more efficient in the production of commodities. Maintaining a reasonable balance of trade remains a challenge for countries with a growing population like India. This is further exacerbated by the challenges associated with inadequate and obsolete logistics infrastructure required to support an efficient distribution of imported food commodities from ports to market catchments.

Some argue that a market-led food distribution system could lead to greater efficiency in food supply chains, but whether it would be able to handle the challenges of vertical and horizontal inequality in terms of food availability to various sections and accessibility to different parts of India requires further public debate.

Relatively slower growth of food grain production and chronic malnutrition are thwarting the long-term food insecurity in India. These have cascading effects on the entire food supply chain including the production, processing, storage, distribution and marketing of food commodities. The Indian Government has been tackling the issue of food insecurity using the line of poverty to ascertain different needs of the populace, which vary with time and place. The estimated population below the poverty line, according to the Planning Commission (now NITI Aayog) is 27.5 per cent to the total population in the BPL category in 2004–5. Population below the poverty line are eligible to procure basic food commodities at a subsidised rate below the market price through PDS. The determination of the optimal poverty line has remained a contentious topic for political debate at the floor of Indian Parliament, but this approach to dealing with food insecurity in India has some merits, provided it is implemented effectively and efficiently.

9.04.3 *Regional supply chain approach*

Regional supply chain approach allows linking areas of production and areas of consumption so that the food distribution across a geographic space can be optimised. Regional approach to food distribution focuses on building integrated agri-supply chains to enhance the efficiency of distribution channels. This approach also helps identify the regions of food deficiency or food surplus and the resultant flows of farm commodities along transport chains. This approach argues for minimising distribution costs of supplying food grains from the food collection centres (warehouses) to 'fair ration shops' or other wholesalers and retailors. It traces the physical movement of products from producers to consumers.

The regional approach is embedded in city-hinterland relationships whereby the interdependencies and functional linkages between key consumption points and production spaces are established. Mapping of agri-supply chains strengthens the internal links of producer–consumer relations, and stabilises production prices and food costs by integrating the commodity supply networks with food deficit areas. The formation of food supply chain clusters and their proper linkages help assess suppliers' selection and location choice and optimise retail networks (Viswanadham 2012).

The links between producers and traders are historically established in India. Local traders of nearby towns often directly visit farmers to procure food grain surpluses at cheaper rates during the harvesting season. Traders then sell the products acquired from farmers at higher rates in local markets. The government intervention through PDS has helped to regulate food purchases from farmers who traditionally have sold their produce to local traders. The Food Corporation of India has been instrumental in facilitating the collection, procurement and distribution of food commodities in rural India.

During the first decade of the 21st century, particularly after the economic liberalisation, there were significant market-led changes in food distribution networks. Agri-supply chains developed by the private sector in larger cities helped balance food supply and demand to consider the profit of producer and supplier and the protection of consumers' interest. Their supply networks contain a four-tier system to link producers with consumers. Farmers (producer), processors, distributors and consumers are the four tiers that are seamlessly interlinked in the food procurement, processing, storage and distribution function (Figure 9.4).

The rise of cities as nodes of substantive consumption of food is shaping the contemporary agriculture production landscape in India. They are also processing and distribution hubs, which play significant role in determining the price-setting mechanism. This has led to the creation of spatial markets that regulate the interplay of demand and supply networks. The mapping of areas of production and consumption and the mechanism through which they are interconnected is paramount to the efficient working of commodity market in India. This would help to identify the food deficit areas, which could then be targeted.

The development of food supply networks has strengthened the links among different stakeholders in three different ways:

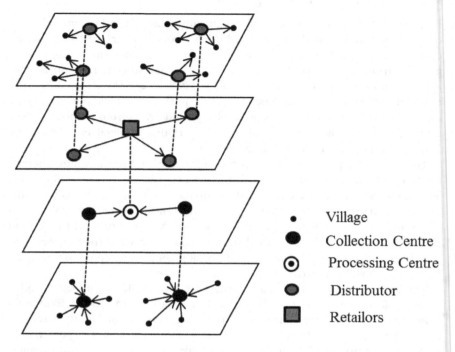

Figure 9.4 Distribution network of a typical farm supply chain (modified after Lazzarini et al. 2001)

Expansion of demand-driven production

The efficient coordination of supply and demand for farm commodities at a given market has led to an expansion of sales volume. Producers have become an integrated part of the supply chain. They now have greater access to information on consumer demand and product pricing, through which they are able to make more informed decisions on what and when to grow. They have started to operate as a contractor in a commercial farming system to produce products for the market. Subsistence farming is thus largely being gradually replaced by commercial farming, but it is still restricted in the vicinity of mega-cities. Producers have expanded the farm production system to not only produce food grains, vegetables and fruits but also allied products such as milk, milk products, fish, poultry and piggery.

Reduction of delivered costs

In a competitive market, the suppliers generally determine the price of products, which is often assessed through market demand and supply conditions. Wholesalers and retailers are also members of commodity supply chains who play a critical role in providing the information of what, where and when a particular commodity is needed. The development of smart food networks, linking farmers, food processing companies and distributors, has made the information more transparent and accessible. This in turn has helped reduce transportation and distribution costs (Van-der-Vorst 2006).

Maintenance of supply–demand balance

Demand–supply equilibrium or near equilibrium is maintained through market mechanism rather than by the government. This has set up a pricing mechanism which determines when, where and at what price farmers should sell their products. Corporate affiliations, contractual affiliations, members from trading communities and cooperatives are the key chain members. However, the corporatisation of farm and the consequent horizontal and vertical integration of supply chains are shaping the agriculture commodity markets, particularly at the downstream end of the supply chains.

9.05 Estimating food consumption levels

Estimating food production per unit of land or input in terms of the volume and composition of food consumption is complex. The food distribution dynamics are heavily dependent on consumption patterns. An accurate set of consumption data is thus an essential requirement to such type of regional analysis where the origin and destination of food distribution are gathered. In India, National Sample Survey Organisation (NSSO) is a government organisation which collects and compiles data on household consumption by conducting questionnaire-based household (HH) surveys. The reliability of data, sample design, data formatting and procedure of data collection are scrutinised and improved to enhance the reliability of consumption statistics. But, it is not completely an error-free procedure and is often subject to numerous caveats. Nonetheless, the data is comprehensive, and collected systematically, scientifically and reliably.

9.05.1 National sample survey data: sample design, data formatting and reliability

The 66th round of survey data, collected during the period between the 1 July 2009 and 30 June 2010, contained questions related to consumption patterns and socio-economic characteristics at a household level. It was administered by NSSO, which is an organisation within the Ministry of Statistics and Program Implementation. The unit-level survey data were compiled and aggregated at a district level using geocoded location. This has enabled mapping of consumption patterns through identification of areas of food surplus or deficit in India.

The sample design was a two-stage process of sample collection. In the first stage, the number of HH samples was determined to cover a minimum proportion of the population of the district enumerated as per the 2001 Census. Two main strata of population, namely urban and rural, were used for sampling. Sampling was adjusted for large size village/towns within the district. The data are arranged into basic strata: urban and rural. In addition, cities with population greater than 10 lakhs formed separate strata in the district.

The second stage of sample identification began at the lower end of the settlement system. The lowest level of settlement unit is the village (used from the list of Village Directory, Census Publication, XA and B, Census 2001), which was considered for HH sample collection to determine the total number of sample size in order to form a hamlet group/Sub-block. The smallest-sized village with less than 1,200 population has only 1 hamlet; villages with 1,200–1,799 population have 3 hamlets/Sub-blocks; villages with 1,800–2,399 have 4; 2,400–2,999 has 5; 3,000–3,599 has 6 and so on.

In case, if samples of HHs were difficult to allocate spatially, the replacement of sample HHs based on the closest metaled road (bitumen/asphalt), and/or the proximity to the nearest infrastructural amenity such as an educational institution or a medical and postal facility is performed. Further, HH statistics of consumption expenditures, during a specific period called reference period, are collected in terms of value (in Rs) and quantity (in kg) of goods and services which:

1   are produced as an output by the number of members in a household,
2   are received by HH as a remuneration and through social transfers, and
3   on consumption of which expenditure is incurred by HH.

A Schedule Type 1.0 for the consumption was prepared to collect HH data. The consumption Schedule follows the item code as given National Industrial Classification Code (NIC) 2004. The Schedule Type 1.0 has the following parts of consumer expenditures (Table 9.2).

Table 9.2 Format for the Schedule Type 1.0 for the collection of data on consumption and expenditure

Schedule Type	Expenditure items	No. of sub-items
1.0:5.1	Consumption of cereals, pulses, milk products, sugar and salt during the last 30 days	46
1.0:5.2	Consumption of edible oils, egg, fish and meat, vegetables, fruits, spices, beverages and processed food during the last 30 days	110
1.0:6	Consumption of energy (fuel, light and HH appliances)	15
1.0:7	Consumption of clothing and bedding etc. during last 365 days	22
1.0:8	Consumption of footwear	6
1.0:9	Expenditure on education and medical goods and services	14
1.0:10	Expenditure on miscellaneous goods and services	36
1.0:11	Expenditure for purchase and construction (including repair and maintenance) of durable goods for domestic use	51
1.0:12	Summary of consumer expenditure	42

Source: NSSO, New Delhi

9.06 Key food consumption patterns (2009–10)

The consumption of the main food items such as cereals, pulses, milk and milk products, vegetables, and fruits (for detail see Table 9.3) are analysed in this section. Main features are based on per capita food consumption statistics calculated by collecting samples of 58,432 rural and urban HHs through a survey conducted by the NSSO. The average value of consumption products was calculated to show the levels of consumption by district or HH. The key highlights of the consumption levels are discussed below.

About one-fourth of the total food grain consumption in India is cereals. Interestingly, it is about same for urban and rural areas (i.e., about Rs 1077/HH in rural and Rs 1050/HH in Urban areas). However, consumption of cereals produced at HH farms is more than 35 per cent to the total food consumption, which is used in home-produced food. Thus, most consumption of cereals is procured locally, whilst the rest is obtained from the local market, which might be sourced from neighbouring regions or overseas.

Table 9.3 Monthly food consumption (Rs per HH) in rural and urban India during the 30 days before survey days (survey conducted in 2009–10).

Item code	Name of the food item	Consumption in rural areas			Consumption in urban areas		
		Home products (Rs)	Total consumption (Rs)	Home products %	Home products (Rs)	Total consumption (Rs)	Home products %
129	Cereals	385	1077	35.74	84	1055	8.05
139	Cereal substitutes	21	75	28	2	59	3.57
159	Pulse and pulse products	41	285	14.38	10	298	3.35
169	Milk and milk products	433	780	55.51	82	829	9.89
179	Sugar	14	201	6.96	4	184	2.17
189	Salt	8	30	26.67	1	31	3.22
199	Edible oil	21	264	7.95	4	283	1.41
209	Egg, fish and meat	33	363	9.09	7	386	1.81
249	Vegetables	51	435	11.72	12	459	2.61
269	Fruits	26	148	17.56	11	179	6.14
279	Fruits (dry)	22	94	23.4	2	109	1.83
289	Spices and processed food	105*	141	74.46	46*	146	31.51
Total		1160	3893	29.8	265	4015	6.6

N.B.: *Figures are provisional

Source: NSSO, 66th Round: Schedule-1.0 (Type-1), Tables 5.1 and5.2

Milk and milk products are the second items consumed in India. Almost 50 per cent of milk products are procured within the local commodity market in rural areas. Milk products, particularly in a vegetarian diet, are of high nutritional value to the rural population. Most farmers in India have cattle which they raise for milk. Dairy farming in most parts of India is a subsidiary farm activity. It is often carried out at a household level instead of for commercial purpose. A part of milk production is also available for sale within the local area, which provides an additional source of income for farmers. Commercial dairy farming however has started to shape market-based farming particularly in the vicinity of large metropolitan cities. Milk and milk products are supplied to more established wholesale and retail networks such as Anand Dairy milk supply in Gujrat, Mother dairy in Delhi, Nilgiris milk scheme in Karnataka and Paras. Milk products manufactured in the Western Uttar Pradesh are good examples to demonstrate the rising milk-oriented economies in the country.

Vegetables and fruits are the third set of items consumed in India. There are however significant differences in the consumption of fruits and vegetables between rural and urban areas. About 11 to 18 per cent of vegetables and fruits consumed in rural areas are grown within the farm, whilst this figure is only 2.6 per cent in urban areas (Table 9.3). Farmers tend to grow cereals, pulses, vegetables, spices and often a few fruit trees to fulfil their household requirements of food. Surplus food grains are supplied to the market. Farmers who are located in the city fringe grow vegetables for their own families as well as for urban markets. Some farmers also operate market gardens and grow vegetables on a commercial scale for sale in urban markets.

The per capita monthly consumption has two key structural components, namely consumption from home products or from the market. In 2009–10, the estimated monthly consumption per capita in rural India was Rs 728, 25 per cent of which constitutes food from home products, which are produced by rural HHs from their farms and processed at home. The main diet of rural HHs consists of home-produced milk and milk products.

In urban areas, producers supply milk within the locality. Residents within a locality in urban areas purchase milk from the producer every morning/evening to fulfil their daily demand (Deka 2011, see Figure 9.5 and 9.6). In urban India, the estimated monthly consumption per capita was slightly higher compared to its rural counterpart (Rs 932); however, it only constitutes 4 per cent of the consumption of home-made products. This led to the obvious conclusion that urban areas have their food procured from the market. Contrary to the conventional wisdom, the findings of this research indicate that urban dwellers do not necessarily consume more food than rural folks.

9.06.1: causes of variation in food consumption – case studies

One could examine the variation in food consumption from two different perspectives: the sectoral and integrative perspectives. The following two case studies

Figure 9.5 Local trading of milk in Guwahati City (Photo Courtesy: Jagdish Chandra Deka)

are presented to discuss the sectoral view to analyse the livelihood and food consumption patterns in India.

The first case study represents the dense forest Plains of Lower Assam (wood economy) while the other case study is from the hills of Meghalaya plateau (hill forest economy). Both are based on surveys which investigated the living conditions and consumption pattern of rural HHs in the forest areas of North Eastern region of India. One was conducted by Narzari (2013) by choosing forest area of about 605 sq km, which lies in the North Western corner of Kokrajhar district, Assam in the lower Brahmaputra valley. It is located at elevation ranging from 80 m to 310 m mean sea level in the foothills of Bhutan Himalayas stretching to the *Bhabar-Tarai* of older alluvial plains.

The second case study was conducted by Daimari (2013) in the Ri-Bhoi district lying in the Southern slopes of Meghalaya plateau with an altitudinal variation ranging from 600 m in its South part along the Brahmaputra plains to 1,000 m from mean sea level in the North part adjoining the upper part of the plateau. It covers about 2,500 sq km, which consists of a variety of physiographical features, rugged terrain, weather conditions, soil types and vegetal cover with the predominance of forest land (Figure 9.7).

The first case has poor road infrastructure and is isolated from the main market centre as it is far from the vicinity of National Highways (NH 31C touches a southern tip of the area but does not have any impact on its economy). The second case has access to better road infrastructure as NH 40 passes through its central part and connects two key urban centres: Guwahati in the North – a

Figure 9.6 Cattle (cow and buffalo) are raised as a part of the family in Indian villages

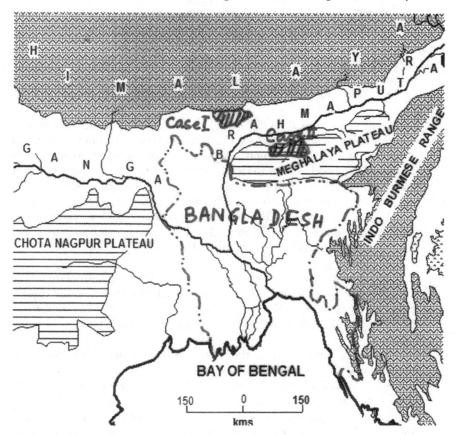

Figure 9.7 Location of surveyed areas in the North East region

regional economic hub of the North East region, and Shillong in the South – a historical cosmopolitan city.

Both cases are tribal dominated. The first case represents Boros, Rabhas and Santhals, which are mostly Hindu tribes; the second case only includes Khasi-Christian tribes. Livelihood and consumption of food are largely influenced by access to natural resources. Market and infrastructure have some impact on the means of livelihood and income levels. Literacy level is significantly higher but does not have much variation across the area. Impact of given determinants is evaluated by analysing HH data related to physical, social, economic and livelihood conditions.

Methodologically, the selection of HHs was based on a 'stratified' sampling technique at two levels: village and HH. First, the sample village selection was done by considering the variation in topographic features (lowland, flood plain and upland *Bhabar* for the first case and river valley, valley-slope and hill-tops for the second case), predominance of tribal society (dominance of major tribes/ communities) and the types of occupation (lumbering, fishing, cultivation and so on). The second level of selection was made at the HH level to consider the size, road accessibility, distance from market and literacy level of HH.

Key findings on the consumption pattern of tribes living in the forest (hills and plains) of the North Eastern region from these surveys are given below.

- Forest hill tribes of Ri-Bhoi district of the plateau spend lesser share of total consumption expenditure on food (56.5 per cent) than the forest plain tribes of Assam (63.8 per cent). Hill tribes spend sufficiently higher share on education (23.6 per cent) than the HHs residing in the forest plains of lower Brahmaputra valley (12–14 per cent) in spite of less rugged topography and high income from forest resources. This may also be due to lower accessibility to education centres in the dense forest. Lesser degree of variability in the share of food consumption to total consumption expenditure (61–7 per cent) shows greater homogeneity in food consumption patterns across the region.
- Ethnicity does not have any significant impact on food consumption in these areas. Most tribal communities have Rice-based food consumption in combination with fish or meat. Not much variety of food is available in rural areas. Rice-based local alcoholic drinks are often part of evening meals among hill tribes.
- Occupation of rural HHs in these areas is largely dependent on forest resources and farming. Access and availability of forest resources are the key factors driving consumption behaviour in tribal areas. As expected, the HHs living adjacent to forests are more dependent on forest resources. HHs also supplement their income by selling forest-based products in local markets. Another study conducted in the Cherrapunji area of Maghalaya plateau confirms the vitality of having access to forest to provide traditional fuel sources (firewood and charcoal). Access to forest resources is found to be a key driver of food consumption among tribal communities (Singh et al. 2014).

A case study of Sikandrabad Tehsil of Bulandshahr district, Uttar Pradesh, situated in the Eastern part of the National Capital Region (NCR) and Delhi shows how surplus crop production and food commodities create '*food complexes*' that influence the types of food consumed within its hinterland. A longitudinal study that requires regular visit to the site shows the structural and spatial changes that have had occurred in these food complexes over time. Changing land use and crop production patterns tend to shape food consumption within the local community. Some of the key changes in food complexes are discussed below:

1   *Wheat-Maize-Millets Food Complex* produces marketable surplus of Wheat and Maize for sale. Maize has commercial value as it is used for many processed food products such as popcorn, cornflakes, chicken and piggery feed.

A variety of Wheat products such as *maida, suji,* and raw materials for bakeries is supplied in the local market.

2   *Milk-Maize-Fodder Complex* represents the predominance of milk and milk products. Dairy is often considered as a subsidiary activity at farms. Maize and Jowar are often grown solely to feed to mulch cattle as fodder. Surplus milk is supplied in the local market to fulfil burgeoning demand in cities within the national capital region.

3   *Vegetable-Fruit Complex* constitutes farming dominated by orchards and market gardens. This complex supplies fruits and vegetables to nearby towns. Potato, cauliflower, chilli, cabbage and other vegetables are grown in market gardens, which operate commercially within the rural urban fringe of larger metropolitan cities.

9.06.2 *Rural versus urban consumption behaviour*

The results from the NSSO data show that consumption of food between rural and urban areas is similar. However there is significant variability in consumption patterns within urban areas as shown by a high coefficient of variability (CV = 135.61 percent). Thus, it can be implied that greater variety of food is consumed in cities and towns. Furthermore, highly skewed per capita monthly consumption (skewness = 15.355) (Table 9.6) suggests inequitable distribution of food consumption. Results of the rank-size rule shows that there is no significant difference in the consumption level between urban and rural districts. Rural and its counterpart urban areas maintain a certain ratio in their per capita consumption (i.e., 1:1.06) throughout India when districts are ranked in an ascending order from low to high. The areas of very high per capita monthly consumption (more than Rs 2,000) such as Punjab and Haryana also do not exhibit much difference in food consumption between rural and urban areas (Figure 9.8).

9.06.3 *Milk supply chains*

Milk production in this region is a subsidiary activity, which generates an additional income for farmers. Surplus Wheat and Rice and other products such as vegetables, fruits and milk and milk products are supplied to Delhi – the national capital and the key metropolitan city in the North Western Great Plains of India. The milk supply chain is regulated by the public agency or operated by private businesses. For instance, there are two milk supply chains, which connect rural suppliers to retail outlets in Delhi and surrounding satellite cities:

1   *Short-haul milk supply chain:* This short-haul milk chain connects rural milk suppliers to local demand in urban areas through locally organised milk processing centres which are often run by local vendors. They prepare milk products such as *khowa,* paneer (cheese) and sweets which are sold in the local

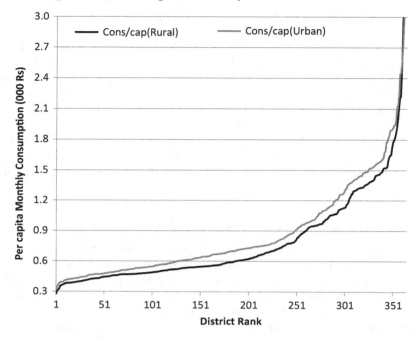

Figure 9.8 Rank-size pattern of per capita monthly consumption in rural and urban areas

market and supplied to Delhi and its satellite towns such as Ghaziabad (Uttar Pradesh), Noida, Faridabad, Gurgaon and Panipath (Haryana).

2   *Long-haul Delhi milk supply chain*: This corporatised and long-hauled milk supply chain extends from Delhi to its surrounding rural–urban hinterland. It functions as a multi-tiered system. At a lower order, farmers are direct suppliers of milk, whereby middle order villages act as a milk collection centre. Small towns are higher order centres where milk preservation centres are established which supply pasteurised milk either to the local consumers through various milk outlets, called milk booths, or directly to Delhi State. These centres also process milk into by-products such as powdered milk, preserved sweets, chocolates, cheese, ice cream, butter and *ghee* which are sold to local, national and international markets (Figure 9.9).

9.06.4 Food consumption and socio-economic correlates

Consumption of food is not only the means of fulfilling the basic needs of human body but also a representation of wealth, power and fulfilment of lifestyle choices. Arguably, food consumption should vary across regions and between sections of

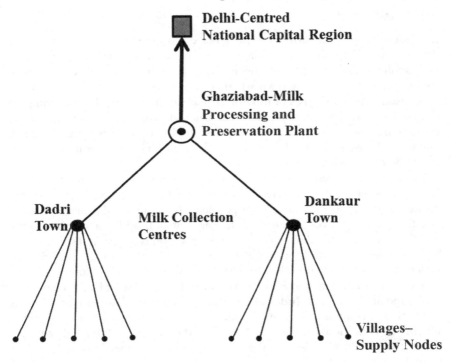

Figure 9.9 Hierarchically structured milk supply networks in Delhi-Dankaur area

society due to differences in physical and economical accessibility based on socio-economic status. Consumption levels are thus compared across different sections of Indian society.

A variety of determinants representing physical, biological and mental health of human body were recognised to influence the dietary habits and consumption behaviour (Parraga 1990). Several other characteristics such as social customs, demographic attributes (e.g. age and sex), institutionalised mind sets (e.g. education and access to health amenities) and economic burdens on HHs (e.g. employment and income) have also been proven to have the potential to affect the levels of food consumption (Sabates et al. 2001, Strauss 1982).

Sabates et al. (2001) developed a scale for estimating endogenously the adult equivalence, which measures per capita expenditure of individual HH. However, the question whether these determinants can be accounted for in explaining the HH consumption in India remains to be evaluated. In the following analysis, four key characteristics, namely education status, gender, economic burden on labour and labour employment in HH are assessed for their impact on consumption behaviour. They are detailed below.

(a) Education status

Education status often drives certain types of consumption behaviour among people. However, there is little empirical evidence to suggest that people who have attained higher education qualifications are more consumptive than their counterparts? It is also unknown whether people with different education status consume different types of food or does it vary by income levels. Using the census data, education attainment levels were categories against the per capita consumption of food. Four key categories of education levels were identified: number of households in a district with diploma or higher qualification; secondary; middle; and primary school.

These categories were then tabulated against the per capita consumption. Education landscape in India in terms of human capital accumulation is spatially fragmented. For instance, the number of people with a graduate diploma and above qualification is largely concentrated in a few large cities. In addition, the share of the number of HHs with a diploma or above qualification is lowest in districts with a high coefficient of variation (CV = 289.13 percent) and high skewedness (14.56). To undertake further analysis of the relationship between the levels of food consumption and education status, an Educational Index (EI) at a district level is computed.

Composite Education Index (EI): Since education standard of HH members is different, a composite Education Index (EI) has been calculated by assigning weights by education status for each of the HH members (Table 9.4, col. -2). A negative weight was given to the category of illiterate members of HH. It is formulated as

$$EI = \sum_{i=1}^{n} ai.Xi \; i = 1, 2, 3, \ldots, n \qquad \ldots \qquad \ldots \qquad \ldots \qquad (9.1)$$

where a refers to assigned weight to ith education category and X is proportional share of population in ith education category. Composite Education Index is computed for Srikakulam district of Andhra Pradesh where the estimated share of primary education population in rural areas is highest (17.22 per cent). While the multiplier factor (weighted score) for the secondary education contains the maximum value in the district (Table 9.4).

(b) Labour force burden (dependency ratio, DR)

A dependency ratio represents the burden of adult working population within the HH. It is computed as the number of dependents in a HH per worker. Thus, it is a dependent/worker ratio. There are two methods to calculate DR: Labour force-based DR, which is calculated the number of active against the non-active labourers in a HH. But active workforce data were neither available at a HH nor at a district level to apply to this method.

The second method is to use an age group-based approach for which census details at a village/district level are available. It is assumed that population in the age cohort of 20 to 59 years is considered as active workers. DR was thus computed by taking simply the ratio of the number of people in the age cohorts (5–19 years and 60+) and aged 20–59 years.

Table 9.4 Assigned integer numbers as per given importance of educational status of HHs.

Category	Assigned integer numbers as weight (based on importance) a_i	% of HH population* X_i	Multiplier factor $a_i.X_i$
1	2	3	4
Illiterate	−0.5	44.93	−22.46
Literate	1	0.15	0.15
Below primary	1	11.78	11.78
Primary	2	17.22	34.44
Middle school	3	8.04	24.12
Secondary school	4	10.81	43.24
Higher secondary	6	4.21	25.26
Diploma	9	0.33	2.97
Graduate	12	2.09	25.08
Post–graduate and above	15	0.44	6.6
Total (i.e., EI)		100	151.18

N.B.: * The figures of the percent shares of HH population are used as example for Rural Srikakulam district of Andhra Pradesh for calculation of EI as formulated above.

Source: NSSO, New Delhi.

(c) **Sex ratio (SR):** Sex ratio is a ratio of females per 100 males.

(d) **Labour employment (share of HH labour engaged in productive work):** It is calculated as the percentage share of HH labour in productive work. It is used as an independent variable to represent the capacity to earn and consume.

A statistical analysis of parametric distribution implies a significantly higher degree of variability of EI and DR in rural as well as in urban areas (Table 9.5). These two are to be considered as independent variables to investigate per capita consumption of HHs.

9.06.5 Education and burden on labour in HH as major socio-economic correlates

A regression model is developed to estimate the effect of EI and DR on per capita monthly food consumption. It includes milk and milk products, fruits, vegetables, sugar, salt, egg and meat (see Table 9.3 for details).

As expected, EI has higher mean value (1348.85) and higher coefficient of variation (CV = 122 percent) in urban areas than rural areas (mean 202.95; CV 47 percent). The direction of distribution as illustrated in Figure 9.10 shows a divergence of per capita consumption towards higher values of EI in both areas, rural and urban. Higher education attainment generally leads to higher levels of food consumption.

However, the degree of divergence is more likely to be higher in urban areas. This is due to the fact that urban areas provide greater access to educational institutions and employment. Education, of course, has been found to be a key

Table 9.5 Statistical parameters of per capita monthly food consumption and socio-economic indicators of HH in rural and urban areas

Statistical parameters	Total consumption per capita (monthly)	Education index	HH sex ratio	HH dependency ratio	% HH labour
Rural area					
Maximum	–	1577.765	1283.105	1.476	67.717
Minimum	–	73.578	525.641	0.477	40.388
Mean	728.107	202.955	945.596	0.867	54.141
SD	458.388	95.394	93.882	0.201	5.512
CV (%)	62.956	47.002	9.928	23.174	10.181
Kurtosis	5.533	112.647	1.301	−0.118	−0.611
Skewness	1.735	7.993	−0.049	0.739	−0.336
Urban area					
Maximum	–	19547.5	1250	1.467	85.714
Minimum	–	0	533.333	0.167	40.541
Mean	931.766	1348.858	942.189	0.522	56.247
S D	1263.645	1647.495	108.087	0.194	5.911
CV (%)	135.618	122.14	11.472	0.004	10.509
Kurtosis	271.898	46.001	0.368	0.497	1.194
Skewness	15.344	5.417	0.281	0.594	0.177

driver of more diversified consumption behaviour (Parraga 1990). The EI seems to be higher in urbanised districts, whilst for rural districts are largely situated at a lower side of the scale in the lowest range (100 to 400 EI value). Most HHs living in rural areas are either illiterate or have attained only basic standards of education. A large proportion of HHs may be below the poverty line, which has lower per capita consumption with less variation. A semi-circular shape of scatteredness of HHs consumption distribution might show this relationship (Figure 9.10).

Distribution of HHs in urban areas has shown an increasing in per capita consumption with increasing scatteredness (Figure 9.10) for two reasons: *first*, a large variation in EI ranging from 400 to 6000 shows the concentration of different types of educational institutions in urban areas. In fact, 80 to 90 per cent of the centres of technical education and institutions of higher learning are located in urban areas; *second*, the lower-income HHs living in urban areas are less likely to educate their children in the institutions of higher learning with quality education due to higher costs.

On the other hand, the average DR is almost equal for both cases: rural and urban (Figure 9.10). However, these distributions follow the convergence of per capita monthly consumption towards higher value of DR. Furthermore, the lesser burden on labour could mean lower dependency ratio. In other words, more active and productive households are likely to earn more and be able to diversify food consumption. DR therefore is inversely related to per capita consumption with its convergence towards the areas of higher DR in rural and urban areas.

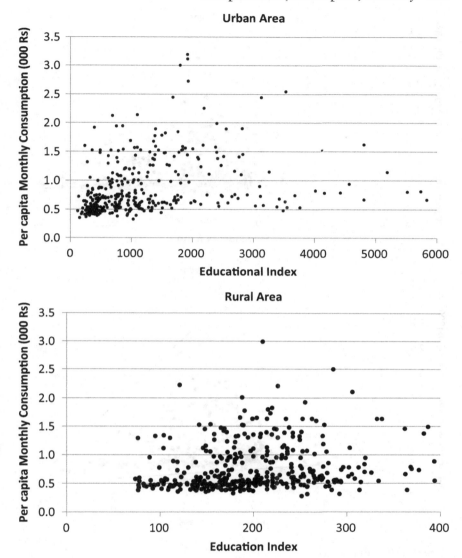

Figure 9.10 Per capita consumption and education status (A) and per capita consumption and dependency ration in rural and urban areas (B)

9.07 Regional variation in per capita food consumption in India

Spatial variation in total annual per capita food consumption (combined rural and urban) shows little similarity to either agricultural growth or productivity levels in India (Figure 9.11). One would expect high farm productivity areas to help increase the scale of food consumption. But it is not the case in most regions. It

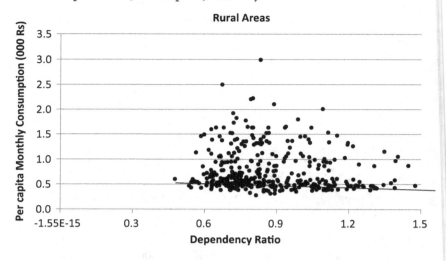

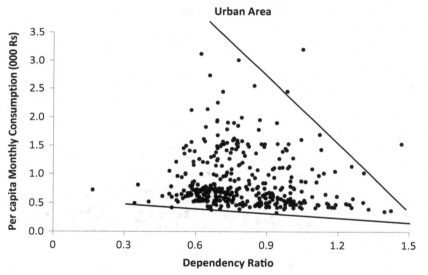

Figure 9.10 (Continued)

may be because agriculture growth and productivity are influenced by the agro-ecological conditions of farms or the intensive use of farm technology to augment land capability, whilst food consumption is largely inelastic and lifestyle driven.

As shown in Figure 9.11, consumption of food in India is also affected by socio-institutionalised food habits, which are particularly exhibited in rural India. Overall, food consumption in India shows two broad spatial patterns.

1   *Firstly,* the wet areas of more than 100 cm of annual rainfall – namely, the Chotanagpur plateau including some districts of Jkarkhand and Chattisgarh;

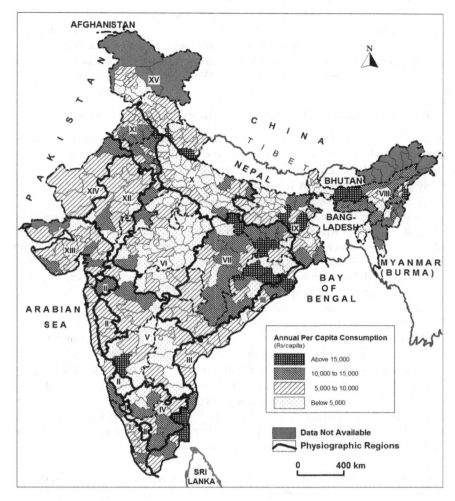

Figure 9.11 Annual per capita food consumption in India

the Kolkata plains including adjoining areas of East coastal Rice belt; Central parts of Tamil Nadu and Brahmaputra Valley of North East region including Rice-dominated districts of its surrounding hills and mountains – have high to very high levels of food consumption (Rs 10,000 and above per capita annually) (Figure 9.11). Inhabitants of these areas consume rice two times a day. Rice is a staple food in coastal humid areas. Fish is relatively more expensive than vegetables but it can be easily available in coastal areas. The share of cereals to total food consumption is larger and the value of food is higher than the other areas of the country.

2   *Secondly*, the semi-arid central region of low rainfall (50–100 cm annually) of the central part of Uttar Pradesh, entire Wheat-dominated Madhya Pradesh,

and Millet-dominated region of Telangana and Andhra Pradesh has very low per capita food consumption (Rs5,000 and below annually). Wheat and Millets are the main food items typically consumed in this region. The value of food consumption is relatively low as these crops are often cheap and readily available at a subsidised rate (especially Wheat through PDS to poor people).

9.07.1 Identification of food surplus/deficit areas and food supply

The identification of food surplus or deficit areas is of strategic importance to ensuring food security in India. Estimation of food deficit for individuals is typically calculated using biophysical measures of calories per unit of time, age or body mass. It is based on minimum nutritional food intake, below which an individual can be classified as undernourished.

Food security from a spatial perspective is often the availability and accessibility of food where and when it is needed. It is estimated through measuring accessibility to food, which could be reflected spatially, economically or culturally. In this analysis, a simple definition of food security is developed through which areas of food deficit/surplus are identified. Food deficit areas represent the state of food insecurity. It is computed as the difference between the amount of food grains produced per unit of land and the amount of food consumed by the population residing within the same area.

Minor adjustment to the supply and demand of food is carried out to improve the proposed theoretical framework. For example, Chakravarti (1970) has estimated the loss of about 16.8 per cent of the total food production from farm to kitchen. That means the effective food availability rate is about 83.2 units of net production instead of 100 units of total production. Some food wastage has been reduced with the use of modern farming technology and logistics applied in crop threshing, food grain transportation and storage. Nonetheless, food wastage remains as a major challenge for food distribution planning.

On the food demand side, total consumption is solely dependent on the demographic characteristics of population. The model has to be adjusted as population in an area has different sets of characteristics. It can vary by age, gender and rural/urban composition. Chakravarti (1970) has estimated that every 100 people in an area having different demographic characteristics equates to 77.3 consumption units. Using 0.832 for food grains production and 0.773 for population conversion as a benchmark, each of the districts were converted into production and consumption units respectively to estimate the usable production of food grains and potential demand for food. This computes the net consumption units, which can now be compared across different regions with varying demographic characteristics. The per capita consumption was computed by the NSSO for rural and urban districts. This has enabled the identification of food surplus (S) or deficit (D) areas in India. The Food Surplus/Deficiency per unit of areal unit (S/D) is simply formulated as:

$$S/D = (0.832TP - TC)/A, \quad \cdots \quad \cdots \quad \cdots \quad \cdots (9.2)$$

where TP is total annual production of food grains including pulses (in Rs), 0.832 is constant for food wastage and A is the area of a particular district (in ha) and TC is total annual consumption (in Rs). TC is defined here as

$$TC = 0.773(Cr.Pr + Cu.Pu), \quad \ldots \quad \ldots \quad \ldots \quad \ldots (9.3)$$

where Cr and Cu are per capita annual consumption rural (r) and urban (u) areas, Pr and Pu are total population in rural and urban areas respectively and 0.773 is demographic constant. If the value of S/D is positive, the districts are classified into areas of food grain surplus otherwise assigned to deficit areas.

Since food surplus or deficit is driven by production and consumption, it is predicated on the basis that the food grains surplus is attributed to higher agricultural productivity and growth. Likewise, food deficiency may be due to rapid urbanisation, which reduces the cultivated land area and increases population pressure per unit of area. India had deficiency of food grains of about Rs 10,172/ha in the year 2010–11. There are 116 districts that have surplus food grains production, which account for an average surplus of Rs 33,767/ha. While the number of food grain deficient districts are 264 (more than double), which account for an average deficiency of about Rs 29,478/ha. Ranking of districts in a descending order according to their food grains surplus/deficiency spectrum demonstrates the contrast between areas of high and low food surplus (Figure 9.12).

Spatial analysis of the results below provides further insights into the mapped data on the scale of food surplus or deficit at the national level in India.

(a) High food surplus region (Rs 50,000/ha annually and above)

This region of high food surplus consists of 20 districts. Fifteen form a contiguous belt stretching from north of Haryana (Ambala and Kurukshetra) through to Western Uttar Pradesh (Upper Ganga-Jamuna doab including Tarai up to Deoria district in the Himalayan Foothills). Soils of this belt are fertile. Wheat, Rice and Sugarcane are the dominating crops. The average surplus food grains production was about Rs 148 thousand per ha in 2006–7 with per capita annual consumption of Rs 7.72 thousand. The average land productivity was Rs 216 thousand per ha, which was much higher than the national average. Moderate population density and high share of urban population in 2011 made this region more agriculturally robust (Table 9.6). The biophysical condition of land also supports higher agriculture production. Rural-dominated food grains consumption also stimulates agriculture growth. Rice and wheat along with milk and its by-products are the key intakes in daily food consumption.

(b) Region of high food deficiency (minus Rs 75,000 per ha annually and below)

This region consists of 26 districts, which are not spatially contiguous, to form a geographic belt. The districts representing the high food deficiency region include

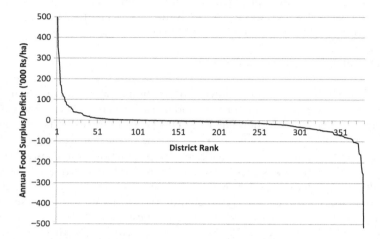

Figure 9.12 Ranking of districts by annual food production (Rs/ha)

Table 9.6 Food grains characteristics of high surplus/deficit areas

	Average values of extremely high areas	Averages of total surplus/ deficit areas
(A) Areas of high surplus food grains (Rs 50,000/ha and above)		
Number of districts	20	116
Surplus food grains (000Rs/ha)	147.87	33.8
Annual per capita consumption (Rs)	7720	6312
Land productivity 2006–7 (000 Rs/ha)	216.15	72.37
Annual agriculture growth (%)	3.12	5.17
Density of total population (persons/sq km)	942	460
Share of urban population to total (%)	32	24.12
(B) Areas of high deficit food grains (Rs –75,000/ha and below)		
Number of districts	26	263
Deficit food grains (000Rs/ha)	123.08	28.63
Annual per capita consumption (Rs)	13151	7988
Land productivity 2006–07 (000 Rs/ha)	50.74	36.39
Annual agriculture growth (%)	1.8	3.98
Density of total population (persons/sq km)	1439	590
Share of urban population to total (%)	41.13	27.67

metropolitan cities, state capitals and large historical towns. They are Dehradun (UttarKhand), Lucknow, Varanasi and Allahabad (Uttar Pradesh), Patna and Gaya (Bihar), Ranchi (Jharkhand), Bhubaneshwar and Catak (Odisha), Maniput central (Maniput), Kamrup (Assam), Howrah (W. Bengal), Bengluru (Karnataka), Thane

(Maharastra), Chikmanglore (Tamil Nadu) and Tiruanathapuram (Karala). These districts are spatially dispersed (Figure 9.13). An average food grains deficiency of Rs 123 thousand per ha was calculated with an average annual per capita consumption of Rs 13.15 thousands. Agriculture productivity and annual agriculture growth were only Rs 50,000/ha and 1.80 per cent respectively with a higher density of population and share of urban population (Table 9.6).

This region of high food grain surpluses is largely rural-dominated with lower per capita consumption, low population density and lesser share of urban population, and higher agriculture productivity than those areas of food grains deficit which characterise high population density and urban population.

Further analysis of data has been carried out to establish relationships between food grains sufficiency/deficiency areas and their attributes. Since land productivity and agriculture growth are associated with high food surplus areas, they are more likely to impact on increased food surplus. In contrast, higher density of

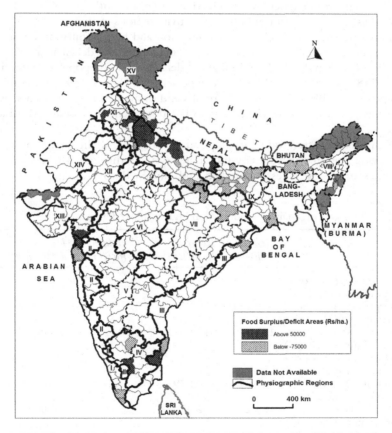

Figure 9.13 Food grains sufficiency and deficiency regions (2009–10)

population and share of urban population tend to create more demand for food supply which leads to food deficient areas.

A statistical analysis is therefore conducted to test these hypotheses and the results are presented in this section. The areas of food grains surplus and higher land productivity are positively correlated at a district level (r = 0.8756, significant at 1 percent level, n = 20). This indicates that high land productivity generates food grains surplus. Areas of upper Ganga-Jamuna doab and Rohilkhand, for example, have high food grains surplus and higher land productivity (Table 9.7).

Interestingly, agriculture growth has an insignificant relationship with food grains surplus (Figure 9.13). These two variables are weakly correlated (r = 0.1844). It is to be noted that the level of surplus food grains regresses more than a half times per ha with a unit of land productivity increase (Figure 9.14).

Contrary, the relationship between land productivity and agriculture growth is inversely correlated in India at a district level (see Chapter 5 for more details). Land productivity is largely dependent on the fertility of land and its biophysical attributes to produce higher yield. Once the land productivity potential is saturated, the growth in agriculture production diminishes with any additional input, which has started to occur in high-productivity regions in India.

As shown in Figure 9.15, rapid urbanisation and high population density per unit of land are equally accountable for creating food grains deficit areas. The relationships between the levels of food grains deficiency, D and population density, P (r = 0.7483) and with the share of urban population, U (r= 0.7797) are significant and positive. Table 9.7 presents the results and shows that food deficiency per ha increases two times in deficient areas with 1.0 per cent increase in urbanisation rate.

Such urban-centred food consumption networks highlight the importance of improving the efficiency of city-hinterland systems through which food commodities can be seamlessly supplied and sustained to fulfil the burgeoning

Table 9.7 Regression analysis conducted in high surplus/deficit areas

Items	Regression origin (a)	Regression coefficient (b)	Correlation coefficient (r)	Degree of determinant (R²)
(A) High surplus food grains areas				
1. Surplus (S) w.r.t. land productivity (Y)	9.131	0.575	0.8757	0.767*
2. Surplus (S) w.r.t. agriculture growth (G)	177.3	–11.66	0.1844	0.034
(B) High deficit food grains areas				
1. Deficit (D) w.r.t. population density (P)	–60.51	0.039	0.7483	0.560**
2. Deficit (D) w.r.t. urban population (U)	–52.25	2.07	0.7797	0.608*

N.B.: Increasing deficit level is considered in conducting regression analysis in present case.
* Significant at .001 and ** signigicant at .005 level.

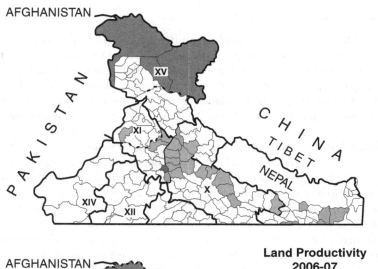

**Land Productivity
2006-07**

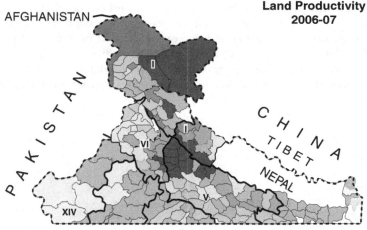

**Annual Agricultural
(2000-01 to 2006-07)**

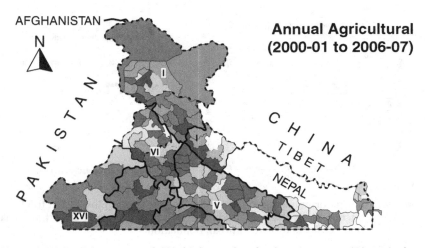

Figure 9.14 Spatial pattern of (A) high surplus food grain areas, (B) agricultural productivity (2006–7) and (C) annual agriculture growth (2000–1 to 2006–7) in the North Western Great Plains

demand for food in cities. Increased urban density and rising population pressure in urban hinterlands are exerting stress on farm land to escalate agriculture productivity per unit of land to mitigate the vulnerability of food crisis in urban areas. This is particularly important in an emergency situation or the occurrence of supply chain disruption. Market-based systems and enhanced logistics infrastructure are needed to tackle the potential food insecurity in city regions of India.

The effects of mass-urbanisation around rapid growth of newly established towns in the rural–urban fringe of large urban agglomerations are changing the agricultural landscape in India. Rapid conversion of farm land into urban land use for residential developments, road infrastructure and commercial use are immensely contributing to the severity of food supply problems in the future. This is because city-regions are not well connected and functionally integrated with hinterlands. Recent infrastructure developments are certainly improving intra-city connectivity. However, little infrastructure has been developed in rural hinterlands. Changing land use pattern and increasing urban population are likely to change consumption behaviour with increasing demand for more and varied sources of food in cities from limited hinterlands with inefficient commodity supply chains. Longer supply chains are increasing the food miles whereby food supply networks need to be expanded through better transportation and logistics infrastructure.

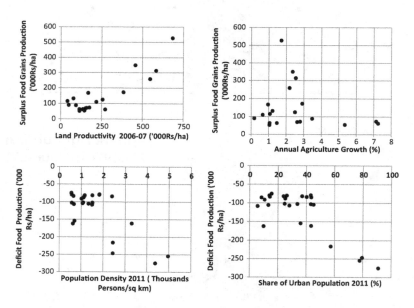

Figure 9.15 Scatter diagrams showing relationship between surplus/deficit food production levels and land productivity, annual agriculture growth, population density and share of urban population

9.08 Summary

This chapter examines the demand and supply of food grain production in India with the aim of developing a spatial methodology to analyse the severity of food insecurity in India. Assessment of food sufficiency or deficiency levels is presented through three key approaches to food distribution from areas of production to areas of consumption. Areas of food sufficiency and deficiency are identified using production and consumption data. From the production side, the production of Rice remained constant and continuous over time. However, the share of Wheat production rose sharply after the Independence on account of two reasons: increasing demand of Wheat products and its processed materials such as *suji, maida,* bread, and confectionaries in urban areas; and the expansion of areas under Wheat cultivation. The share of production of Millets, Jowar and Bajara declined sharply over time due to low relative prices and changing consumption behaviour.

From the consumption side, cereals is a significant share of about one-fourth of food consumption and about one-third of it is home produced in rural areas. The cereal–non-cereal consumption ratio was 33:67 for rural areas, while it was 24:76 for urban areas. This indicates the growing importance of non-cereal diets in India. Milk and milk products are also vital elements in the Indian diet. Wheat-based bread (locally called *roti/chapati*); milk and milk products such as butter, cheese, toned milk, butter-milk, curd and home-made sweets; pulses and vegetables and meat in rare occasions are the major elements of food intake in India.

The amount of quantity of food consumed in rural and urban areas is similar. The rural-urban food consumption ratio is 1:1.06, which indicates no difference in consumption behaviour between rural and urban population. Contrary to the conventional wisdom, urban dwellers are not necessarily more consumptive than their rural counterparts.

The analysis of case studies highlighted that access to forest resources and transport infrastructure drives the consumption behaviour in remote and hilly districts of the North Eastern region of India. Higher education attainment generally leads to higher levels of food consumption. Burden on HH labour tends to decrease per capita food consumption. Rapid urbanisation, expansion of urban infrastructure and reduction in cultivable area in the vicinity of mega-cities increase the demand for food in urban areas. As a result, most high food deficient areas are located in the vicinity of large metropolitan cities where the market gardens and cultivated areas are increasingly shrinking. The areas of high food surplus are largely concentrated in Sivaliks (foodhills of Haryana), Deoria district of Uttar Pradesh, Upper Ganga–Jamuna doab and Rohilkhand. The areas of high food grains surpluses are largely rural-dominated with low population density and share of urban population, and higher agriculture productivity than those areas of food grains deficit. The spatial methodology developed in this chapter provides a systematic base for undertaking the analysis of more complex spatial dynamics of food insecurity. Evidence gathered in the analysis is useful to planners and governmental agencies for developing innovative spatially integrated plans and policy to strengthen the efficiency of food distribution systems in India.

10 Conclusion

10.01 Introduction

Agriculture is the 'culture' of Indian society. Agriculture is embedded as a part of rural living. Changes in agriculture production mode and the concomitant division of land have long been affected by social evolution and technological change. Yet, even in the globalised world, value and belief systems continue to drive what food is grown, who grows them, what technologies are employed and who consumes what products.

Food production is regulated and socially institutionalised. There are social rules, cultural norms and institutional frameworks from ancient times on the division of labour. Traditionally, they were controlled and regulated by value systems, which were socially fractured, culturally divisive and spatially fragmented. Biophysical properties of land, changing market conditions and labour markets have been the key drivers of agriculture production and land productivity. In recent decades, agricultural systems and the underlying farm practices in India have been shaped by globalisation, liberalisation and deregulation of the economy through improved access to global competitive markets, commercialisation and the deployment of innovative farm technology.

The trajectory of the contemporary Indian agricultural landscape is the product of various evolutionary stages within which rules, norms and guidelines on land use and farming practices were established and governed. Land ownership and the right to cultivate were reinforced through a 'power sharing' and control schema, which first allocated and then assigned the right to work in various occupations to various social groups. India thus developed a 'poly-cyclic' agriculture system, which emerged from a simple 'socially organised ecosystem' of the Harappan culture in the Indus valley civilisation, to an 'administrative-heavy hierarchical feudal system' during the medieval period when agriculture was practiced under closed-land management control, through to a 'modern quasi-market based system' with limited and selective access to global commodity markets. Agriculture in India continues to evolve and transit towards an industrialised production system, which is driven by commercialisation, mechanisation and market-led mass-production of commodities. But its speed, intensity and magnitude of change in the agriculture production systems significantly vary across India.

This chapter summarises the key findings and discusses their potential policy implications for agriculture development in India. Results are synthesised and thematically presented to redress the challenges of globalisation, liberalisation and deregulation. Policy implications and responses are highlighted at a strategic level and are formulated from a regional perspective.

10.02 Agriculture production, yield and growth

Agriculture growth and productivity show significant regional variability in India. The annual average growth of the agricultural sector was recorded much lower at 3 per cent relative to other sectors despite the growing diversification of agricultural practices and infrastructure. This growth however was not uniform. There were substantial areal and sectoral differences, which were recognised as a key concern by many studies. NSSO (2010) also noted the negative effects of liberalisation such as the increasing gap between social groups or areas.

The growth in crop area and crop yield drove the agriculture growth and change in cropping patterns. Expansion of land under cultivation and the growing share of non-food grains positively influenced the rate of agriculture growth. Effects of rural road networks and higher relative prices of commercial crops shifted the focus from the 'production-oriented' to 'profit-oriented' growth model. This indicates a shift to improve functional linkages between farms and the market. Recent decline in the average annual agriculture growth from 4 per cent in 2006–07 to 2 per cent in 2011–12 is however seen as a major challenge.

Regional patterns of agricultural growth are governed by the biophysical factors of land and the use of farm technology in India. Spatial shift of agriculture growth clusters first began from Punjab-Haryana and Gujrat during the Green Revolution, expanded to the Maharastra-Karnataka region in the Post-Green Revolution and then percolated through to coastal areas of Deltaic Narrow Plains and the Interior Deccan during the 1980s in the Pre-Liberalisation phase. The Post-Liberalisation phase has seen agriculture growth permeating through to the North-East hills, Siwaliks, Himachal Himalayas and foreland plateaus of Deccan (Malwa-Bundelkhand-Banghelkhand and Chotanagpur including the Thar).

Many empirical studies have found a restricted impact of the Green Revolution in selected regions of India. In contrast, other regions of the country experienced a net decline in the per capita agricultural output and the rise in intra-regional inequalities (Mohapatra 1982: 217–218). Increasing intra-regional disparities however indicate diversified agricultural land use patterns. It is because of the positive effects of Green Revolution technology, which enabled extending the cultivated area and accelerated yield of Wheat crop in the Great Plains – the home of the Green Revolution (Bhalla and Alagh 1979a and 1979b, Mohapatra 1982: 241–243). With the greater emphasis placed on self-sustained growth of agriculture to maximise production in the fifth through to the seventh five-year-plan periods, the Indian Government should have considered adopting the strategy to optimise production based on land potential.

Agriculture growth patterns concur with the findings of previous studies. A comprehensive analysis of agricultural growth was conducted by Bhat and Learmonth (1968) using district-wide data of agricultural output growth (1951–4 to 1958–61) and land productivity for 1950–4 to establish their areal association with the physiographic regions of India. They concluded that the areas of high productivity are more likely to have lower growth rates particularly in the fertile Great Plains of India. In contrast, Western Madhya Pradesh and parts of the black-soil plateau of Maharashtra characterised by low agricultural productivity registered high growth rate (Bhat and Learmonth 1968). Cotton is widely grown in these areas, which tends to respond well to market demand because of its commercial value. Using the data over the first three five-year plans, Nath (1969) concluded that the regional variability in agricultural growth components such as crop area and crop yield is hard to explain using infrastructure-related parameters. In addition, he asserted that there was no significant effect on moisture index and irrigation on agricultural growth and productivity during the 1950s.

Agriculture growth modelling identified the key drivers, which have significant impact on agriculture growth at a farm level. A robust agriculture growth model was developed that integrated two previously discrete functions: *production function*, which assessed the impact of increasing farm technology, labour and land potential for growth; and *the input pulse function*, which evaluated the depreciated impact of farm investments on agriculture growth over time. Applications of science and technology in farming in alignment with ecological conditions of land are recommended as a suitable approach for productivity enhancement. Besides the use of agricultural technology (which is considered in the form of capital intensity by economists), land capacity should also be taken into account. Productive capacity of land should be one of the criteria for the assessment of production–efficiency frontier.

Using a case study of Greater Ganga Plains, agriculture growth was modelled across different sizes of farm. The evidence suggests that excess labour supply in rural areas reduced labour productivity in small and marginal-sized farms and creates disguised unemployment. This is attested through high IIOR in small and marginal-sized farms. This led to an increased pressure for out-migration of unskilled workers to urban labour markets, which in turn dumped down the wages in urban areas but increased income for rural households.

The benefits of land consolidation and cooperative farming have been recognised by small and marginal farm owners. The farms on high land potential have the capacity to absorb additional labour in farm operations to help reach the full potential of land. Larger farms in the upper part of the Great Plains of India (Punjab, Haryana and Western Uttar Pradesh) are much more productive and market-driven. The use of high-capacity harvesters, tractors and thrashers has increased farm productivity. Commercial cultivation of cash crops has led to additional savings for farmers and thus further investment in farm to enhance production. The market-driven farm production thus has proven to be a successful strategy in a few regions, which has helped many farmers to opt out of subsistence farming and break the '*vicious circle of poverty*' in India.

10.03 Labour and land productivity

Spatial variability in land and labour productivity was measured and visualised across different agriculture regions in India. There are significant regional changes in land productivity (output per unit of cultivated land) over time. During the Pre-Liberalisation phase, higher productivity was achieved in the Great Plains and Coastal Deltaic areas through to the Himalayan Foothills, Mumbai-Ahamdabad Cotton and Groundnut belts of Gujrat and Maharastra. The Meghalaya-Manipur hills of North East India have also improved land productivity after economic liberalisation.

The impact of production factors such as biophysical properties of farm land, labour force involved in farming and the capital (in the form of technology) invested in farm activities has contributed immensely to the regional variability in agriculture productivity. The crop price has also become an important factor of land productivity. In addition, increased share of commercial crops has augmented land productivity differences. Land intensification and expansion of commercial farming in other parts of India such as hill areas of the North East have made agriculture more productive and market oriented. Agriculture growth and productivity however have shown an inverse relationship in recent decades whereby low-productivity areas exhibit higher growth. The changing growth-productivity relationship has reduced regional gaps in productivity levels.

Labour productivity (output per person of agriculture work force) is a vital component of agriculture growth. Spatiality of labour markets tends to influence labour productivity. The inter-regional labour productivity gaps were reduced over time during the Post-Liberalisation phase when productivity levels increased in low-productivity areas such as Rajasthan in the West, Himachal and Uttrakhand mountains in the North and most of hill districts in the North East region. Nevertheless, the overall regional patterns of labour productivity remained unchanged during the Post-Liberalisation phase.

Unlimited supply of labour and the rising labour pressure on finite land resources increased labour intensity (agriculture workers per unit of cultivated land). This in turn diminished labour productivity due to additional burden of excessive supply of labour in rural India. Overall, agriculture efficiency and productivity gap were affected by the potential productivity of land, which varies due to the differences in biophysical characteristics of land. But it is also driven by the ability of each region to harness the potential of farm technology, innovations and the prudential deployment of skilled labour.

10.04 Regional convergence and spill-over effects

The policy debate on regional economic development was rejuvenated to revisit its policy relevance in a globalised and competitive world. For example, should agriculture growth be equitably dispersed or should it be concentrated in few high-performing growth areas to achieve high-efficiency standards? Did economic liberalisation and trade deregulation converge or diverge agriculture growth in rural India?

Agriculture productivity increase has diverged at a rate of 0.631 times with the use of per unit of land potential in India. The rate of productivity increase has been relatively high (β = 1.08) in Mumbai-based Western Plateau Region (IX). High productivity increases in the North Eastern Hills Region (IIb) is achieved by harnessing the full land potential through an intensive use of modern horti-culture techniques, especially applied on valley slopes. Technology-driven com-mercial crop farming has a positive effect on productivity of Rice in Assam plains in the North East (IIa), which in turn reduces the gap between developed and under-developed areas.

In India, high agriculture growth and increased farm productivity were pre-dominately driven by land potential and technology adoption. Regional varia-tion in agriculture productivity was much higher in Punjab and Upper Ganga Plains. However, the intra-regional variation in productivity within the Lower Ganga Plains (Bihar-West Bengal Region), as shown by the productivity gap, was equally high. High beta-coefficients indicate regional convergence in Pun-jab, Gujrat plains and Himachal-Uttrakhand. Convergence was stronger in high-productivity regions surrounded by low-productivity regions, which shows the prevalence of 'spill-over' or neighbourhood effect.

This 'trickle down' process of growth was further exacerbated by the grow-ing size of non-farm allied activities in rural areas, the rapid emergence of mar-ket towns (mandies), which act as distribution centres, and the expansion of infrastructure in rural India. Intra-regional variation in the productivity increase has however risen. The propensity for regional convergence was high in high-productivity regions in India. Furthermore, the diffusion of technological inno-vation from high- to low-productivity areas and the seasonal mobility of labour force from low- to high-productivity areas drove regional convergence in agri-cultural performance, which reduced the gap between high-productivity and low-productivity regions. However, agriculture growth is subject to the dimin-ishing law of return, whereby return reduces the rate of increasing growth in high growth areas.

Inter-regional differences in land and labour productivity in India is an inherent effect of the physiographical characteristics and agro-climatic conditions. How-ever, these inter-regional differences in productivity levels were accelerated due to the effect of high-productivity increase in low-productivity areas. If the effects of physiographical and agro-climatic conditions remained constant over time, the changes in productivity levels generated due to technological enhancement in low-productivity areas and market reforms during the Post-Liberalisation phase would be a key policy concern for regional planners due to the adverse impact of regional growth inequalities. The adoption of technology in few progressive regions was instrumental in mitigating inter-regional productivity differences, whilst in others technology escalated the gap between high- and low-performing regions. Similarly, the effects of market around key city-regions were strong, which escalated the disparity in regional productivity. This was an outcome of the differences in city-periphery interdependencies and functional connectedness.

Technology and the maturity of market also affected the process of regional convergence. There is where a policy intervention to disperse equitable growth to achieve inclusive growth should be permitted. Technology and market caused regional divergence in the initial stage of agricultural development, but technological maturity and improved access to market led to regional convergence whereby low-performing regions began to catch up with high-performing regions. But this trajectory is manifested in few more progressive regions, which are well resourced and better connected with key urban agglomerations in India.

10.05 Hierarchically nested agriculture regions

Regions are fundamental units for agriculture development and resource planning. An innovative technique has been developed which considers proximity of multi-dimensional set of agriculture attributes and spatial arrangement of areal units for optimal partitioning of areal units to assimilate them to form new multi-scaled regional boundaries. Hierarchically nested agricultural regions were generated using agro-ecological, agricultural commodities, crop potential and techno-organisational characteristics. Broadly, five macro-regions were delineated following a purely biophysical basis of agriculture regionalisation, assuming the higher impact of topographical properties of land on agriculture activities. These regions include: Deccan Plateau, Great Plains, Coastal plains, Western Himalayas and Rajasthan plains.

Meso- and micro-agricultural regions in India are hierarchically structured, which are tiered due to the interplay of various factors of production. Micro-agricultural regions are most dependent on the development of growth centres and mandi towns, which have strong bearing on agricultural growth and productivity and the development of rural road networks. This new regionalisation approach does not undermine the physiographical basis for delineating agriculture regions in India. The key purpose is to improve efficiency and effectiveness of policy intervention and planning process in the context of emerging globalised competitive economic order, whereby regions are constantly changing in response to the functional requirements of the key consumption hubs in an open commodity market.

Arguably, the macro-regional frame of agricultural regionalisation represents the broader biophysical attributes of land, which sets out the carrying capacity thresholds and the limits to growth, whilst the meso- and micro-regional frames reflect market functions that integrate rural–urban economies as a single interlocking economic system.

Two key processes have changed the regional structures of the Indian agriculture system. The *first* is the diminishing importance of embedded biophysical constraints of land, which in the past has dictated the nature and characteristics of agriculture practices in India. Yet, they provide the macro-regional framework within which the Indian agricultural system has evolved. The *second* is the sectoral shift in the Indian agricultural economy from farm to non-farm-based activities.

Recent advancement and economic restructuring have resulted in rapid increase of non-farm activities either undertaken at a farm and/or off-farm locations within rural areas. This has blurred the rural–urban duality while strengthening the nexus between cities and their hinterlands. The key changes in rural economy include more frequent rural–urban labour mobility, shift in capital investment predominately from rural to urban areas, non-farm employment generation in rural areas and the stagnancy of agricultural growth.

Framing region-specific agricultural policies to drive the national agenda for agriculture development makes sense. Yet, the choice of spatial unit that provides the basis for regional planning and agriculture development is not formally settled. The state in India is often considered as an appropriate unit for evaluating agricultural performance and for developing regional investment strategy. Indeed, states in India are largely 'language-based' sub-division of politico-administrative identities rather than based on 'economic functional differentiation'. Furthermore, state boundaries do not necessarily correspond to agro-ecological regions, which broadly define the prevailing agricultural systems in India. Such dichotomy of political boundaries in the backdrop of agro-ecological regions for agricultural planning and policy formulation and execution hinders the path of increasing capacity to improve productivity levels of land and to reduce regional inequalities in agricultural performance.

10.06 Spatial markets, rural infrastructure and technology

During the 1990s, the issue of agricultural productivity enhancement became critical when the agricultural sector was reformed as a part of the overall economic liberalisation. The New Economic Policy of 1991 reformed the regulations on international trade, foreign direct investment and fiscal restructuring in the financial and public sectors. The Reserve Bank of India introduced new regulations to reform the banking credit system, which favoured small and medium-sized farms (Kalirajan et al 2001, Mahadevan 2003). In spite of these reforms, the share of agriculture commodities to total export declined from 19 per cent in 1990–1 to 10 per cent in 2004–5. It was envisaged that competitive rural markets and deregulated financial and banking systems would increase the production of high-value and value-added crops and the concomitant development of agro-processing centres and allied activities in rural areas at a farm level. This in turn would increase productivity and reduce regional disparities. In addition, the deregulated market would strengthen the effects of '*agglomeration economies*', which partition the Indian agriculture systems into regional mosaics, each representing a self-contained and quasi-functioning city region to improve the linkages between production and consumption nodes.

Emerging new market centres or 'mandies' have also added market efficiency to the key commodity chains, reducing distribution costs and the taxes levied on inter-regional transportation of goods. Relaxed terms of trade for exporting or importing agricultural products, emergence of horticulture and cash crops, and growing participation in profit-oriented 'contract farming' have added a market-centred dimension to agricultural production system in India.

The development of 'quadrilateral' national road networks in India has connected the places and accelerated the pace of agriculture growth. It has helped overcome the physiographical constraints of land and socio-cultural trade barriers across states. Newly created rural road networks have connected farms to their respective markets, which have reduced transport costs and increased competitive prices of farm products and thereby enhanced farm operational efficiency.

The diffusion of modern farm technology has significant impact on the rural labour market. Mechanisation of farm operations has replaced labour by eliminating basic operational tasks that farmers used to traditionally perform at farms. Some skills which were deemed essential in traditional farming have become redundant, while new skills have emerged which are needed in operating technology-driven farm production. Technology has also affected labour mobility and employment patterns. Farmers have shifted to other industrial sectors or sought employment in urban labour markets. This has augmented the geographic mobility of farm labourers from villages to towns and from one economic region to others either for survival or progress. Inter-regional labour mobility has reduced the gap between developed and under-developed regions, but it has created a set of new challenges in both labour-surplus and labour-deficit regions. More geo-targeted educational campaigns and awareness programs need to be deployed to help farmers understand the value of technology in improving effectiveness and efficiency of farming practices.

Technological progress and liberalisation have increased market potential by intensifying greater concentration of farm activities and by amplifying spatial disparities in agricultural growth and productivity. Economic liberalisation and privatisation have affected all segments of food supply chains which were involved in the seamless transportation of farm products to processing centres and through to the consumption nodes. The distribution and density of agricultural activities and the market accessibility through improved transport and communication networks were shaped by the policies driven by a neo-liberal political agenda. In this neo-spatial structure of agriculture landscape, distance, which is often captured through time and monetary cost, has become a functional rather than physical barrier to the mobility of goods and services. With the rise of globalised production networks, locations are value-add foci which help in the vertical integration of food supply chains. Each of these nodes is a low-cost production or processing location in global commodity chains. Reduction of production costs and increasing product price at farm gate are highly dependent on efficient transportation means and the reliability of freight networks.

10.07 Spatiality of food insecurity

Food security has been argued as a fundamental human right. Despite of this, there are millions of those who are malnourished or undernourished. A new approach to examine the spatiality of food insecurity has been developed that considers both production and consumption of food at a small area level. From the supply perspective, the production of all grain crops was analysed over time. The share of Rice to total grain production remained constant while Wheat production rose sharply after the Independence. It was due to the increased demand of Wheat products such as suji, maida, bread, and confectionaries in urban areas and the expansion of areas under Wheat cultivation. The share of Millets, Jowar and Bajara to total production however has declined.

Case studies demonstrated changing consumption behaviour in two different socio-ecological settings. Access to forest resources and education attainment tends to increase food consumption whilst an induced burden on household labour decrease per capital food consumption in remote and hilly districts of North East India. In contrast, rapid urbanisation, expansion of urban infrastructure and reduction in cultivable area in the vicinity of mega-cities tend to increase the demand for food in urban areas.

High food deficient areas were generally located in the vicinity of large metropolitan cities where market gardens and cultivated areas have shrunk. The areas of high food surplus were largely concentrated in Sivaliks (foothills of Haryana), Deoria district of Uttar Pradesh, Upper Ganga–Jamuna doab and Rohilkhand. In contrast, the areas of high food grains surplus were largely rural-dominated with low population density and high agriculture productivity.

There is no doubt that the deployment of long-term strategies for food security is vital for the future prosperity of India. The major objectives of food strategy include improvement in farm productivity and satisfactory growth of food grain production relative to the size of population growth, meeting the acceptable nutritional intake of food by all sections of society, the minimum availability of the basic food commodities and the provision of adequate security of food supply in case of a poor harvest, a significant price fluctuation in the global market or an occurrence of a natural disaster (Adamowicz 1988). Evidence gathered in the analysis would be useful to planners and governmental agencies in developing new spatially integrated plans and area-specific policies to strengthen the efficiency of food distribution systems in India.

10.08 Policy implications

Economic liberalisation and regulatory reforms in India have shaped the agriculture production landscape. These reforms aimed at helping the agriculture industry to alleviate rural poverty and unemployment, promote free and fair trade practices, improve the quality of life of farmers, secure food supplies and create a buoyant market to compete in a global marketplace. Therefore, tariffs were harmonised and restrictions on internal trade and import tariffs on agricultural commodities were reduced to enhance India's competitiveness to be able to harness the potential of free and unrestricted global trade. However, the economic reforms also implemented measures to reduce per capita government expenditure on rural areas, cut subsidies on fertiliser, decrease public investment in rural infrastructure, agriculture and irrigation, and reduce access to rural credit.

Yet, the agriculture industry is challenged by anachronistic farming methods, increased complexity of global production systems, service inadequacy by dilapidated rural infrastructure and the burgeoning but unfulfilled demand for food from the domestic market. India as a key supplier of food commodities to the global commodity markets is yet to be realised. It is unanimously conceded that increased global competitiveness in cross-border trade, coupled with an inefficient rural infrastructure to support transportation of agriculture commodities, impedes the prospect of India entering into the global commodity markets.

Given the recent emphasis on inclusive growth in the public policy arena, where the focus is placed on the development of all sectors of the economy and across all sections of the society. There are significant policy implications of regional variability in agriculture production, growth and productivity on achieving inclusive growth in India. Arguably, the policy promoting regional convergence is one of the vital components of the inclusive growth strategy. The key to the policy of inclusive growth is to reduce regional disparities in agriculture development. Nonetheless, the spatial variability in land potential based on ecological limits and thresholds have created marked regional imbalances in agriculture growth because of the spatial variability in resource endowments. This thus potentially contradicts the basic premise of the inclusive growth strategy.

In the frame of our existing political and economic systems (i.e., Centre–State relationship under the federal system), two models of regional growth have been widely known. The *'productivity-oriented'* growth model argues for micro-economic reforms to enhance land and labour productivity. It emphasises utilising the productive capacity of land potential and rural labour to enhance productivity-driven growth in rural India. This model inclusively maintains the regional economic hierarchies to reinforce existing Centre–State government relationships in the allocation resource. Centre Government is largely responsible for building the critical infrastructure (such as road, electricity, drinking water, health and education) to rural populace to help access life-enhancing opportunities to create self-sustained growth contained within regions. The *'investment-oriented'* growth model argues for promoting rural economic growth through market reforms via a reduction in import and export tariffs, quota and trade barriers. It emphasises liberalisation, privatisation and deregulation of the economy to attract the interest of private enterprises and multinational corporations to invest in rural infrastructure through foreign direct investment. This could be a long-term strategic investment or through a private-public partnership to build mega-infrastructure projects.

Prior to the Green Revolution, Indian agriculture was largely under the control of biophysical factors of land. Agricultural regions were in complete alignment with agro-climatic regions of the country. With the transformation of local agricultural economy to non-market economy after the Green Revolution, structural changes and regulatory reforms to boost food grain production and productivity to supply basic food to the large population base became inevitable. At that time, agricultural production process and practices were deeply influenced by land potential as dictated by the biophysical characteristics of land. However, it was the beginning of market-oriented regional agricultural economy with the rapid emergence of mandi towns. Market-based regional formation of agricultural commodity markets were much awaited when the policies to promote economic liberalisation and deregulation were introduced in 1990s.

The overall food grain production increased to meet the burgeoning demand of the increasing population in India. But the agricultural development models pursued by the government led to greater rural–urban and rural–rural divide. It was particularly pronounced after the introduction of Green Revolution technology. India has struggled to increase crop yields, which is below world standards. The lack of knowledge or awareness of the benefits of modern agricultural technology among the farming community is the key barrier to agricultural innovation in India. Fragmented farming practices and thus the inability to achieve economies of scale and scope make farming less competitive.

The Central Government continued to provide financial help through subsidies. However, the model has proven to be less effective to maintain inter-industry linkages and sectoral integration and sustain economic stimulus to support regional agriculture growth. Many development schemes such as Block Development Schemes were unsustainable because of a heavy burden from subsidies. They were eventually abandoned or merged with the National scheme, namely, MENREGA. The benefits of privatisation and deregulation were largely restricted to the services economy. In addition, the "Pick-and-Choose" sector policy of economic development strengthened trade relations to fulfil the required demand of increasing population and helped India to enter in services industries such as IT and Call-Centre Operations (Business Processing Outsourcing) to fulfil global requirements. Ironically, the primary sector is often overlooked and is deemed less strategic to attract investment to innovate farming practices. It therefore could not harness the potential and did not even attain half of the average national annual growth, which was about 7 to 8 per cent per year during the first decade of this century.

Increasing economic disparities and regional inequalities in agriculture economic systems and wide-spread rural unemployment are the potential consequences of the Post-Liberalisation phase in India. There is no strong evidence to show that *ad-hoc* public investment and agriculture subsidies maintained under the poverty alleviation programs and employment guarantee schemes had made any significant impact on boosting labour productivity and poverty reduction in rural India. Increasing income disparities, widening regional inequalities and stagnant agricultural productivity continue to impede India's progress towards inclusive growth. Rising inflation, regular disruptions of commodity chains, erratic and variant domestic demand for food and the rising trade imbalances are some of the key challenges for India's agriculture sector.

Government liberalisation policies created two key changes in agricultural development which led to major structural reforms from a regional perspective. *Firstly*, the regional agricultural growth and productivity started to be driven by metropolitan market economies. The linkages became much more integrated during the Liberalisation phase (the 2000s) when connectivity of transport infrastructure and quality of logistics services became much more efficient. Agriculture is now considered as a market activity, which has brought structural changes in agriculture practices such as changes in cropping pattern, farm commercialisation and land use intensification. Farmer's income from allied activities performed at farms has also increased. Development of market facilities and transport and communication hubs has helped in the intensive use of farm inputs (seed-fertiliser-machine tools used for agriculture) on the one hand and has facilitated the trade of surplus farm products to the market on the other.

The liberalisation policies promoted the development of market infrastructure to support an efficient distribution of agricultural products from farms to end consumers. New agricultural growth centres in rural areas have emerged which provide impetus for agricultural growth and productivity boost within their hinterlands. It is to be highlighted here that because of structural changes in agriculture in the Liberalisation and Post-Liberalisation phases, the agricultural growth and productivity, which were initially controlled by the quality of biophysical attributes of land (e.g. relief, agro-climate conditions and soils), have accelerated via market forces and have improved by the efficiency of regional transport networks. As the basis of regional frame changed from agro-ecological to market-led systems, the regional hierarchy of agricultural system is also increasingly becoming dependent on market centres and their '*spheres of influence*'.

Secondly, understanding the shift in the structure and growth processes of agricultural activities is relevant to get further insights into distance-dependent agricultural growth within the confinement of market regions. Location of farms deeply underpins growth processes, migration of agricultural labour force, supply of surplus farm products, scale of non-farm activities at farms and the nature of contract farming. These changes however differ in different market regions due to the interplay of demand–supply relationships. However, the issues of rural employment, poverty alleviation, fair prices of agricultural products and reduction in input costs are tightly bounded with the macro-structural changes of the economy.

Creation of common multi-purpose infrastructure for health, sanitation, logistics and education in the newly emerging market centres, development of wholesale markets or mandies, provision of high-capacity market facilities, increased farm revenues through market interventions, such as a reduction in market taxes and municipal taxes on agricultural products, have the potential to increase agricultural growth and productivity at a farm level. These changes will have the potential to promote inclusive development and help to delineate a proper path for rural development through which urban growth in mega-cities can permeate to rural hinterlands.

Progress in seed-fertiliser technology, rapid development in Information Technology and removal of fertiliser subsidies were the driving forces to push rural wealth to rural non-farm activities. There was a gradual shift in the labour and wealth from rural areas to nearby urban centres where the elasticity of investment in non-agricultural activities (like trade, transport, manufacturing and services) became much lucrative compared to investment in farm activities. Traditionally, there was investment flow from urban to rural areas in commercial farming, but most of it was restricted to rural–urban fringe in the vicinity of large metropolitan cities.

The landless agricultural labour forces, which were largely unskilled and uneducated, needed higher wages to compensate for increased costs of living in rural areas. Since non-agricultural activities in urban areas have much higher wages even for unskilled workers, this resulted in mass-migration of landless rural labourers initially to regional cities and then to mega-cities. Such migration created new labour markets, which have established stronger rural–urban economic linkages and strengthened market interdependencies. Consequently, the agricultural system in India became much more productive and integrated with improved linkages to market centres. Commercialisation of cropping, diversification of farm income, shifting of disguised unemployed agriculture labour to allied activities, inland movement of agribusinesses in rural areas and migration of landless workers to urban areas were inevitable outcomes of liberalisation policy. With these drastic changes, the agriculture industry in India is now being seen as a catalyst to help integrate rural and urban economies within its regional framework (World Development Report 2008). However, the inefficiency in the spatial organisation of production and distribution of food networks became an emerging issue when public distribution systems (PDS) showed little success in facilitating fair or equitable access to basic food commodities to all sections of the Indian society in rural and urban areas.

Self-sustained agricultural growth models must adopt the 'optima-limit concept' of neo–determinism. This approach is based on environmental factors of agricultural growth rather than the 'equilibrium theory of profit maximization'. Optima limit model follows agro-ecological criteria of agricultural production efficiency, while the equilibrium theory argues the agricultural growth on the basis of income elasticity of the production demand. The regional study of agricultural growth processes must be operationalised on the basis of delimiting homogeneous agro-ecological regions of the country rather than using states as the homogeneous agro-ecological regions, which, hence, is less likely to provide the realistic estimation of land capability and potential.

Inefficient and insufficient infrastructure to support the production and distribution of food commodities in India is also a key contributor to low agricultural productivity and waste. Market-led infrastructure to support agri-businesses should be developed using the population-centred demand and mapped agricultural growth potential and 'yield gaps' of various crops. Socio-economic barriers such as land tenancy, size of operational landholdings, price mechanism and consumption habits often inhibit technology adoption and behaviour change in rural India. The lack of entrepreneurial capability and risk-taking behaviour also prohibit the adoption of innovative farm technologies to improve farming practices and enhance farm productivity.

A new planning paradigm and policy shift is now required to tackle some of these emerging issues in order to enhance the efficient functioning of the commodity market in India, which integrates global demand for food with localised production systems to competitively generate food surplus. Micro-level planning is indicative of empowering farmers to define the perimeter of their own individual problems and deploy strategies to redress them at a farm level. Hence, it is argued that the processing and distribution of agricultural products should be planned at a farm level. This argument is based on the premise of 'shifting responsibility' to the person responsible for making the decision. In doing so, the farmers would be able to seek out opportunities to diversify farm income and may change behaviour and decisions in terms of switching their economic base primarily from subsistence to other farming options and choices in rural India. This would help to mitigate risks such as those associated with monsoonal uncertainty or market failure. Such farm-level structural changes would strengthen farmers' decision making in shaping the spatio-functional organisation of farming practices to align with the production of agricultural commodities to demand-led regional, national and international markets.

Rural-urban economic disparities and income inequality in most of the Asian countries including India has widened. Globalised production networks and the resultant economies of agglomeration in strategic regions have been more likely to benefit services and knowledge economies whilst reducing the contribution of the agricultural sector to GDP. Market-led agricultural systems have also accelerated the polarisation of agricultural growth in areas of competitive advantages (Nurul-Amin 1994). This change has increased the gap between high- and low-performing agriculture regions. With a large population base of India (1.2 billion in 2011) with much higher density (i.e., 378 persons/sq km), there has been sufficient supply of skilled and unskilled labour force to work in agriculture and allied sectors of the economy. However, in order to fulfil the basic demand for food, India needs to increase the scale of production and productivity of key cereals (e.g. Wheat, Rice, Pulses), commercialise rural agricultural production practices (e.g. fruits, animal products such as meat, milk, milk products), modernise farming methods and technology, and expand non-agricultural activities in rural areas. Rural agricultural economies have less income elasticity of demand than urban goods produced at urban market centres (NSSO 2010, Suryakant 2010). Therefore, there needs to be proper spatial organisation of rural agricultural activities in tune with growing urban economies and commodity markets.

It is equally important to ensure rural India receives significant investment in rural infrastructure, and obtains fair and competitive prices for produce. Reinforced land and tenure reforms, combined with attracting and fostering agro-processing and allied industries in rural areas, are crucial. Such a suite of investment strategies also needs equitable access to credit for farm assets and infrastructure.

Future research will explore new research frontiers, which will simulate future agriculture growth patterns and generate regional plans and policy interventions. This will enable creating regional freight networks to connect food surplus areas with food deficit areas through dedicated transport corridors and food distribution and processing centres. This in turn will help to integrate regional planning objectives with national economic goals and targets.

Bibliography

Acharya, S. (2012): *India after the Global Crisis*, Orient Black Swan, Hyderabad: 110–114.

Adamowicz, M. (1988): Gran Production and Food Security in Arab Countries, *Agricultural Economics*. 2(1): 39–56.

Aggarwal, P. K., Kalran, N., Singh, A. K. and Sinha, S. K. (1994): Analyzing the Limitation Set by Climatic Factors, Genotype, Water and Nitrogen Availability on Productivity of Wheat I: The Model Description, Parameterization and Validation, *Field Crops Research*. 38(1): 73–91.

Agrawal, R. and Gisselquist, R. (1999): *Geography and Agricultural Productivity in India: Implications for Tamil Nadu, Harvard Institute for International Development*, Report Submitted to State Government of Tamil Nadu, Channai: 1–4.

Agriculture Commission (1964): Division of the Country in Homogeneous Crop Regions, *Agricultural Situation of India*. XIX(5): 453–471.

Aigner, D. J., Lovell, C. A. K. and Schmidt, P. (1977): Formulation and Estimation of Stochastic Frontier Production Function, *Journal of Econometrics*. 6: 21–37.

Alagh, Y. K. (1989): *Draft Guidelines for Plans at the Agro-Climatic Regions*, Planning Commission, Government of India, New Delhi.

Amedeo, D. (1969): An Optimisation Approach to the Identification of a System of Regions, in M. D. Thomas (ed): Papers of the Regional Science Association, XXIII: 25–44.

Amedeo, D. and Golledge, R. G. (1975): *An Introduction to Scientific Reasoning of Geography*, John Willey and Sons, Inc., New York: 160–170.

Anbumozhi, V., Reddy, V. R., Lu, Y.-C. and Yamaji, E. (2003): The Role of Crop Simulation Models in Agricultural Research and Development – A Review, *Agricultural Engineering Journal*. 12(1 and 2): 1–18.

Baker, D. N., Hesketh, J. D. and Duncan, W. G. (1972): Simulation of Growth in Cotton I: Gross Photosynthesis, Respiration and Growth, *Crop Science*. 12, 431–435.

Baker, O. E. (1928): Agricultural Regions of North America, *Economic Geography*. 4:44–73, 399–433.

Barro, R. J. and Sala-i-Martin, X. (1992): Covergence, *The Journal of Political Economy*. 100(2): 223–251.

Basu, D. N. and Guha, G. S. (1996) (eds): *Agro-Climatic Regional Planning in India* (Vol. I), Concept Publishing Co., New Delhi: 27–61.

Bernard, A. B. and Jones, C. I. (1995): *Productivity and Convergence across U.S. States and Industries (Version 4.0)*. Online www.bing.com/search?q=productivity+convergence and FORM = AWRE downloaded on 25.5.2012.

Berry, B. J. L. (1961): A Method for Deriving Milti-Factor Uniform Regions, *Polish Geographic Review*. 33(2): 263–282.

Berry, B. J. L. (1964): Approaches and Regional Analysis: A Synthesis, *Annals of the Association of American Geographers*. 54: 2–11.

Berry, B. J. L. (1965): Identification of Delineating Regions, in W. D. Wood and R. S. Thomas (eds): *Areas of Economic Stress in Canada*, Industrial Relations Centre, Queen's University, Kingston, Ontario.

Berry, B. J. L., Conkling, E. C. and Ray, D. M. (1993): *The Global Economy: Resource Use, Locational Choice and International Trade*, Prentice Hall, Englewood Cliffs, NJ.

Berry, B. J. L. and Rao, V. L. S. P. (1968): *Duality in the Regional Structure of Andhra Pradesh*, paper presented and discussed in the Session of 21st IGC, New Delhi.

Bhalla, G. S. (1988): *Regional Pattern of Agricultural Development in India as an Index of Natural Resource Use*, Paper presented in Indo-Soviet Seminar on Rational Utilization of Natural Resources and Regional Development, organised by CSRD, JNU, New Delhi.

Bhalla, G. S. and Alagh, Y. K. (1979a): Labour Productivity in Indian Agriculture, *Economic and Political Weekly*. Annual Number: 825–834.

Bhalla, G. S. and Alagh, Y. K. (1979b): *Performance of Indian Agriculture*, Starling Publishers, New Delhi: 40–61 and Table-11.

Bhalla, G. S. and Tyagi, D. S. (1989): *Patterns in Indian Agricultural Development: A District Level Study*, Institute for Studies in Industrial Development, New Delhi.

Bhat, L. S. and Das, B. N. (1968): *Land Use Planning Regions of India*, Monograph, Indian Statistical Institute, New Delhi.

Bhat, L. S and Learmonth, A. T. A. (1968): Recent Contribution to Economic Geography of India, *Economic Geography*. 44(3): 189–201.

Bhatia, B. M. (1988): *Indian Agriculture – A Policy Perspective*, Sage Publications Inc., New Delhi.

Bhatia, S. S. (1967): A New Measurement of Agricultural Efficiency in Uttar Pradesh, India, *Economic Geography*. 43 (3): 244–260.

Binswanger, H. P. (1978): Induced Technological Change: Evolution of Thought, in H. P. Binswanger and V. W. Rattan (eds): *Induced Innovation*, John Hopkins University Press, Baltimore, MD: 19–21.

Blomstrom, M. and Wolff, E. N. (1989): *Multinational Corporations and Productivity Convergence in Mexico*, Working Paper No. 3141, National Bureau of Economic Research.

Bunge, W. (1962): Theoretical Geography, Series – C, *Lund Studies in Geography*, Lund(No. 1): 14–26.

Casetti, E. (1964): *Classificatory and Regional Analysis by Discriminant Iterations*, Technical Report No. 12, Contract NONR 1228(26), North Western University, Evanston, IL.

Casetti, E. (1966): Analysis of Spatial Association by Trigonometric Polynomials, *Canadian Geographer*. 10(3): 199–204.

Census of India (1952): *Office of the Registrar General, Publication Division, paper no 2*. New Delhi.

Chakravarti, A. K. (1970): Foodgrain Sufficiency Pattern in India, *Geographical Review*. 60 (2): 208–228.

Chakravarty, A. K. (1976): The Impact of HYV Programme of Foodgrain Production in India, *Canadian Geographer*. 20: 199–223.

Chatterjee, S. P. (1964): *Map of Physiographic Divisions of India* (I Edn), National Atlas Organisation, Calcutta.

Chattopadhyaya, B. and Raza, M. (1975): Regional Development: An Analytical Frame, *Indian Journal of Regional Science*. 7(1)

Chaudhary, G. and Bhattacharyya, D. (2012): Retail Reloaded, *Hindustan Times Business Daily* (News paper), New-Delhi Oct 27, 2012: 23–25.

Chhetri, A., Arrowsmith C., Chhetri P. and Corcoran J (2013): *Mapping Spatial Tourism and Hospitality Clusters: An Application of Spatial Autocorrelation Techniques*, Tourism Analysis.

Chhetri, P., Corcoran J. and Hall, C. M. (2008): Modelling the spatial patterns of tourism-related employment for South East Queensland – A spatial econometric approach, *Tourism Recreation Research*. 33 (1): 25-38.

Cuadrado-Roura, J. R., Navarro, T. M. and Yserte, R. G. (2000): Regional Productivity Pattern in Europe: An Alternative Approach, *The Annals of Regional Science*. 34: 365–384.

Daimari, M. S. (2013): *Livelihood Pattern in Ri-Bhoi District of Meghalaya*, Ph.D. Thesis submitted to the Department of Geography, North- Eastern Hill University, Shillong: 107–148.

Dandekar, V. M and Rath, N. (1971): Poverty in India, *Economic and Political Weekly*. VI(1): 25–48 and VI(2): 106–146.

Dantawala, M. L. (1987): Growth and Equity in Agriculture, *Indian Journal of Agricultural Economics*. 42(2): 149–159.

Das, M. M. (1984): *Peasant Agriculture in Assam: A Structural Analysis*, Inter- India Publicatios, New Delhi: 131–173.

Dayal, E. (1984): Agricultural Development in India – A Spatial Analysis, *Annals of the Association of American Geographers*. 74(1): 98–123.

Deka, J.C. (2011): *Socio-Economic Study of Milk Producer Communities in Greater Guwahati Region*, Assam Ph.D. Thesis submitted to the Department of Geography, North-Eastern Hill University, Shillong.

DeWit, C. T., Brouwer, R. and Vries, F. W. T. P. (1969): The Simulation of Photosynthesis Systems I: Models and Methods. *Proceedings, IPB/PP Technical Meeting*, Pudoc, Wageningen.

Dogra, B. (1981, Nov 1): How Green Was Our Revolution, *The Hindustan Times (Sunday Magazine)*. LVIII(300): 1.

Douglas, P. H. and Cobb, C. W. (1928): A Theory of Production, *American Economic Review*. 18(Supplement), c.f. G. Tintner (1952): *Econometrics*, John Willey and Sons, Inc., New York: 51–52.

Dyson, T. (1996): *Population and Food: Global Trends and Future Prospects*. Routledge, London and New York.

FAO (2010): *Feeding the World*, viewed on 22 March 2016, http://www.fao.org/docrep/015/i2490e/i2490e03a.pdf

FAO (2015): The State of Food Insecurity in the World 2014. Strengthening the enabling environment for food security and nutrition, *International Fund for Agricultural Development, World Food Program. 2015*. Rome, viewed on 22 March 2016, http://www.fao.org/3/a4ef2d16-70a7-460a-a9ac-2a65a533269a/i4646e.pdf

Francisco, S. A. and Routray, J. K. (1992): *Road Transport and Rural Development – A Case Study in the Phillipines*, Dimensions of Human Supplements Development, Asian Institute of Technology, Bangkok: 27–29.

Friedmann, J. (1966): *Regional Development Policy: A Case Study of Venezuela*, MIT Press, Cambridge.

Gopal, L. and Srivastawa, V. C. (2008): History of Agriculture in India upto c 1200 AD, in D. P. Chattopadhyay (General editor): *History of Science, Philosophy and culture in India* (Vol. V, Part 1), Centre for the Studies in Civilisations, Delhi.

Gorski, T. and Gorska, K. (2003): The Effects of Scale on Crop Yield Variability, *Agricultural Systems.* 78: 425–434.

Goswami, P. C. (1988): *The Economic Development of Assam,* Kalyani Publications, New Delhi: 159–172.

Griffith, T. (1940): *Australia: A Study of Warm Environment and their Effect on British Settlement,* Methuen and Co. Ltd., London.

Grigg, D. (1965): The Logic of Regional Systems, *Annals of the Association of American Geographers.* 55(3): 465–491.

Grigg, D. (1967): Regions, Models and Classes, in R. J. Chorley and P. Hagget (eds): *Integrated Models in Geography,* Methuen and Co. Ltd., London: 494–500.

Groniger, W. (Undated): *Debating Development – A Historical Analysis of the Sasakawa Global 2000 project in Ghana,* Master thesis submitted to the Department of International Relations in Historical Perspective.

Grosjean, M. and Messerli, B. (1988): African Mountains and Highlands – Potential and Constraints, *Mountain Research and Development.* 8(2/3): 111–122.

Gupta, S. P. (1968): Agricultural Regionalisation of India, in P. Sen Gupta and G. Sdasyuk (1968), *Economic Regionalisation of India – Problems and Approaches, Monograph Series (Vol. I, No. 8),* Registrar General and Ex-officio Census Commissioner for India, New Delhi.

Hagen, E. E. (1975): *The Economics of Development,* Richard D. Irwin Inc., London: 162–213.

Hagen, E. E. (1975): *The Economics of Development,* Richard D. Irwin, Inc., Homewood, IL: 250–258.

Hall, P. (1966) (ed): *Von Thunen's Isolated State,* Translated by C. M. Warthenberg, Pargamon, Oxford.

Hayami, Y. (2001): *Economic Development* (II Edn), Oxford University Press, New Delhi: 221–229.

Hicks, J. R. (1932): *The Theory of Wages,* Macmillan, London.

Hine, J. L. and Riverson, J. D. N. (1984): The Impact of Feeder Road Investment on Accessibility and Agricultural Development in Ghana, *International Journal for Development Technology.* 2(1): 65–72.

Huntington, E. (1915): *Civilization and Climate,* Yale University Press, New Haven, CT: 173.

Ingersent, K. and Ghatak, S. (1984): *Agriculture and Economic Development.* Prentice Hall and Harvester Wheatsheaf. ISBN 10: 0710801378 ISBN 13: 9780710801371.

Jain, N. (2013): Heart for Art's Sake: Reviving India's Crafts, *Airports India Magazine.* 1(8): 9–14.

Johnston, B. F. (1980): Socio-Economic Aspects of Improved Animal Drawn Implements and Mechanization in Semi- Arid East Africa, in *Proceedings of International Workshop on Socio- Economic Constraints to Development of Semi Arid Tropical Agriculture, ICRISAT, Patancheru, India,* 221–233.

Kang, S. Z., Lu, Z., Liang, Y. L. and Caia, H. J. (2002): Effects of Limited Irrigation on Yield and Water Use Efficiency of Winter Wheat in the Loess Plateau of China, *Agricultural Water Management.* 55: 203–216.

Kang, S. Z., Lu, Z., Liang, Y. L. and Dawes, W. (2003): Simulation of Winter Wheat Yield and Water Use Efficiency in the Loess Plateau of China Using WAVES, *Agricultural Systems.* 78: 355–367.

Kalirajan, K. P., Mythili, G. and Shankar, U. (2001) (eds): *Accelerating Growth through Globalisation of Indian Agriculture*, Macmillan, India.

King, L. J. (1969): *Statistical Analysis in Geography*, Prentice-Hall, Englewood Cliffs, NJ: 198–204.

Kiniry, J. R., Bean, B., Xie, Y. and Chen, P.-Y. (2004): Maize Yield Potential: Critical Processes and Simulation Modeling in a High Yielding Environment, *Agricultural Systems*. 82(1): 45–56.

Kumar, A. (1986, April): Imbalances in Pulse Productivity, *Agricultural Situation in India*. XLI: 23–27.

Kumar, V., Dhaliwal, R. K. and Kaur, M. (2015): Scientists Perception Regarding Effect of Climate Change on Agriculture, *Indian Journal of Soil Conservation*. 43(2): 192–196.

Kuriyan, G. (1942): Discussion on Regional Scheme for India with M. B. Pithawala and K. S. Ahmad, *Indian Geographical Journal*. 17(I): 71, c.f. Spate O. H. K. and Learmonth, A. T. A. (1967): *India and Pakistan* (III Edn), Methuen and Co. Ltd., London:407–423.

Kuznets, S. (1964): Economic Growth and Contribution of Agriculture, in C. K. Eicher and L. W. Witt (eds): *Agriculture in Economic Development*, McGraw Hill, New York.

Mahadevan, R. (2003): Productivity Growth in Indian Agriculture: The Role of Globalisation and Economic Reform, *Asia-Pacific Development Journal*. 10(2): 57–72.

Manjunath, K. R. and Potdar, M. B. (2004): Wheat Growth Profile: Satellite Monitoring and Crop Yield Modeling, *Journal of the Indian Society of Remote Sensing*. 32(1): 91–102.

Malik, S. J. (2005): *Agricultural Growth and Rural Poverty: A Review of the Evidence*, *Asian Development Bank*, Pakistan Resident Mission Working Paper No 2: 23–31.

Mall, R. K. and Singh, K. K. (2000): Climate Variability and Wheat Yield Progress in Punjab Using CERES-Wheat and WTGROWS models, *VayuMandal*. 3–4: 91–102.

Mani, K. P. 1996: Some Reflections on the Capital Formation in Indian Agriculture, *Indian Journal of Agricultural Economics*. 51(4): 572.

Mankiw, N. G., Romer, D. and Weil, D. N. (1992): A Contribution to the Empirics of Economic Growth, *Quarterly Journal of Economics*. 107: 407–437.

Mathur, A. (2003): National and Regional Growth Performance in the Indian Economy: A Sectoral Analysis, in A. C. Mohapatra and C. R. Pathak (eds), *Economic Liberalisation and Regional Disparities in India*, Star Publishing House, Shillong: 3–41.

Mathur, P. N. and Gupta, M. P. (1985): *National Demonstrations Project – An Overview*, Publication and Information Division, ICAR, New Delhi.

McCarty, H. H. and Lindbarg, J. (1967): *Preface to Economic Geography*, Prentice Hall, Englewood Cliffs, NJ.

McCunn, A. and Huffman, W. E. (1999): Convergence in U.S. Productivity Growth for Agriculture – Implications of Inter-State Research Spillovers for Funding Agriculture Research, *American Journal of Agricultural Economics*. 82(2): 370–388.

Miller, J. W. (1966): *The Economics of Agricultural Development*, Vakils, Feffer and Simons, Bombay.

Minhas, B. S. and Vaidyanathan, A. (1965): Growth of Agricultural Output in India, 1951–4 to 1958–61: An Analysis of Compolent Elements, *Journal of Indian Society of Agricultural Statistics*. XVIII(2): 230–252.

Ministry of Agriculture (1991): *Statistics at a Glance*, Department of Agriculture and Cooperatation, Government of India, New Delhi: Table- 14.2.

Minten, B. (2011): *The Quiet Revolution in India's Food Supply Chains*, IFPRI Discussion Paper 01115, New Delhi.

Misra, S. D. (1970): *Regions of India*, National Book Trust, New Delhi.

Mohapatra, A. C. (1982): *Regional Inequality in Indian*, Unpublished Ph. D. Thesis submitted to North-Eastern Hill University, Shillong: 220–243.

Monmonier, M.S. (1972): Contiguity-Biased Class-Interval Selection: A Method for Simplifying Pattern on Statistical Maps, *Geographical Review*, Vol. LXII (2): 203–228.

Moumita, T. (2013): *Crop Productivity and Farm Income in Tinsukhia District of Assam*, Unpublished Ph.D. Thesis submitted to Department of Geography, North Eastern Hill University, Shilling.

Myrdal, G. (1957): *Economic Theory and Underdeveloped Regions*, Duckworth, London.

Nag, P. (2010) (ed): *Atlas of Agricultural Resources of India*, National Atlas and Thematic Mapping Organisation, Kolkata: 60–69.

Narzari, G. S. (2013): *Forest Related Activities for Livelihood in Ripu Reserve Forest*, Ph.D. Thesis submitted to the Department of Geography, North Eastern Hill University, Shillong: 132–138.

Nath, V. (1954): *Resource Development Regions and Division of India*, Report submitted to Planning Commission, New Delhi.

Nath, V. (1969): The Growth of Indian Agriculture: A Regional Analysis, *The Geographical Review*. LIX(3): 348–372.

Navadkar, D. S., Amale, A. J., Gulave, C. M. and Nannaware, V. M. (2012): Economics of Production and Marketing of Kharif Maize in Ahamadnagar District of Maharastra State, *Agricultural Situation in India*. LXIX(6): 309–316.

NSSO (2010): *National Sample Survey Organisation*, Ministry of planning, Government of India, New Delhi.

NCERT (2007): *Themes in Indian History*, National Council of Educational Research and Training (NCERT), New Delhi.

Neha, J. (2013): Heart for Art's Sake: Reviving India's Crafts, *Airports India Magazine*. 1(8): 9–14.

Nurkse, R. (1953): *Problems of Capital Formation in Underdeveloped Countries*, Oxford University Press, New York.

Nurul-Amin, A. T. M. (1994): *Economic Logic of Resource Flows between the Rural-Agricultural and the Urban-Industrial Sector-Consequences for Human Settlements, Income Distribution and Living*, HSD Working Paper No 50, The School of Environment, Resources and Development, Asian Institute of Technology, Bangkok.

O'Hare, G. (1997): The Indian Monsoon, *Geography*. 82(3): 218–230 and 82(4): 335–352.

Pal, M. N. (1961): Quantitative Delimitations of Regions, *Bombay Geographical Magazine*. 8/9: 69–82.

Pal, M. N. (1963): A Method of Regional Analysis of Economic Development with Special Reference to South India, *Journal of Regional Science*. 5(1)

Pal, M. N. (1968): *Quantitative Delineation of Regions*, paper presented in the Session of 21st IGC., New Delhi.

Pal, M. N. (1975): Regional Disparities in the Level of Development in India, *Indian Journal of Regional Science*. VII(1): 35–52.

Panda, B. 2006: Rural Non Farm Employment in India and Thailand, *Asian Pacific.* 34(6): 609–624.

Park, J. M. (1970): *Fortran IV Program for Q-Mode Cluster Analysis on Distance Function with Printed Dendogram*, Computer Contribution No. 46, Kansas State Geographical Survey.

Parraga, I. M. (1990): Determinants of Food Consumption, *Journal of American Dietetic Association.* 90(5): 661–663.

Perroux, F. (1950): Economic Space: Theory and Applications. *Quartley Journal of Economic*, 64: 89–104.

Prasad, C., Choudhary, B. and Nayar, B. B. (1987): *First Line Transfer of Technology Project*, Publication and Information Division, ICAR, New Delhi.

Randhawa, N. S. and Sundaram, K. V. (1990): *Small Farmers Development in Asia and the Pacific- Some Lessons for Strategy Formulation and Planning*, FAO Economic and development paper No. 87. FAO/UN Rome.

Rao, M. G., Shand, R. T. and Kalirajan, K. P. (1999, March): Convergence of Income across States, *Economic and Political Weekly.* 27: 769–778.

Rao, V. L. S. P. and Bhat, L. S. (1964): A Regional Framework for Resource Development, *Bombay Geographical Magazine.* 10(1)

Rasson, J. P. et al (1988): *A New Approach for a Natural Measurement of Proximities also for Non Disjoint Training Sets and for Any Dimension of Space*, III Meeting of Euro Working group on Location Analysis, Sevilla, Spain.

Rasson, J. P. et al (1989): *The Supervised Classification Problems – What Happens with a New Hypothesis?* IV Meeting of Euro Working group on Location Analysis, Chios, Greece.

Raza, M. (1981): Regional Disparities in India, in N. Mohammad (ed): *Perspectives in Agricultural Geography* (Vol. IV), Concept Publishing Co., New Delhi: 103–144.

Raza, M. and Kundu, A. (1975): Discordance between Industrialisation and Urbanisation in India- Some Aspects, *Proceedings of Indo- USSR Joint Seminar, Moscow.*

Raza, M., Kundu, A. and Nangia, S. (1975): Urban Rural Continuum in India, *Indian and Foreign Review.* 12(15)

Reardon, T. and Minten, B. (2011): The Quiet Revolution in India's Food Supply Chains, *Internatonal Food PolicyResearch Institute, Discussion Paper 01115, New Delhi*

Re-emerging World Advisory Services (2012): *NSSO Household Expenditure Survey 66th Round – a Critique*, downloaded from www.re-emergingworld.com on 25th May 2012.

Regional Survey Unit (1968): *Indian Statistical Institute, Regional Planning Division*, New Delhi

Rodan, P. N. R. (1943, June): Problems of Industrialisation of Eastern and South Eastern Europe, *Economic Journal.* 53: 202–211.

Sabates, R., Gould, B. W. and Villarreal, H. J. (2001): Household Composition and Food Expenditure: A Cross – Country Comparison, *Food Policy* (Elsevier). 26(6): 571–586.

Schwartzberg, J. E. (1978): *A Historical Atlas of South Asia.*, ed. Association for Asian Studies Reference Series, 2. University of Chicago Press, Chicago, xxxix + 352 pp.

Sdasyuk, G. (1968): The Concepts of General Economic Regionalisation as Developed in India, in P. Sen Gupta and G. Sdasyuk (1968), *Economic Regionalisation of India – Problems and Approaches, Monograph Series, Vol. I* (No. 8), Registrar General and Ex-officio Census Commissioner for India, New Delhi.

Shrestha, R. P. and Naikaset, S. (2003): Agro-Spectral Models for Estimating Dry Season Rice Yield in the Bangkok Plain of Thailand, *Asian Journal of Geo-Informatics.* 4(1): 11–19.

Siddiq, E. A. (2000): *Bridging the Rice Yield Gap in India, in Report at the Expert Consultation on Bridging the Rice Yield Gap in Asia and the Pacific, Bangkok (Thailand).* Online http://www.fao.org/docrep/003/x6905e/x 6905e09.htm.

Simpson, G. G. (1961): *Principles of Animal Taxonomy,* Columbia University Press, New York.

Singer, H. W. (1949, March): Economic Progress in Under Developed Countries, *Social Research.* 16: 1–11.

Singh, B. (1985): *Convocation Address (24th Convocation),* Indian Agricultural Research Institute, New Delhi.

Singh, J. (1971): Agricultural Colonisation of Cultivable Land in India, *The Deccan Geographer.* IX(2): 135–149.

Singh, J. (1974): *The Green Revolution in India: How Green It Is,* Vishal Publications, Kurukshetra.

Singh, R. L. (1971) (ed): *India – A Regional Geography,* National Geographical Society of India, Varanasi.

Singh, S. (1994): *Agricultural Development in India – A Regional Analysis,* Kaushal Publications, Shillong: 103–142.

Singh, S. (1994): *Agricultural Development in India – A Regional Analysis,* Kaushal Publications, Shillong: 55–66.

Singh, S. (1988): *Rural Development and Planning,* Shree Publishing House, New Delhi (Reprinted)

Singh, S. (2000): Modelling Structure and Function of Agricultural Yield Potential, *Transactions of the Institute of Indian Geographers.* 22(2): 1–15.

Singh, S. (2002): Optimizing the Spatial Structure of the Agricultural Production Function, *Geographical Analysis.* 34(3): 229–244.

Singh, S. (2006): Predicting Summer Rice Yield Based on Biophysical and Technological Parameters on Monsoon Lands of Brahmaputra Valley, India, *International Agricultural Engineering Journal.* 15(2–3): 91–107.

Singh, S. (2007): Regional Dimensions of Agricultural Growth Potentials, in A. Mohammad, A. Munir and H. Rehman (eds): *Fifty Years of Indian Agriculture* (Vol. I) *(Production and Self-Sufficiency),* Concept Publishing Co., New Delhi: 138–153.

Singh, S. (2012): Regional Dimensions of Agricultural Development, in A. Shukla (ed): *Paradigm of Regional Planning and Development,* Deep & Deep Publications Pvt. Ltd, New Delhi: 3–28.

Singh, S. and Chhetri, P. (2011): Regional Structural of Indian Agriculture – An Analysis of Post – Liberalisation Phase, *Journal of Business and Economics* (USA). 2(4): 302–314.

Singh, S. and Chhetri, P. (2013, June): Regional Processes and Patterns of Agricultural Growth in India after Economic Liberalisation, *Agricultural Situation in India, New Delhi.* LXX(3).

Singh, S., Hayashi, T., Hiambok Jones Syiemlieh, H.J., Cajee, L. and Toru Terao, T. (2011): Weather Variability and Rainfall Pattern of 'Sidr' Post - Monsoon Cyclonic Storm of 15th November 2007 in the Meghalaya Plateau, India. *Current Science,* 100(10): 1522–1531.

Singh, S. and Sharma, B. (2007): Changing Pattern of Agricultural Productivity in Brahmaputra Valley, *Indian Journal of Agricultural Economics.* 62(1): 139–151.

Singh, S., Sharma, B. and Dey, P. P. (2006): Predicting Summer Rice Yield Based on Biophysical and Technological Parameters on Monsoon Lands of Brahmaputra Valley, India, *International Agricultural Engineering Journal* (Bangkok). 15(2–3): 91–107.

Singh, S., Syiemlieh, H. J. and Dey, P. P. (2009–10): Weather Variability and Summer Rice Yield in Wet Monsoon Environment of Upper Brahmaputra Valley, *VayuMandal (Bulletin of Indian Meteorological Society)*. 35 and 36(1–4): 46–59.

Singh, S., Syiemlieh, H. J., Soja, R., Prokop, P., Starkel, L. and Kumar Y. (2014): Socio-Economic Determinants of the Use of Water and Fuel Resources in the Degraded Environment of Cherrapunji Area, India, *Geographical Review of India*. 76(1): 82–94.

Singh, S. and Zoram, K. (2015): Economic Liberalisation and Agricultural Productivity, *Agricultural Situation in India*. LXXII(5): 21–28.

Sokal, R. R. and Sneath, P. H. A. (1963): *Principles of Numerical Taxonomy*, W.H. Freeman, San Francisco: 169–215.

Somasekharan, J., Prasad, S. and Roy, V. P. N. (2011): Convergence Hypothesis: Some Dynamics and Explanations of Agricultural Growth across Indian States, *Agricultural Economics Research Review*. 24(July–December issue): 211–216.

Somra, S. S. and Singh, K. (2010): *Growth Globalisation and Agriculture in India*, Bookwell Publications, New Delhi: 3–4.

Spate, O. H. K., Learmonth, A. T. A and Farmer, B. H. (1967): *India, Pakistan and Ceylone: The Regions* (III Edn), Methuen and Co. Ltd., London.

Sri, P. (2012): Disparities in Agricultural Development in Madhya Pradesh, in Shukla, A. (ed): *Paradigms of Regional Planning and Development*, Deep and Deep Publications Pvt. Ltd., New Delhi: 29–51.

Srivastav, N. and Dubey, A. (2002): Rural Non-Farm Employment in India- Spatial Variations and Temporal Change, *The Indian Journal of Labour Economics*. 45(4): 745–758.

Stamp, L. D. (1928): The Natural Regions of India, *Geography*. 14: 502–506.

Strauss, J. (1982): Determinants of Food Consumption in Rural Sierra Leone: Application of the Quadratic Expenditure System to the Consumer-Leisure Component of a Household – Firm Model, *Journal of Development Economics* (Elsevier). 11(3): 327–253.

Sundaram, K. V. (2007): The Small Farmer Development Strategies for the Next Millennium, in A. Mohammad, A. Munir, H. Rehman (eds): *Fifth Years of Indian Agriculture* (Vol. I), Concept Publishing Co., New Delhi: 46–60.

Suryakant, (2010): Development, Disparity and Emerging Governance Issues and Challenges in Post Reforms India, in S. Nagia, M. M. Jha, S. Mishra, H. Ramachandran and M. Velayutham (eds): *Development Concerns in the 21stCentury*, Concept Publishing Co., New Delhi: 73–88.

Spillman, W. J. (1922): Application of the Law of Diminishing Returns to Some Fertilizer and Seed Data, *Journal of Fertilizer Economics*. 5: 36–52.

Spillman, W. J. (1933): *Exponential Yield Function*, c.f. Alber, R., Adams, J. S. and Gould, P. (1971): *Spatial Organisation*, Prentice Hall, Englewood Cliffs, NJ: 143.

Subash, S., Bino-Paul, G. D. and Ramanathan, A. (2004): Technical Efficiency in Rice Production – An Application of Stochastic Frontier Analysis, *Indian Journal of Regional Science*. XXXVI(1): 118–126.

Talukdar M. (2013): *Crop productivity and Farm Income in Tinsukhia District of Assam*, unpublished Ph.D. Thesis submitted to Department of Geography, North Eastern Hill University, Shilling.

Thakur, B. R. and Sharma, D. D. (2010): Changing Cropping Pattern in Tribal Areas of Himachal Pradesh – A Spatio-Temporal Analysis, *Annals of the National Association of Geographers India*. XXX(2): 24–39.

Thakur, M. C. (1987): Agricultural Labour Productivity in Western Uttar Pradesh, *Geographical Review of India*. 49(1): 33–41.

Thakur, S. K. (2007): New Economic World: Whither Old Wine in New Bottle, in B. Thakur, G. Pomeroy, C. Cusack and S. K. Thakur (eds): *City, Society and Planning* (Vol. 3), Concept Publishing Co., New Delhi: 100–121.

Thomas, S. M. and Mani, K. P. (2015): Institutional Credit for Agriculture in India since Reforms, *Agricultural Situation in India*. LXXII(5): 14–20.

Van-der-Vorst, J. G. A. J. (2006): Performance Measurement in Agri-Food Supply-Chain Networks, in C. J. M. Ondersteijn, J. H. M. Wijnandas, R. B. M. Huirne and O. V. Kooten (eds): *Quantifying the Agri-Food Supply Chain*, Springer, The Netherland: 13–24.

Varadarajan, S. (1986): Prospects for Pulses in Tamil Nadu, *Agricultural Situations in India*. XLI(8): 641–646.

Verma, P. C. (1974): Measurement of Regional Development in Bangladesh, *Indian Journal of Regional Science*. VI(1): 1–12.

Vijayshankar, P. S. (2016): Going through the Grain, *The Hindu: A Daily News Paper* (Noida/Delhi Edn), Feb 5 Friday: 10.

Visser, S. (1980): Technological Change and the Spatial Structure of Agriculture, *Economic Geography*. 56(4): 311–319.

Visser, S. (1982): On Agricultural Location Theory, *Geographical Analysis*. 14(2): 167–176.

Viswanadham, N. (2012): *Can India Be the Food Basket for the World?* Working Paper.

Ward, J. H. (1963): Hierarchical Grouping to Optimise an Objective Function, *Journal of American Statistical Association*. 58: 236–244.

Whittlesey, D. (1936): Major Agricultural Regions of the Earth, *Annals of the American Association of Geographers*. XXVI(1): 199–240.

The World Bank (2016): Food Production Index, World Bank Group, viewed on 20 March 2016, http://data.worldbank.org/indicator/AG.PRD.FOOD.XD.

World Development Report (1982): *International Development Trends Agriculture and Economic Development; World Development Indicators*, World Bank Group, Washington, DC. http://documents.worldbank.org/curated/en/1982/01/173 87645/world-development-report-1982.

World Development Report (2008): *Agriculture for Development*, The World Bank, Washington DC: 118–137.

WRI (World Resources Institute) (2013): *The Global Food Challenge Explained in 18 Graphics*, viewed on 16 March 2016, http://www.wri.org/blog/2013/12/global-food-challenge-explained-18-graphics).

Zebler, L. (1958): Decision Making in Regional Construction, *Annals of the American Association of Geographers*. 48: 140–148.

Zegar, J. S. and Florianczyk, Z. (2003): Main Problems of Agriculture and Rural Areas in Poland in the Period of Transformation and Integration with European Union, in J. Banski and J. Owsinski (eds): *Alternatives for European Rural Areas*, Institute of Agriculture and Food Economics and the Institute of Geography and Spatial Organisation, Polish Academy of Sciences, Warsawa: 6–18.

Zobler, L. (1972): *The Use of Numerical Taxonomy to Evaluate Soil Resources, International Geography, Vol. I (Abstract of papers submitted to 22nd IGC)*, University of Toronto Press, Paper No. P0322: 289–290.

Author index

Note: word 'n' after a page refers to two or more than two names in reference

Subject index

Printed in the United States
By Bookmasters